Textbook Outlines, Highlights, and Practice Quizzes

Physics: Principles with Applications

by Douglas C. Giancoli, 7th Edition

All "Just the Facts101" Material Written or Prepared by Cram101 Textbook Reviews

---

Title Page

STUDYING MADE EASY

This Facts101 notebook is designed to make studying easier and increase your comprehension of the textbook material. Instead of starting with a blank notebook and trying to write down everything discussed in class lectures, you can use this Facts101 textbook notebook and annotate your notes along with the lecture.

Our goal is to give you the best tools for success.

For a supreme understanding of the course, pair your notebook with our online tools. Should you decide you prefer jtf101.com as your study tool,

we'd like to offer you a trade...

Our Trade In program is a simple way for us to keep our promise and provide you the best studying tools, regardless of where you purchased your Facts101 textbook notebook. As long as your notebook is in *Like New Condition**, you can send it back to us and we will immediately give you a JustTheFacts101.com account free for 120 days!

Let The **Trade In** *Begin!*

THREE SIMPLE STEPS TO TRADE:

1. Go to www.jtf101.com/tradein and fill out the packing slip information.
2. Submit and print the packing slip and mail it in with your Facts101 textbook notebook.
3. Activate your account after you receive your email confirmation.

* Books must be returned in *Like New Condition*, meaning there is no damage to the book including, but not limited to; ripped or torn pages, markings or writing on pages, or folded / creased pages. Upon receiving the book, Facts101 will inspect it and reserves the right to terminate your free Facts101.com account and return your textbook notebook at the owners expense.

"Just the Facts101" is a Content Technologies publication and tool designed to give you all the facts from your textbooks. Visit JustTheFacts101.com for the full practice test for each of your chapters for virtually any of your textbooks.

Facts101 has built custom study tools specific to your textbook. We provide all of the factual testable information and unlike traditional study guides, we will never send you back to your textbook for more information.

YOU WILL NEVER HAVE TO HIGHLIGHT A BOOK AGAIN!

Facts101 StudyGuides

All of the information in this StudyGuide is written specifically for your textbook. We include the key terms, places, people, and concepts... the information you can expect on your next exam!

Want to take a practice test?

Throughout each chapter of this StudyGuide you will find links to JustTheFacts101.com where you can select specific chapters to take a complete test on, or you can subscribe and get practice tests for up to 12 of your textbooks, along with other exclusive Jtf101.com tools like problem solving labs and reference libraries.

JustTheFacts101.com

Only Jtf101.com gives you the outlines, highlights, and PRACTICE TESTS specific to your textbook. JustTheFacts101.com is an online application where you'll discover study tools designed to make the most of your limited study time.

By purchasing this book, you get 50% off the normal monthly subscription fee!. Just enter the promotional code **'DK73DW22805'** on the Jtf101.com registration screen.

www.JustTheFacts101.com

ISBN(s): 9781490246475. PUBX-6.201434

Physics: Principles with Applications
Douglas C. Giancoli, 7th

CONTENTS

1. INTRODUCTION, MEASUREMENT, ESTIMATING

CHAPTER OUTLINE: KEY TERMS, PEOPLE, PLACES, CONCEPTS

Planck time

Laser

Aristotle

Mercury

Theory

Interpolation

Velocity

Protractor

Scientific notation

Speed of light

Kilogram

Pixel

Polaroid

Solid angle

Area

Micrometer

Symmetry

Triangulation

Dimensional analysis

Pendulum

Light-year

1. INTRODUCTION, MEASUREMENT, ESTIMATING

CHAPTER OUTLINE: KEY TERMS, PEOPLE, PLACES, CONCEPTS

	Planck
	Planck length
	String theory
	Compact disc
	Nautical mile

CHAPTER HIGHLIGHTS & NOTES: KEY TERMS, PEOPLE, PLACES, CONCEPTS

Planck time	In physics, the Planck time is the unit of time in the system of natural units known as Planck units. It is the time required for light to travel, in a vacuum, a distance of 1 Planck length. The unit is named after Max Planck, who was the first to propose it.
Laser	A laser is a device that emits light through a process of optical amplification based on the stimulated emission of electromagnetic radiation. The term 'laser' originated as an acronym for Light Amplification by Stimulated Emission of Radiation. Lasers differ from other sources of light because they emit light coherently.
Aristotle	Aristotle was a Greek philosopher born in Stagirus, northern Greece, in 384 BCE. His father, Nicomachus, died when Aristotle was a child, whereafter he lived under a guardian's care. At eighteen, he joined Plato's Academy in Athens and remained there until the age of thirty-seven (c. 347 BCE). His writings cover many subjects - including physics, biology, zoology, metaphysics, logic, ethics, aesthetics, poetry, theater, music, rhetoric, linguistics, politics and government - and constitute the first comprehensive system of Western philosophy.
Mercury	Mercury is a chemical element with the symbol Hg and atomic number 80. It is commonly known as quicksilver and was formerly named hydrargyrum (from Greek 'hydr-' water and 'argyros' silver). A heavy, silvery d-block element, mercury is the only metal that is liquid at standard conditions for temperature and pressure; the only other element that is liquid under these conditions is bromine, though metals such as caesium, gallium, and rubidium melt just above room temperature. With a freezing point of -38.83 °C and boiling point of 356.73 °C, mercury has one of the narrowest ranges of its liquid state of any metal.

Theory	Theory is a system of ideas intended to explain something, such as a single or collection of fact, event(s), or phenomen(a)(on). Typically, a theory is developed through the use of contemplative and rational forms of abstract and generalized thinking. Furthermore, a theory is often based on general principles that are independent of the thing being explained.
Interpolation	In the mathematical field of numerical analysis, interpolation is a method of constructing new data points within the range of a discrete set of known data points. In engineering and science, one often has a number of data points, obtained by sampling or experimentation, which represent the values of a function for a limited number of values of the independent variable. It is often required to interpolate (i.e. estimate) the value of that function for an intermediate value of the independent variable.
Velocity	Velocity is the rate of change of the position of an object, equivalent to a specification of its speed and direction of motion, e.g. 60 km/h to the north. Velocity is an important concept in kinematics, the branch of classical mechanics which describes the motion of bodies. Velocity is a vector physical quantity; both magnitude and direction are required to define it.
Protractor	A protractor is a square, circular or semicircular measuring instrument, typically made of transparent plastic or glass, for measuring angles. Most protractors measure angles in degrees (°). Radian-scale protractors measure angles in radians.
Scientific notation	Scientific notation is a way of writing numbers that are too big or too small to be conveniently written in decimal form. Scientific notation has a number of useful properties and is commonly used in calculators and by scientists, mathematicians and engineers. In scientific notation all numbers are written in the form of $a \times 10^b$ (a times ten raised to the power of b), where the exponent b is an integer, and the coefficient a is any real number, called the significand or mantissa.
Speed of light	The speed of light in vacuum, commonly denoted c, is a universal physical constant important in many areas of physics. Its value is exactly 299,792,458 metres per second, a figure that is exact because the length of the metre is defined from this constant and the international standard for time. This is approximately 186,282.4 miles per second, or about 671 million miles per hour.
Kilogram	The kilogramme, is the base unit of mass in the International System of Units (SI) and is defined as being equal to the mass of the International Prototype of the Kilogram. The avoirdupois (or international) pound, used in both the Imperial system and U.S. customary units, is defined as exactly 0.45359237 kg, making one kilogram approximately equal to 2.2046 avoirdupois pounds.

1. INTRODUCTION, MEASUREMENT, ESTIMATING

CHAPTER HIGHLIGHTS & NOTES: KEY TERMS, PEOPLE, PLACES, CONCEPTS

Pixel	In digital imaging, a pixel, or pel, is a physical point in a raster image, or the smallest addressable element in a display device; so it is the smallest controllable element of a picture represented on the screen. The address of a pixel corresponds to its physical coordinates. LCD pixels are manufactured in a two-dimensional grid, and are often represented using dots or squares, but CRT pixels correspond to their timing mechanisms and sweep rates.
Polaroid	Polaroid is the trademark for a type of synthetic plastic sheet which is used as a polarizer or polarizing filter, made by Polaroid Corporation.
Solid angle	In geometry, a solid angle is the two-dimensional angle in three-dimensional space that an object subtends at a point. It is a measure of how large the object appears to an observer looking from that point. In the International System of Units (SI), a solid angle is a dimensionless unit of measurement called a steradian (symbol: sr).
Area	Area is a quantity that expresses the extent of a two-dimensional surface or shape, or planar lamina, in the plane. Area can be understood as the amount of material with a given thickness that would be necessary to fashion a model of the shape, or the amount of paint necessary to cover the surface with a single coat. It is the two-dimensional analog of the length of a curve (a one-dimensional concept) or the volume of a solid (a three-dimensional concept).
Micrometer	A micrometer, sometimes known as a micrometer screw gauge, is a device incorporating a calibrated screw used widely for precise measurement of small distances in mechanical engineering and machining as well as most mechanical trades, along with other metrological instruments such as dial, vernier, and digital calipers. Micrometers are usually, but not always, in the form of calipers (opposing ends joined by a frame), which is why micrometer caliper is another common name. The spindle is a very accurately machined screw.
Symmetry	In physics, symmetry includes all features of a physical system that exhibit the property of symmetry--that is, under certain transformations, aspects of these systems are otherwise 'unchanged', according to a particular observation. A symmetry of a physical system is a physical or mathematical feature of the system (observed or intrinsic) that is 'preserved' under some change. A family of particular transformations may be continuous (such as rotation of a circle) or discrete (e.g., reflection of a bilaterally symmetric figure, or rotation of a regular polygon).
Triangulation	In trigonometry and geometry, triangulation is the process of determining the location of a point by measuring angles to it from known points at either end of a fixed baseline, rather than measuring distances to the point directly . The point can then be fixed as the third point of a triangle with one known side and two known angles.

Dimensional analysis

In physics and all science, dimensional analysis is the analysis of the relationships between different physical quantities by identifying their dimensions. The dimension of any physical quantity is the combination of the basic physical dimensions that compose it, although the definitions of basic physical dimensions may vary. Some fundamental physical dimensions, based on the SI system of units, are length, mass, time, and electric charge.

Pendulum

A pendulum is a weight suspended from a pivot so that it can swing freely. When a pendulum is displaced sideways from its resting equilibrium position, it is subject to a restoring force due to gravity that will accelerate it back toward the equilibrium position. When released, the restoring force combined with the pendulum's mass causes it to oscillate about the equilibrium position, swinging back and forth.

Light-year

A light-year, sometimes written light year, lightyear, or Light-year is an astronomical unit of length equal to just under 10 trillion kilometres (or about 6 trillion miles). As defined by the International Astronomical Union (IAU), a light-year is the distance that light travels in vacuum in one Julian year.

The light-year is most often used when expressing distances to stars and other distances on a galactic scale, especially in non-specialist and popular science publications.

Planck

Max Karl Ernst Ludwig Planck, FRS was a German theoretical physicist who originated quantum theory, which won him the Nobel Prize in Physics in 1918.

Planck made many contributions to theoretical physics, but his fame rests primarily on his role as originator of the quantum theory. This theory revolutionized human understanding of atomic and subatomic processes, just as Albert Einstein's theory of relativity revolutionized the understanding of space and time.

Planck length

In physics, the Planck length, denoted l_P, is a unit of length, equal to 1.616199×10^{-35} metres. It is a base unit in the system of Planck units, developed by physicist Max Planck. The Planck length can be defined from three fundamental physical constants: the speed of light in a vacuum, Planck's constant, and the gravitational constant.

String theory

In physics, string theory is a theoretical framework in which the point-like particles of particle physics are replaced by one-dimensional objects called strings. In string theory, the different types of observed elementary particles arise from the different quantum states of these strings. In addition to the types of particles postulated by the standard model of particle physics, string theory naturally incorporates gravity, and is therefore a candidate for a theory of everything, a self-contained mathematical model that describes all fundamental forces and forms of matter.

Compact disc

Compact disc, or CD for short, is a digital optical disc data storage format.

CHAPTER HIGHLIGHTS & NOTES: KEY TERMS, PEOPLE, PLACES, CONCEPTS

The format was originally developed to store and play back sound recordings only (CD-DA), but was later adapted for storage of data (CD-ROM). Several other formats were further derived from these, including write-once audio and data storage (CD-R), rewritable media (CD-RW), Video Compact Disc Super Video Compact Disc Photo CD, PictureCD, CD-i, and Enhanced Music CD. Audio CDs and audio CD players have been commercially available since October 1982.

Nautical mile

The nautical mile is a unit of length that is approximately one minute of arc measured along any meridian. By international agreement it has been set at 1,852 metres exactly (about 6,076 feet).

It is a non-SI unit (although accepted for use in the International System of Units by the BIPM) used especially by navigators in the shipping and aviation industries, and also in polar exploration.

CHAPTER QUIZ: KEY TERMS, PEOPLE, PLACES, CONCEPTS

1. In physics, the _________ is the unit of time in the system of natural units known as Planck units. It is the time required for light to travel, in a vacuum, a distance of 1 Planck length. The unit is named after Max Planck, who was the first to propose it.

   a. Geometrized unit system
   b. Planck angular frequency
   c. Planck charge
   d. Planck time

2. _________ is a system of ideas intended to explain something, such as a single or collection of fact, event(s), or phenomen(a)(on). Typically, a _________ is developed through the use of contemplative and rational forms of abstract and generalized thinking. Furthermore, a _________ is often based on general principles that are independent of the thing being explained.

   a. Theory
   b. Berkelium
   c. Beryllium
   d. Bismuth

3. . A _________ is a device that emits light through a process of optical amplification based on the stimulated emission of electromagnetic radiation. The term '_________' originated as an acronym for Light Amplification by Stimulated Emission of Radiation. _________s differ from other sources of light because they emit light coherently.

   a. Chloride
   b. Bromide
   c. Borohydride

4. In the mathematical field of numerical analysis, _________ is a method of constructing new data points within the range of a discrete set of known data points.

   In engineering and science, one often has a number of data points, obtained by sampling or experimentation, which represent the values of a function for a limited number of values of the independent variable. It is often required to interpolate (i.e. estimate) the value of that function for an intermediate value of the independent variable.

   a. Interpolation
   b. Colorburst
   c. Component video
   d. Component video sync

5. In physics and all science, _________ is the analysis of the relationships between different physical quantities by identifying their dimensions. The dimension of any physical quantity is the combination of the basic physical dimensions that compose it, although the definitions of basic physical dimensions may vary. Some fundamental physical dimensions, based on the SI system of units, are length, mass, time, and electric charge.

   a. 1s Slater-type function
   b. Dimensional analysis
   c. Legendre transformation
   d. Gravitational two-body problem

ANSWER KEY
1. INTRODUCTION, MEASUREMENT, ESTIMATING

1. d
2. a
3. d
4. a
5. b

2. DESCRIBING MOTION: KINEMATICS IN ONE DIMENSION

CHAPTER OUTLINE: KEY TERMS, PEOPLE, PLACES, CONCEPTS

- Kinematics
- Linear motion
- Particle
- Point particle
- Internal combustion
- Average speed
- Displacement
- Velocity
- Instantaneous
- Air resistance
- Free fall
- Gravity
- Acceleration
- Terminal velocity
- Terminal
- Quadratic equation
- Symmetry
- Quadratic formula
- Tangent

2. DESCRIBING MOTION: KINEMATICS IN ONE DIMENSION

CHAPTER HIGHLIGHTS & NOTES: KEY TERMS, PEOPLE, PLACES, CONCEPTS

Kinematics

Kinematics is the branch of classical mechanics which describes the motion of points, bodies and systems of bodies (groups of objects) without consideration of the causes of motion. The term is the English version of A.M. Ampère's cinématique, which he constructed from the Greek ????µa, kinema (movement, motion), derived from ???e??, kinein (to move).

The study of kinematics is often referred to as the geometry of motion.

Linear motion

Linear motion is motion along a straight line, and can therefore be described mathematically using only one spatial dimension. The linear motion can be of two types: uniform linear motion with constant velocity or zero acceleration; non uniform linear motion with variable velocity or non-zero acceleration. The motion of a particle (a point-like object) along a line can be described by its position x, which varies with t (time).

Particle

In the physical sciences, a particle is a small localized object to which can be ascribed several physical or chemical properties such as volume or mass. The word is rather general in meaning, and is refined as needed by various scientific fields. Something that is composed of particles may be referred to as particulate, although this term is generally used to refer to a suspension of unconnected particles, rather than a connected particle aggregation.

Point particle

A point particle is an idealization of particles heavily used in physics. Its defining feature is that it lacks spatial extension: being zero-dimensional, it does not take up space. A point particle is an appropriate representation of any object whose size, shape, and structure is irrelevant in a given context.

Internal combustion

The internal combustion engine is an engine in which the combustion of a fuel occurs with an oxidizer (usually air) in a combustion chamber that is an integral part of the working fluid flow circuit. In an internal combustion engine (ICE) the expansion of the high-temperature and high-pressure gases produced by combustion apply direct force to some component of the engine. The force is applied typically to pistons, turbine blades, or a nozzle.

Average speed

In everyday use and in kinematics, the speed of an object is the magnitude of its velocity ; it is thus a scalar quantity. The average speed of an object in an interval of time is the distance travelled by the object divided by the duration of the interval; the instantaneous speed is the limit of the average speed as the duration of the time interval approaches zero.

Like velocity, speed has the dimensions of a length divided by a time; the SI unit of speed is the metre per second, but the most usual unit of speed in everyday usage is the kilometre per hour or, in the US and the UK, miles per hour.

Displacement

In fluid mechanics, displacement occurs when an object is immersed in a fluid, pushing it out of the way and taking its place.

The volume of the fluid displaced can then be measured, and from this the volume of the immersed object can be deduced (the volume of the immersed object will be exactly equal to the volume of the displaced fluid).

An object that sinks displaces an amount of fluid equal to the object's volume.

Velocity	Velocity is the rate of change of the position of an object, equivalent to a specification of its speed and direction of motion, e.g. 60 km/h to the north. Velocity is an important concept in kinematics, the branch of classical mechanics which describes the motion of bodies. Velocity is a vector physical quantity; both magnitude and direction are required to define it.
Instantaneous	An instant is an infinitesimal moment in time, a moment whose passage is instantaneous. The continuous nature of time and its infinite divisibility was addressed by Aristotle in his Physics, where he wrote on Zeno's paradoxes. The philosopher and mathematician Bertrand Russell was still seeking to define the exact nature of an instant thousands of years later.
Air resistance	In fluid dynamics, drag (sometimes called air resistance, a type of friction, or fluid resistance, another type of friction) refers to forces acting opposite to the relative motion of any object moving with respect to a surrounding fluid. This can exist between two fluid layers (or surfaces) or a fluid and a solid surface. Unlike other resistive forces, such as dry friction, which are nearly independent of velocity, drag forces depend on velocity.
Free fall	In Newtonian physics, free fall is any motion of a body where its weight is the only force acting upon it. In the context of general relativity where gravitation is reduced to a space-time curvature, a body in free fall has no force acting on it and it moves along a geodesic
Gravity	In chemistry, gravity is the density of a fluid, particularly a fuel. It is expressed in degrees, with lower numbers indicating heavier liquids and higher numbers indicating lighter liquids. See specific gravity and API gravity.
Acceleration	In physics, acceleration is the rate at which the velocity of a body changes with time. Velocity and acceleration are vector quantities, with magnitude, direction, and add according to the parallelogram law. As described by Newton's Second Law, acceleration is caused by a net force; the force, as a vector, is equal to the product of the mass of the object being accelerated (scalar) and the acceleration.
Terminal velocity	The terminal velocity of a falling object is the velocity of the object when the sum of the drag force and buoyancy equals the downward force of gravity (F_G) acting on the object. Since the net force on the object is zero, the object has zero acceleration.

Terminal

In the context of telecommunications, a terminal is a device which ends a telecommunications link and is the point at which a signal enters and/or leaves a network. Examples of equipment containing network terminations are telephones, fax machines, computer terminals and network devices, printers and workstations.

Quadratic equation

In elementary algebra, a quadratic equation is any equation having the form $ax^2 + bx + c = 0$

where x represents an unknown, and a, b, and c are constants with a not equal to 0. If a = 0, then the equation is linear, not quadratic. The constants a, b, and c are called, respectively, the quadratic coefficient, the linear coefficient and the constant or free term.

Symmetry

In physics, symmetry includes all features of a physical system that exhibit the property of symmetry--that is, under certain transformations, aspects of these systems are otherwise 'unchanged', according to a particular observation. A symmetry of a physical system is a physical or mathematical feature of the system (observed or intrinsic) that is 'preserved' under some change.

A family of particular transformations may be continuous (such as rotation of a circle) or discrete (e.g., reflection of a bilaterally symmetric figure, or rotation of a regular polygon).

Quadratic formula

In basic algebra, the quadratic formula is the solution of the quadratic equation. There are other ways to solve the quadratic equation instead of using the quadratic formula, such as factoring, completing the square, or graphing. However, using the quadratic formula is often the most convenient way.

Tangent

In geometry, the tangent line (or simply the tangent) to a plane curve at a given point is the straight line that 'just touches' the curve at that point. Informally, it is a line through a pair of infinitely close points on the curve. More precisely, a straight line is said to be a tangent of a curve y = f(x) at a point x = c on the curve if the line passes through the point (c, f(c)) on the curve and has slope f(c) where f is the derivative of f.

2. DESCRIBING MOTION: KINEMATICS IN ONE DIMENSION

CHAPTER QUIZ: KEY TERMS, PEOPLE, PLACES, CONCEPTS

1. In physics, _________ includes all features of a physical system that exhibit the property of _________--that is, under certain transformations, aspects of these systems are otherwise 'unchanged', according to a particular observation. A _________ of a physical system is a physical or mathematical feature of the system (observed or intrinsic) that is 'preserved' under some change.

   A family of particular transformations may be continuous (such as rotation of a circle) or discrete (e.g., reflection of a bilaterally symmetric figure, or rotation of a regular polygon).

   a. Symmetry
   b. Bloch wave
   c. Bohr magneton
   d. Bohr model

2. In elementary algebra, a _________ is any equation having the form $ax^2 + bx + c = 0$

   where x represents an unknown, and a, b, and c are constants with a not equal to 0. If a = 0, then the equation is linear, not quadratic. The constants a, b, and c are called, respectively, the quadratic coefficient, the linear coefficient and the constant or free term.

   a. Bernstein polynomial
   b. Quadratic equation
   c. Bombieri norm
   d. Bracket polynomial

3. _________ is the branch of classical mechanics which describes the motion of points, bodies and systems of bodies (groups of objects) without consideration of the causes of motion. The term is the English version of A.M. Ampère's cinématique, which he constructed from the Greek ????µa, kinema (movement, motion), derived from ???e??, kinein (to move).

   The study of _________ is often referred to as the geometry of motion.

   a. Binet equation
   b. Bucket argument
   c. Center-of-momentum frame
   d. Kinematics

4.. In everyday use and in kinematics, the speed of an object is the magnitude of its velocity ; it is thus a scalar quantity. The _________ of an object in an interval of time is the distance travelled by the object divided by the duration of the interval; the instantaneous speed is the limit of the _________ as the duration of the time interval approaches zero.

   Like velocity, speed has the dimensions of a length divided by a time; the SI unit of speed is the metre per second, but the most usual unit of speed in everyday usage is the kilometre per hour or, in the US and the UK, miles per hour.

   a. Instantaneous speed

b. action Force
c. Algebraic topology
d. Average speed

5. _________ is motion along a straight line, and can therefore be described mathematically using only one spatial dimension. The _________ can be of two types: uniform _________ with constant velocity or zero acceleration; non uniform _________ with variable velocity or non-zero acceleration. The motion of a particle (a point-like object) along a line can be described by its position x , which varies with t (time).

a. Linear motion
b. Bucket argument
c. Center-of-momentum frame
d. Central force

ANSWER KEY
2. DESCRIBING MOTION: KINEMATICS IN ONE DIMENSION

---

1. a

2. b

3. d

4. d

5. a

---

3. KINEMATICS IN Two DIMENSIONS; VECTORS

CHAPTER OUTLINE: KEY TERMS, PEOPLE, PLACES, CONCEPTS

- Kinematics
- Parabola
- Projectile motion
- Projectile
- Scalar
- Velocity
- Displacement
- Resultant
- Pythagorean theorem
- Component
- Resolution
- Sine
- Tangent
- Symmetry
- Relative velocity
- Aristotle
- Contact force
- Gravitational force
- Gravity
- Friction
- Inertia

3. KINEMATICS IN Two DIMENSIONS; VECTORS

CHAPTER OUTLINE: KEY TERMS, PEOPLE, PLACES, CONCEPTS

- Net force
- Kilogram
- Dyne
- Acceleration
- Laser
- Normal force
- Point particle
- Atwood machine
- Pulley
- Accelerometer
- Mechanical advantage
- Coefficient
- Kinetics
- Statics
- Planck time
- Rock climbing

Kinematics

Kinematics is the branch of classical mechanics which describes the motion of points, bodies and systems of bodies (groups of objects) without consideration of the causes of motion. The term is the English version of A.M. Ampère's cinématique, which he constructed from the Greek ????μa, kinema (movement, motion), derived from ???e??, kinein (to move).

The study of kinematics is often referred to as the geometry of motion.

Parabola

A parabola is a two-dimensional, mirror-symmetrical curve, which is approximately U-shaped when oriented as shown in the diagram, but which can be in any orientation in its plane. It fits any of several superficially different mathematical descriptions which can all be proved to define curves of exactly the same shape.

One description of a parabola involves a point (the focus) and a line (the directrix).

Projectile motion

Projectile motion is a form of motion in which an object or particle is thrown obliquely near the earth's surface, and it moves along a curved path under the action of gravity only.The path followed by a projectile motion is called its trajectory. Projectile motion only occurs when there is one force applied at the beginning of the trajectory, after which there is no force in operation apart from gravity.

Projectile

A projectile is any object projected into space by the exertion of a force. Although any object in motion through space (for example a thrown baseball) may be referred to as a projectile, the term more commonly refers to a ranged weapon. Mathematical equations of motion are used to analyze projectile trajectory.

Scalar

In physics, a scalar is a one-dimensional physical quantity, i.e. one that can be described by a single real number (sometimes signed, often with units), unlike (or as a special case of) vectors, tensors, etc. which are described by several numbers which characterize magnitude and direction. Formally, a scalar is unchanged by coordinate system rotations or reflections (in Newtonian mechanics), or by Lorentz transformations or space-time translations (in relativity).

Velocity

Velocity is the rate of change of the position of an object, equivalent to a specification of its speed and direction of motion, e.g. 60 km/h to the north. Velocity is an important concept in kinematics, the branch of classical mechanics which describes the motion of bodies.

Velocity is a vector physical quantity; both magnitude and direction are required to define it.

Displacement

In fluid mechanics, displacement occurs when an object is immersed in a fluid, pushing it out of the way and taking its place. The volume of the fluid displaced can then be measured, and from this the volume of the immersed object can be deduced (the volume of the immersed object will be exactly equal to the volume of the displaced fluid).

3. KINEMATICS IN Two DIMENSIONS; VECTORS

CHAPTER HIGHLIGHTS & NOTES: KEY TERMS, PEOPLE, PLACES, CONCEPTS

Resultant

In mathematics, the resultant of two polynomials is a polynomial expression of their coefficients, which is equal to zero if and only if the polynomials have a common root, or, equivalently, a common factor (over their field of coefficients). In some older texts, the resultant is also called eliminant.

The resultant is widely used in number theory, either directly or through the discriminant, which is essentially the resultant of a polynomial and its derivative.

Pythagorean theorem

In mathematics, the Pythagorean theorem--or Pythagoras' theorem--is a relation in Euclidean geometry among the three sides of a right triangle. It states that the square of the hypotenuse (the side opposite the right angle) is equal to the sum of the squares of the other two sides. The theorem can be written as an equation relating the lengths of the sides a, b and c, often called the Pythagorean equation: $a^2 + b^2 = c^2$

where c represents the length of the hypotenuse, and a and b represent the lengths of the other two sides.

Component

In thermodynamics, a component is a chemically-independent constituent of a system. The number of components represents the minimum number of independent species necessary to define the composition of all phases of the system.

Calculating the number of components in a system is necessary, for example, when applying Gibbs' phase rule in determination of the number of degrees of freedom of a system.

Resolution

Resolution in terms of electron density is a measure of the resolvability in the electron density map of a molecule. In X-ray crystallography, resolution is the highest resolvable peak in the diffraction pattern. While cryo-electron microscopy is a frequency space comparison of two halves of the data, which strives to correlate with the X-ray definition.

Sine

In mathematics, the sine function is a trigonometric function of an angle. The sine of an angle is defined in the context of a right triangle: it is the ratio of the length of the side that is opposite to the angle divided by the hypotenuse.

Trigonometric functions are commonly defined as ratios of two sides of a right triangle containing the angle, and can equivalently be defined as the lengths of various line segments from a unit circle.

Tangent

In geometry, the tangent line (or simply the tangent) to a plane curve at a given point is the straight line that 'just touches' the curve at that point. Informally, it is a line through a pair of infinitely close points on the curve. More precisely, a straight line is said to be a tangent of a curve y = f(x) at a point x = c on the curve if the line passes through the point (c, f(c)) on the curve and has slope f(c) where f

Symmetry

In physics, symmetry includes all features of a physical system that exhibit the property of symmetry--that is, under certain transformations, aspects of these systems are otherwise 'unchanged', according to a particular observation. A symmetry of a physical system is a physical or mathematical feature of the system (observed or intrinsic) that is 'preserved' under some change.

A family of particular transformations may be continuous (such as rotation of a circle) or discrete (e.g., reflection of a bilaterally symmetric figure, or rotation of a regular polygon).

Relative velocity

The relative velocity $\vec{v}_{\mathrm{BA}}$ is the velocity of an object or observer B in the rest frame of another object or observer A, if it is constant, $\vec{v}_{\mathrm{BA}} = -\vec{v}_{\mathrm{AB}}$

where $\vec{v}_{\mathrm{AB}}$ is A's velocity in the rest frame of B.

Aristotle

Aristotle was a Greek philosopher born in Stagirus, northern Greece, in 384 BCE. His father, Nicomachus, died when Aristotle was a child, whereafter he lived under a guardian's care. At eighteen, he joined Plato's Academy in Athens and remained there until the age of thirty-seven (c. 347 BCE). His writings cover many subjects - including physics, biology, zoology, metaphysics, logic, ethics, aesthetics, poetry, theater, music, rhetoric, linguistics, politics and government - and constitute the first comprehensive system of Western philosophy.

Contact force

In physics, a contact force is a force that acts at the point of contact between two objects, in contrast to body forces. Contact forces are described by Newton's laws of motion, as with all other forces in dynamics.

Contact force is the force in which an object comes in contact with another object.

Gravitational force

Gravitation, or gravity, is a natural phenomenon by which all physical bodies attract each other. It is most commonly recognized and experienced as the agent that gives weight to physical objects, and causes physical objects to fall toward the ground when dropped from a height.

It is hypothesized that the gravitational force is mediated by a massless spin-2 particle called the graviton.

Gravity

In chemistry, gravity is the density of a fluid, particularly a fuel. It is expressed in degrees, with lower numbers indicating heavier liquids and higher numbers indicating lighter liquids. See specific gravity and API gravity.

Friction

Friction is the force resisting the relative motion of solid surfaces, fluid layers, and material elements sliding against each other. There are several types of friction: like fluid friction, dry friction, and sliding friction.•Dry friction resists relative lateral motion of two solid surfaces in contact.

3. KINEMATICS IN Two DIMENSIONS; VECTORS

CHAPTER HIGHLIGHTS & NOTES: KEY TERMS, PEOPLE, PLACES, CONCEPTS

Inertia

Inertia is the resistance of any physical object to any change in its motion . In other words, it is the tendency of objects to keep moving in a straight line at constant linear velocity. The principle of inertia is one of the fundamental principles of classical physics that are used to describe the motion of objects and how they are affected by externally applied forces.

Net force

In physics, net force is the overall force acting on an object. In order to calculate the net force, the body is isolated and interactions with the environment or constraints are introduced as forces and torques forming a free-body diagram.

The net force does not have the same effect on the movement of the object as the original system forces, unless the point of application of the net force and an associated torque are determined so that they form the resultant force and torque.

Kilogram

The kilogramme, is the base unit of mass in the International System of Units (SI) and is defined as being equal to the mass of the International Prototype of the Kilogram. The avoirdupois (or international) pound, used in both the Imperial system and U.S. customary units, is defined as exactly 0.45359237 kg, making one kilogram approximately equal to 2.2046 avoirdupois pounds.

The gram was originally defined in 1795 as the mass of one cubic centimeter of water at 4°C, making the kilogram equal to the mass of one liter of water.

Dyne

In physics, the dyne is a unit of force specified in the centimetre-gram-second (CGS) system of units, a predecessor of the modern SI. One dyne is equal to 10 μN (micronewtons), or to 10 nsn (nanosthenes) in the old metre-tonne-second system of units. Equivalently, the dyne is defined as 'the force required to accelerate a mass of one gram at a rate of one centimetre per second squared':1 dyn = 1 $g \cdot cm/s^2 = 10^{-5}\ kg \cdot m/s^2 = 10^{-5}$ N1 Newton = 1 $kg \cdot m/s^2 = 10^5\ g \cdot cm/s^2 = 10^{\ 5}$ dyne

The dyne per centimetre is the unit traditionally used to measure surface tension. For example, the surface tension of distilled water is 72 dyn/cm at 25 °C (77 °F); in SI units this is 72×10^{-3} N/m or 72 mN/m.

Acceleration

In physics, acceleration is the rate at which the velocity of a body changes with time. Velocity and acceleration are vector quantities, with magnitude, direction, and add according to the parallelogram law. As described by Newton's Second Law, acceleration is caused by a net force; the force, as a vector, is equal to the product of the mass of the object being accelerated (scalar) and the acceleration.

Laser

A laser is a device that emits light through a process of optical amplification based on the stimulated emission of electromagnetic radiation. The term 'laser' originated as an acronym for Light Amplification by Stimulated Emission of Radiation. Lasers differ from other sources of light because they emit light coherently.

Normal force

In mechanics, the normal force F_n is the component, perpendicular to the surface of contact, of the contact force exerted on an object by, for example, the surface of a floor or wall, preventing the object from penetrating the surface.

The normal force is one of the components of the ground reaction force and may coincide with it, for example considering a person standing still on the ground, in which case the ground reaction force reduces to the normal force. In another common situation, if an object hits a surface with some speed, and the surface can withstand it, the normal force provides for a rapid deceleration, which will depend on the flexibility of the surface.

Point particle

A point particle is an idealization of particles heavily used in physics. Its defining feature is that it lacks spatial extension: being zero-dimensional, it does not take up space. A point particle is an appropriate representation of any object whose size, shape, and structure is irrelevant in a given context.

Atwood machine

The Atwood machine was invented in 1784 by Rev. George Atwood as a laboratory experiment to verify the mechanical laws of motion with constant acceleration. Atwood's machine is a common classroom demonstration used to illustrate principles of classical mechanics.

The ideal Atwood Machine consists of two objects of mass m_1 and m_2, connected by an inextensible massless string over an ideal massless pulley.

Pulley

A pulley is a wheel on an axle that is designed to support movement of a cable or belt along its circumference. Pulleys are used in a variety of ways to lift loads, apply forces, and to transmit power.

A pulley is also called a sheave or drum and may have a groove between two flanges around its circumference.

Accelerometer

An accelerometer is a device that measures proper acceleration. The proper acceleration measured by an accelerometer is not necessarily the coordinate acceleration (rate of change of velocity). Instead, the accelerometer sees the acceleration associated with the phenomenon of weight experienced by any test mass at rest in the frame of reference of the accelerometer device.

Mechanical advantage

Mechanical advantage is a measure of the force amplification achieved by using a tool, mechanical device or machine system. Ideally, the device preserves the input power and simply trades off forces against movement to obtain a desired amplification in the output force. The model for this is the law of the lever.

Coefficient

In mathematics, a coefficient is a multiplicative factor in some term of an expression ; it is usually a number, but in any case does not involve any variables of the expression. For instance in

$$7x^2 - 3xy + 1.5 + y$$

the first two terms respectively have the coefficients 7 and -3. The third term 1.5 is a constant. The final term does not have any explicitly written coefficient, but is considered to have coefficient 1, since multiplying by that factor would not change the term.

Kinetics

In physics and engineering, kinetics is a term for the branch of classical mechanics that is concerned with the relationship between the motion of bodies and its causes, namely forces and torques. Since the mid-20th century, the term 'dynamics' (or 'analytical dynamics') has largely superseded 'kinetics' in physics text books; the term 'kinetics' is still used in engineering.

In mechanics, the Kinetics is deduced from Kinematics by the introduction of the concept of mass.

Statics

Statics is the branch of mechanics that is concerned with the analysis of loads on physical systems in static equilibrium, that is, in a state where the relative positions of subsystems do not vary over time, or where components and structures are at a constant velocity. When in static equilibrium, the system is either at rest, or its center of mass moves at constant velocity.

By Newton's first law, this situation implies that the net force and net torque (also known as moment of force) on every part of the system is zero.

Planck time

In physics, the Planck time is the unit of time in the system of natural units known as Planck units. It is the time required for light to travel, in a vacuum, a distance of 1 Planck length. The unit is named after Max Planck, who was the first to propose it.

Rock climbing

Rock climbing is an activity in which participants climb up, down or across natural rock formations or artificial rock walls. The goal is to reach the summit of a formation or the endpoint of a pre-defined route without falling. To successfully complete a climb, one must return to the base of the route safely.

1. In mathematics, the _________ of two polynomials is a polynomial expression of their coefficients, which is equal to zero if and only if the polynomials have a common root, or, equivalently, a common factor (over their field of coefficients). In some older texts, the _________ is also called eliminant.

   The _________ is widely used in number theory, either directly or through the discriminant, which is essentially the _________ of a polynomial and its derivative.

   a. Bernstein polynomial
   b. Binomial type
   c. Bombieri norm
   d. Resultant

2. The _________ $\vec{v}_{\rm BA}$ is the velocity of an object or observer B in the rest frame of another object or observer A, if it is constant, $\vec{v}_{\rm BA} = -\vec{v}_{\rm AB}$

   where $\vec{v}_{\rm AB}$ is A's velocity in the rest frame of B.

   a. Binet equation
   b. Bucket argument
   c. Relative velocity
   d. Central force

3. A _________ is any object projected into space by the exertion of a force. Although any object in motion through space (for example a thrown baseball) may be referred to as a _________, the term more commonly refers to a ranged weapon. Mathematical equations of motion are used to analyze _________ trajectory.

   a. Projectile
   b. Ballistic gelatin
   c. Ballistic limit
   d. Ballistic missile

4. _________ is a measure of the force amplification achieved by using a tool, mechanical device or machine system. Ideally, the device preserves the input power and simply trades off forces against movement to obtain a desired amplification in the output force. The model for this is the law of the lever.

   a. Mechanical advantage
   b. Belt friction
   c. Buckling
   d. Cam and groove

5. . _________ is a form of motion in which an object or particle is thrown obliquely near the earth's surface, and it moves along a curved path under the action of gravity only.The path followed by a _________ is called its trajectory.

_________ only occurs when there is one force applied at the beginning of the trajectory, after which there is no force in operation apart from gravity.

a. Banked turn
b. Belt friction
c. Buckling
d. Projectile motion

ANSWER KEY
3. KINEMATICS IN Two DIMENSIONS; VECTORS

---

1. d

2. c

3. a

4. a

5. d

---

4. DYNAMICS: NEWTON`S LAWS OF MOTION MOTION; GRAVITATION

CHAPTER OUTLINE: KEY TERMS, PEOPLE, PLACES, CONCEPTS

- Circular motion
- Centripetal
- Kinematics
- Frequency
- Period
- Centrifugal force
- Radius of curvature
- Action at a distance
- Gravitational force
- Gravity
- Symmetry
- Gravitational constant
- Apparent weight
- Free fall
- Weightlessness
- Celestial sphere
- Ellipse
- Mercury
- Neptune
- Uranus
- Planets

4. DYNAMICS: NEWTON`S LAWS OF MOTION MOTION; GRAVITATION

CHAPTER OUTLINE: KEY TERMS, PEOPLE, PLACES, CONCEPTS

	Perturbation
	Determinism
	Electromagnetic force
	Grand Unified Theory
	Lunar eclipse
	Nuclear force
	Solar eclipse
	Strong nuclear force
	Electromagnetic
	Black hole
	Milky Way

CHAPTER HIGHLIGHTS & NOTES: KEY TERMS, PEOPLE, PLACES, CONCEPTS

Circular motion

In physics, circular motion is a movement of an object along the circumference of a circle or rotation along a circular path. It can be uniform, with constant angular rate of rotation (and constant speed), or non-uniform with a changing rate of rotation. The rotation around a fixed axis of a three-dimensional body involves circular motion of its parts.

Centripetal

Centripetal force is a force that makes a body follow a curved path: its direction is always orthogonal to the velocity of the body, toward the fixed point of the instantaneous center of curvature of the path. Centripetal force is generally the cause of circular motion.

In simple terms, centripetal force is defined as a force which keeps a body moving with a uniform speed along a circular path and is directed along the radius towards the centre.

Kinematics	Kinematics is the branch of classical mechanics which describes the motion of points, bodies and systems of bodies (groups of objects) without consideration of the causes of motion. The term is the English version of A.M. Ampère's cinématique, which he constructed from the Greek ????μa, kinema (movement, motion), derived from ???e??, kinein (to move). The study of kinematics is often referred to as the geometry of motion.
Frequency	Frequency is the number of occurrences of a repeating event per unit time. It is also referred to as temporal frequency, which emphasizes the contrast to spatial frequency and angular frequency. The period is the duration of one cycle in a repeating event, so the period is the reciprocal of the frequency.
Period	In the periodic table of the elements, elements are arranged in a series of rows (or periods) so that those with similar properties appear in a column. Elements of the same period have the same number of electron shells; with each group across a period, the elements have one more proton and electron and become less metallic. This arrangement reflects the periodic recurrence of similar properties as the atomic number increases.
Centrifugal force	Centrifugal force is the apparent force that draws a rotating body away from the center of rotation. It is caused by the inertia of the body as the body's path is continually redirected. In Newtonian mechanics, the term centrifugal force is used to refer to one of two distinct concepts: an inertial force (also called a 'fictitious' force) observed in a non-inertial reference frame, and a reaction force corresponding to a centripetal force.
Radius of curvature	Radius of curvature has specific meaning and sign convention in optical design. A spherical lens or mirror surface has a center of curvature located in (x, y, z) either along or decentered from the system local optical axis. The vertex of the lens surface is located on the local optical axis.
Action at a distance	In physics, action at a distance is the nonlocal interaction of objects that are separated in space. This term was used most often in the context of early theories of gravity and electromagnetism to describe how an object responds to the influence of distant objects. More generally 'action at a distance' describes the failure of early atomistic and mechanistic theories which sought to reduce all physical interaction to collision.
Gravitational force	Gravitation, or gravity, is a natural phenomenon by which all physical bodies attract each other. It is most commonly recognized and experienced as the agent that gives weight to physical objects, and causes physical objects to fall toward the ground when dropped from a height. It is hypothesized that the gravitational force is mediated by a massless spin-2 particle called the graviton.

4. DYNAMICS: NEWTON`S LAWS OF MOTION MOTION; GRAVITATION

CHAPTER HIGHLIGHTS & NOTES: KEY TERMS, PEOPLE, PLACES, CONCEPTS

Gravity

In chemistry, gravity is the density of a fluid, particularly a fuel. It is expressed in degrees, with lower numbers indicating heavier liquids and higher numbers indicating lighter liquids. See specific gravity and API gravity.

Symmetry

In physics, symmetry includes all features of a physical system that exhibit the property of symmetry--that is, under certain transformations, aspects of these systems are otherwise 'unchanged', according to a particular observation. A symmetry of a physical system is a physical or mathematical feature of the system (observed or intrinsic) that is 'preserved' under some change.

A family of particular transformations may be continuous (such as rotation of a circle) or discrete (e.g., reflection of a bilaterally symmetric figure, or rotation of a regular polygon).

Gravitational constant

The gravitational constant, approximately 6.67×10^{-11} $N\cdot^{2}$ and denoted by letter G, is an empirical physical constant involved in the calculation(s) of gravitational force between two bodies. It usually appears in Sir Isaac Newton's law of universal gravitation, and in Albert Einstein's theory of general relativity. It is also known as the universal gravitational constant, Newton's constant, and colloquially as Big G. It should not be confused with 'little g' (g), which is the local gravitational field (equivalent to the free-fall acceleration), especially that at the Earth's surface.

Apparent weight

In physics, apparent weight is a property of objects that corresponds to how heavy an object is. The apparent weight of an object will differ from the weight of an object whenever the force of gravity acting on the object is not balanced by an equal but opposite normal force. By definition, the weight of an object is equal to the magnitude of the force of gravity acting on it.

Free fall

In Newtonian physics, free fall is any motion of a body where its weight is the only force acting upon it. In the context of general relativity where gravitation is reduced to a space-time curvature, a body in free fall has no force acting on it and it moves along a geodesic

Weightlessness

Weightlessness, or an absence of 'weight', is in fact an absence of stress and strain resulting from externally applied forces, typically contact forces from floors, seats, beds, scales, and the like. Counterintuitively, a uniform gravitational field does not by itself cause stress or strain, and a body in free fall in such an environment experiences no g-force acceleration and feels weightless. This is also termed zero-g.

Celestial sphere

In astronomy and navigation, the celestial sphere is an imaginary sphere of arbitrarily large radius, concentric with Earth. All objects in the observer's sky can be thought of as projected upon the inside surface of the celestial sphere, as if it were the underside of a dome or a hemispherical screen. The celestial sphere is a practical tool for spherical astronomy, allowing observers to plot positions of objects in the sky when their distances are unknown or unimportant.

Ellipse	In mathematics, an ellipse is a curve on a plane surrounding two focal points such that a straight line drawn from one of the focal points to any point on the curve and then back to the other focal point has the same length for every point on the curve. As such, it is a generalization of a circle which is a special type of an ellipse that has both focal points at the same location. The shape of an ellipse is represented by its eccentricity which for an ellipse can be any number from 0 (the limiting case of a circle) to arbitrarily close to but less than 1.
Mercury	Mercury is a chemical element with the symbol Hg and atomic number 80. It is commonly known as quicksilver and was formerly named hydrargyrum (from Greek 'hydr-' water and 'argyros' silver). A heavy, silvery d-block element, mercury is the only metal that is liquid at standard conditions for temperature and pressure; the only other element that is liquid under these conditions is bromine, though metals such as caesium, gallium, and rubidium melt just above room temperature. With a freezing point of -38.83 °C and boiling point of 356.73 °C, mercury has one of the narrowest ranges of its liquid state of any metal.
Neptune	Neptune is the eighth and farthest planet from the Sun in the Solar System. It is the fourth-largest planet by diameter and the third-largest by mass. Among the gaseous planets in the solar system, Neptune is the most dense.
Uranus	Ices: Uranus is the seventh planet from the Sun. It has the third-largest planetary radius and fourth-largest planetary mass in the Solar System. Uranus is similar in composition to Neptune, and both are of different chemical composition than the larger gas giants Jupiter and Saturn.
Planets	A planet (from Ancient Greek ?st?? p?a??t??, meaning 'wandering star') is an astronomical object orbiting a star or stellar remnant that is massive enough to be rounded by its own gravity, is not massive enough to cause thermonuclear fusion, and has cleared its neighbouring region of planetesimals. The term planet is ancient, with ties to history, science, mythology, and religion. The planets were originally seen by many early cultures as divine, or as emissaries of deities.
Perturbation	In astronomy, perturbation is the complex motion of a massive body subject to forces other than the gravitational attraction of a single other massive body. The other forces can include a third (fourth, fifth, etc). body, resistance, as from an atmosphere, and the off-center attraction of an oblate or otherwise misshapen body.
Determinism	Determinism is a philosophical position stating that for everything that happens there are conditions such that, given those conditions, nothing else could happen. 'There are many determinisms, depending upon what pre-conditions are considered to be determinative of an event.' Deterministic theories throughout the history of philosophy have sprung from diverse motives and considerations, some of which overlap.

CHAPTER HIGHLIGHTS & NOTES: KEY TERMS, PEOPLE, PLACES, CONCEPTS

Electromagnetic force	Electromagnetism, or the electromagnetic force is one of the four fundamental interactions in nature, the other three being the strong interaction, the weak interaction, and gravitation. This force is described by electromagnetic fields, and has innumerable physical instances including the interaction of electrically charged particles and the interaction of uncharged magnetic force fields with electrical conductors. The word electromagnetism is a compound form of two Greek terms, ??e?t???, elektron, 'amber', and μa???t??, magnetes, 'magnet'.
Grand Unified Theory	A Grand Unified Theory is a model in particle physics in which at high energy, the three gauge interactions of the Standard Model which define the electromagnetic, weak, and strong interactions, are merged into one single interaction characterized by one larger gauge symmetry and thus one unified coupling constant. In contrast, the experimentally supported Standard Model of particle physics is based on three independent interactions, symmetries and coupling constants. Models that do not unify all interactions using one simple Lie group as the gauge symmetry, but do so using semisimple groups, can exhibit similar properties and are sometimes referred to as Grand Unified Theories as well.
Lunar eclipse	A lunar eclipse occurs when the Moon passes directly behind the Earth into its umbra . This can occur only when the Sun, Earth, and Moon are aligned (in 'syzygy') exactly, or very closely so, with the Earth in the middle. Hence, a lunar eclipse can only occur the night of a full moon.
Nuclear force	The nuclear force is the force between two or more nucleons. Its fundamental laws and constants are unknown unlike the Coulomb and Newton laws. It is responsible for binding protons and neutrons into atomic nuclei.
Solar eclipse	As seen from the Earth, a solar eclipse is a type of eclipse that occurs when the Moon passes between the Sun and Earth, and the Moon fully or partially blocks the Sun. This can happen only at new moon, when the Sun and the Moon are in conjunction as seen from Earth in an alignment referred to as syzygy. In a total eclipse, the disk of the Sun is fully obscured by the Moon.
Strong nuclear force	In particle physics, the strong interaction (also called the strong force, strong nuclear force, nuclear strong force or color force) is one of the four fundamental interactions of nature, the others being electromagnetism, the weak interaction and gravitation. At atomic scale, it is about 100 times stronger than electromagnetism, which in turn is orders of magnitude stronger than the weak force interaction and gravitation. It ensures the stability of ordinary matter, in confining the elementary particles quarks into hadrons such as the proton and neutron, the largest components of the mass of ordinary matter.
Electromagnetic	Electromagnetic is a prefix used to specialise many technical terms that involve electromagnetism.

CHAPTER HIGHLIGHTS & NOTES: KEY TERMS, PEOPLE, PLACES, CONCEPTS

Black hole	A black hole is a region of spacetime from which gravity prevents anything, including light, from escaping. The theory of general relativity predicts that a sufficiently compact mass will deform spacetime to form a black hole. Around a black hole, there is a mathematically defined surface called an event horizon that marks the point of no return.
Milky Way	The Milky Way is the galaxy that contains our Solar System. Its name 'milky' is derived from its appearance as a dim glowing band arching across the night sky in which the naked eye cannot distinguish individual stars. The term 'Milky Way' is a translation of the Classical Latin via lactea, from the Greek ?a?a??a? ?????? (pr.

CHAPTER QUIZ: KEY TERMS, PEOPLE, PLACES, CONCEPTS

1. In physics, _________ is a movement of an object along the circumference of a circle or rotation along a circular path. It can be uniform, with constant angular rate of rotation (and constant speed), or non-uniform with a changing rate of rotation. The rotation around a fixed axis of a three-dimensional body involves _________ of its parts.

   a. Central angle
   b. Bevel
   c. Conformal map
   d. Circular motion

2. _________, or an absence of 'weight', is in fact an absence of stress and strain resulting from externally applied forces, typically contact forces from floors, seats, beds, scales, and the like. Counterintuitively, a uniform gravitational field does not by itself cause stress or strain, and a body in free fall in such an environment experiences no g-force acceleration and feels weightless. This is also termed zero-g.

   a. Blackett effect
   b. CLIO
   c. Coriolis field
   d. Weightlessness

3. . _________ is the number of occurrences of a repeating event per unit time. It is also referred to as temporal _________, which emphasizes the contrast to spatial _________ and angular _________. The period is the duration of one cycle in a repeating event, so the period is the reciprocal of the _________.

   a. Frequency
   b. Background noise
   c. Bass trap

4. _________ force is a force that makes a body follow a curved path: its direction is always orthogonal to the velocity of the body, toward the fixed point of the instantaneous center of curvature of the path. _________ force is generally the cause of circular motion.

   In simple terms, _________ force is defined as a force which keeps a body moving with a uniform speed along a circular path and is directed along the radius towards the centre.

   a. gravitational
   b. Gravitational force
   c. scanning tunneling
   d. Centripetal

5. _________ is the branch of classical mechanics which describes the motion of points, bodies and systems of bodies (groups of objects) without consideration of the causes of motion. The term is the English version of A.M. Ampère's cinématique, which he constructed from the Greek ????μa, kinema (movement, motion), derived from ???e??, kinein (to move).

   The study of _________ is often referred to as the geometry of motion.

   a. Binet equation
   b. Bucket argument
   c. Center-of-momentum frame
   d. Kinematics

ANSWER KEY
4. DYNAMICS: NEWTON`S LAWS OF MOTION MOTION; GRAVITATION

1. d
2. d
3. a
4. d
5. d

---

5. WORK AND ENERGY

CHAPTER OUTLINE: KEY TERMS, PEOPLE, PLACES, CONCEPTS

- Conservation law
- Conserved quantity
- Momentum
- Joule
- Kinetic energy
- Kinetics
- Potential energy
- Gravitational
- Roller coaster
- Restoring force
- Conservative force
- Conservation of energy
- Energy conservation
- Mechanical energy
- Transformation
- Thermal energy
- Horsepower
- Watt
- Efficiency
- Kilowatt-hour

5. WORK AND ENERGY

CHAPTER HIGHLIGHTS & NOTES: KEY TERMS, PEOPLE, PLACES, CONCEPTS

Conservation law	In physics, a conservation law states that a particular measurable property of an isolated physical system does not change as the system evolves. One particularly important physical result concerning conservation laws is Noether's theorem, which states that there is a one-to-one correspondence between conservation laws and differentiable symmetries of physical systems. For example, the conservation of energy follows from the time-invariance of physical systems, and the fact that physical systems behave the same regardless of how they are oriented in space gives rise to the conservation of angular momentum.
Conserved quantity	In mathematics, a conserved quantity of a dynamical system is a function H of the dependent variables that is a constant along each trajectory of the system. A conserved quantity can be a useful tool for qualitative analysis. Not all systems have conserved quantities, however the existence has nothing to do with linearity (a simplifying trait in a system) which means that finding and examining conserved quantities can be useful in understanding nonlinear systems.
Momentum	In classical mechanics, linear momentum or translational momentum is the product of the mass and velocity of an object. For example, a heavy truck moving fast has a large momentum--it takes a large and prolonged force to get the truck up to this speed, and it takes a large and prolonged force to bring it to a stop afterwards. If the truck were lighter, or moving more slowly, then it would have less momentum.
Joule	The joule, symbol J, is a derived unit of energy, work, or amount of heat in the International System of Units. It is equal to the energy expended (or work done) in applying a force of one newton through a distance of one metre (1 newton metre or N·m), or in passing an electric current of one ampere through a resistance of one ohm for one second. It is named after the English physicist James Prescott Joule.
Kinetic energy	In physics, the kinetic energy of an object is the energy which it possesses due to its motion. It is defined as the work needed to accelerate a body of a given mass from rest to its stated velocity. Having gained this energy during its acceleration, the body maintains this kinetic energy unless its speed changes.
Kinetics	In physics and engineering, kinetics is a term for the branch of classical mechanics that is concerned with the relationship between the motion of bodies and its causes, namely forces and torques. Since the mid-20th century, the term 'dynamics' (or 'analytical dynamics') has largely superseded 'kinetics' in physics text books; the term 'kinetics' is still used in engineering. In mechanics, the Kinetics is deduced from Kinematics by the introduction of the concept of mass.
Potential energy	In physics, potential energy is the energy of an object or a system due to the position of the body or the arrangement of the particles of the system. The SI unit for measuring work and energy is the joule (symbol J).

Gravitational	Gravitation, or gravity, is a natural phenomenon by which all physical bodies attract each other. It is most commonly recognized and experienced as the agent that gives weight to physical objects, and causes physical objects to fall toward the ground when dropped from a height. It is hypothesized that the gravitational force is mediated by a massless spin-2 particle called the graviton.
Roller coaster	The roller coaster is a popular amusement ride developed for amusement parks and modern theme parks. LaMarcus Adna Thompson obtained a patent regarding roller coasters on January 20, 1885, which were made out of wood, but this patent is considerably later than the 'Russian mountains' described below. In essence a specialized railroad system, a roller coaster consists of a track that rises in designed patterns, sometimes with one or more inversions (such as vertical loops) that briefly turn the rider upside down.
Restoring force	Restoring force, in a physics context, is a variable force that gives rise to an equilibrium in a physical system. If the system is perturbed away from the equilibrium, the restoring force will tend to bring the system back toward equilibrium. The restoring force is a function only of position of the mass or particle.
Conservative force	A conservative force is a force with the property that the work done in moving a particle between two points is independent of the taken path. Equivalently, if a particle travels in a closed loop, the net work done (the sum of the force acting along the path multiplied by the distance travelled) by a conservative force is zero. A conservative force is dependent only on the position of the object.
Conservation of energy	In physics, the law of conservation of energy states that the total energy of an isolated system cannot change--it is said to be conserved over time. Energy can be neither created nor destroyed, but can change form, for instance chemical energy can be converted to kinetic energy in the explosion of a stick of dynamite. A consequence of the law of conservation of energy is that a perpetual motion machine of the first kind cannot exist.
Energy conservation	Energy conservation refers to reducing energy through using less of an energy service. Energy conservation differs from efficient energy use, which refers to using less energy for a constant service. For example, driving less is an example of energy conservation.
Mechanical energy	In the physical sciences, mechanical energy is the sum of potential energy and kinetic energy. It is the energy associated with the motion and position of an object.

5. WORK AND ENERGY

CHAPTER HIGHLIGHTS & NOTES: KEY TERMS, PEOPLE, PLACES, CONCEPTS

Transformation

In mathematics, a transformation could be any function mapping a set X to another set or to itself. However, often the set X has some additional algebraic or geometric structure and the term 'transformation' refers to a function from X to itself that preserves this structure.

Examples include linear transformations and affine transformations, rotations, reflections and translations.

Thermal energy

Thermal energy is the part of the total potential energy and kinetic energy of an object or sample of matter that results in the system temperature. It is represented by the variable Q, and can be measured in Joules. This quantity may be difficult to determine or even meaningless unless the system has attained its temperature only through warming (heating), and not been subjected to work input or output, or any other energy-changing processes.

Horsepower

Horsepower is the name of several units of measurement of power, the rate at which work is done. The most common conversion factor, especially for electrical power, is 1 hp = 746 watts. The term was adopted in the late 18th century by Scottish engineer James Watt to compare the output of steam engines with the power of draft horses.

Watt

The watt is a derived unit of power in the International System of Units (SI) defined as one joule per second, measures the rate of energy conversion or transfer.

Efficiency

Efficiency in general, describes the extent to which time, effort or cost is well used for the intended task or purpose. It is often used with the specific purpose of relaying the capability of a specific application of effort to produce a specific outcome effectively with a minimum amount or quantity of waste, expense, or unnecessary effort. 'Efficiency' has widely varying meanings in different disciplines.

Kilowatt-hour

The kilowatt hour, or kilowatt-hour, is a unit of energy equal to 1000 watt-hours or 3.6 megajoules. For constant power, energy in watt-hours is the product of power in watts and time in hours. The kilowatt-hour is most commonly known as a billing unit for energy delivered to consumers by electric utilities.

1. _________ is the name of several units of measurement of power, the rate at which work is done. The most common conversion factor, especially for electrical power, is 1 hp = 746 watts. The term was adopted in the late 18th century by Scottish engineer James Watt to compare the output of steam engines with the power of draft horses.

   a. Complexity
   b. Continuous predicate
   c. Daydream
   d. Horsepower

2. In physics, a _________ states that a particular measurable property of an isolated physical system does not change as the system evolves.

   One particularly important physical result concerning _________s is Noether's theorem, which states that there is a one-to-one correspondence between _________s and differentiable symmetries of physical systems. For example, the conservation of energy follows from the time-invariance of physical systems, and the fact that physical systems behave the same regardless of how they are oriented in space gives rise to the conservation of angular momentum.

   a. 1s Slater-type function
   b. Bloch wave
   c. Conservation law
   d. Bohr model

3. In mathematics, a _________ of a dynamical system is a function H of the dependent variables that is a constant along each trajectory of the system. A _________ can be a useful tool for qualitative analysis. Not all systems have _________(ies), however the existence has nothing to do with linearity (a simplifying trait in a system) which means that finding and examining _________(ies) can be useful in understanding nonlinear systems.

   a. Boolean delay equation
   b. Brjuno number
   c. Conserved quantity
   d. Cellular automaton

4. In classical mechanics, linear _________ or translational _________ is the product of the mass and velocity of an object. For example, a heavy truck moving fast has a large _________--it takes a large and prolonged force to get the truck up to this speed, and it takes a large and prolonged force to bring it to a stop afterwards. If the truck were lighter, or moving more slowly, then it would have less _________.

   a. Banked turn
   b. Momentum
   c. Buckling
   d. Cam and groove

5.. The _________, symbol J, is a derived unit of energy, work, or amount of heat in the International System of Units.

5. WORK AND ENERGY

It is equal to the energy expended (or work done) in applying a force of one newton through a distance of one metre (1 newton metre or N·m), or in passing an electric current of one ampere through a resistance of one ohm for one second. It is named after the English physicist James Prescott _________.

a. 3-manifold
b. Belt friction
c. Buckling
d. Joule

ANSWER KEY
5. WORK AND ENERGY

1. d
2. c
3. c
4. b
5. d

---

6. LINEAR MOMENTUM

CHAPTER OUTLINE: KEY TERMS, PEOPLE, PLACES, CONCEPTS

- Linear momentum
- Collision
- Isolated system
- Impulse
- Elastic collision
- Inelastic collision
- Relative velocity
- Cloud chamber
- Symmetry
- Center of mass
- Human body
- Particle
- Neutrino

6. LINEAR MOMENTUM

CHAPTER HIGHLIGHTS & NOTES: KEY TERMS, PEOPLE, PLACES, CONCEPTS

Linear momentum	In classical mechanics, linear momentum or translational momentum is the product of the mass and velocity of an object. For example, a heavy truck moving fast has a large momentum--it takes a large and prolonged force to get the truck up to this speed, and it takes a large and prolonged force to bring it to a stop afterwards. If the truck were lighter, or moving more slowly, then it would have less momentum.
Collision	A collision is an isolated event in which two or more moving bodies exert forces on each other for a relatively short time. Although the most common colloquial use of the word 'collision' refers to accidents in which two or more objects collide, the scientific use of the word 'collision' implies nothing about the magnitude of the forces. Some examples of physical interactions that scientists would consider collisions:•An insect touches its antenna to the leaf of a plant.
Isolated system	In the natural sciences an isolated system is a physical system without any external exchange - neither matter nor energy can enter or exit, but can only move around inside. Truly isolated systems cannot exist in nature, other than allegedly the universe itself, and they are thus hypothetical concepts only. It obeys, in particular, to the first of the conservation laws: its total energy - mass stays constant.
Impulse	In classical mechanics, the impulse of force is defined as the product of the average force multiplied by the time it is exerted. Impulse is a vector quantity since force is a vector quantity. The SI unit of impulse is the newton second (N·s) or, in base units, the kilogram meter per second (kg·m/s).
Elastic collision	An elastic collision is an encounter between two bodies in which the total kinetic energy of the two bodies after the encounter is equal to their total kinetic energy before the encounter. Elastic collisions occur only if there is no net conversion of kinetic energy into other forms. During the collision of small objects, kinetic energy is first converted to potential energy associated with a repulsive force between the particles (when the particles move against this force, i.e. the angle between the force and the relative velocity is obtuse), then this potential energy is converted back to kinetic energy (when the particles move with this force, i.e. the angle between the force and the relative velocity is acute).
Inelastic collision	An inelastic collision, in contrast to an elastic collision, is a collision in which kinetic energy is not conserved. In collisions of macroscopic bodies, some kinetic energy is turned into vibrational energy of the atoms, causing a heating effect, and the bodies are deformed.

Relative velocity

The relative velocity $\vec{v}_{\mathrm{BA}}$ is the velocity of an object or observer B in the rest frame of another object or observer A, if it is constant, $\vec{v}_{\mathrm{BA}} = -\vec{v}_{\mathrm{AB}}$

where $\vec{v}_{\mathrm{AB}}$ is A's velocity in the rest frame of B.

Cloud chamber

The cloud chamber, also known as the Wilson chamber, is a particle detector used for detecting ionizing radiation.

In its most basic form, a cloud chamber is a sealed environment containing a supersaturated vapor of water or alcohol. When a charged particle (for example, an alpha or beta particle) interacts with the mixture, it ionizes it.

Symmetry

In physics, symmetry includes all features of a physical system that exhibit the property of symmetry--that is, under certain transformations, aspects of these systems are otherwise 'unchanged', according to a particular observation. A symmetry of a physical system is a physical or mathematical feature of the system (observed or intrinsic) that is 'preserved' under some change.

A family of particular transformations may be continuous (such as rotation of a circle) or discrete (e.g., reflection of a bilaterally symmetric figure, or rotation of a regular polygon).

Center of mass

In physics, the center of mass of a distribution of mass in space is the unique point where the weighted relative position of the distributed mass sums to zero. The distribution of mass is balanced around the center of mass and the average of the weighted position coordinates of the distributed mass defines its coordinates. Calculations in mechanics are often simplified when formulated with respect to the center of mass.

Human body

The human body is the entire structure of a human being and comprises a head, neck, trunk, two arms and hands and two legs and feet. Every part of the body is composed of various types of cell. At maturity, the estimated number of cells in the body is given as 37.2 trillion.

Particle

In the physical sciences, a particle is a small localized object to which can be ascribed several physical or chemical properties such as volume or mass. The word is rather general in meaning, and is refined as needed by various scientific fields. Something that is composed of particles may be referred to as particulate, although this term is generally used to refer to a suspension of unconnected particles, rather than a connected particle aggregation.

Neutrino

A neutrino is an electrically neutral, weakly interacting elementary subatomic particle with half-integer spin. The neutrino is denoted by the Greek letter ? (nu). All evidence suggests that neutrinos have mass but that their mass is tiny even by the standards of subatomic particles.

6. LINEAR MOMENTUM

CHAPTER QUIZ: KEY TERMS, PEOPLE, PLACES, CONCEPTS

1. An _________ is an encounter between two bodies in which the total kinetic energy of the two bodies after the encounter is equal to their total kinetic energy before the encounter. _________s occur only if there is no net conversion of kinetic energy into other forms.

   During the collision of small objects, kinetic energy is first converted to potential energy associated with a repulsive force between the particles (when the particles move against this force, i.e. the angle between the force and the relative velocity is obtuse), then this potential energy is converted back to kinetic energy (when the particles move with this force, i.e. the angle between the force and the relative velocity is acute).

   a. Binet equation
   b. Bucket argument
   c. Center-of-momentum frame
   d. Elastic collision

2. In the natural sciences an _________ is a physical system without any external exchange - neither matter nor energy can enter or exit, but can only move around inside. Truly _________s cannot exist in nature, other than allegedly the universe itself, and they are thus hypothetical concepts only. It obeys, in particular, to the first of the conservation laws: its total energy - mass stays constant.

   a. Backdraft
   b. Batteryless radio
   c. Bennett acceptance ratio
   d. Isolated system

3. A _________ is an isolated event in which two or more moving bodies exert forces on each other for a relatively short time.

   Although the most common colloquial use of the word '_________' refers to accidents in which two or more objects collide, the scientific use of the word '_________' implies nothing about the magnitude of the forces.

   Some examples of physical interactions that scientists would consider _________s:•An insect touches its antenna to the leaf of a plant.

   a. Collision
   b. Belt friction
   c. Buckling
   d. Cam and groove

4. . In classical mechanics, _________ or translational momentum is the product of the mass and velocity of an object. For example, a heavy truck moving fast has a large momentum--it takes a large and prolonged force to get the truck up to this speed, and it takes a large and prolonged force to bring it to a stop afterwards. If the truck were lighter, or moving more slowly, then it would have less momentum.

   a. Linear momentum

b. Berge conjecture
c. Berge knot
d. Branched surface

5. In classical mechanics, the _________ of force is defined as the product of the average force multiplied by the time it is exerted. _________ is a vector quantity since force is a vector quantity. The SI unit of _________ is the newton second (N·s) or, in base units, the kilogram meter per second (kg·m/s).

a. Binet equation
b. Impulse
c. Center-of-momentum frame
d. Central force

ANSWER KEY
6. LINEAR MOMENTUM

1. d
2. d
3. a
4. a
5. b

---

7. ROTATIONAL MOTION

CHAPTER OUTLINE: KEY TERMS, PEOPLE, PLACES, CONCEPTS

- Kinematics
- Rigid body
- Angular displacement
- Angular velocity
- Instantaneous
- Angular acceleration
- Frequency
- Hertz
- Period
- Rotation
- Rotation period
- Statics
- Joule
- Moment of inertia
- Pulley
- Kinetics
- Angular momentum
- Neutron star
- Neutron
- Symmetry
- Atwood machine

7. ROTATIONAL MOTION

CHAPTER OUTLINE: KEY TERMS, PEOPLE, PLACES, CONCEPTS

	Flywheel
	Solar eclipse

CHAPTER HIGHLIGHTS & NOTES: KEY TERMS, PEOPLE, PLACES, CONCEPTS

Kinematics

Kinematics is the branch of classical mechanics which describes the motion of points, bodies and systems of bodies (groups of objects) without consideration of the causes of motion. The term is the English version of A.M. Ampère's cinématique, which he constructed from the Greek ????μa, kinema (movement, motion), derived from ???e??, kinein (to move).

The study of kinematics is often referred to as the geometry of motion.

Rigid body

In physics, a rigid body is an idealization of a solid body in which deformation is neglected. In other words, the distance between any two given points of a rigid body remains constant in time regardless of external forces exerted on it. Even though such an object cannot physically exist due to relativity, objects can normally be assumed to be perfectly rigid if they are not moving near the speed of light.

Angular displacement

Angular displacement of a body is the angle in radians through which a point or line has been rotated in a specified sense about a specified axis.

When an object rotates about its axis, the motion cannot simply be analyzed as a particle, since in circular motion it undergoes a changing velocity and acceleration at any time (t). When dealing with the rotation of an object, it becomes simpler to consider the body itself rigid.

Angular velocity

In physics, the angular velocity is defined as the rate of change of angular displacement and is a vector quantity which specifies the angular speed (rotational speed) of an object and the axis about which the object is rotating. The SI unit of angular velocity is radians per second, although it may be measured in other units such as degrees per second, degrees per hour, etc. Angular velocity is usually represented by the symbol omega (?, rarely O).

Instantaneous

An instant is an infinitesimal moment in time, a moment whose passage is instantaneous.

The continuous nature of time and its infinite divisibility was addressed by Aristotle in his Physics, where he wrote on Zeno's paradoxes.

Angular acceleration	Angular acceleration is the rate of change of angular velocity. In SI units, it is measured in radians per second squared (rad/s^2), and is usually denoted by the Greek letter alpha (a).
Frequency	Frequency is the number of occurrences of a repeating event per unit time. It is also referred to as temporal frequency, which emphasizes the contrast to spatial frequency and angular frequency. The period is the duration of one cycle in a repeating event, so the period is the reciprocal of the frequency.
Hertz	The hertz is the unit of frequency in the International System of Units (SI). It is defined as the number of cycles per second of a periodic phenomenon. One of its most common uses is the description of the sine wave, particularly those used in radio and audio applications, such as the frequency of musical tones.
Period	In the periodic table of the elements, elements are arranged in a series of rows (or periods) so that those with similar properties appear in a column. Elements of the same period have the same number of electron shells; with each group across a period, the elements have one more proton and electron and become less metallic. This arrangement reflects the periodic recurrence of similar properties as the atomic number increases.
Rotation	In geometry and linear algebra, a rotation is a transformation in a plane or in space that describes the motion of a rigid body around a fixed point. A rotation is different from a translation, which has no fixed points, and from a reflection, which 'flips' the bodies it is transforming. A rotation and the above-mentioned transformations are isometries; they leave the distance between any two points unchanged after the transformation.
Rotation period	The rotation period of an astronomical object is the time that it takes to complete one revolution around its axis of rotation relative to the background stars. It differs from the planet's solar day, which includes an extra fractional rotation needed to accommodate the portion of the planet's orbital period during one day.
Statics	Statics is the branch of mechanics that is concerned with the analysis of loads on physical systems in static equilibrium, that is, in a state where the relative positions of subsystems do not vary over time, or where components and structures are at a constant velocity. When in static equilibrium, the system is either at rest, or its center of mass moves at constant velocity. By Newton's first law, this situation implies that the net force and net torque (also known as moment of force) on every part of the system is zero.
Joule	The joule, symbol J, is a derived unit of energy, work, or amount of heat in the International System of Units. It is equal to the energy expended (or work done) in applying a force of one newton through a distance of one metre (1 newton metre or N·m), or in passing an electric current of one ampere through a resistance of one ohm for one second.

7. ROTATIONAL MOTION

CHAPTER HIGHLIGHTS & NOTES: KEY TERMS, PEOPLE, PLACES, CONCEPTS

Moment of inertia	Moment of inertia is the mass property of a rigid body that defines the torque needed for a desired change in angular velocity about an axis of rotation. Moment of inertia depends on the shape of the body and may be different around different axes of rotation. A larger moment of inertia around a given axis requires more torque to increase the rotation, or to stop the rotation, of a body about that axis.
Pulley	A pulley is a wheel on an axle that is designed to support movement of a cable or belt along its circumference. Pulleys are used in a variety of ways to lift loads, apply forces, and to transmit power. A pulley is also called a sheave or drum and may have a groove between two flanges around its circumference.
Kinetics	In physics and engineering, kinetics is a term for the branch of classical mechanics that is concerned with the relationship between the motion of bodies and its causes, namely forces and torques. Since the mid-20th century, the term 'dynamics' (or 'analytical dynamics') has largely superseded 'kinetics' in physics text books; the term 'kinetics' is still used in engineering. In mechanics, the Kinetics is deduced from Kinematics by the introduction of the concept of mass.
Angular momentum	In physics, angular momentum, moment of momentum, or rotational momentum is the amount of rotation an object has, taking into account its mass and shape. It is a vector quantity that represents the product of a body's rotational inertia and rotational velocity about a particular axis. The angular momentum of a system of particles (e.g. a rigid body) is the sum of angular momenta of the individual particles.
Neutron star	A neutron star is a type of stellar remnant that can result from the gravitational collapse of a massive star during a Type II, Type Ib or Type Ic supernova event. Such stars are composed almost entirely of neutrons, which are subatomic particles without net electrical charge and with slightly larger mass than protons. Neutron stars are very hot and are supported against further collapse by quantum degeneracy pressure due to the phenomenon described by the Pauli exclusion principle.
Neutron	The neutron is a subatomic hadron particle that has the symbol n or n0, no net electric charge and a mass slightly larger than that of a proton. With the exception of hydrogen-1, nuclei of atoms consist of protons and neutrons, which are therefore collectively referred to as nucleons. The number of protons in a nucleus is the atomic number and defines the type of element the atom forms.
Symmetry	In physics, symmetry includes all features of a physical system that exhibit the property of symmetry--that is, under certain transformations, aspects of these systems are otherwise 'unchanged', according to a particular observation.

7. ROTATIONAL MOTION

CHAPTER HIGHLIGHTS & NOTES: KEY TERMS, PEOPLE, PLACES, CONCEPTS

A symmetry of a physical system is a physical or mathematical feature of the system (observed or intrinsic) that is 'preserved' under some change.

A family of particular transformations may be continuous (such as rotation of a circle) or discrete (e.g., reflection of a bilaterally symmetric figure, or rotation of a regular polygon).

Atwood machine

The Atwood machine was invented in 1784 by Rev. George Atwood as a laboratory experiment to verify the mechanical laws of motion with constant acceleration. Atwood's machine is a common classroom demonstration used to illustrate principles of classical mechanics.

The ideal Atwood Machine consists of two objects of mass m_1 and m_2, connected by an inextensible massless string over an ideal massless pulley.

Flywheel

A flywheel is a rotating mechanical device that is used to store rotational energy. Flywheels have a significant moment of inertia and thus resist changes in rotational speed. The amount of energy stored in a flywheel is proportional to the square of its rotational speed.

Solar eclipse

As seen from the Earth, a solar eclipse is a type of eclipse that occurs when the Moon passes between the Sun and Earth, and the Moon fully or partially blocks the Sun. This can happen only at new moon, when the Sun and the Moon are in conjunction as seen from Earth in an alignment referred to as syzygy. In a total eclipse, the disk of the Sun is fully obscured by the Moon.

CHAPTER QUIZ: KEY TERMS, PEOPLE, PLACES, CONCEPTS

1. The _________ of an astronomical object is the time that it takes to complete one revolution around its axis of rotation relative to the background stars. It differs from the planet's solar day, which includes an extra fractional rotation needed to accommodate the portion of the planet's orbital period during one day.

   a. Binary system
   b. Rotation period
   c. Dynamic method
   d. Dynamical lifetime

2. . The _________ is the unit of frequency in the International System of Units (SI). It is defined as the number of cycles per second of a periodic phenomenon. One of its most common uses is the description of the sine wave, particularly those used in radio and audio applications, such as the frequency of musical tones.

   a. Revolutions per minute

b. 3-manifold
c. Hertz
d. Beat

3. The _________ was invented in 1784 by Rev. George Atwood as a laboratory experiment to verify the mechanical laws of motion with constant acceleration. Atwood's machine is a common classroom demonstration used to illustrate principles of classical mechanics.

   The ideal _________ consists of two objects of mass m_1 and m_2, connected by an inextensible massless string over an ideal massless pulley.

   a. Friedrich Oskar Giesel
   b. Atwood machine
   c. Sibplaz
   d. The Aluminum Association

4. _________ is the branch of classical mechanics which describes the motion of points, bodies and systems of bodies (groups of objects) without consideration of the causes of motion. The term is the English version of A.M. Ampère's cinématique, which he constructed from the Greek ????µa, kinema (movement, motion), derived from ???e??, kinein (to move).

   The study of _________ is often referred to as the geometry of motion.

   a. Kinematics
   b. Bucket argument
   c. Center-of-momentum frame
   d. Central force

5. _________ is the mass property of a rigid body that defines the torque needed for a desired change in angular velocity about an axis of rotation. _________ depends on the shape of the body and may be different around different axes of rotation. A larger _________ around a given axis requires more torque to increase the rotation, or to stop the rotation, of a body about that axis.

   a. Moment of inertia
   b. Belt friction
   c. Buckling
   d. Cam and groove

ANSWER KEY
7. ROTATIONAL MOTION

1. b
2. c
3. b
4. a
5. a

---

8. STATIC EQUILIBRIUM; ELASTICITY AND FRACTURE

CHAPTER OUTLINE: KEY TERMS, PEOPLE, PLACES, CONCEPTS

Statics

Mechanical advantage

Symmetry

Center of mass

Intervertebral disc

Neutral

Unstable

Elasticity

Bulk modulus

Shear modulus

Strength of materials

Shear stress

Safety factor

Shear strength

8. STATIC EQUILIBRIUM; ELASTICITY AND FRACTURE

CHAPTER HIGHLIGHTS & NOTES: KEY TERMS, PEOPLE, PLACES, CONCEPTS

Statics	Statics is the branch of mechanics that is concerned with the analysis of loads on physical systems in static equilibrium, that is, in a state where the relative positions of subsystems do not vary over time, or where components and structures are at a constant velocity. When in static equilibrium, the system is either at rest, or its center of mass moves at constant velocity. By Newton's first law, this situation implies that the net force and net torque (also known as moment of force) on every part of the system is zero.
Mechanical advantage	Mechanical advantage is a measure of the force amplification achieved by using a tool, mechanical device or machine system. Ideally, the device preserves the input power and simply trades off forces against movement to obtain a desired amplification in the output force. The model for this is the law of the lever.
Symmetry	In physics, symmetry includes all features of a physical system that exhibit the property of symmetry--that is, under certain transformations, aspects of these systems are otherwise 'unchanged', according to a particular observation. A symmetry of a physical system is a physical or mathematical feature of the system (observed or intrinsic) that is 'preserved' under some change. A family of particular transformations may be continuous (such as rotation of a circle) or discrete (e.g., reflection of a bilaterally symmetric figure, or rotation of a regular polygon).
Center of mass	In physics, the center of mass of a distribution of mass in space is the unique point where the weighted relative position of the distributed mass sums to zero. The distribution of mass is balanced around the center of mass and the average of the weighted position coordinates of the distributed mass defines its coordinates. Calculations in mechanics are often simplified when formulated with respect to the center of mass.
Intervertebral disc	Intervertebral discs lie between adjacent vertebrae in the spine. Each disc forms a cartilaginous joint to allow slight movement of the vertebrae, and acts as a ligament to hold the vertebrae together.
Neutral	Neutral and neutrallty may mean the following:
Unstable	In numerous fields of study, the component of instability within a system is generally characterized by some of the outputs or internal states growing without bounds. Not all systems that are not stable are unstable; systems can also be marginally stable or exhibit limit cycle behavior. In control theory, a system is unstable if any of the roots of its characteristic equation has real part greater than zero (or if zero is a repeated root).

Elasticity

In physics, elasticity is the tendency of solid materials to return to their original shape after being deformed. Solid objects will deform when forces are applied on them. If the material is elastic, the object will return to its initial shape and size when these forces are removed.

Bulk modulus

The bulk modulus of a substance measures the substance's resistance to uniform compression. It is defined as the ratio of the infinitesimal pressure increase to the resulting relative decrease of the volume. Its SI unit is the pascal, and its dimensional form is $kg^1L^{-1}T^{-2}$.

Shear modulus

In materials science, shear modulus or modulus of rigidity, denoted by G, or sometimes S or μ, is defined as the ratio of shear stress to the shear strain: $G \stackrel{\mathrm{def}}{=} \frac{\tau_{xy}}{\gamma_{xy}} = \frac{F/A}{\Delta x/l} = \frac{Fl}{A\Delta x}$

where $\tau_{xy} = F/A$ = shear stress; F is the force which acts A is the area on which the force actsin engineering, $\gamma_{xy} = \Delta x/l = \tan\theta$ = shear strain. Elsewhere, $\gamma_{xy} = \theta$ Δx is the transverse displacement l is the initial length

Shear modulus' derived SI unit is the pascal (Pa), although it is usually expressed in gigapascals (GPa) or in thousands of pounds per square inch (ksi). Its dimensional form is $M^1L^{-1}T^{-2}$.

Strength of materials

Mechanics of materials, also called strength of materials, is a subject which deals with the behavior of objects withstanding stresses and strains. This theory was established on the basis of mathematical modeling in first and second principal stress, specifically because types of stress state in construction parts such beam and shell are possible to approximate as one or two dimensional one. An important founding pioneer in mechanics of materials was Stephen Timoshenko.

Shear stress

A shear stress, denoted τ, is defined as the component of stress coplanar with a material cross section. Shear stress arises from the force vector component parallel to the cross section. Normal stress, on the other hand, arises from the force vector component perpendicular or antiparallel to the material cross section on which it acts.

Safety factor

In a toroidal fusion power reactor, the magnetic fields confining the plasma are formed in a helical shape, winding around the interior of the reactor. The safety factor, labeled q or q(r), is the ratio of the times a particular magnetic field line travels around a toroidal confinement area's 'long way' (toroidally) to the 'short way' (poloidally).

The term 'safety' refers to the resulting stability of the plasma; plasmas that rotate around the torus poloidally about the same number of times as toroidally are inherently less susceptible to certain instabilities.

8. STATIC EQUILIBRIUM; ELASTICITY AND FRACTURE

CHAPTER HIGHLIGHTS & NOTES: KEY TERMS, PEOPLE, PLACES, CONCEPTS

Shear strength	Shear strength is a term used in soil mechanics to describe the magnitude of the shear stress that a soil can sustain. The shear resistance of soil is a result of friction and interlocking of particles, and possibly cementation or bonding at particle contacts. Due to interlocking, particulate material may expand or contract in volume as it is subject to shear strains.

CHAPTER QUIZ: KEY TERMS, PEOPLE, PLACES, CONCEPTS

1. _________ and neutrality may mean the following:

a. reactor
b. Neutral
c. 3-manifold
d. Coccydynia

2. _________ is the branch of mechanics that is concerned with the analysis of loads on physical systems in _________ (s) equilibrium, that is, in a state where the relative positions of subsystems do not vary over time, or where components and structures are at a constant velocity. When in _________(s) equilibrium, the system is either at rest, or its center of mass moves at constant velocity.

By Newton's first law, this situation implies that the net force and net torque (also known as moment of force) on every part of the system is zero.

a. Flapping counter-torque
b. Die Glocke
c. Giovanni Modanese
d. Statics

3. _________ is a measure of the force amplification achieved by using a tool, mechanical device or machine system. Ideally, the device preserves the input power and simply trades off forces against movement to obtain a desired amplification in the output force. The model for this is the law of the lever.

a. Banked turn
b. Belt friction
c. Buckling
d. Mechanical advantage

4.. A _________, denoted τ, is defined as the component of stress coplanar with a material cross section. _________ arises from the force vector component parallel to the cross section. Normal stress, on the other hand, arises from the force vector component perpendicular or antiparallel to the material cross section on which it acts.

a. Bending moment
b. Bimoment
c. Cauchy elastic material
d. Shear stress

5. In materials science, _________ or modulus of rigidity, denoted by G, or sometimes S or μ, is defined as the ratio of shear stress to the shear strain: $G \stackrel{\text{def}}{=} \frac{\tau_{xy}}{\gamma_{xy}} = \frac{F/A}{\Delta x/l} = \frac{Fl}{A\Delta x}$

where $\tau_{xy} = F/A$ = shear stress; F is the force which acts A is the area on which the force actsin engineering, $\gamma_{xy} = \Delta x/l = \tan\theta$ = shear strain. Elsewhere, $\gamma_{xy} = \theta$ Δx is the transverse displacement l is the initial length

_________' derived SI unit is the pascal (Pa), although it is usually expressed in gigapascals (GPa) or in thousands of pounds per square inch (ksi). Its dimensional form is $M^1L^{-1}T^{-2}$.

a. Shear modulus
b. Flamant solution
c. Liquid metal embrittlement
d. Michell solution

ANSWER KEY
8. STATIC EQUILIBRIUM; ELASTICITY AND FRACTURE

---

1. b
2. d
3. d
4. d
5. a

---

9. FLUIDS

CHAPTER OUTLINE: KEY TERMS, PEOPLE, PLACES, CONCEPTS

Colloid

Density

Liquid crystal

Plasma

Specific gravity

Pressure head

Atmosphere

Atmospheric pressure

Straw

Mechanical advantage

Hydraulics

Barometer

Vacuum pump

Archimedes

Buoyancy

Apparent weight

Fluid dynamics

Laminar flow

Plate tectonics

Eddy current

Viscosity

9. FLUIDS

CHAPTER OUTLINE: KEY TERMS, PEOPLE, PLACES, CONCEPTS

______ Drag

______ Boundary layer

______ Curveball

______ Coefficient

______ Gradient

______ Velocity

______ Surface tension

______ Cohesion

______ Surfactant

______ Circulating pump

______ Centrifugal pump

______ Hydraulic press

______ Human body

______ Drinking fountain

______ Heartbeat

9. FLUIDS

CHAPTER HIGHLIGHTS & NOTES: KEY TERMS, PEOPLE, PLACES, CONCEPTS

Colloid

A colloid is a substance microscopically dispersed throughout another substance.

The dispersed-phase particles have a diameter of between approximately 1 and 1000 nanometers. Such particles are normally invisible in an optical microscope, though their presence can be confirmed with the use of an ultramicroscope or an electron microscope.

Density

The density, or more precisely, the volumetric mass density, of a substance is its mass per unit volume. The symbol most often used for density is ? (the lower case Greek letter rho).

Mathematically, density is defined as mass divided by volume: $\rho = \frac{m}{V}$,

where ? is the density, m is the mass, and V is the volume.

Liquid crystal

Liquid crystals are matter in a state that has properties between those of conventional liquid and those of solid crystal. For instance, a liquid crystal may flow like a liquid, but its molecules may be oriented in a crystal-like way. There are many different types of liquid-crystal phases, which can be distinguished by their different optical properties (such as birefringence).

Plasma

Plasma is one of the four fundamental states of matter (the others being solid, liquid, and gas). It comprises the major component of the Sun. Heating a gas may ionize its molecules or atoms (reducing or increasing the number of electrons in them), thus turning it into a plasma, which contains charged particles: positive ions and negative electrons or ions.

Specific gravity

Specific gravity is the ratio of the density of a substance to the density of a reference substance. Apparent specific gravity is the ratio of the weight of a volume of the substance to the weight of an equal volume of the reference substance. The reference substance is nearly always water for liquids or air for gases.

Pressure head

Pressure head is a term used in fluid mechanics to represent the internal energy of a fluid due to the pressure exerted on its container. It may also be called static pressure head or simply static head (but not static head pressure). It is mathematically expressed as: $\psi = \frac{p}{\gamma} = \frac{p}{\rho g}$

where ψ is pressure head; p is fluid pressure (force per unit area, often as Pa units); and γ is the specific weight (force per unit volume, typically N/m^3 units) ρ is the density of the fluid (mass per unit volume, typically kg/m^3) g is acceleration due to gravity (rate of change of velocity, given in m/s^2)

Note that in this equation, the pressure term is gauge pressure, not absolute pressure.

9. FLUIDS

CHAPTER HIGHLIGHTS & NOTES: KEY TERMS, PEOPLE, PLACES, CONCEPTS

Atmosphere	The standard atmosphere is an international reference pressure defined as 101325 Pa and used as a unit of pressure.
Atmospheric pressure	Atmospheric pressure is the force per unit area exerted on a surface by the weight of air above that surface in the atmosphere of Earth . In most circumstances atmospheric pressure is closely approximated by the hydrostatic pressure caused by the weight of air above the measurement point. On a given plane, low-pressure areas have less atmospheric mass above their location, whereas high-pressure areas have more atmospheric mass above their location.
Straw	Straw is an agricultural by-product, the dry stalks of cereal plants, after the grain and chaff have been removed. Straw makes up about half of the yield of cereal crops such as barley, oats, rice, rye and wheat. It has many uses, including fuel, livestock bedding and fodder, thatching and basket -making.
Mechanical advantage	Mechanical advantage is a measure of the force amplification achieved by using a tool, mechanical device or machine system. Ideally, the device preserves the input power and simply trades off forces against movement to obtain a desired amplification in the output force. The model for this is the law of the lever.
Hydraulics	Hydraulics is a topic in applied science and engineering dealing with the mechanical properties of liquids. At a very basic level hydraulics is the liquid version of pneumatics. Fluid mechanics provides the theoretical foundation for hydraulics, which focuses on the engineering uses of fluid properties.
Barometer	A barometer is a scientific instrument used in meteorology to measure atmospheric pressure. Pressure tendency can forecast short term changes in the weather. Numerous measurements of air pressure are used within surface weather analysis to help find surface troughs, high pressure systems, and frontal boundaries.
Vacuum pump	A vacuum pump is a device that removes gas molecules from a sealed volume in order to leave behind a partial vacuum. The first vacuum pump was invented in 1650 by Otto von Guericke, and was preceded by the suction pump, which dates to antiquity.
Archimedes	Archimedes of Syracuse was a Greek mathematician, physicist, engineer, inventor, and astronomer. Although few details of his life are known, he is regarded as one of the leading scientists in classical antiquity. Among his advances in physics are the foundations of hydrostatics, statics and an explanation of the principle of the lever.
Buoyancy	In science, buoyancy is an upward force exerted by a fluid that opposes the weight of an immersed object. In a column of fluid, pressure increases with depth as a result of the weight of the overlying fluid. Thus a column of fluid, or an object submerged in the fluid, experiences greater pressure at the bottom of the column than at the top.

9. FLUIDS

CHAPTER HIGHLIGHTS & NOTES: KEY TERMS, PEOPLE, PLACES, CONCEPTS

Apparent weight	In physics, apparent weight is a property of objects that corresponds to how heavy an object is. The apparent weight of an object will differ from the weight of an object whenever the force of gravity acting on the object is not balanced by an equal but opposite normal force. By definition, the weight of an object is equal to the magnitude of the force of gravity acting on it.
Fluid dynamics	In physics, fluid dynamics is a subdiscipline of fluid mechanics that deals with fluid flow--the natural science of fluids in motion. It has several subdisciplines itself, including aerodynamics (the study of air and other gases in motion) and hydrodynamics (the study of liquids in motion). Fluid dynamics has a wide range of applications, including calculating forces and moments on aircraft, determining the mass flow rate of petroleum through pipelines, predicting weather patterns, understanding nebulae in interstellar space and reportedly modelling fission weapon detonation.
Laminar flow	Laminar flow occurs when a fluid flows in parallel layers, with no disruption between the layers. At low velocities the fluid tends to flow without lateral mixing, and adjacent layers slide past one another like playing cards. There are no cross currents perpendicular to the direction of flow, nor eddies or swirls of fluids.
Plate tectonics	Plate tectonics is a scientific theory that describes the large-scale motions of Earth's lithosphere. The model builds on the concepts of continental drift, developed during the first few decades of the 20th century. The geoscientific community accepted the theory after the concepts of seafloor spreading were developed in the late 1950s and early 1960s.
Eddy current	Eddy currents are electric currents induced within conductors by a changing magnetic field in the conductor. These circulating eddies of current have inductance and thus induce magnetic fields. These fields can cause repulsive, attractive, propulsion, drag, and heating effects.
Viscosity	The viscosity of a fluid is a measure of its resistance to gradual deformation by shear stress or tensile stress. For liquids, it corresponds to the informal notion of 'thickness'. For example, honey has a higher viscosity than water.
Drag	In fluid dynamics, drag refers to forces which act on a solid object in the direction of the relative fluid flow velocity. Unlike other resistive forces, such as dry friction, which is nearly independent of velocity, drag forces depend on velocity. Drag forces always decrease fluid velocity relative to the solid object in the fluid's path.
Boundary layer	In physics and fluid mechanics, a boundary layer is the layer of fluid in the immediate vicinity of a bounding surface where the effects of viscosity are significant. In the Earth's atmosphere, the planetary boundary layer is the air layer near the ground affected by diurnal heat, moisture or momentum transfer to or from the surface. On an aircraft wing the boundary layer is the part of the flow close to the wing, where viscous forces distort the surrounding non-viscous flow.

Curveball

The curveball is a type of pitch in baseball thrown with a characteristic grip and hand movement that imparts forward spin to the ball causing it to dive in a downward path as it approaches the plate. Its close relatives are the slider and the slurve. The 'curve' of the ball varies from pitcher to pitcher.

Coefficient

In mathematics, a coefficient is a multiplicative factor in some term of an expression ; it is usually a number, but in any case does not involve any variables of the expression. For instance in $7x^2 - 3xy + 1.5 + y$

the first two terms respectively have the coefficients 7 and -3. The third term 1.5 is a constant. The final term does not have any explicitly written coefficient, but is considered to have coefficient 1, since multiplying by that factor would not change the term.

Gradient

In mathematics, the gradient is a generalization of the usual concept of derivative to the functions of several variables. If $f(x_1, .. x_n)$ is a differentiable function of several variables, also called 'scalar field', its gradient is the vector of the n partial derivatives of f. It is thus a vector-valued function also called vector field.

Velocity

Velocity is the rate of change of the position of an object, equivalent to a specification of its speed and direction of motion, e.g. 60 km/h to the north. Velocity is an important concept in kinematics, the branch of classical mechanics which describes the motion of bodies.

Velocity is a vector physical quantity; both magnitude and direction are required to define it.

Surface tension

Surface tension is a contractive tendency of the surface of a liquid that allows it to resist an external force. It is revealed, for example, in the floating of some objects on the surface of water, even though they are denser than water, and in the ability of some insects (e.g. water striders) to run on the water surface. This property is caused by cohesion of similar molecules, and is responsible for many of the behaviors of liquids.

Cohesion

Cohesion is the component of shear strength of a rock or soil that is independent of interparticle friction.

In soils, true cohesion is caused by following:•Electrostatic forces in stiff overconsolidated clays •Cementing by Fe_2O_3, $CaCO_3$, NaCl, etc.

There can also be apparent cohesion. This is caused by:•Negative capillary pressure (which is lost upon wetting)•Pore pressure response during undrained loading (which is lost through time)•Root cohesion

Some typical values of soil cohesion for different soils can be found on Geotechdata.info database.

9. FLUIDS

CHAPTER HIGHLIGHTS & NOTES: KEY TERMS, PEOPLE, PLACES, CONCEPTS

Surfactant	Surfactants are compounds that lower the surface tension between two liquids or between a liquid and a solid. Surfactants may act as detergents, wetting agents, emulsifiers, foaming agents, and dispersants.
Circulating pump	A circulating pump - a device that causes the flow of liquid in circuits (primary or secondary) of heating or cooling installations. The circulating pumps are used only as centrifugal pumps. The basic elements of the centrifugal pump are coiled housing with two ports, suction and discharge, and what is more, blade rotor mounted on a shaft driven be an electric motor.
Centrifugal pump	Centrifugal pumps are a sub-class of dynamic axisymmetric work-absorbing turbomachinery. Centrifugal pumps are used to transport fluids by the conversion of rotational kinetic energy to the hydrodynamic energy of the fluid flow. The rotational energy typically comes from an engine or electric motor.
Hydraulic press	A hydraulic press is a machine using a hydraulic cylinder to generate a compressive force. It uses the hydraulic equivalent of a mechanical lever, and was also known as a Bramah press after the inventor, Joseph Bramah, of England. He invented and was issued a patent on this press in 1795. As Bramah (who is also known for his development of the flush toilet) installed toilets, he studied the existing literature on the motion of fluids and put this knowledge into the development of the press.
Human body	The human body is the entire structure of a human being and comprises a head, neck, trunk, two arms and hands and two legs and feet. Every part of the body is composed of various types of cell. At maturity, the estimated number of cells in the body is given as 37.2 trillion.
Drinking fountain	A drinking fountain, also called a water fountain or bubbler, is a fountain designed to provide drinking water. It consists of a basin with either continuously running water or a tap. The drinker bends down to the stream of water and swallows water directly from the stream.
Heartbeat	Heartbeat in computer science is a periodic signal generated by hardware or software to indicate normal operation or to synchronize other parts of a system. Usually a heartbeat is sent between machines at a regular interval of the order of seconds. If a heartbeat isn't received for a time--usually a few heartbeat intervals--the machine that should have sent the heartbeat is assumed to have failed.

1. The _________ is the entire structure of a human being and comprises a head, neck, trunk, two arms and hands and two legs and feet. Every part of the body is composed of various types of cell. At maturity, the estimated number of cells in the body is given as 37.2 trillion.

   a. 3-manifold
   b. Bleed screw
   c. Human body
   d. Cut-off factor

2. _________ is a term used in fluid mechanics to represent the internal energy of a fluid due to the pressure exerted on its container. It may also be called static _________ or simply static head (but not static head pressure). It is mathematically expressed as: $\psi = \frac{p}{\gamma} = \frac{p}{\rho g}$

   where ψ is _________; p is fluid pressure (force per unit area, often as Pa units); and γ is the specific weight (force per unit volume, typically N/m^3 units) ρ is the density of the fluid (mass per unit volume, typically kg/m^3) g is acceleration due to gravity (rate of change of velocity, given in m/s^2)

   Note that in this equation, the pressure term is gauge pressure, not absolute pressure.

   a. Pressure head
   b. Brazier effect
   c. Decompression
   d. Discharge pressure

3. A _________ is a machine using a hydraulic cylinder to generate a compressive force. It uses the hydraulic equivalent of a mechanical lever, and was also known as a Bramah press after the inventor, Joseph Bramah, of England. He invented and was issued a patent on this press in 1795. As Bramah (who is also known for his development of the flush toilet) installed toilets, he studied the existing literature on the motion of fluids and put this knowledge into the development of the press.

   a. Banjo fitting
   b. Hydraulic press
   c. Brake fluid
   d. Cut-off factor

4. . A _________ is a substance microscopically dispersed throughout another substance.

   The dispersed-phase particles have a diameter of between approximately 1 and 1000 nanometers. Such particles are normally invisible in an optical microscope, though their presence can be confirmed with the use of an ultramicroscope or an electron microscope.

   a. Band diagram

b. Band mapping
c. Bethe ansatz
d. Colloid

5. In physics, _________ is a subdiscipline of fluid mechanics that deals with fluid flow--the natural science of fluids in motion. It has several subdisciplines itself, including aerodynamics (the study of air and other gases in motion) and hydrodynamics (the study of liquids in motion). _________ has a wide range of applications, including calculating forces and moments on aircraft, determining the mass flow rate of petroleum through pipelines, predicting weather patterns, understanding nebulae in interstellar space and reportedly modelling fission weapon detonation.

    a. Bending moment
    b. Bimoment
    c. Fluid dynamics
    d. Cauchy momentum equation

ANSWER KEY
9. FLUIDS

1. c
2. a
3. b
4. d
5. c

---

10. OSCILLATIONS AND WAVES

CHAPTER OUTLINE: KEY TERMS, PEOPLE, PLACES, CONCEPTS

- Vibration
- Restoring force
- Amplitude
- Displacement
- Frequency
- Hertz
- Period
- Harmonic oscillator
- Harmonic
- Simple harmonic motion
- Acceleration
- Angular displacement
- Pendulum clock
- Pendulum
- Natural frequency
- Resonance
- Forced
- Mechanical wave
- Wave Motion
- Continuous wave
- Tsunami

10. OSCILLATIONS AND WAVES

CHAPTER OUTLINE: KEY TERMS, PEOPLE, PLACES, CONCEPTS

Wavelength

Pulse

Pulse wave

Trough

Velocity

Compression

Longitudinal wave

Transverse wave

Rarefaction

Bulk modulus

Surface wave

Earthquake

Wave power

Intensity

Plane wave

Reflection

Transmission

Interference

Standing wave

Overtone

Fundamental frequency

10. OSCILLATIONS AND WAVES

CHAPTER OUTLINE: KEY TERMS, PEOPLE, PLACES, CONCEPTS

	Refraction
	Diffraction
	Molecular vibration
	Total internal reflection
	Wave packet

CHAPTER HIGHLIGHTS & NOTES: KEY TERMS, PEOPLE, PLACES, CONCEPTS

Vibration	Vibration is a mechanical phenomenon whereby oscillations occur about an equilibrium point. The oscillations may be periodic such as the motion of a pendulum or random such as the movement of a tire on a gravel road. Vibration is occasionally 'desirable'.
Restoring force	Restoring force, in a physics context, is a variable force that gives rise to an equilibrium in a physical system. If the system is perturbed away from the equilibrium, the restoring force will tend to bring the system back toward equilibrium. The restoring force is a function only of position of the mass or particle.
Amplitude	The amplitude of a periodic variable is a measure of its change over a single period . There are various definitions of amplitude, which are all functions of the magnitude of the difference between the variable's extreme values. In older texts the phase is sometimes called the amplitude.
Displacement	In fluid mechanics, displacement occurs when an object is immersed in a fluid, pushing it out of the way and taking its place. The volume of the fluid displaced can then be measured, and from this the volume of the immersed object can be deduced (the volume of the immersed object will be exactly equal to the volume of the displaced fluid). An object that sinks displaces an amount of fluid equal to the object's volume.
Frequency	Frequency is the number of occurrences of a repeating event per unit time. It is also referred to as temporal frequency, which emphasizes the contrast to spatial frequency and angular frequency.

10. OSCILLATIONS AND WAVES

CHAPTER HIGHLIGHTS & NOTES: KEY TERMS, PEOPLE, PLACES, CONCEPTS

Hertz	The hertz is the unit of frequency in the International System of Units (SI). It is defined as the number of cycles per second of a periodic phenomenon. One of its most common uses is the description of the sine wave, particularly those used in radio and audio applications, such as the frequency of musical tones.
Period	In the periodic table of the elements, elements are arranged in a series of rows (or periods) so that those with similar properties appear in a column. Elements of the same period have the same number of electron shells; with each group across a period, the elements have one more proton and electron and become less metallic. This arrangement reflects the periodic recurrence of similar properties as the atomic number increases.
Harmonic oscillator	In classical mechanics, a harmonic oscillator is a system that, when displaced from its equilibrium position, experiences a restoring force, F, proportional to the displacement, x: $\vec{F} = -k\vec{x}$ where k is a positive constant. If F is the only force acting on the system, the system is called a simple harmonic oscillator, and it undergoes simple harmonic motion: sinusoidal oscillations about the equilibrium point, with a constant amplitude and a constant frequency . If a frictional force (damping) proportional to the velocity is also present, the harmonic oscillator is described as a damped oscillator.
Harmonic	A harmonic of a wave is a component frequency of the signal that is an integer multiple of the fundamental frequency, i.e. if the fundamental frequency is f, the harmonics have frequencies 2f, 3f, 4f, .
Simple harmonic motion	In mechanics and physics, simple harmonic motion is a type of periodic motion where the restoring force is directly proportional to the displacement. It can serve as a mathematical model of a variety of motions, such as the oscillation of a spring. In addition, other phenomena can be approximated by simple harmonic motion, including the motion of a simple pendulum as well as molecular vibration.
Acceleration	In physics, acceleration is the rate at which the velocity of a body changes with time. Velocity and acceleration are vector quantities, with magnitude, direction, and add according to the parallelogram law. As described by Newton's Second Law, acceleration is caused by a net force; the force, as a vector, is equal to the product of the mass of the object being accelerated (scalar) and the acceleration.
Angular displacement	Angular displacement of a body is the angle in radians through which a point or line has been rotated in a specified sense about a specified axis.

When an object rotates about its axis, the motion cannot simply be analyzed as a particle, since in circular motion it undergoes a changing velocity and acceleration at any time (t). When dealing with the rotation of an object, it becomes simpler to consider the body itself rigid.

Pendulum clock

A pendulum clock is a clock that uses a pendulum, a swinging weight, as its timekeeping element. The advantage of a pendulum for timekeeping is that it is a harmonic oscillator; it swings back and forth in a precise time interval dependent on its length, and resists swinging at other rates. From its invention in 1656 by Christiaan Huygens until the 1930s, the pendulum clock was the world's most precise timekeeper, accounting for its widespread use.

Pendulum

A pendulum is a weight suspended from a pivot so that it can swing freely. When a pendulum is displaced sideways from its resting equilibrium position, it is subject to a restoring force due to gravity that will accelerate it back toward the equilibrium position. When released, the restoring force combined with the pendulum's mass causes it to oscillate about the equilibrium position, swinging back and forth.

Natural frequency

Natural frequency is the frequency at which a system tends to oscillate in the absence of any driving or damping force.

Free vibrations of any elastic body is called natural vibration and happens at a frequency called natural frequency. Natural vibrations are different from forced vibration which happen at frequency of applied force (forced frequency).

Resonance

In physics, resonance is the tendency of a system to oscillate with greater amplitude at some frequencies than at others. Frequencies at which the response amplitude is a relative maximum are known as the system's resonant frequencies, or resonance frequencies. At these frequencies, even small periodic driving forces can produce large amplitude oscillations, because the system stores vibrational energy.

Forced

Forced is a local and online co-op action role-playing game developed by Beta Dwarf Entertainment, released in October 2013 for Windows, OS X and Linux through the Steam platform.

Mechanical wave

A mechanical wave is a wave that propagates as an oscillation of matter, and therefore transfers energy through a medium. While waves can move over long distances, the movement of the medium of transmission--the material--is limited. Therefore, oscillating material does not move far from its initial equilibrium position.

Wave Motion

Wave Motion is a peer-reviewed scientific journal publishing papers on the physics of waves - with emphasis on the areas of acoustics, optics, geophysics, seismology, electromagnetic theory, solid and fluid mechanics.

Original research articles on analytical, numerical and experimental aspects of wave motion are covered.

Since the journal's establishment in 1979, the editor in chief has been Jan D. Achenbach.

Continuous wave

A continuous waveform is an electromagnetic wave of constant amplitude and frequency; and in mathematical analysis, of infinite duration. Continuous wave is also the name given to an early method of radio transmission, in which a carrier wave is switched on and off. Information is carried in the varying duration of the on and off periods of the signal, for example by Morse code in early radio.

Tsunami

A tsunami is a series of water waves caused by the displacement of a large volume of a body of water, generally an ocean or a large lake. Earthquakes, volcanic eruptions and other underwater explosions (including detonations of underwater nuclear devices), landslides, glacier calvings, meteorite impacts and other disturbances above or below water all have the potential to generate a tsunami.

Wavelength

In physics, the wavelength of a sinusoidal wave is the spatial period of the wave--the distance over which the wave's shape repeats. It is usually determined by considering the distance between consecutive corresponding points of the same phase, such as crests, troughs, or zero crossings, and is a characteristic of both traveling waves and standing waves, as well as other spatial wave patterns. Wavelength is commonly designated by the Greek letter lambda (?).

Pulse

In physics, a pulse is a single disturbance that moves through a medium from one point to the next point.

Pulse wave

A pulse wave or pulse train is a kind of non-sinusoidal waveform that is similar to a square wave, but does not have the symmetrical shape associated with a perfect square wave. It is a term common to synthesizer programming, and is a typical waveform available on many synthesizers. The exact shape of the wave is determined by the duty cycle of the oscillator.

Trough

A 'trough' is an elongated region of relatively low atmospheric pressure, often associated with fronts.

Unlike fronts, there is not a universal symbol for a trough on a weather chart. The weather charts in some countries or regions mark troughs by a line.

Velocity

Velocity is the rate of change of the position of an object, equivalent to a specification of its speed and direction of motion, e.g. 60 km/h to the north. Velocity is an important concept in kinematics, the branch of classical mechanics which describes the motion of bodies.

Velocity is a vector physical quantity; both magnitude and direction are required to define it.

10. OSCILLATIONS AND WAVES

Compression	In mechanics, compression is the application of balanced inward forces to different points on a material or structure, that is, forces with no net sum or torque directed so as to reduce its size in one or more directions. It is contrasted with tension or traction, the application of balanced outward ('pulling') forces; and with shearing forces, directed so as to displace layers of the material parallel to each other. The compressive strength of materials and structures is an important engineering consideration.
Longitudinal wave	Longitudinal waves, also known as 'l-waves', are waves in which the displacement of the medium is in the same direction as, or the opposite direction to, the direction of travel of the wave. Mechanical longitudinal waves are also called compressional waves or compression waves, because they produce compression and rarefaction when traveling through a medium. The other main type of wave is the transverse wave, in which the displacements of the medium are at right angles to the direction of propagation.
Transverse wave	A transverse wave is a moving wave that consists of oscillations occurring perpendicular to the direction of energy transfer. If a transverse wave is moving in the positive x-direction, its oscillations are in up and down directions that lie in the y-z plane. Light is an example of a transverse wave.
Rarefaction	Rarefaction is the reduction of an item's density, the opposite of compression. Like compression, which can travel in waves (sound waves, for instance), rarefaction waves also exist in nature. A common rarefaction wave is the area of low relative pressure following a shock wave .
Bulk modulus	The bulk modulus of a substance measures the substance's resistance to uniform compression. It is defined as the ratio of the infinitesimal pressure increase to the resulting relative decrease of the volume. Its SI unit is the pascal, and its dimensional form is $kg^1L^{-1}T^{-2}$.
Surface wave	In physics, a surface wave is a mechanical wave that propagates along the interface between differing media, usually two fluids with different densities. A surface wave can also be an electromagnetic wave guided by a refractive index gradient. In radio transmission, a ground wave is a surface wave that propagates close to the surface of the Earth.
Earthquake	An earthquake is the result of a sudden release of energy in the Earth's crust that creates seismic waves. The seismicity, seismism or seismic activity of an area refers to the frequency, type and size of earthquakes experienced over a period of time. Earthquakes are measured using observations from seismometers.
Wave power	Wave energy is the transport of energy by ocean surface waves, and the capture of that energy to do useful work - for example, electricity generation, water desalination, or the pumping of water . Machinery able to exploit wave power is generally known as a wave energy converter (WEC).

10. OSCILLATIONS AND WAVES

CHAPTER HIGHLIGHTS & NOTES: KEY TERMS, PEOPLE, PLACES, CONCEPTS

Intensity	In physics, intensity is the power transferred per unit area. In the SI system, it has units watts per metre squared (W/m^2). It is used most frequently with waves (e.g. sound or light), in which case the average power transfer over one period of the wave is used.
Plane wave	In the physics of wave propagation, a plane wave is a constant-frequency wave whose wavefronts (surfaces of constant phase) are infinite parallel planes of constant peak-to-peak amplitude normal to the phase velocity vector. It is not possible in practice to have a true plane wave; only a plane wave of infinite extent will propagate as a plane wave. However, many waves are approximately plane waves in a localized region of space.
Reflection	Reflection is the change in direction of a wavefront at an interface between two different media so that the wavefront returns into the medium from which it originated. Common examples include the reflection of light, sound and water waves. The law of reflection says that for specular reflection the angle at which the wave is incident on the surface equals the angle at which it is reflected.
Transmission	A machine consists of a power source and a power transmission system, which provides controlled application of the power. Merriam-Webster defines transmission as an assembly of parts including the speed-changing gears and the propeller shaft by which the power is transmitted from an engine to a live axle. Often transmission refers simply to the gearbox that uses gears and gear trains to provide speed and torque conversions from a rotating power source to another device.
Interference	In physics, interference is a phenomenon in which two waves superimpose to form a resultant wave of greater or lower amplitude. Interference usually refers to the interaction of waves that are correlated or coherent with each other, either because they come from the same source or because they have the same or nearly the same frequency. Interference effects can be observed with all types of waves, for example, light, radio, acoustic and surface water waves.
Standing wave	In physics, a standing wave - also known as a stationary wave - is a wave that remains in a constant position. This phenomenon can occur because the medium is moving in the opposite direction to the wave, or it can arise in a stationary medium as a result of interference between two waves traveling in opposite directions. In the second case, for waves of equal amplitude traveling in opposing directions, there is on average no net propagation of energy.
Overtone	An overtone is any frequency higher than the fundamental frequency of a sound. Using the model of Fourier analysis, the fundamental and the overtones together are called partials. Harmonics, or more precisely, harmonic partials, are partials whose frequencies are integer multiples of the fundamental (including the fundamental which is 1 times itself).

Fundamental frequency	The fundamental frequency, often referred to simply as the fundamental, is defined as the lowest frequency of a periodic waveform. In terms of a superposition of sinusoids (e.g. Fourier series), the fundamental frequency is the lowest frequency sinusoidal in the sum. In some contexts, the fundamental is usually abbreviated as f_0 (or FF), indicating the lowest frequency counting from zero.
Refraction	Refraction is the change in direction of a wave due to a change in its transmission medium. Refraction is essentially a surface phenomenon. The phenomenon is mainly in governance to the law of conservation of energy and momentum.
Diffraction	Diffraction refers to various phenomena which occur when a wave encounters an obstacle. In classical physics, the diffraction phenomenon is described as the apparent bending of waves around small obstacles and the spreading out of waves past small openings. Similar effects occur when a light wave travels through a medium with a varying refractive index, or a sound wave travels through one with varying acoustic impedance.
Molecular vibration	A molecular vibration occurs when atoms in a molecule are in periodic motion while the molecule as a whole has constant translational and rotational motion. The frequency of the periodic motion is known as a vibration frequency, and the typical frequencies of molecular vibrations range from less than 10^{12} to approximately 10^{14} Hz. In general, a molecule with N atoms has 3N - 6 normal modes of vibration, but a linear molecule has 3N - 5 such modes, as rotation about its molecular axis cannot be observed.
Total internal reflection	Total internal reflection is a phenomenon that happens when a propagating wave strikes a medium boundary at an angle larger than a particular critical angle with respect to the normal to the surface. If the refractive index is lower on the other side of the boundary and the incident angle is greater than the critical angle, the wave cannot pass through and is entirely reflected. The critical angle is the angle of incidence above which the total internal reflectance occurs.
Wave packet	In physics, a wave packet is a short 'burst' or 'envelope' of localized wave action that travels as a unit. A wave packet can be analyzed into, or can be synthesized from, an infinite set of component sinusoidal waves of different wavenumbers, with phases and amplitudes such that they interfere constructively only over a small region of space, and destructively elsewhere. Depending on the evolution equation, the wave packet's envelope may remain constant or it may change (dispersion) while propagating.

10. OSCILLATIONS AND WAVES

CHAPTER QUIZ: KEY TERMS, PEOPLE, PLACES, CONCEPTS

1. A _________ is a clock that uses a pendulum, a swinging weight, as its timekeeping element. The advantage of a pendulum for timekeeping is that it is a harmonic oscillator; it swings back and forth in a precise time interval dependent on its length, and resists swinging at other rates. From its invention in 1656 by Christiaan Huygens until the 1930s, the _________ was the world's most precise timekeeper, accounting for its widespread use.

   a. Blackburn pendulum
   b. Bob
   c. Centrifugal pendulum absorber
   d. Pendulum clock

2. In physics, a _________ is a single disturbance that moves through a medium from one point to the next point.

   a. Beta particle
   b. Pulse
   c. Cosmic ray
   d. Dose profile

3. In mechanics, _________ is the application of balanced inward forces to different points on a material or structure, that is, forces with no net sum or torque directed so as to reduce its size in one or more directions. It is contrasted with tension or traction, the application of balanced outward ('pulling') forces; and with shearing forces, directed so as to displace layers of the material parallel to each other. The compressive strength of materials and structures is an important engineering consideration.

   a. Bending moment
   b. Compression
   c. Cauchy elastic material
   d. Cauchy momentum equation

4. In physics, a _________ is a mechanical wave that propagates along the interface between differing media, usually two fluids with different densities. A _________ can also be an electromagnetic wave guided by a refractive index gradient. In radio transmission, a ground wave is a _________ that propagates close to the surface of the Earth.

   a. Carrier-to-noise-density ratio
   b. Cassegrain reflector
   c. Surface wave
   d. Clutter

5. . A '_________' is an elongated region of relatively low atmospheric pressure, often associated with fronts.

   Unlike fronts, there is not a universal symbol for a _________ on a weather chart. The weather charts in some countries or regions mark _________s by a line.

   a. Bowen ratio
   b. Capping inversion

c. Carnot cycle

d. Trough

ANSWER KEY
10. OSCILLATIONS AND WAVES

1. d
2. b
3. b
4. c
5. d

---

11. SOUND

CHAPTER OUTLINE: KEY TERMS, PEOPLE, PLACES, CONCEPTS

- Loudness
- Speed of sound
- Supersonic speed
- Decibel
- Intensity
- Amplitude
- Sensitivity
- Octave
- Harmonic
- Overtone
- Fundamental frequency
- Sounding board
- Waveform
- Quality
- Fourier analysis
- Interference
- Spectrum
- Doppler effect
- Bow wave
- Mach number
- Radar

11. SOUND

CHAPTER OUTLINE: KEY TERMS, PEOPLE, PLACES, CONCEPTS

	Redshift
	Shock wave
	Sonic boom
	Medical imaging
	Ultrasound

CHAPTER HIGHLIGHTS & NOTES: KEY TERMS, PEOPLE, PLACES, CONCEPTS

Loudness	Loudness is the characteristic of a sound that is primarily a psychological correlate of physical strength . More formally, it is defined as 'that attribute of auditory sensation in terms of which sounds can be ordered on a scale extending from quiet to loud'. Loudness, a subjective measure, is often confused with objective measures of sound strength such as sound pressure, sound pressure level (in decibels), sound intensity or sound power.
Speed of sound	The speed of sound is the distance travelled during a unit of time by a sound wave propagating through an elastic medium. In dry air at 20 °C (68 °F), the speed of sound is 343.2 metres per second (1,126 ft/s). This is 1,236 kilometres per hour (768 mph), or about a kilometre in three seconds or a mile in five seconds.
Supersonic speed	Supersonic speed is a rate of travel of an object that exceeds the speed of sound . For objects traveling in dry air of a temperature of 20 °C (68 °F) at sea level, this speed is approximately 343 m/s, 1,125 ft/s, 768 mph, 667 knots, or 1,235 km/h. Speeds greater than five times the speed of sound (Mach 5) are often referred to as hypersonic.
Decibel	The decibel is a logarithmic unit used to express the ratio between two values of a physical quantity (usually measured in units of power or intensity). One of these quantities is often a reference value, and in this case the dB can be used to express the absolute level of the physical quantity. The decibel is also commonly used as a measure of gain or attenuation, the ratio of input and output powers of a system, or of individual factors that contribute to such ratios.
Intensity	In physics, intensity is the power transferred per unit area. In the SI system, it has units watts per metre squared (W/m^2). It is used most frequently with waves (e.g.

11. SOUND

Amplitude

The amplitude of a periodic variable is a measure of its change over a single period . There are various definitions of amplitude, which are all functions of the magnitude of the difference between the variable's extreme values. In older texts the phase is sometimes called the amplitude.

Sensitivity

The sensitivity of an electronic device, such as a communications system receiver, or detection device, such as a PIN diode, is the minimum magnitude of input signal required to produce a specified output signal having a specified signal-to-noise ratio, or other specified criteria.

Sensitivity is sometimes improperly used as a synonym for responsivity.

The sensitivity of a microphone is usually expressed as the sound field strength in decibels relative to 1 V/Pa (Pa = N/m^2) or as the transfer factor in millivolts per pascal (mV/Pa) into an open circuit or into a 1 kilohm load.

Octave

In electronics, an octave is a doubling or halving of a frequency. The term is derived from the Western musical scale (an octave is a doubling in frequency) and is therefore common in audio electronics. (The prefix octa-, denoting eight, has no direct significance).

Harmonic

A harmonic of a wave is a component frequency of the signal that is an integer multiple of the fundamental frequency, i.e. if the fundamental frequency is f, the harmonics have frequencies 2f, 3f, 4f, .

Overtone

An overtone is any frequency higher than the fundamental frequency of a sound. Using the model of Fourier analysis, the fundamental and the overtones together are called partials. Harmonics, or more precisely, harmonic partials, are partials whose frequencies are integer multiples of the fundamental (including the fundamental which is 1 times itself).

Fundamental frequency

The fundamental frequency, often referred to simply as the fundamental, is defined as the lowest frequency of a periodic waveform. In terms of a superposition of sinusoids (e.g. Fourier series), the fundamental frequency is the lowest frequency sinusoidal in the sum. In some contexts, the fundamental is usually abbreviated as f_0 (or FF), indicating the lowest frequency counting from zero.

Sounding board

A sounding board is a structure placed above or behind a pulpit or other speaking platform which helps to project the sound of the speaker. The structure may be specially shaped to assist the projection, for example, being formed as a parabolic reflector. In the typical setting of a church building, the sounding board may be ornately carved or constructed.

Waveform

A waveform is the shape and form of a signal such as a wave moving in a physical medium or an abstract representation.

In many cases the medium in which the wave is being propagated does not permit a direct visual image of the form. In these cases, the term 'waveform' refers to the shape of a graph of the varying quantity against time or distance.

Quality

In response theory, the quality of an excited system is related to the number of excitation frequencies to which it can respond. In the case of a homogeneous, isotropic system, the quality is proportional to the FWHM.

This sense of the phrase is the precursor of the usage of the word in music theory. In music theory, quality is the number of harmonics of a fundamental frequency of an instrument (the higher the quality, the richer the sound).

Fourier analysis

In mathematics, Fourier analysis is the study of the way general functions may be represented or approximated by sums of simpler trigonometric functions. Fourier analysis grew from the study of Fourier series, and is named after Joseph Fourier, who showed that representing a function as a sum of trigonometric functions greatly simplifies the study of heat transfer.

Today, the subject of Fourier analysis encompasses a vast spectrum of mathematics.

Interference

In physics, interference is a phenomenon in which two waves superimpose to form a resultant wave of greater or lower amplitude. Interference usually refers to the interaction of waves that are correlated or coherent with each other, either because they come from the same source or because they have the same or nearly the same frequency. Interference effects can be observed with all types of waves, for example, light, radio, acoustic and surface water waves.

Spectrum

A spectrum is a condition that is not limited to a specific set of values but can vary infinitely within a continuum. The word was first used scientifically within the field of optics to describe the rainbow of colors in visible light when separated using a prism; it has since been applied by analogy to many fields other than optics. Thus, one might talk about the spectrum of political opinion, or the spectrum of activity of a drug, or the autism spectrum.

Doppler effect

The Doppler effect who proposed it in 1842 in Prague, is the change in frequency of a wave (or other periodic event) for an observer moving relative to its source. It is commonly heard when a vehicle sounding a siren or horn approaches, passes, and recedes from an observer. The received frequency is higher (compared to the emitted frequency) during the approach, it is identical at the instant of passing by, and it is lower during the recession.

Bow wave

A bow wave is the wave that forms at the bow of a ship when it moves through the water. As the bow wave spreads out, it defines the outer limits of a ship's wake.

Mach number

In fluid mechanics, Mach number is a dimensionless quantity representing the ratio of speed of an object moving through a fluid and the local speed of sound.

$$\mathrm{M} = \frac{v}{v_{\mathrm{sound}}}$$

whereM is the Mach number,v is the velocity of the source relative to the medium, andv_{sound} is the speed of sound in the medium.

Mach number varies by the composition of the surrounding medium and also by local conditions, especially temperature and pressure. The Mach number can be used to determine if a flow can be treated as an incompressible flow.

Radar

Radar is an object detection system which uses radio waves to determine the range, altitude, direction, or speed of objects. It can be used to detect aircraft, ships, spacecraft, guided missiles, motor vehicles, weather formations, and terrain. The radar dish or antenna transmits pulses of radio waves or microwaves which bounce off any object in their path.

Redshift

In physics, redshift happens when light or other electromagnetic radiation from an object moving away from the observer is increased in wavelength, or shifted to the red end of the spectrum. In general, whether or not the radiation is within the visible spectrum, 'redder' means an increase in wavelength - equivalent to a lower frequency and a lower photon energy, in accordance with, respectively, the wave and quantum theories of light.

Redshifts are an example of the Doppler effect, familiar in the change in the apparent pitches of sirens and frequency of the sound waves emitted by speeding vehicles.

Shock wave

A shock wave is a type of propagating disturbance. Like an ordinary wave, it carries energy and can propagate through a medium (solid, liquid, gas or plasma) or in some cases in the absence of a material medium, through a field such as the electromagnetic field. Shock waves are characterized by an abrupt, nearly discontinuous change in the characteristics of the medium.

Sonic boom

A sonic boom is the sound associated with the shock waves created by an object traveling through the air faster than the speed of sound. Sonic booms generate enormous amounts of sound energy, sounding much like an explosion. The crack of a supersonic bullet passing overhead is an example of a sonic boom in miniature.

Medical imaging

Medical imaging is the technique and process used to create images of the human body for clinical purposes (medical procedures seeking to reveal, diagnose, or examine disease) or medical science (including the study of normal anatomy and physiology). Although imaging of removed organs and tissues can be performed for medical reasons, such procedures are not usually referred to as medical imaging, but rather are a part of pathology.

11. SOUND

CHAPTER HIGHLIGHTS & NOTES: KEY TERMS, PEOPLE, PLACES, CONCEPTS

Ultrasound	Ultrasound is an oscillating sound pressure wave with a frequency greater than the upper limit of the human hearing range. Ultrasound is thus not separated from 'normal' (audible) sound based on differences in physical properties, only the fact that humans cannot hear it. Although this limit varies from person to person, it is approximately 20 kilohertz (20,000 hertz) in healthy, young adults.

CHAPTER QUIZ: KEY TERMS, PEOPLE, PLACES, CONCEPTS

1. A _________ is a structure placed above or behind a pulpit or other speaking platform which helps to project the sound of the speaker. The structure may be specially shaped to assist the projection, for example, being formed as a parabolic reflector. In the typical setting of a church building, the _________ may be ornately carved or constructed.

   a. Sounding board
   b. Background noise
   c. Bass trap
   d. Beat

2. In physics, _________ is the power transferred per unit area. In the SI system, it has units watts per metre squared (W/m^2). It is used most frequently with waves (e.g. sound or light), in which case the average power transfer over one period of the wave is used.

   a. Bahtinov mask
   b. Intensity
   c. Beam diameter
   d. Beam divergence

3. In electronics, an _________ is a doubling or halving of a frequency. The term is derived from the Western musical scale (an _________ is a doubling in frequency) and is therefore common in audio electronics. (The prefix octa-, denoting eight, has no direct significance).

   a. 3D sound localization
   b. Background noise
   c. Bass trap
   d. Octave

4. . _________ is the characteristic of a sound that is primarily a psychological correlate of physical strength . More formally, it is defined as 'that attribute of auditory sensation in terms of which sounds can be ordered on a scale extending from quiet to loud'.

_________, a subjective measure, is often confused with objective measures of sound strength such as sound pressure, sound pressure level (in decibels), sound intensity or sound power.

a. Loudness
b. Background noise
c. Bass trap
d. Beat

5. In physics, _________ is a phenomenon in which two waves superimpose to form a resultant wave of greater or lower amplitude. _________ usually refers to the interaction of waves that are correlated or coherent with each other, either because they come from the same source or because they have the same or nearly the same frequency. _________ effects can be observed with all types of waves, for example, light, radio, acoustic and surface water waves.

a. Bifluoride
b. Bisulfide
c. Interference
d. Borohydride

ANSWER KEY
11. SOUND

---

1. a
2. b
3. d
4. a
5. c

---

12. TEMPERATURE AND KINETIC THEORY

CHAPTER OUTLINE: KEY TERMS, PEOPLE, PLACES, CONCEPTS

- Atom
- Kinetic theory
- Atomic theory
- Atomic mass
- Brownian
- Brownian motion
- Molecular weight
- Molecule
- Expansion joint
- Bimetallic strip
- Boiling point
- Celsius
- Fahrenheit
- Kelvin scale
- Thermal contact
- Thermal equilibrium
- Thermodynamics
- Zeroth law of thermodynamics
- Human body
- Thermal
- Thermal expansion

12. TEMPERATURE AND KINETIC THEORY

CHAPTER OUTLINE: KEY TERMS, PEOPLE, PLACES, CONCEPTS

- Coefficient
- Equation of state
- Gas laws
- Liquefaction
- Absolute zero
- Ideal gas
- Ideal gas law
- Gas constant
- Boltzmann constant
- Velocity
- Average speed
- Root-mean-square speed
- Critical point
- Phase transition
- Dry ice
- Liquid crystal
- Phase diagram
- Sublimation
- Superfluidity
- Vapor
- Triple point

12. TEMPERATURE AND KINETIC THEORY

CHAPTER OUTLINE: KEY TERMS, PEOPLE, PLACES, CONCEPTS

______ Condensation

______ Evaporation

______ Vapor pressure

______ Humidity

______ Partial pressure

______ Relative humidity

______ Dew point

______ Diffusion

______ Diffusion equation

______ Escape velocity

______ Regelation

CHAPTER HIGHLIGHTS & NOTES: KEY TERMS, PEOPLE, PLACES, CONCEPTS

Atom	The atom is a basic unit of matter that consists of a dense central nucleus surrounded by a cloud of negatively charged electrons. The atomic nucleus contains a mix of positively charged protons and electrically neutral neutrons, which means 'uncuttable' or 'the smallest indivisible particle of matter'. Although the Indian and Greek concepts of the atom were based purely on philosophy, modern science has retained the name coined by Democritus.
Kinetic theory	The kinetic theory of gases describes a gas as a large number of small particles, all of which are in constant, random motion. The rapidly moving particles constantly collide with each other and with the walls of the container. Kinetic theory explains macroscopic properties of gases, such as pressure, temperature, viscosity, thermal conductivity, and volume, by considering their molecular composition and motion.

Atomic theory	In chemistry and physics, atomic theory is a scientific theory of the nature of matter, which states that matter is composed of discrete units called atoms, as opposed to the earlier concept which held that matter could be divided into any arbitrarily small quantity. It began as a philosophical concept in ancient Greece (Democritus) and entered the scientific mainstream in the early 19th century when discoveries in the field of chemistry showed that matter did indeed behave as if it were made up of particles. The word 'atom' (from the ancient Greek adjective atomos, 'indivisible'.
Atomic mass	The atomic mass is the mass of an atomic particle, sub-atomic particle, or molecule. It may be expressed in unified atomic mass units; by international agreement, 1 atomic mass unit is defined as 1/12 of the mass of a single carbon-12 atom (at rest). When expressed in such units, the atomic mass is called the relative isotopic mass .
Brownian	Robert Brown FRSE FRS FLS MWS was a Scottish botanist and palaeobotanist who made important contributions to botany largely through his pioneering use of the microscope. His contributions include one of the earliest detailed descriptions of the cell nucleus and cytoplasmic streaming; the observation of Brownian motion; early work on plant pollination and fertilisation, including being the first to recognise the fundamental difference between gymnosperms and angiosperms; and some of the earliest studies in palynology. He also made numerous contributions to plant taxonomy, including the erection of a number of plant families that are still accepted today; and numerous Australian plant genera and species, the fruit of his exploration of that continent with Matthew Flinders.
Brownian motion	Brownian motion or pedesis is the random motion of particles suspended in a fluid (a liquid or a gas) resulting from their collision with the quick atoms or molecules in the gas or liquid. The term 'Brownian motion' can also refer to the mathematical model used to describe such random movements, which is often called a particle theory. In 1827, the botanist Robert Brown, looking through a microscope at particles found in pollen grains in water, noted that the particles moved through the water but was not able to determine the mechanisms that caused this motion.
Molecular weight	Molecular mass or molecular weight refers to the mass of a molecule. It is calculated as the sum of the mass of each constituent atom multiplied by the number of atoms of that element in the molecular formula. The molecular mass of small to medium size molecules, measured by mass spectrometry, determines stoichiometry.
Molecule	A molecule is an electrically neutral group of two or more atoms held together by chemical bonds. Molecules are distinguished from ions by their lack of electrical charge.

12. TEMPERATURE AND KINETIC THEORY

CHAPTER HIGHLIGHTS & NOTES: KEY TERMS, PEOPLE, PLACES, CONCEPTS

Expansion joint

An expansion joint or movement joint is an assembly designed to safely absorb the heat-induced expansion and contraction of construction materials, to absorb vibration, to hold parts together, or to allow movement due to ground settlement or earthquakes. They are commonly found between sections of buildings, bridges, sidewalks, railway tracks, piping systems, ships, and other structures.

Building faces, concrete slabs, and pipelines expand and contract due to warming and cooling from seasonal variation, or due to other heat sources.

Bimetallic strip

A bimetallic strip is used to convert a temperature change into mechanical displacement. The strip consists of two strips of different metals which expand at different rates as they are heated, usually steel and copper, or in some cases steel and brass. The strips are joined together throughout their length by riveting, brazing or welding.

Boiling point

The boiling point of a substance is the temperature at which the vapor pressure of the liquid equals the pressure surrounding the liquid and the liquid changes into a vapor.

A liquid in a vacuum has a lower boiling point than when that liquid is at atmospheric pressure. A liquid at high-pressure has a higher boiling point than when that liquid is at atmospheric pressure.

Celsius

Celsius, also known as centigrade, is a scale and unit of measurement for temperature. It is named after the Swedish astronomer Anders Celsius who developed a similar temperature scale. The degree Celsius can refer to a specific temperature on the Celsius scale as well as a unit to indicate a temperature interval, a difference between two temperatures or an uncertainty.

Fahrenheit

Fahrenheit is a temperature scale based on one proposed in 1724 by the physicist Daniel Gabriel Fahrenheit after whom the scale is named. The scale is defined by two fixed points: the temperature at which water freezes into ice is defined as 32 degrees, and the boiling point of water is defined to be 212 degrees. On Fahrenheit's original scale the lower defining point was the freezing point of brine, defined as zero degrees.

Kelvin scale

The kelvin is a unit of measurement for temperature. It is one of the seven base units in the International System of Units (SI) and is assigned the unit symbol K. The Kelvin scale is an absolute, thermodynamic temperature scale using as its null point absolute zero, the temperature at which all thermal motion ceases in the classical description of thermodynamics. The kelvin is defined as the fraction $^{1}/_{273.16}$ of the thermodynamic temperature of the triple point of water (exactly 0.01 °C or 32.018 °F).

Thermal contact

In heat transfer and thermodynamics, a thermodynamic system is said to be in thermal contact with another system if it can exchange energy with it through the process of heat. Perfect thermal isolation is an idealization as real systems are always in thermal contact with their environment to some extent.

Thermal equilibrium

In physics, the phrase thermal equilibrium is used sometimes in the common parlance of the ordinary language of physical discourse, and sometimes as a specialized technical term in thermodynamics.

As common parlance, the phrase refers to steady states of temperature, which may be spatial or temporal. The meaning varies from occasion to occasion, as with all ordinary language usages.

Thermodynamics

Thermodynamics is a branch of natural science concerned with heat and its relation to energy and work. It defines macroscopic variables (such as temperature, internal energy, entropy, and pressure) that characterize materials and radiation, and explains how they are related and by what laws they change with time. Thermodynamics describes the average behavior of very large numbers of microscopic constituents, and its laws can be derived from statistical mechanics.

Zeroth law of thermodynamics

The zeroth law of thermodynamics states that if two systems are each in thermal equilibrium with a third system, they are also in thermal equilibrium with each other.

Two systems are said to be in the relation of thermal equilibrium if they are linked by a wall permeable only to heat, and do not change over time. As a convenience of language, systems are sometimes also said to be in a relation of thermal equilibrium if they are not linked so as to be able to transfer heat to each other, but would not do so if they were connected by a wall permeable only to heat.

Human body

The human body is the entire structure of a human being and comprises a head, neck, trunk, two arms and hands and two legs and feet. Every part of the body is composed of various types of cell. At maturity, the estimated number of cells in the body is given as 37.2 trillion.

Thermal

A thermal column (or thermal) is a column of rising air in the lower altitudes of the Earth's atmosphere. Thermals are created by the uneven heating of the Earth's surface from solar radiation, and are an example of convection, specifically atmospheric convection. The Sun warms the ground, which in turn warms the air directly above it.

Thermal expansion

Thermal expansion is the tendency of matter to change in volume in response to a change in temperature.

When a substance is heated, its particles begin moving more and thus usually maintain a greater average separation. Materials which contract with increasing temperature are unusual; this effect is limited in size, and only occurs within limited temperature ranges .

Coefficient

In mathematics, a coefficient is a multiplicative factor in some term of an expression ; it is usually a number, but in any case does not involve any variables of the expression. For instance in $7x^2 - 3xy + 1.5 + y$

the first two terms respectively have the coefficients 7 and -3. The third term 1.5 is a constant. The final term does not have any explicitly written coefficient, but is considered to have coefficient 1, since multiplying by that factor would not change the term.

Equation of state

In physics and thermodynamics, an equation of state is a relation between state variables. More specifically, an equation of state is a thermodynamic equation describing the state of matter under a given set of physical conditions. It is a constitutive equation which provides a mathematical relationship between two or more state functions associated with the matter, such as its temperature, pressure, volume, or internal energy.

Gas laws

The early gas laws were developed at the end of the 18th century, when scientists began to realize that relationships between the pressure, volume and temperature of a sample of gas could be obtained which would hold for all gases. Gases behave in a similar way over a wide variety of conditions because to a good approximation they all have molecules which are widely spaced, and nowadays the equation of state for an ideal gas is derived from kinetic theory. The earlier gas laws are now considered as special cases of the ideal gas equation, with one or more of the variables held constant.

Liquefaction

Liquefaction, sometimes liquification, generally refers to the process of becoming a liquid or liquid-like.

Absolute zero

Absolute zero is the lowest temperature possible. More formally, it is the temperature at which entropy reaches its minimum value. The laws of thermodynamics state that absolute zero cannot be reached using only thermodynamic means.

Ideal gas

An ideal gas is a theoretical gas composed of a set of randomly moving, non-interacting point particles. The ideal gas concept is useful because it obeys the ideal gas law, a simplified equation of state, and is amenable to analysis under statistical mechanics.

At normal conditions such as standard temperature and pressure, most real gases behave qualitatively like an ideal gas.

Ideal gas law

The ideal gas law is the equation of state of a hypothetical ideal gas. It is a good approximation to the behaviour of many gases under many conditions, although it has several limitations. It was first stated by Émile Clapeyron in 1834 as a combination of Boyle's law and Charles's law.

Gas constant

The gas constant is a physical constant which is featured in many fundamental equations in the physical sciences, such as the ideal gas law and the Nernst equation.

It is equivalent to the Boltzmann constant, but expressed in units of energy per temperature increment per mole (rather than energy per temperature increment per particle).

12. TEMPERATURE AND KINETIC THEORY

Boltzmann constant

The Boltzmann constant is a physical constant relating energy at the individual particle level with temperature. It is the gas constant R divided by the Avogadro constant N_A: $k = \frac{R}{N_{\rm A}}.$

It has the same dimension . Introducing the Boltzmann constant transforms the ideal gas law into an alternative form: $PV = NkT$

where N is the number of molecules of gas.

Velocity

Velocity is the rate of change of the position of an object, equivalent to a specification of its speed and direction of motion, e.g. 60 km/h to the north. Velocity is an important concept in kinematics, the branch of classical mechanics which describes the motion of bodies.

Velocity is a vector physical quantity; both magnitude and direction are required to define it.

Average speed

In everyday use and in kinematics, the speed of an object is the magnitude of its velocity ; it is thus a scalar quantity. The average speed of an object in an interval of time is the distance travelled by the object divided by the duration of the interval; the instantaneous speed is the limit of the average speed as the duration of the time interval approaches zero.

Like velocity, speed has the dimensions of a length divided by a time; the SI unit of speed is the metre per second, but the most usual unit of speed in everyday usage is the kilometre per hour or, in the US and the UK, miles per hour.

Root-mean-square speed

Root-mean-square speed is the measure of the speed of particles in a gas that is most convenient for problem solving within the kinetic theory of gases. It is defined as the square root of the average velocity-squared of the molecules in a gas. It is given by the formula $v_{\rm rms} = \sqrt{\frac{3RT}{M_m}}$

where v_{rms} is the root mean square of the speed in meters per second, M_m is the molar mass of the gas in kilograms per mole, R is the molar gas constant, and T is the temperature in kelvin.

Critical point

In physical chemistry, thermodynamics, chemistry and condensed matter physics, a critical point, also known as a critical state, occurs under conditions at which no phase boundaries exist. There are multiple types of critical points, including vapor-liquid critical points and liquid-liquid critical points.

Phase transition

A phase transition is the transformation of thermodynamic system from one phase or state of matter to another.

A phase of a thermodynamic system and the states of matter have uniform physical properties.

During a phase transition of a given medium certain properties of the medium change, often discontinuously, as a result of some external condition, such as temperature, pressure, and others.

Dry ice

Dry ice, sometimes referred to as 'cardice' or as 'card ice', is the solid form of carbon dioxide. It is used primarily as a cooling agent. Its advantages include lower temperature than that of water ice and not leaving any residue (other than incidental frost from moisture in the atmosphere).

Liquid crystal

Liquid crystals are matter in a state that has properties between those of conventional liquid and those of solid crystal. For instance, a liquid crystal may flow like a liquid, but its molecules may be oriented in a crystal-like way. There are many different types of liquid-crystal phases, which can be distinguished by their different optical properties (such as birefringence).

Phase diagram

A phase diagram in physical chemistry, engineering, mineralogy, and materials science is a type of chart used to show conditions at which thermodynamically distinct phases can occur at equilibrium. In mathematics and physics, 'phase diagram' is used with a different meaning: a synonym for a phase space.

Sublimation

Sublimation is the transition of a substance directly from the solid to the gas phase without passing through an intermediate liquid phase. Sublimation is an endothermic phase transition that occurs at temperatures and pressures below a substance's triple point in its phase diagram. The reverse process of sublimation is desublimation, or deposition.

Superfluidity

Superfluidity is a state of matter in which the matter behaves like a fluid with zero viscosity; where it appears to exhibit the ability to self-propel and travel in a way that defies the forces of gravity and surface tension. While this characteristic was originally discovered in liquid helium, it is also found in astrophysics, high-energy physics, and theories of quantum gravity. The phenomenon is related to the Bose-Einstein condensation, but it is not identical: not all Bose-Einstein condensates can be regarded as superfluids, and not all superfluids are Bose-Einstein condensates.

Vapor

A vapor or vapour (British spelling) is a substance in the gas phase at a temperature lower than its critical point. This means that the vapor can be condensed to a liquid or to a solid by increasing its pressure without reducing the temperature.

For example, water has a critical temperature of 374 °C (647 K), which is the highest temperature at which liquid water can exist.

Triple point

In thermodynamics, the triple point of a substance is the temperature and pressure at which the three phases of that substance coexist in thermodynamic equilibrium. For example, the triple point of mercury occurs at a temperature of -38.8344 °C and a pressure of 0.2 mPa.

Condensation

Condensation is the change of the physical state of matter from gas phase into liquid phase, and is the reverse of vaporization. It can also be defined as the change in the state of water vapor to water/any liquid when in contact with any surface. When the transition happens from the gaseous phase into the solid phase directly, the change is called deposition.

Evaporation

Evaporation is a type of vaporization of a liquid that occurs from the surface of a liquid into a gaseous phase that is not saturated with the evaporating substance. The other type of vaporization is boiling, which is characterized by bubbles of saturated vapor forming in the liquid phase. Steam produced in a boiler is another example of evaporation occurring in a saturated vapor phase.

Vapor pressure

Vapor pressure or equilibrium vapor pressure is the pressure exerted by a vapor in thermodynamic equilibrium with its condensed phases at a given temperature in a closed system. The equilibrium vapor pressure is an indication of a liquid's evaporation rate. It relates to the tendency of particles to escape from the liquid (or a solid).

Humidity

Humidity is the amount of water vapor in the air. Water vapor is the gaseous state of water and is invisible. Humidity indicates the likelihood of precipitation, dew, or fog.

Partial pressure

In a mixture of gases, each gas has a partial pressure which is the hypothetical pressure of that gas if it alone occupied the volume of the mixture at the same temperature. The total pressure of an ideal gas mixture is the sum of the partial pressures of each individual gas in the mixture.

It relies on the following isotherm relation: $V_x \times p_{tot} = V_{tot} \times p_x$ •V_x is the partial volume of any individual gas component (X)•V_{tot} is the total volume in gas mixture•p_x is the partial pressure of gas X•p_{tot} is the total pressure of gas mixture•n_x is the amount of substance of a gas (X)•n_{tot} is the total amount of substance in gas mixture

The partial pressure of a gas is a measure of thermodynamic activity of the gas's molecules.

Relative humidity

Relative humidity is the ratio of the partial pressure of water vapor in an air-water mixture to the saturated vapor pressure of water at a prescribed temperature. The relative humidity of air depends on temperature and the pressure of the system of interest.

Dew point

The dew point is the temperature below which the water vapor in air at constant barometric pressure condenses into liquid water at the same rate at which it evaporates. The condensed water is called dew when it forms on a solid surface.

The dew point is a water-to-air saturation temperature.

Diffusion

Diffusion, in acoustics and architectural engineering, is the efficacy by which sound energy is spread evenly in a given environment. A perfectly diffusive sound space is one that has certain key acoustic properties which are the same anywhere in the space.

12. TEMPERATURE AND KINETIC THEORY

CHAPTER HIGHLIGHTS & NOTES: KEY TERMS, PEOPLE, PLACES, CONCEPTS

Diffusion equation

The diffusion equation is a partial differential equation which describes density dynamics in a material undergoing diffusion. It is also used to describe processes exhibiting diffusive-like behaviour, for instance the 'diffusion' of alleles in a population in population genetics.

Escape velocity

In physics, escape velocity is the speed at which the kinetic energy plus the gravitational potential energy of an object is zero. It is the speed needed to 'break free' from the gravitational attraction of a massive body, without further propulsion.

For a spherically symmetric body, the escape velocity at a given distance is calculated by the formula

$$v_e = \sqrt{\frac{2GM}{r}},$$

where G is the universal gravitational constant ($G = 6.67\times10^{-11}\ m^3\ kg^{-1}\ s^{-2}$), M the mass of the planet, star or other body, and r the distance from the center of gravity.

Regelation

Regelation is the phenomenon of melting under pressure and freezing again when the pressure is reduced. Many sources state that regelation can be demonstrated by looping a fine wire around a block of ice, with a heavy weight attached to it. The pressure exerted on the ice slowly melts it locally, permitting the wire to pass through the entire block.

CHAPTER QUIZ: KEY TERMS, PEOPLE, PLACES, CONCEPTS

1. Robert Brown FRSE FRS FLS MWS was a Scottish botanist and palaeobotanist who made important contributions to botany largely through his pioneering use of the microscope. His contributions include one of the earliest detailed descriptions of the cell nucleus and cytoplasmic streaming; the observation of _________ motion; early work on plant pollination and fertilisation, including being the first to recognise the fundamental difference between gymnosperms and angiosperms; and some of the earliest studies in palynology. He also made numerous contributions to plant taxonomy, including the erection of a number of plant families that are still accepted today; and numerous Australian plant genera and species, the fruit of his exploration of that continent with Matthew Flinders.

   a.
   b. Cubical atom
   c. Brownian
   d. Hydrogen atom

2. In chemistry and physics, _________ is a scientific theory of the nature of matter, which states that matter is composed of discrete units called atoms, as opposed to the earlier concept which held that matter could be divided into any arbitrarily small quantity. It began as a philosophical concept in ancient Greece (Democritus) and entered the scientific mainstream in the early 19th century when discoveries in the field of chemistry showed that matter did indeed behave as if it were made up of particles.

   The word 'atom' (from the ancient Greek adjective atomos, 'indivisible'.

   a. Potential well
   b. Atomic theory
   c. Position operator
   d. Physical Review A

3. The _________ of gases describes a gas as a large number of small particles, all of which are in constant, random motion. The rapidly moving particles constantly collide with each other and with the walls of the container. _________ explains macroscopic properties of gases, such as pressure, temperature, viscosity, thermal conductivity, and volume, by considering their molecular composition and motion.

   a. Backdraft
   b. Batteryless radio
   c. Kinetic theory
   d. Binodal

4. A _________ column (or _________) is a column of rising air in the lower altitudes of the Earth's atmosphere. _________s are created by the uneven heating of the Earth's surface from solar radiation, and are an example of convection, specifically atmospheric convection. The Sun warms the ground, which in turn warms the air directly above it.

   a. Thermal
   b. Convection heater
   c. Convection microwave
   d. Convection oven

5. In physical chemistry, thermodynamics, chemistry and condensed matter physics, a _________, also known as a critical state, occurs under conditions at which no phase boundaries exist. There are multiple types of _________s, including vapor-liquid _________s and liquid-liquid _________s.

   a. Boiling point
   b. Friedrich Oskar Giesel
   c. Kuznetsov NK-14
   d. Critical point

ANSWER KEY
12. TEMPERATURE AND KINETIC THEORY

---

1. c

2. b

3. c

4. a

5. d

---

13. HEAT

CHAPTER OUTLINE: KEY TERMS, PEOPLE, PLACES, CONCEPTS

- Calorie
- Kilocalorie
- Mechanical equivalent of heat
- Energy transfer
- Internal energy
- Thermal energy
- Calorimetry
- Closed system
- Conservation of energy
- Energy conservation
- Isolated system
- Thermal equilibrium
- Thermal
- Calorimeter
- Boiling point
- Heat of fusion
- Heat of vaporization
- Latent heat
- Melting point
- Phase transition
- Vaporization

13. HEAT

CHAPTER OUTLINE: KEY TERMS, PEOPLE, PLACES, CONCEPTS

- Heat transfer
- Thermal conductivity
- Gradient
- Human body
- Convection
- Forced convection
- Natural convection
- R-value
- Thermal resistance
- Emissivity
- Thermal radiation
- Radiation
- Medical imaging
- Solar constant
- Solar energy
- Thermography
- Heat capacity
- Skin conductance

13. HEAT

CHAPTER HIGHLIGHTS & NOTES: KEY TERMS, PEOPLE, PLACES, CONCEPTS

Calorie	The name calorie is used for two units of energy. •The small calorie or gram calorie is the approximate amount of energy needed to raise the temperature of one gram of water by one degree Celsius.•The large calorie, kilogram calorie, dietary calorie, nutritionist's calorie, nutritional calorie or food calorie is the amount of energy needed to raise the temperature of one kilogram of water by one degree Celsius. The large calorie is thus equal to 1000 small calories or one kilocalorie. Although these units are part of the metric system, they now have been superseded in the International System of Units by the joule.
Kilocalorie	The name calorie is used for two units of energy. •The small calorie or gram calorie is the approximate amount of energy needed to raise the temperature of one gram of water by one degree Celsius.•The large calorie, kilogram calorie, dietary calorie, nutritionist's calorie, nutritional calorie or food calorie (symbol: Cal, equiv: kcal) is the amount of energy needed to raise the temperature of one kilogram of water by one degree Celsius. The large calorie is thus equal to 1000 small calories or one kilocalorie. Although these units are part of the metric system, they now have been superseded in the International System of Units by the joule.
Mechanical equivalent of heat	In the history of science, the mechanical equivalent of heat was a concept that had an important part in the development and acceptance of the conservation of energy and the establishment of the science of thermodynamics in the 19th century. The concept stated that motion and heat are mutually interchangeable and that in every case, a given amount of work would generate the same amount of heat, provided the work done is totally converted to heat energy.
Energy transfer	In the physical sciences, an energy transfer or energy exchange from one system to another is said to occur when an amount of energy crosses the boundary between them, thus increasing the energy content of one system while decreasing the energy content of the other system by the same amount. The transfer is characterized by the quantity of energy transferred, which can be specified in energy units such as the joule (J), in combination with the direction of the transfer, which can be specified as in (to) or out of (from) one system or the other. The transfer occurs in a process which changes the state of each system.
Internal energy	In thermodynamics, the internal energy is the total energy contained by a thermodynamic system. It is the energy needed to create the system but excludes the energy to displace the system's surroundings, any energy associated with a move as a whole, or due to external force fields. Internal energy has two major components, kinetic energy and potential energy.

13. HEAT

Thermal energy

Thermal energy is the part of the total potential energy and kinetic energy of an object or sample of matter that results in the system temperature. It is represented by the variable Q, and can be measured in Joules. This quantity may be difficult to determine or even meaningless unless the system has attained its temperature only through warming (heating), and not been subjected to work input or output, or any other energy-changing processes.

Calorimetry

Calorimetry is the science or act of measuring changes in parameters of chemical reactions, physical changes and phase transitions, for the purpose of deriving the heat or heat transfer associated with those changes. Calorimetry is performed with a calorimeter. The word calorimetry is derived from the Latin word calor, meaning heat and the Greek word µ?t??? (metron), meaning measure.

Closed system

The term closed system refers to a physical system that is closed to certain types of transfers in or out of the system. The specification of what types of transfers are excluded, is different in different contexts.

Conservation of energy

In physics, the law of conservation of energy states that the total energy of an isolated system cannot change--it is said to be conserved over time. Energy can be neither created nor destroyed, but can change form, for instance chemical energy can be converted to kinetic energy in the explosion of a stick of dynamite.

A consequence of the law of conservation of energy is that a perpetual motion machine of the first kind cannot exist.

Energy conservation

Energy conservation refers to reducing energy through using less of an energy service. Energy conservation differs from efficient energy use, which refers to using less energy for a constant service. For example, driving less is an example of energy conservation.

Isolated system

In the natural sciences an isolated system is a physical system without any external exchange - neither matter nor energy can enter or exit, but can only move around inside. Truly isolated systems cannot exist in nature, other than allegedly the universe itself, and they are thus hypothetical concepts only. It obeys, in particular, to the first of the conservation laws: its total energy - mass stays constant.

Thermal equilibrium

In physics, the phrase thermal equilibrium is used sometimes in the common parlance of the ordinary language of physical discourse, and sometimes as a specialized technical term in thermodynamics.

As common parlance, the phrase refers to steady states of temperature, which may be spatial or temporal. The meaning varies from occasion to occasion, as with all ordinary language usages.

13. HEAT

CHAPTER HIGHLIGHTS & NOTES: KEY TERMS, PEOPLE, PLACES, CONCEPTS

Thermal	A thermal column (or thermal) is a column of rising air in the lower altitudes of the Earth's atmosphere. Thermals are created by the uneven heating of the Earth's surface from solar radiation, and are an example of convection, specifically atmospheric convection. The Sun warms the ground, which in turn warms the air directly above it.
Calorimeter	In particle physics, a calorimeter is an experimental apparatus that measures the energy of particles. Most particles enter the calorimeter and initiate a particle shower and the particles' energy is deposited in the calorimeter, collected, and measured. The energy may be measured in its entirety, requiring total containment of the particle shower, or it may be sampled.
Boiling point	The boiling point of a substance is the temperature at which the vapor pressure of the liquid equals the pressure surrounding the liquid and the liquid changes into a vapor. A liquid in a vacuum has a lower boiling point than when that liquid is at atmospheric pressure. A liquid at high-pressure has a higher boiling point than when that liquid is at atmospheric pressure.
Heat of fusion	The enthalpy of fusion or heat of fusion is the change in enthalpy resulting from heating a given quantity of a substance to change its state from a solid to a liquid. The temperature at which this occurs is the melting point. The 'enthalpy' of fusion is a latent heat, because during melting the introduction of heat cannot be observed as a temperature change, as the temperature remains constant during the process.
Heat of vaporization	The enthalpy of vaporization also known as the (latent) heat of vaporization or heat of evaporation, is the enthalpy change required to transform a given quantity of a substance from a liquid into a gas at a given pressure (often atmospheric pressure, as in STP). It is often measured at the normal boiling point of a substance; although tabulated values are usually corrected to 298 K, the correction is often smaller than the uncertainty in the measured value. The heat of vaporization is temperature-dependent, though a constant heat of vaporization can be assumed for small temperature ranges and for reduced temperature $T_r \ll 1.0$. The heat of vaporization diminishes with increasing temperature and it vanishes completely at the critical temperature ($T_r=1$) because above the critical temperature the liquid and vapor phases no longer exist, since the substance is a supercritical fluid.
Latent heat	Latent heat is the heat released or absorbed by a body or a thermodynamic system during a constant-temperature process. A typical example is a change of state of matter, meaning a phase transition such as the melting of ice or the boiling of water. The term was introduced around 1762 by Scottish chemist Joseph Black.

13. HEAT

Melting point

The melting point of a solid is the temperature at which it changes state from solid to liquid at atmospheric pressure. At the melting point the solid and liquid phase exist in equilibrium. The melting point of a substance depends (usually slightly) on pressure and is usually specified at standard pressure.

Phase transition

A phase transition is the transformation of thermodynamic system from one phase or state of matter to another.

A phase of a thermodynamic system and the states of matter have uniform physical properties.

During a phase transition of a given medium certain properties of the medium change, often discontinuously, as a result of some external condition, such as temperature, pressure, and others.

Vaporization

Vaporization of an element or compound is a phase transition from the liquid phase to gas phase. There are two types of vaporization: evaporation and boiling.

Evaporation is a phase transition from the liquid phase to gas phase that occurs at temperatures below the boiling temperature at a given pressure.

Heat transfer

Heat transfer is a discipline of thermal engineering that concerns the generation, use, conversion, and exchange of thermal energy and heat between physical systems. As such, heat transfer is involved in almost every sector of the economy. Heat transfer is classified into various mechanisms, such as thermal conduction, thermal convection, thermal radiation, and transfer of energy by phase changes.

Thermal conductivity

In physics, thermal conductivity is the property of a material to conduct heat. It is evaluated primarily in terms of Fourier's Law for heat conduction.

Heat transfer occurs at a higher rate across materials of high thermal conductivity than across materials of low thermal conductivity.

Gradient

In mathematics, the gradient is a generalization of the usual concept of derivative to the functions of several variables. If $f(x_1, .. x_n)$ is a differentiable function of several variables, also called 'scalar field', its gradient is the vector of the n partial derivatives of f. It is thus a vector-valued function also called vector field.

Human body

The human body is the entire structure of a human being and comprises a head, neck, trunk, two arms and hands and two legs and feet. Every part of the body is composed of various types of cell. At maturity, the estimated number of cells in the body is given as 37.2 trillion.

Convection

Convection is the concerted, collective movement of groups or aggregates of molecules within fluids and rheids, either through advection or through diffusion or as a combination of both of them.

Convection of mass cannot take place in solids, since neither bulk current flows nor significant diffusion can take place in solids. Diffusion of heat can take place in solids, but that is called heat conduction.

Forced convection

Forced convection is a mechanism, or type of transport in which fluid motion is generated by an external source . It should be considered as one of the main methods of useful heat transfer as significant amounts of heat energy can be transported very efficiently and this mechanism is found very commonly in everyday life, including central heating, air conditioning, steam turbines and in many other machines. Forced convection is often encountered by engineers designing or analyzing heat exchangers, pipe flow, and flow over a plate at a different temperature than the stream (the case of a shuttle wing during re-entry, for example).

Natural convection

Natural convection is a mechanism, or type of heat transport, in which the fluid motion is not generated by any external source but only by density differences in the fluid occurring due to temperature gradients. In natural convection, fluid surrounding a heat source receives heat, becomes less dense and rises. The surrounding, cooler fluid then moves to replace it.

R-value

The Lankford coefficient (also called Lankford value, R-value, or plastic strain ratio) is a measure of the plastic anisotropy of a rolled sheet metal. This scalar quantity is used extensively as an indicator of the formability of recrystallized low-carbon steel sheets.

Thermal resistance

Thermal resistance is a heat property and a measurement of a temperature difference by which an object or material resists a heat flow (heat per time unit or thermal resistance). Thermal resistance is the reciprocal of thermal conductance. •Thermal resistance R has the units $(m^2K)/W$.•Specific thermal resistance or specific thermal resistivity $R_?$ in (K·m)/W is a material constant.•Absolute thermal resistance R_{th} in K/W is a specific property of a component.

Emissivity

The emissivity of a material is the relative ability of its surface to emit energy by radiation. It is the ratio of energy radiated by a particular material to energy radiated by a black body at the same temperature. A true black body would have an $e = 1$ while any real object would have $e < 1$. Emissivity is a dimensionless quantity.

Thermal radiation

Thermal radiation is electromagnetic radiation generated by the thermal motion of charged particles in matter. All matter with a temperature greater than absolute zero emits thermal radiation. When the temperature of the body is greater than absolute zero, interatomic collisions cause the kinetic energy of the atoms or molecules to change.

Radiation

In physics, radiation is a process in which energetic particles or energetic waves travel through a vacuum, or through matter-containing media that are not required for their propagation. Waves of a mass filled medium itself, such as water waves or sound waves, are usually not considered to be forms of 'radiation' in this sense.

Medical imaging	Medical imaging is the technique and process used to create images of the human body for clinical purposes (medical procedures seeking to reveal, diagnose, or examine disease) or medical science (including the study of normal anatomy and physiology). Although imaging of removed organs and tissues can be performed for medical reasons, such procedures are not usually referred to as medical imaging, but rather are a part of pathology. As a discipline and in its widest sense, it is part of biological imaging and incorporates Radiology, Magnetic Resonance Imaging, Nuclear medicine, medical Ultrasonography or Ultrasound, Endoscopy, Elastography, Tactile Imaging, Thermography and medical photography.
Solar constant	The solar constant, a measure of flux density, is the amount of incoming solar electromagnetic radiation per unit area that would be incident on a plane perpendicular to the rays, at a distance of one astronomical unit (AU) (roughly the mean distance from the Sun to the Earth). The solar constant includes all types of solar radiation, not just the visible light. It is measured by satellite to be roughly 1.361 kilowatts per square meter (kW/m^2) at solar minimum and approximately 0.1% greater (roughly 1.362 kW/m^2) at solar maximum.
Solar energy	Solar energy, radiant light and heat from the sun, is harnessed using a range of ever-evolving technologies such as solar heating, solar photovoltaics, solar thermal electricity, solar architecture and artificial photosynthesis. Solar technologies are broadly characterized as either passive solar or active solar depending on the way they capture, convert and distribute solar energy. Active solar techniques include the use of photovoltaic panels and solar thermal collectors to harness the energy.
Thermography	Thermography or thermology is the medical science that derives diagnostic indications from highly detailed and sensitive infrared images of the human body. Thermology is sometimes referred to as medical infrared imaging or tele-thermology and utilizes highly resolute and sensitive thermographic cameras.
Heat capacity	Heat capacity, or thermal capacity, is the measurable physical quantity of heat energy required to change the temperature of an object or body by a given amount. The SI unit of heat capacity is joule per kelvin, $\frac{J}{K}$ and the dimensional form is $M^1L^2T^{-2}T^{-1}$. Heat capacity is an extensive property of matter, meaning it is proportional to the size of the system.
Skin conductance	Skin conductance, also known as galvanic skin response, electrodermal response (EDR), psychogalvanic reflex (PGR), skin conductance response (SCR) or skin conductance level (SCL), is a method of measuring the electrical conductance of the skin, which varies with its moisture level.

13. HEAT

CHAPTER HIGHLIGHTS & NOTES: KEY TERMS, PEOPLE, PLACES, CONCEPTS

This is of interest because the sweat glands are controlled by the sympathetic nervous system, so skin conductance is used as an indication of psychological or physiological arousal. Therefore, if the sympathetic branch of the autonomic nervous system is highly aroused, then sweat gland activity will also increase, which in turn increases skin conductance.

CHAPTER QUIZ: KEY TERMS, PEOPLE, PLACES, CONCEPTS

1. In the natural sciences an _________ is a physical system without any external exchange - neither matter nor energy can enter or exit, but can only move around inside. Truly _________s cannot exist in nature, other than allegedly the universe itself, and they are thus hypothetical concepts only. It obeys, in particular, to the first of the conservation laws: its total energy - mass stays constant.

   a. Backdraft
   b. Isolated system
   c. Bennett acceptance ratio
   d. Binodal

2. _________ is the technique and process used to create images of the human body for clinical purposes (medical procedures seeking to reveal, diagnose, or examine disease) or medical science (including the study of normal anatomy and physiology). Although imaging of removed organs and tissues can be performed for medical reasons, such procedures are not usually referred to as _________, but rather are a part of pathology.

   As a discipline and in its widest sense, it is part of biological imaging and incorporates Radiology, Magnetic Resonance Imaging, Nuclear medicine, medical Ultrasonography or Ultrasound, Endoscopy, Elastography, Tactile Imaging, Thermography and medical photography.

   a. Background subtraction
   b. Bicubic interpolation
   c. Medical imaging
   d. Black balance

3. . The term _________ refers to a physical system that is closed to certain types of transfers in or out of the system. The specification of what types of transfers are excluded, is different in different contexts.

   a. Backdraft
   b. Batteryless radio
   c. Closed system

4. _________ is electromagnetic radiation generated by the thermal motion of charged particles in matter. All matter with a temperature greater than absolute zero emits _________. When the temperature of the body is greater than absolute zero, interatomic collisions cause the kinetic energy of the atoms or molecules to change.

 a. Back scattering alignment
 b. Thermal radiation
 c. Creeping wave
 d. Cyclotron radiation

5. The name _________ is used for two units of energy. •The small _________ or gram _________ is the approximate amount of energy needed to raise the temperature of one gram of water by one degree Celsius.•The large _________, kilogram _________, dietary _________, nutritionist's _________, nutritional _________ or food _________ is the amount of energy needed to raise the temperature of one kilogram of water by one degree Celsius. The large _________ is thus equal to 1000 small _________s or one kilo_________.

 Although these units are part of the metric system, they now have been superseded in the International System of Units by the joule.

 a. Kilocalorie
 b. Kilowatt-hour
 c. Calorie
 d. Berge conjecture

ANSWER KEY
13. HEAT

---

1. b

2. c

3. c

4. b

5. c

---

14. THE LAWS OF THERMODYNAMICS

CHAPTER OUTLINE: KEY TERMS, PEOPLE, PLACES, CONCEPTS

- Thermodynamics
- Conservation of energy
- Energy conservation
- First law of thermodynamics
- Internal energy
- Adiabatic
- Human body
- Second law of thermodynamics
- Heat engine
- Steam engine
- Internal combustion
- Operating temperature
- Efficiency
- Carnot cycle
- Reversible process
- Absolute zero
- Third law of thermodynamics
- Heat pump
- Coefficient of performance
- Entropy
- Order and disorder

14. THE LAWS OF THERMODYNAMICS

CHAPTER OUTLINE: KEY TERMS, PEOPLE, PLACES, CONCEPTS

	Degradation
	Solar energy
	Thermal pollution
	Turbine
	Thermal
	Geothermal energy
	Nuclear fission
	Nuclear fusion
	Wind power

CHAPTER HIGHLIGHTS & NOTES: KEY TERMS, PEOPLE, PLACES, CONCEPTS

Thermodynamics	Thermodynamics is a branch of natural science concerned with heat and its relation to energy and work. It defines macroscopic variables (such as temperature, internal energy, entropy, and pressure) that characterize materials and radiation, and explains how they are related and by what laws they change with time. Thermodynamics describes the average behavior of very large numbers of microscopic constituents, and its laws can be derived from statistical mechanics.
Conservation of energy	In physics, the law of conservation of energy states that the total energy of an isolated system cannot change--it is said to be conserved over time. Energy can be neither created nor destroyed, but can change form, for instance chemical energy can be converted to kinetic energy in the explosion of a stick of dynamite. A consequence of the law of conservation of energy is that a perpetual motion machine of the first kind cannot exist.
Energy conservation	Energy conservation refers to reducing energy through using less of an energy service. Energy conservation differs from efficient energy use, which refers to using less energy for a constant service.

14. THE LAWS OF THERMODYNAMICS

CHAPTER HIGHLIGHTS & NOTES: KEY TERMS, PEOPLE, PLACES, CONCEPTS

First law of thermodynamics	The first law of thermodynamics is a version of the law of conservation of energy, adapted for thermodynamic systems. The law of conservation of energy states that the total energy of an isolated system is constant; energy can be transformed from one form to another, but cannot be created or destroyed. The first law of thermodynamics recognizes a particular form of energy called internal energy.
Internal energy	In thermodynamics, the internal energy is the total energy contained by a thermodynamic system. It is the energy needed to create the system but excludes the energy to displace the system's surroundings, any energy associated with a move as a whole, or due to external force fields. Internal energy has two major components, kinetic energy and potential energy.
Adiabatic	An adiabatic process is a process that occurs without the transfer of heat or matter between a system and its surroundings. A key concept in thermodynamics, adiabatic transfer provides a rigorous conceptual basis for the theory used to expound the first law of thermodynamics. It is also key in a practical sense, that many rapid chemical and physical processes are described using the adiabatic approximation; such processes are usually followed or preceded by events that do involve heat transfer.
Human body	The human body is the entire structure of a human being and comprises a head, neck, trunk, two arms and hands and two legs and feet. Every part of the body is composed of various types of cell. At maturity, the estimated number of cells in the body is given as 37.2 trillion.
Second law of thermodynamics	The second law of thermodynamics states that the entropy of an isolated system never decreases, because isolated systems spontaneously evolve toward thermodynamic equilibrium--the state of maximum entropy. Equivalently, perpetual motion machines of the second kind are impossible. The second law is an empirically validated postulate of thermodynamics, but it can be understood and explained using the underlying quantum statistical mechanics, together with the assumption of low-entropy initial conditions in the distant past of a system results from an infinitesimal transfer of heat to a closed system divided by the common temperature of the system and the surroundings which supply the heat.
Heat engine	In thermodynamics, a heat engine is a system that performs the conversion of heat or thermal energy to mechanical work. It does this by bringing a working substance from a higher state temperature to a lower state temperature. A heat 'source' generates thermal energy that brings the working substance to the high temperature state.
Steam engine	A steam engine is a heat engine that performs mechanical work using steam as its working fluid. Using boiling water to produce mechanical motion goes back about 2,000 years, but early devices were not practical.

14. THE LAWS OF THERMODYNAMICS

Internal combustion	The internal combustion engine is an engine in which the combustion of a fuel occurs with an oxidizer (usually air) in a combustion chamber that is an integral part of the working fluid flow circuit. In an internal combustion engine (ICE) the expansion of the high-temperature and high-pressure gases produced by combustion apply direct force to some component of the engine. The force is applied typically to pistons, turbine blades, or a nozzle.
Operating temperature	An operating temperature is the temperature at which an electrical or mechanical device operates. The device will operate effectively within a specified temperature range which varies based on the device function and application context, and ranges from the minimum operating temperature to the maximum operating temperature. Outside this range of safe operating temperatures the device may fail.
Efficiency	Efficiency in general, describes the extent to which time, effort or cost is well used for the intended task or purpose. It is often used with the specific purpose of relaying the capability of a specific application of effort to produce a specific outcome effectively with a minimum amount or quantity of waste, expense, or unnecessary effort. 'Efficiency' has widely varying meanings in different disciplines.
Carnot cycle	The Carnot cycle is a theoretical thermodynamic cycle proposed by Nicolas Léonard Sadi Carnot in 1823 and expanded by in the 1830s and 40s. It can be shown that it is the most efficient cycle for converting a given amount of thermal energy into work, or conversely, creating a temperature difference (e.g. refrigeration) by doing a given amount of work. Every single thermodynamic system exists in a particular state.
Reversible process	In thermodynamics, a reversible process, or reversible cycle if the process is cyclic, is a process that can be 'reversed' by means of infinitesimal changes in some property of the system without entropy production . Due to these infinitesimal changes, the system is in thermodynamic equilibrium throughout the entire process. Since it would take an infinite amount of time for the reversible process to finish, perfectly reversible processes are impossible.
Absolute zero	Absolute zero is the lowest temperature possible. More formally, it is the temperature at which entropy reaches its minimum value. The laws of thermodynamics state that absolute zero cannot be reached using only thermodynamic means.
Third law of thermodynamics	The third law of thermodynamics is sometimes stated as follows:' The entropy of a perfect crystal, at absolute zero kelvin, is exactly equal to zero. ' At zero kelvin the system must be in a state with the minimum possible energy, and this statement of the third law holds true if the perfect crystal has only one minimum energy state.

14. THE LAWS OF THERMODYNAMICS

Heat pump

A heat pump is a device that provides heat energy from a source of heat to a destination called a 'heat sink'. Heat pumps are designed to move thermal energy opposite to the direction of spontaneous heat flow by absorbing heat from a cold space and release it to a warmer one, and vice-versa. A heat pump uses some amount of external power to accomplish the work of transferring energy from the heat source to the heat sink.

Coefficient of performance

The coefficient of performance of a heat pump is a ratio of heating or cooling provided to electrical energy consumed. Higher Coefficient of performances equate to lower operating costs. The Coefficient of performance may exceed 1, because it is a ratio of output:loss, unlike the thermal efficiency ratio of output:input energy.

Entropy

In thermodynamics, entropy is a measure of the number of specific ways in which a thermodynamic system may be arranged, often taken to be a measure of disorder, or a measure of progressing towards thermodynamic equilibrium. The entropy of an isolated system never decreases, because isolated systems spontaneously evolve towards thermodynamic equilibrium, which is the state of maximum entropy.

Entropy was originally defined for a thermodynamically reversible process

as $\Delta S = \int \frac{dQ_{rev}}{T}$

where the entropy is found from the uniform thermodynamic temperature of a closed system dividing an incremental reversible transfer of heat into that system .

Order and disorder

In physics, the terms order and disorder designate the presence or absence of some symmetry or correlation in a many-particle system.

In condensed matter physics, systems typically are ordered at low temperatures; upon heating, they undergo one or several phase transitions into less ordered states. Examples for such an order -disorder transition are:•the melting of ice: solid-liquid transition, loss of crystalline order;•the demagnetization of iron by heating above the Curie temperature: ferromagnetic-paramagnetic transition, loss of magnetic order.

The degree of freedom that is ordered or disordered can be translational (crystalline ordering), rotational (ferroelectric ordering), or a spin state (magnetic ordering).

Degradation

In telecommunication, degradation, which may be categorized as either 'graceful' or 'catastrophic', has the following meanings:•The deterioration in quality, level, or standard of performance of a functional unit.•In communications, a condition in which one or more of the required performance parameters fall outside predetermined limits, resulting in a lower quality of service.

There are several forms and causes of degradation in electric signals, both in the time domain and in the physical domain, including runt pulse, voltage spike, jitter, wander, swim, drift, glitch, ringing, crosstalk, antenna effect, and phase noise.

Degradation usually refers to reduction in quality of an analog or digital signal. When a signal is being transmitted or received, it undergoes changes which are undesirable.

Solar energy

Solar energy, radiant light and heat from the sun, is harnessed using a range of ever-evolving technologies such as solar heating, solar photovoltaics, solar thermal electricity, solar architecture and artificial photosynthesis.

Solar technologies are broadly characterized as either passive solar or active solar depending on the way they capture, convert and distribute solar energy. Active solar techniques include the use of photovoltaic panels and solar thermal collectors to harness the energy.

Thermal pollution

Thermal pollution is the degradation of water quality by any process that changes ambient water temperature.

A common cause of thermal pollution is the use of water as a coolant by power plants and industrial manufacturers. When water used as a coolant is returned to the natural environment at a higher temperature, the change in temperature decreases oxygen supply, and affects ecosystem composition.

Turbine

A turbine is a rotary mechanical device that extracts energy from a fluid flow and converts it into useful work. A turbine is a turbomachine with at least one moving part called a rotor assembly, which is a shaft or drum with blades attached. Moving fluid acts on the blades so that they move and impart rotational energy to the rotor.

Thermal

A thermal column (or thermal) is a column of rising air in the lower altitudes of the Earth's atmosphere. Thermals are created by the uneven heating of the Earth's surface from solar radiation, and are an example of convection, specifically atmospheric convection. The Sun warms the ground, which in turn warms the air directly above it.

Geothermal energy

Geothermal energy is thermal energy generated and stored in the Earth. Thermal energy is the energy that determines the temperature of matter. The geothermal energy of the Earth's crust originates from the original formation of the planet (20%) and from radioactive decay of minerals (80%).

Nuclear fission

In nuclear physics and nuclear chemistry, nuclear fission is either a nuclear reaction or a radioactive decay process in which the nucleus of a particle splits into smaller parts .

14. THE LAWS OF THERMODYNAMICS

CHAPTER HIGHLIGHTS & NOTES: KEY TERMS, PEOPLE, PLACES, CONCEPTS

The fission process often produces free neutrons and photons (in the form of gamma rays), and releases a very large amount of energy even by the energetic standards of radioactive decay.

Nuclear fission of heavy elements was discovered on December 17, 1938 by Otto Hahn and his assistant Fritz Strassmann, and explained theoretically in January 1939 by Lise Meitner and her nephew Otto Robert Frisch.

Nuclear fusion

In nuclear physics, nuclear fusion is a nuclear reaction in which two or more atomic nuclei collide at a very high speed and join to form a new type of atomic nucleus. During this process, matter is not conserved because some of the mass of the fusing nuclei is converted to photons (energy). Fusion is the process that powers active or 'main sequence' stars.

Wind power

Wind power is the conversion of wind energy into a useful form of energy, such as using wind turbines to make electrical power, windmills for mechanical power, windpumps for water pumping or drainage, or sails to propel ships.

Large wind farms consist of hundreds of individual wind turbines which are connected to the electric power transmission network. For new constructions, onshore wind is an inexpensive source of electricity, competitive with or in many places cheaper than fossil fuel plants.

CHAPTER QUIZ: KEY TERMS, PEOPLE, PLACES, CONCEPTS

1. The _________ states that the entropy of an isolated system never decreases, because isolated systems spontaneously evolve toward thermodynamic equilibrium--the state of maximum entropy. Equivalently, perpetual motion machines of the second kind are impossible.

   The second law is an empirically validated postulate of thermodynamics, but it can be understood and explained using the underlying quantum statistical mechanics, together with the assumption of low-entropy initial conditions in the distant past of a system results from an infinitesimal transfer of heat to a closed system divided by the common temperature of the system and the surroundings which supply the heat.

   a. Bisulfide
   b. Second law of thermodynamics
   c. Buffering agent
   d. Carbonate alkalinity

2. . In thermodynamics, the _________ is the total energy contained by a thermodynamic system.

It is the energy needed to create the system but excludes the energy to displace the system's surroundings, any energy associated with a move as a whole, or due to external force fields. _________ has two major components, kinetic energy and potential energy.

a. Fugacity
b. Internal energy
c. Helmholtz free energy
d. Bisulfide

3. _________ refers to reducing energy through using less of an energy service. _________ differs from efficient energy use, which refers to using less energy for a constant service. For example, driving less is an example of _________.

a. Energy conservation
b. Buffer solution
c. Buffering agent
d. Carbonate alkalinity

4. _________ is a branch of natural science concerned with heat and its relation to energy and work. It defines macroscopic variables (such as temperature, internal energy, entropy, and pressure) that characterize materials and radiation, and explains how they are related and by what laws they change with time. _________ describes the average behavior of very large numbers of microscopic constituents, and its laws can be derived from statistical mechanics.

a. Bisulfide
b. Buffer solution
c. Thermodynamics
d. Carbonate alkalinity

5. _________ in general, describes the extent to which time, effort or cost is well used for the intended task or purpose. It is often used with the specific purpose of relaying the capability of a specific application of effort to produce a specific outcome effectively with a minimum amount or quantity of waste, expense, or unnecessary effort. '_________' has widely varying meanings in different disciplines.

a. Algebraic topology
b. Critical point
c. Efficiency
d. Flash point

ANSWER KEY
14. THE LAWS OF THERMODYNAMICS

---

1. b
2. b
3. a
4. c
5. c

---

15. ELECTRIC CHARGE AND ELECTRIC FIELD

CHAPTER OUTLINE: KEY TERMS, PEOPLE, PLACES, CONCEPTS

- Electric charge
- Electron
- Neutron
- Proton
- Semiconductor
- Ultrasound
- Electroscope
- Electrometer
- Symmetry
- Electrostatics
- Coulomb
- Electrostatic units
- Elementary charge
- Permittivity
- Statcoulomb
- Elementary particle
- Quantization
- Electric field
- Vector field
- Gravitational field
- Gravitational

15. ELECTRIC CHARGE AND ELECTRIC FIELD

CHAPTER OUTLINE: KEY TERMS, PEOPLE, PLACES, CONCEPTS

______	Faraday cage
______	Van de Graaff generator
______	Cytosine
______	Hydrogen bond
______	Hydrogen
______	Kinetics
______	Cloning
______	Photoconductivity
______	Electric flux
______	Charge density
______	Gravity

CHAPTER HIGHLIGHTS & NOTES: KEY TERMS, PEOPLE, PLACES, CONCEPTS

Electric charge	Electric charge is the physical property of matter that causes it to experience a force when close to other electrically charged matter. There are two types of electric charges - positive and negative. Positively charged substances are repelled from other positively charged substances, but attracted to negatively charged substances; negatively charged substances are repelled from negative and attracted to positive.
Electron	The electron is a subatomic particle with a negative elementary electric charge. Electrons belong to the first generation of the lepton particle family, and are generally thought to be elementary particles because they have no known components or substructure. The electron has a mass that is approximately 1/1836 that of the proton.
Neutron	The neutron is a subatomic hadron particle that has the symbol n or n0, no net electric charge and a mass slightly larger than that of a proton.

15. ELECTRIC CHARGE AND ELECTRIC FIELD

With the exception of hydrogen-1, nuclei of atoms consist of protons and neutrons, which are therefore collectively referred to as nucleons. The number of protons in a nucleus is the atomic number and defines the type of element the atom forms.

Proton

The proton is a subatomic particle with the symbol p or p+ and a positive electric charge of 1 elementary charge. One or more protons are present in the nucleus of each atom. The number of protons in each atom is its atomic number.

Semiconductor

A semiconductor is a material which has electrical conductivity to a degree between that of a metal and that of an insulator (such as glass). Semiconductors are the foundation of modern electronics, including transistors, solar cells, light-emitting diodes (LEDs), quantum dots and digital and analog integrated circuits.

A semiconductor may have a number of unique properties, one of which is the ability to change conductivity by the addition of impurities ('doping') or by interaction with another phenomenon, such as an electric field or light; this ability makes a semiconductor very useful for constructing a device that can amplify, switch, or convert an energy input.

Ultrasound

Ultrasound is an oscillating sound pressure wave with a frequency greater than the upper limit of the human hearing range. Ultrasound is thus not separated from 'normal' (audible) sound based on differences in physical properties, only the fact that humans cannot hear it. Although this limit varies from person to person, it is approximately 20 kilohertz (20,000 hertz) in healthy, young adults.

Electroscope

An electroscope is an early scientific instrument that is used to detect the presence and magnitude of electric charge on a body. It was the first electrical measuring instrument. The first electroscope, a pivoted needle called the versorium, was invented by British physician William Gilbert around 1600. The pith-ball electroscope and the gold-leaf electroscope are two classical types of electroscope that are still used in physics education to demonstrate the principles of electrostatics.

Electrometer

An electrometer is an electrical instrument for measuring electric charge or electrical potential difference. There are many different types, ranging from historical handmade mechanical instruments to high-precision electronic devices. Modern electrometers based on vacuum tube or solid-state technology can be used to make voltage and charge measurements with very low leakage currents, down to 1 femtoampere.

Symmetry

In physics, symmetry includes all features of a physical system that exhibit the property of symmetry--that is, under certain transformations, aspects of these systems are otherwise 'unchanged', according to a particular observation. A symmetry of a physical system is a physical or mathematical feature of the system (observed or intrinsic) that is 'preserved' under some change.

Electrostatics

Electrostatics is a branch of physics that deals with the phenomena and properties of stationary or slow-moving electric charges with no acceleration.

Since classical antiquity, it has been known that some materials such as amber attract lightweight particles after rubbing. The Greek word for amber, ??e?t??? electron, was the source of the word 'electricity'.

Coulomb

The coulomb is the SI derived unit of electric charge (symbol: Q or q). It is defined as the charge transported by a constant current of one ampere in one second: $1\ \mathrm{C} = 1\ \mathrm{A} \times 1\ \mathrm{s}$

One coulomb is also the amount of excess charge on the positive side of a capacitor of one farad charged to a potential difference of one volt: $1\ \mathrm{C} = 1\ \mathrm{F} \times 1\ \mathrm{V}$

Electrostatic units

The electrostatic system of units is a system of units used to measure electrical quantities of electric charge, electric current, and voltage within the centimeter-gram-second system of metric units. In electrostatic units, electrical charge is defined by the force that it exerts on other charges. Although the CGS units have mostly been supplanted by the MKSA (meter-kilogram-second-ampere) or International System of Units (SI) units, the electrostatic units are still in occasional use in some applications, most notably in certain fields of physics such as in particle physics and astrophysics.

Elementary charge

The elementary charge, usually denoted as e, is the electric charge carried by a single proton, or equivalently, the negation of the electric charge carried by a single electron. This elementary charge is a fundamental physical constant. To avoid confusion over its sign, e is sometimes called the elementary positive charge.

Permittivity

In electromagnetism, absolute permittivity is the measure of the resistance that is encountered when forming an electric field in a medium. In other words, permittivity is a measure of how an electric field affects, and is affected by, a dielectric medium. The permittivity of a medium describes how much electric field (more correctly, flux) is 'generated' per unit charge in that medium.

Statcoulomb

The statcoulomb or franklin (Fr) or electrostatic unit of charge (esu) is the physical unit for electrical charge used in the centimetre-gram-second system of units (cgs) and Gaussian units. It is a derived unit given by1 statC = 1 $g^{1/2}\ cm^{3/2}\ s^{-1}$ = 1 $erg^{1/2}\ cm^{1/2}$.

The SI system of units uses the coulomb (C) instead. The conversion between C and statC is different in different contexts.

Elementary particle

In particle physics, an elementary particle or fundamental particle is a particle whose substructure is unknown, thus it is not known to be composed of other particles.

Known elementary particles include the fundamental fermions (quarks, leptons, antiquarks, and antileptons), which generally are 'matter particles' and 'antimatter particles', as well as the fundamental bosons (gauge bosons and Higgs boson), which generally are 'force particles' that mediate interactions among fermions. A particle containing two or more elementary particles is a composite particle.

Quantization

In physics, quantization is the process of transition from a classical understanding of physical phenomena to a newer understanding known as 'quantum mechanics'. It is a procedure for constructing a quantum field theory starting from a classical field theory. This is a generalization of the procedure for building quantum mechanics from classical mechanics.

Electric field

An electric field is generated by electrically charged particles and time-varying magnetic fields. The electric field describes the electric force experienced by a motionless positively electrically charged test particle at any point in space relative to the source(s) of the field. The concept of an electric field was introduced by Michael Faraday.

Vector field

In vector calculus, a vector field is an assignment of a vector to each point in a subset of Euclidean space. A vector field in the plane, for instance, can be visualized as a collection of arrows with a given magnitude and direction each attached to a point in the plane. Vector fields are often used to model, for example, the speed and direction of a moving fluid throughout space, or the strength and direction of some force, such as the magnetic or gravitational force, as it changes from point to point.

Gravitational field

In physics, a gravitational field is a model used to explain the influence that a massive body extends into the space around itself, producing a force on another massive body. Thus, a gravitational field is used to explain gravitational phenomena, and is measured in newtons per kilogram (N/kg). In its original concept, gravity was a force between point masses.

Gravitational

Gravitation, or gravity, is a natural phenomenon by which all physical bodies attract each other. It is most commonly recognized and experienced as the agent that gives weight to physical objects, and causes physical objects to fall toward the ground when dropped from a height.

It is hypothesized that the gravitational force is mediated by a massless spin-2 particle called the graviton.

Faraday cage

A Faraday cage or Faraday shield is an enclosure formed by conducting material or by a mesh of such material. Such an enclosure blocks external static and non-static electric fields by channeling electricity through the mesh, providing constant voltage on all sides of the enclosure. Since the difference in voltage is the measure of electrical potential, no current flows through the space.

Van de Graaff generator

A Van de Graaff generator is an electrostatic generator which uses a moving belt to accumulate very high amounts of electrical potential on a hollow metal globe on the top of the stand.

It was invented by American physicist Robert J. Van de Graaff in 1929. The potential difference achieved in modern Van de Graaff generators can reach 5 megavolts. A tabletop version can produce on the order of 100,000 volts and can store enough energy to produce a visible spark.

Cytosine

Cytosine is one of the four main bases found in DNA and RNA, along with adenine, guanine, and thymine (uracil in RNA). It is a pyrimidine derivative, with a heterocyclic aromatic ring and two substituents attached (an amine group at position 4 and a keto group at position 2). The nucleoside of cytosine is cytidine.

Hydrogen bond

A hydrogen bond is the electromagnetic attractive interaction between polar molecules in which hydrogen is bound to a highly electronegative atom, such as nitrogen (N), oxygen (O) or fluorine (F). The name hydrogen bond is something of a misnomer, as it is not a true bond but a particularly strong dipole-dipole attraction, and should not be confused with a covalent bond.

These hydrogen-bond attractions can occur between molecules (intermolecular) or within different parts of a single molecule (intramolecular).

Hydrogen

Hydrogen is a chemical element with chemical symbol H and atomic number 1. With an atomic weight of 1.00794 u, hydrogen is the lightest element and its monatomic form (H) is the most abundant chemical substance, constituting roughly 75% of the Universe's baryonic mass. Non-remnant stars are mainly composed of hydrogen in its plasma state.

At standard temperature and pressure, hydrogen is a colorless, odorless, tasteless, non-toxic, nonmetallic, highly combustible diatomic gas with the molecular formula H_2.

Kinetics

In physics and engineering, kinetics is a term for the branch of classical mechanics that is concerned with the relationship between the motion of bodies and its causes, namely forces and torques. Since the mid-20th century, the term 'dynamics' (or 'analytical dynamics') has largely superseded 'kinetics' in physics text books; the term 'kinetics' is still used in engineering.

In mechanics, the Kinetics is deduced from Kinematics by the introduction of the concept of mass.

Cloning

In biology, cloning is the process of producing similar populations of genetically identical individuals that occurs in nature when organisms such as bacteria, insects or plants reproduce asexually. Cloning in biotechnology refers to processes used to create copies of DNA fragments (molecular cloning), cells (cell cloning), or organisms. The term also refers to the production of multiple copies of a product such as digital media or software.

Photoconductivity

Photoconductivity is an optical and electrical phenomenon in which a material becomes more electrically conductive due to the absorption of electromagnetic radiation such as visible light, ultraviolet light, infrared light, or gamma radiation.

15. ELECTRIC CHARGE AND ELECTRIC FIELD

CHAPTER HIGHLIGHTS & NOTES: KEY TERMS, PEOPLE, PLACES, CONCEPTS

When light is absorbed by a material such as a semiconductor, the number of free electrons and electron holes increases and raises its electrical conductivity. To cause excitation, the light that strikes the semiconductor must have enough energy to raise electrons across the band gap, or to excite the impurities within the band gap.

Electric flux

In electromagnetism, electric flux is the rate of flow of the electric field through a given area. Electric flux is proportional to the number of electric field lines going through a virtual surface. If the electric field is uniform, the electric flux passing through a surface of vector area S is $\Phi_E = \mathbf{E} \cdot \mathbf{S} = ES\cos\theta,$

where E is the electric field, E is its magnitude, S is the area of the surface, and ? is the angle between the electric field lines and the normal (perpendicular) to S.

Charge density

In electromagnetism, charge density is a measure of electric charge per unit volume of space, in one, two or three dimensions. More specifically: the linear, surface, or volume charge density is the amount of electric charge per unit length, surface area, or volume, respectively. The respective SI units are $C\cdot m^{-1}$, $C\cdot m^{-2}$ or $C\cdot m^{-3}$.

Gravity

In chemistry, gravity is the density of a fluid, particularly a fuel. It is expressed in degrees, with lower numbers indicating heavier liquids and higher numbers indicating lighter liquids. See specific gravity and API gravity.

CHAPTER QUIZ: KEY TERMS, PEOPLE, PLACES, CONCEPTS

1. The _________, usually denoted as e, is the electric charge carried by a single proton, or equivalently, the negation of the electric charge carried by a single electron. This _________ is a fundamental physical constant. To avoid confusion over its sign, e is sometimes called the elementary positive charge.

   a. Elementary charge
   b. Coulomb
   c. Bifluoride
   d. Bisulfide

2. . A _________ or Faraday shield is an enclosure formed by conducting material or by a mesh of such material. Such an enclosure blocks external static and non-static electric fields by channeling electricity through the mesh, providing constant voltage on all sides of the enclosure.

Since the difference in voltage is the measure of electrical potential, no current flows through the space.

a. Barometric light
b. Charge density
c. Coefficients of potential
d. Faraday cage

3. _________ is the physical property of matter that causes it to experience a force when close to other electrically charged matter. There are two types of _________s - positive and negative. Positively charged substances are repelled from other positively charged substances, but attracted to negatively charged substances; negatively charged substances are repelled from negative and attracted to positive.

a. Electric charge
b. Cathode ray
c. Cavity perturbation theory
d. Charge conservation

4. The _________ is a subatomic particle with a negative elementary electric charge. _________s belong to the first generation of the lepton particle family, and are generally thought to be elementary particles because they have no known components or substructure. The _________ has a mass that is approximately 1/1836 that of the proton.

a. Electron
b. Laplace expansion
c. Hollow-cathode lamp
d. K-beta

5. The _________ is a subatomic hadron particle that has the symbol n or n0, no net electric charge and a mass slightly larger than that of a proton. With the exception of hydrogen-1, nuclei of atoms consist of protons and _________s, which are therefore collectively referred to as nucleons. The number of protons in a nucleus is the atomic number and defines the type of element the atom forms.

a. Baryon
b. Baryonic dark matter
c. Delta baryon
d. Neutron

ANSWER KEY
15. ELECTRIC CHARGE AND ELECTRIC FIELD

---

1. a
2. d
3. a
4. a
5. d

---

16. ELECTRIC POTENTIAL

CHAPTER OUTLINE: KEY TERMS, PEOPLE, PLACES, CONCEPTS

- Voltage
- Electric potential
- Electric potential energy
- Potential energy
- Volt
- Gravitational potential
- Breakdown voltage
- Electric field
- Equipotential surface
- Capacitance
- Capacitor
- Condenser
- Dipole
- Farad
- Dielectric strength
- Dielectric
- Permittivity
- Byte
- Digital signal
- Pixel
- Sampling rate

16. ELECTRIC POTENTIAL

CHAPTER OUTLINE: KEY TERMS, PEOPLE, PLACES, CONCEPTS

	Bandwidth
	Anode
	Cathode
	Cathode ray tube
	Thermionic emission
	Light-emitting diode
	Active matrix
	Oscilloscope
	Refresh rate
	Thin-film transistor
	Molecule

CHAPTER HIGHLIGHTS & NOTES: KEY TERMS, PEOPLE, PLACES, CONCEPTS

Voltage	Voltage, electrical potential difference, electric tension or electric pressure is the electric potential difference between two points, or the difference in electric potential energy of a unit charge transported between two points. Voltage is equal to the work done per unit charge against a static electric field to move the charge between two points. A voltage may represent either a source of energy (electromotive force), or lost, used, or stored energy (potential drop).
Electric potential	In classical electromagnetism, the electric potential at a point is the amount of electric potential energy that a unitary point charge would have when located at that point. The electric potential at a point is equal to the electric potential energy, or volts .

16. ELECTRIC POTENTIAL

CHAPTER HIGHLIGHTS & NOTES: KEY TERMS, PEOPLE, PLACES, CONCEPTS

Electric potential energy	Electric potential energy, or electrostatic potential energy, is a potential energy that results from conservative Coulomb forces and is associated with the configuration of a particular set of point charges within a defined system. An object may have electric potential energy by virtue of two key elements: its own electric charge and its relative position to other electrically charged objects. The term 'electric potential energy' is used to describe the potential energy in systems with time-variant electric fields, while the term 'electrostatic potential energy' is used to describe the potential energy in systems with time-invariant electric fields.
Potential energy	In physics, potential energy is the energy of an object or a system due to the position of the body or the arrangement of the particles of the system. The SI unit for measuring work and energy is the joule (symbol J). The term potential energy was coined by the 19th century Scottish engineer and physicist William Rankine, although it has links to Greek philosopher Aristotle's concept of potentiality.
Volt	The volt is the SI derived unit for electric potential (voltage), electric potential difference, and electromotive force. The volt is named in honour of the Italian physicist Alessandro Volta (1745-1827), who invented the voltaic pile, possibly the first chemical battery.
Gravitational potential	In classical mechanics, the gravitational potential at a location is equal to the work per unit mass that is done by the force of gravity to move an object to a fixed reference location. It is analogous to the electric potential with mass playing the role of charge. The reference location, where the potential is zero, is by convention infinitely far away from any mass, resulting in a negative potential at any finite distance.
Breakdown voltage	The breakdown voltage of an insulator is the minimum voltage that causes a portion of an insulator to become electrically conductive. The breakdown voltage of a diode is the minimum reverse voltage to make the diode conduct in reverse. Some devices (such as TRIACs) also have a forward breakdown voltage.
Electric field	An electric field is generated by electrically charged particles and time-varying magnetic fields. The electric field describes the electric force experienced by a motionless positively electrically charged test particle at any point in space relative to the source(s) of the field. The concept of an electric field was introduced by Michael Faraday.
Equipotential surface	Equipotential surfaces are surfaces of constant scalar potential. They are used to visualize an (n)-dimensional scalar potential function in (n-1) dimensional space. The gradient of the potential, denoting the direction of greatest increase, is perpendicular to the surface.
Capacitance	Capacitance is the ability of a body to store an electrical charge.

Any object that can be electrically charged exhibits capacitance. A common form of energy storage device is a parallel-plate capacitor.

Capacitor

A capacitor is a passive two-terminal electrical component used to store energy electrostatically in an electric field. The forms of practical capacitors vary widely, but all contain at least two electrical conductors separated by a dielectric (insulator); for example, one common construction consists of metal foils separated by a thin layer of insulating film. Capacitors are widely used as parts of electrical circuits in many common electrical devices.

Condenser

A Condenser is an optical lens which renders a divergent beam from a point source into a parallel or converging beam to illuminate an object. In the context of microscopy, the parallel illumination scheme is known as Köhler illumination whereas the converging illumination scheme is known as critical illumination.

It is an essential part of any imaging device, such as microscopes, enlargers, slide projectors, and telescopes.

Dipole

In physics, there are several kinds of dipole:

Dipoles can be characterized by their dipole moment, a vector quantity. For the simple electric dipole given above, the electric dipole moment points from the negative charge towards the positive charge, and has a magnitude equal to the strength of each charge times the separation between the charges. (To be precise: for the definition of the dipole moment one should always consider the 'dipole limit', where e.g. the distance of the generating charges should converge to 0, while simultaneously the charge strength should diverge to infinity in such a way that the product remains a positive constant).

Farad

The farad is the SI derived unit of electrical capacitance. It is named after the English physicist Michael Faraday.

Dielectric strength

In physics, the term dielectric strength has the following meanings:

The theoretical dielectric strength of a material is an intrinsic property of the bulk material and is dependent on the configuration of the material or the electrodes with which the field is applied. The 'intrinsic dielectric strength' is measured using pure materials under ideal laboratory conditions. At breakdown, the electric field frees bound electrons.

Dielectric

A dielectric material (dielectric for short) is an electrical insulator that can be polarized by an applied electric field. When a dielectric is placed in an electric field, electric charges do not flow through the material as they do in a conductor, but only slightly shift from their average equilibrium positions causing dielectric polarization.

16. ELECTRIC POTENTIAL

CHAPTER HIGHLIGHTS & NOTES: KEY TERMS, PEOPLE, PLACES, CONCEPTS

Permittivity

In electromagnetism, absolute permittivity is the measure of the resistance that is encountered when forming an electric field in a medium. In other words, permittivity is a measure of how an electric field affects, and is affected by, a dielectric medium. The permittivity of a medium describes how much electric field (more correctly, flux) is 'generated' per unit charge in that medium.

Byte

The byte is a unit of digital information in computing and telecommunications that most commonly consists of eight bits. Historically, the byte was the number of bits used to encode a single character of text in a computer and for this reason it is the smallest addressable unit of memory in many computer architectures. The size of the byte has historically been hardware dependent and no definitive standards existed that mandated the size.

Digital signal

A digital signal is a physical signal that is a representation of a sequence of discrete values, for example of an arbitrary bit stream, or of a digitized (sampled and analog-to-digital converted) analog signal. The term digital signal can refer to either of the following:•any continuous-time waveform signal used in digital communication, representing a bit stream or other sequence of discrete values•a pulse train signal that switches between a discrete number of voltage levels or levels of light intensity, also known as a line coded signal or baseband transmission, for example a signal found in digital electronics or in serial communications, or a pulse code modulation (PCM) representation of a digitized analog signal.

A signal that is generated by means of a digital modulation method (digital passband transmission), to be transferred between modems, is in the first case considered as a digital signal, and in the second case as converted to an analog signal.

Pixel

In digital imaging, a pixel, or pel, is a physical point in a raster image, or the smallest addressable element in a display device; so it is the smallest controllable element of a picture represented on the screen. The address of a pixel corresponds to its physical coordinates. LCD pixels are manufactured in a two-dimensional grid, and are often represented using dots or squares, but CRT pixels correspond to their timing mechanisms and sweep rates.

Sampling rate

The sampling rate, sample rate, or sampling frequency defines the number of samples per unit of time (usually seconds) taken from a continuous signal to make a discrete signal. For time-domain signals, the unit for sampling rate is hertz (inverse seconds, 1/s, s^{-1}), sometimes noted as Sa/s or S/s (samples per second). The reciprocal of the sampling frequency is the sampling period or sampling interval, which is the time between samples.

Bandwidth

In computer networking and computer science, bandwidth, network bandwidth, data bandwidth, or digital bandwidth is a measurement of bit-rate of available or consumed data communication resources expressed in bits per second or multiples of it .

Note that in textbooks on signal processing, wireless communications, modem data transmission, digital communications, electronics, etc., the word 'bandwidth' is used to refer to analog signal bandwidth measured in hertz. The connection is that according to Hartley's law, the digital data rate limit (or channel capacity) of a physical communication link is proportional to its bandwidth in hertz.

Anode | An anode is an electrode through which electric current flows into a polarized electrical device. The direction of electric current is, by convention, opposite to the direction of electron flow. In other words, the electrons flow from the anode into, for example, an electrical circuit.

Cathode | A cathode is an electrode through which electric current flows out of a polarized electrical device. The direction of electric current is, by convention, opposite to the direction of electron flow--thus, electrons are considered to flow toward the cathode electrode while current flows away from it. This convention is sometimes remembered using the mnemonic CCD for cathode current departs.

Cathode ray tube | The cathode ray tube is a vacuum tube containing one or more electron guns (a source of electrons or electron emitter) and a fluorescent screen used to view images. It has a means to accelerate and deflect the electron beam(s) onto the screen to create the images. The images may represent electrical waveforms (oscilloscope), pictures (television, computer monitor), radar targets or others.

Thermionic emission | Thermionic emission is the heat-induced flow of charge carriers from a surface or over a potential-energy barrier. This occurs because the thermal energy given to the carrier overcomes the binding potential, also known as work function of the metal. The charge carriers can be electrons or ions, and in older literature are sometimes referred to as 'thermions'.

Light-emitting diode | A light-emitting diode is a semiconductor light source. Light emitting diodes are used as indicator lamps in many devices and are increasingly used for general lighting. Appearing as practical electronic components in 1962, early Light emitting diodes emitted low-intensity red light, but modern versions are available across the visible, ultraviolet, and infrared wavelengths, with very high brightness.

Active matrix | Active matrix is a type of addressing scheme used in flat panel displays. In this method of switching individual elements (pixels) of a flat panel display, each pixel is attached to a transistor and capacitor which actively maintain the pixel state while other pixels are being addressed. This is to be contrasted with the older passive matrix technology in which each pixel must maintain its state passively, without being driven by circuitry.

16. ELECTRIC POTENTIAL

CHAPTER HIGHLIGHTS & NOTES: KEY TERMS, PEOPLE, PLACES, CONCEPTS

Oscilloscope	An oscilloscope, previously called an oscillograph, and informally known as a scope, CRO (for cathode-ray oscilloscope), or DSO (for the more modern digital storage oscilloscope), is a type of electronic test instrument that allows observation of constantly varying signal voltages, usually as a two-dimensional graph of one or more electrical potential differences using the vertical or y-axis, plotted as a function of time . This way, many types of signals can be converted to voltages and displayed. Oscilloscopes are used to observe the change of an electrical signal over time, such that voltage and time describe a shape which is continuously graphed against a calibrated scale.
Refresh rate	The refresh rate is the number of times in a second that a display hardware updates it buffer. This is distinct from the measure of frame rate in that the refresh rate includes the repeated drawing of identical frames, while frame rate measures how often a video source can feed an entire frame of new data to a display. For example, most movie projectors advance from one frame to the next one 24 times each second.
Thin-film transistor	A thin-film transistor is a special kind of field-effect transistor made by depositing thin films of an active semiconductor layer as well as the dielectric layer and metallic contacts over a supporting (but non-conducting) substrate. A common substrate is glass, because the primary application of Thin film transistors is in liquid-crystal displays. This differs from the conventional transistor, where the semiconductor material typically is the substrate, such as a silicon wafer.
Molecule	A molecule is an electrically neutral group of two or more atoms held together by chemical bonds. Molecules are distinguished from ions by their lack of electrical charge. However, in quantum physics, organic chemistry, and biochemistry, the term molecule is often used less strictly, also being applied to polyatomic ions.

1. An _________, previously called an oscillograph, and informally known as a scope, CRO (for cathode-ray _________), or DSO (for the more modern digital storage _________), is a type of electronic test instrument that allows observation of constantly varying signal voltages, usually as a two-dimensional graph of one or more electrical potential differences using the vertical or y-axis, plotted as a function of time . This way, many types of signals can be converted to voltages and displayed.

   _________s are used to observe the change of an electrical signal over time, such that voltage and time describe a shape which is continuously graphed against a calibrated scale.

   a. BNC 575
   b. Breadboard
   c. Bus analyzer
   d. Oscilloscope

2. _________, or electrostatic potential energy, is a potential energy that results from conservative Coulomb forces and is associated with the configuration of a particular set of point charges within a defined system. An object may have _________ by virtue of two key elements: its own electric charge and its relative position to other electrically charged objects.

   The term '_________' is used to describe the potential energy in systems with time-variant electric fields, while the term 'electrostatic potential energy' is used to describe the potential energy in systems with time-invariant electric fields.

   a. Backup battery
   b. Electric potential energy
   c. CAIDI
   d. CAIFI

3. _________s are surfaces of constant scalar potential. They are used to visualize an (n)-dimensional scalar potential function in (n-1) dimensional space. The gradient of the potential, denoting the direction of greatest increase, is perpendicular to the surface.

   a. Block and bleed manifold
   b. Equipotential surface
   c. Buoyancy
   d. Capillary surface

4. . In computer networking and computer science, _________, network _________, data _________, or digital _________ is a measurement of bit-rate of available or consumed data communication resources expressed in bits per second or multiples of it .

   Note that in textbooks on signal processing, wireless communications, modem data transmission, digital communications, electronics, etc., the word '_________' is used to refer to analog signal _________ measured in hertz. The connection is that according to Hartley's law, the digital data rate limit (or channel capacity) of a physical communication link is proportional to its _________ in hertz.

a. Bandwidth
b. Bismuthide
c. Bisulfide
d. Borohydride

5. In physics, _________ is the energy of an object or a system due to the position of the body or the arrangement of the particles of the system. The SI unit for measuring work and energy is the joule (symbol J).

The term _________ was coined by the 19th century Scottish engineer and physicist William Rankine, although it has links to Greek philosopher Aristotle's concept of potentiality.

a. Potential energy
b. Die Glocke
c. Giovanni Modanese
d. Gravitational interaction of antimatter

ANSWER KEY
16. ELECTRIC POTENTIAL

1. d
2. b
3. b
4. a
5. a

---

17. ELECTRIC CURRENTS

CHAPTER OUTLINE: KEY TERMS, PEOPLE, PLACES, CONCEPTS

- Electric current
- Electroscope
- Electrode
- Electrolyte
- Ampere
- Ampere-hour
- Resistor
- Voltage drop
- Semiconductor
- Temperature coefficient
- Speaker wire
- Electric power
- Heating element
- Resistance thermometer
- Thermistor
- Watt
- Short circuit
- Extension cord
- Alternating current
- Direct current
- Voltage

17. ELECTRIC CURRENTS

CHAPTER OUTLINE: KEY TERMS, PEOPLE, PLACES, CONCEPTS

	Drift velocity
	Electric field
	Dendrite
	Superconductivity
	Transition temperature
	Action potential
	Conductance
	Strain gauge

CHAPTER HIGHLIGHTS & NOTES: KEY TERMS, PEOPLE, PLACES, CONCEPTS

Electric current	An electric current is a flow of electric charge. In electric circuits this charge is often carried by moving electrons in a wire. It can also be carried by ions in an electrolyte, or by both ions and electrons such as in a plasma.
Electroscope	An electroscope is an early scientific instrument that is used to detect the presence and magnitude of electric charge on a body. It was the first electrical measuring instrument. The first electroscope, a pivoted needle called the versorium, was invented by British physician William Gilbert around 1600. The pith-ball electroscope and the gold-leaf electroscope are two classical types of electroscope that are still used in physics education to demonstrate the principles of electrostatics.
Electrode	An electrode is an electrical conductor used to make contact with a nonmetallic part of a circuit . The word was coined by the scientist Michael Faraday from the Greek words elektron (meaning amber, from which the word electricity is derived) and hodos, a way.
Electrolyte	An electrolyte is a compound that ionizes when dissolved in suitable ionizing solvents such as water. This includes most soluble salts, acids, and bases. Some gases, such as hydrogen chloride, under conditions of high temperature or low pressure can also function as electrolytes.
Ampere	The ampere, often shortened to amp, is the SI unit of electric current (quantity symbol: I,

i) and is one of the seven SI base units. It is named after André-Marie Ampère (1775-1836), French mathematician and physicist, considered the father of electrodynamics.

In practical terms, the ampere is a measure of the amount of electric charge passing a point in an electric circuit per unit time, with 6.241×10^{18} electrons (or one coulomb) per second, constituting one ampere.

Ampere-hour

An ampere-hour or amp-hour is a unit of electric charge, with sub-units milliampere-hour and milliampere-second (mA·s). One ampere-hour is equal to 3600 coulomb. The ampere-hour is frequently used in measurements of electrochemical systems such as electroplating and electrical batteries.

Resistor

A resistor is a passive two-terminal electrical component that implements electrical resistance as a circuit element.

The current through a resistor is in direct proportion to the voltage across the resistor's terminals.

This relationship is represented by Ohm's law: $I = \frac{V}{R}$

where I is the current through the conductor in units of amperes, V is the potential difference measured across the conductor in units of volts, and R is the resistance of the conductor in units of ohms.

Voltage drop

Voltage drop describes how the supplied energy of a voltage source is reduced as electric current moves through the passive elements of an electrical circuit. Voltage drops across internal resistances of the source, across conductors, across contacts, and across connectors are undesired; supplied energy is lost (dissipated). Voltage drops across loads and across other active circuit elements are desired; supplied energy performs useful work.

Semiconductor

A semiconductor is a material which has electrical conductivity to a degree between that of a metal and that of an insulator (such as glass). Semiconductors are the foundation of modern electronics, including transistors, solar cells, light-emitting diodes (LEDs), quantum dots and digital and analog integrated circuits.

A semiconductor may have a number of unique properties, one of which is the ability to change conductivity by the addition of impurities ('doping') or by interaction with another phenomenon, such as an electric field or light; this ability makes a semiconductor very useful for constructing a device that can amplify, switch, or convert an energy input.

Temperature coefficient

The temperature coefficient is the relative change of a physical property when the temperature is changed by 1 Kelvin.

17. ELECTRIC CURRENTS

In the following formula, let R be the physical property to be measured and T be the temperature at which the property is measured. T_0 is the reference temperature, and ?T is the difference between T and T_0.

Speaker wire

Speaker wire is used to make the electrical connection between loudspeakers and audio amplifiers. Modern speaker wire consists of two or more electrical conductors individually insulated by plastic (such as PVC, PE or Teflon) or, less commonly, rubber. The two wires are electrically identical, but are marked to identify the correct audio signal polarity.

Electric power

Electric power is the rate at which electric energy is transferred by an electric circuit. The SI unit of power is the watt, one joule per second.

Electric power is usually produced by electric generators, but can also be supplied by chemical sources such as electric batteries.

Heating element

A heating element converts electricity into heat through the process of resistive or Joule heating. Electric current passing through the element encounters resistance, resulting in heating of the element. Unlike the Peltier Effect this process is independent of the direction of current flow.

Resistance thermometer

Resistance thermometers, also called resistance temperature detectors, are sensors used to measure temperature by correlating the resistance of the RTD element with temperature. Most RTD elements consist of a length of fine coiled wire wrapped around a ceramic or glass core. The element is usually quite fragile, so it is often placed inside a sheathed probe to protect it.

Thermistor

A thermistor is a type of resistor whose resistance varies significantly with temperature, more so than in standard resistors. The word is a portmanteau of thermal and resistor. Thermistors are widely used as inrush current limiters, temperature sensors, self-resetting overcurrent protectors, and self-regulating heating elements.

Watt

The watt is a derived unit of power in the International System of Units (SI) defined as one joule per second, measures the rate of energy conversion or transfer.

Short circuit

A short circuit is an electrical circuit that allows a current to travel along an unintended path, often where essentially no (or a very low) electrical impedance is encountered. The electrical opposite of a short circuit is an 'open circuit', which is an infinite resistance between two nodes. It is common to misuse 'short circuit' to describe any electrical malfunction, regardless of the actual problem.

Extension cord

An extension cord, power extender, or extension lead is a length of flexible electrical power cable with a plug on one end and one or more sockets on the other end (usually of the same type as the plug). The term usually refers to mains (household AC) extensions but is also used to refer to extensions for other types of cabling.

Alternating current	In alternating current, the flow of electric charge periodically reverses direction. In direct current (DC, also dc), the flow of electric charge is only in one direction. The abbreviations AC and DC are often used to mean simply alternating and direct, as when they modify current or voltage.
Direct current	Direct current is the unidirectional flow of electric charge. Direct current is produced by sources such as batteries, thermocouples, solar cells, and commutator-type electric machines of the dynamo type. Direct current may flow in a conductor such as a wire, but can also flow through semiconductors, insulators, or even through a vacuum as in electron or ion beams.
Voltage	Voltage, electrical potential difference, electric tension or electric pressure is the electric potential difference between two points, or the difference in electric potential energy of a unit charge transported between two points. Voltage is equal to the work done per unit charge against a static electric field to move the charge between two points. A voltage may represent either a source of energy (electromotive force), or lost, used, or stored energy (potential drop).
Drift velocity	The drift velocity is the average velocity that a particle, such as an electron, attains due to an electric field. It can also be referred to as axial drift velocity since particles defined are assumed to be moving along a plane. In general, an electron will 'rattle around' in a conductor at the Fermi velocity randomly.
Electric field	An electric field is generated by electrically charged particles and time-varying magnetic fields. The electric field describes the electric force experienced by a motionless positively electrically charged test particle at any point in space relative to the source(s) of the field. The concept of an electric field was introduced by Michael Faraday.
Dendrite	A crystal dendrite is a crystal that develops with a typical multi-branching tree-like form. Dendritic crystal growth is very common and illustrated by snowflake formation and frost patterns on a window. Dendritic crystallization forms a natural fractal pattern.
Superconductivity	Superconductivity is a phenomenon of exactly zero electrical resistance and expulsion of magnetic fields occurring in certain materials when cooled below a characteristic critical temperature. It was discovered by Dutch physicist Heike Kamerlingh Onnes on April 8, 1911 in Leiden. Like ferromagnetism and atomic spectral lines, superconductivity is a quantum mechanical phenomenon.
Transition temperature	Transition temperature is the temperature at which a material changes from one crystal state to another. For example, when rhombic sulfur is heated above 96°C it changes form into monoclinic sulfur. When cooled below 96°C it reverts to rhombic sulfur.
Action potential	In physiology, an action potential is a short-lasting event in which the electrical membrane potential of a cell rapidly rises and falls, following a consistent trajectory.

17. ELECTRIC CURRENTS

CHAPTER HIGHLIGHTS & NOTES: KEY TERMS, PEOPLE, PLACES, CONCEPTS

Action potentials occur in several types of animal cells, called excitable cells, which include neurons, muscle cells, and endocrine cells, as well as in some plant cells. In neurons, they play a central role in cell-to-cell communication.

Conductance

In graph theory the conductance of a graph G= measures how 'well-knit' the graph is: it controls how fast a random walk on G converges to a uniform distribution. The conductance of a graph is often called the Cheeger constant of a graph as the analog of its counterpart in spectral geometry. Since electrical networks are intimately related to random walks with a long history in the usage of the term 'conductance', this alternative name helps avoid possible confusion.

Strain gauge

A strain gauge is a device used to measure strain on an object. Invented by Edward E. Simmons and Arthur C. Ruge in 1938, the most common type of strain gauge consists of an insulating flexible backing which supports a metallic foil pattern. The gauge is attached to the object by a suitable adhesive, such as cyanoacrylate.

CHAPTER QUIZ: KEY TERMS, PEOPLE, PLACES, CONCEPTS

1. An _________ is a flow of electric charge. In electric circuits this charge is often carried by moving electrons in a wire. It can also be carried by ions in an electrolyte, or by both ions and electrons such as in a plasma.

   a. Electric current
   b. Bismuthide
   c. Bisulfide
   d. Borohydride

2. _________, electrical potential difference, electric tension or electric pressure is the electric potential difference between two points, or the difference in electric potential energy of a unit charge transported between two points. _________ is equal to the work done per unit charge against a static electric field to move the charge between two points. A _________ may represent either a source of energy (electromotive force), or lost, used, or stored energy (potential drop).

   a. Voltage
   b. Cathode ray
   c. Cavity perturbation theory
   d. Charge conservation

3. . The _________ is the average velocity that a particle, such as an electron, attains due to an electric field. It can also be referred to as axial _________ since particles defined are assumed to be moving along a plane. In general, an electron will 'rattle around' in a conductor at the Fermi velocity randomly.

a. Band mapping
b. Bethe ansatz
c. Bilbao Crystallographic Server
d. Drift velocity

4. _________s, also called resistance temperature detectors, are sensors used to measure temperature by correlating the resistance of the RTD element with temperature. Most RTD elements consist of a length of fine coiled wire wrapped around a ceramic or glass core. The element is usually quite fragile, so it is often placed inside a sheathed probe to protect it.

a. Bleeder resistor
b. Resistance thermometer
c. Force-sensing resistor
d. Humistor

5. A _________ is a passive two-terminal electrical component that implements electrical resistance as a circuit element.

The current through a _________ is in direct proportion to the voltage across the _________'s terminals. This relationship is represented by Ohm's law: $I = \frac{V}{R}$

where I is the current through the conductor in units of amperes, V is the potential difference measured across the conductor in units of volts, and R is the resistance of the conductor in units of ohms.

a. Bleeder resistor
b. Digital potentiometer
c. Force-sensing resistor
d. Resistor

ANSWER KEY
17. ELECTRIC CURRENTS

---

1. a

2. a

3. d

4. b

5. d

---

18. DC CIRCUITS

CHAPTER OUTLINE: KEY TERMS, PEOPLE, PLACES, CONCEPTS

- Alternating current
- Electromotive force
- Internal resistance
- Terminal
- Voltage divider
- Electric current
- Voltage drop
- RC circuit
- Time constant
- Ammeter
- Digital voltmeter
- Galvanometer
- Sensitivity
- Multimeter
- Ohmmeter
- Bridge circuit
- Wheatstone bridge
- Potentiometer

Alternating current	In alternating current, the flow of electric charge periodically reverses direction. In direct current (DC, also dc), the flow of electric charge is only in one direction. The abbreviations AC and DC are often used to mean simply alternating and direct, as when they modify current or voltage.
Electromotive force	Electromotive force, also called emf, is the voltage developed by any source of electrical energy such as a battery or dynamo. The word 'force' in this case is not used to mean mechanical force, measured in newtons, but a potential, or energy per unit of charge, measured in volts. In electromagnetic induction, emf can be defined around a closed loop as the electromagnetic work that would be transferred to a unit of charge if it travels once around that loop.
Internal resistance	A practical electrical power source which is a linear electric circuit may, according to Thévenin's theorem, be represented as an ideal voltage source in series with an impedance. This resistance is termed the internal resistance of the source. When the power source delivers current, the measured e.m.f.
Terminal	In the context of telecommunications, a terminal is a device which ends a telecommunications link and is the point at which a signal enters and/or leaves a network. Examples of equipment containing network terminations are telephones, fax machines, computer terminals and network devices, printers and workstations.
Voltage divider	In electronics or EET, a voltage divider is a linear circuit that produces an output voltage (V_{out}) that is a fraction of its input voltage (V_{in}). Voltage division refers to the partitioning of a voltage among the components of the divider. An example of a voltage divider consists of two resistors in series or a potentiometer.
Electric current	An electric current is a flow of electric charge. In electric circuits this charge is often carried by moving electrons in a wire. It can also be carried by ions in an electrolyte, or by both ions and electrons such as in a plasma.
Voltage drop	Voltage drop describes how the supplied energy of a voltage source is reduced as electric current moves through the passive elements of an electrical circuit. Voltage drops across internal resistances of the source, across conductors, across contacts, and across connectors are undesired; supplied energy is lost (dissipated). Voltage drops across loads and across other active circuit elements are desired; supplied energy performs useful work.

18. DC CIRCUITS

CHAPTER HIGHLIGHTS & NOTES: KEY TERMS, PEOPLE, PLACES, CONCEPTS

RC circuit

A resistor-capacitor circuit (RC circuit), or RC filter or RC network, is an electric circuit composed of resistors and capacitors driven by a voltage or current source. A first order RC circuit is composed of one resistor and one capacitor and is the simplest type of RC circuit.

RC circuits can be used to filter a signal by blocking certain frequencies and passing others.

Time constant

In physics and engineering, the time constant, usually denoted by the Greek letter τ , is the parameter characterizing the response to a step input of a first-order, linear time-invariant (LTI) system. The time constant is the main characteristic unit of a first-order LTI (linear time-invariant) system.

In the time domain, the usual choice to explore the time response is through the step response to a step input, or the impulse response to a Dirac delta function input.

Ammeter

An ammeter is a measuring instrument used to measure the electric current in a circuit. Electric currents are measured in amperes (A), hence the name. Instruments used to measure smaller currents, in the milliampere or microampere range, are designated as milliammeters or microammeters.

Digital voltmeter

A voltmeter is an instrument used for measuring electrical potential difference between two points in an electric circuit. Analog voltmeters move a pointer across a scale in proportion to the voltage of the circuit; digital voltmeters give a numerical display of voltage by use of an analog to digital converter.

Voltmeters are made in a wide range of styles.

Galvanometer

A galvanometer is a type of sensitive ammeter: an instrument for detecting electric current. It is an analog electromechanical actuator that produces a rotary deflection of some type of pointer in response to electric current flowing through its coil in a magnetic field.

Galvanometers were the first instruments used to detect and measure electric currents.

Sensitivity

The sensitivity of an electronic device, such as a communications system receiver, or detection device, such as a PIN diode, is the minimum magnitude of input signal required to produce a specified output signal having a specified signal-to-noise ratio, or other specified criteria.

Sensitivity is sometimes improperly used as a synonym for responsivity.

The sensitivity of a microphone is usually expressed as the sound field strength in decibels relative to 1 V/Pa (Pa = N/m^2) or as the transfer factor in millivolts per pascal (mV/Pa) into an open circuit or into a 1 kilohm load.

Multimeter	A multimeter or a multitester, also known as a VOM, is an electronic measuring instrument that combines several measurement functions in one unit. A typical multimeter would include basic features such as the ability to measure voltage, current, and resistance. Analog multimeters use a microammeter whose pointer moves over a scale calibrated for all the different measurements that can be made.
Ohmmeter	An ohmmeter is an electrical instrument that measures electrical resistance, the opposition to an electric current. Micro-ohmmeters (microhmmeter or microohmmeter) make low resistance measurements. Megohmmeters (aka megaohmmeter or in the case of a trademarked device Megger) measure large values of resistance.
Bridge circuit	A bridge circuit is a type of electrical circuit in which two circuit branches are 'bridged' by a third branch connected between the first two branches at some intermediate point along them. The bridge was originally developed for laboratory measurement purposes and one of the intermediate bridging points is often adjustable when so used. Bridge circuits now find many applications, both linear and non-linear, including in instrumentation, filtering and power conversion.
Wheatstone bridge	A Wheatstone bridge is an electrical circuit used to measure an unknown electrical resistance by balancing two legs of a bridge circuit, one leg of which includes the unknown component. Its operation is similar to the original potentiometer. It was invented by Samuel Hunter Christie in 1833 and improved and popularized by Sir Charles Wheatstone in 1843. One of the Wheatstone bridge's initial uses was for the purpose of soils analysis and comparison.
Potentiometer	A potentiometer is an instrument for measuring the potential in a circuit. Before the introduction of the moving coil and digital volt meters, potentiometers were used in measuring voltage, hence the '-meter' part of their name. The method was described by Johann Christian Poggendorff around 1841 and became a standard laboratory measuring technique.

18. DC CIRCUITS

CHAPTER QUIZ: KEY TERMS, PEOPLE, PLACES, CONCEPTS

1. An _________ is a flow of electric charge. In electric circuits this charge is often carried by moving electrons in a wire. It can also be carried by ions in an electrolyte, or by both ions and electrons such as in a plasma.

   a. Electric current
   b. Bismuthide
   c. Bisulfide
   d. Borohydride

2. A _________ is an instrument for measuring the potential in a circuit. Before the introduction of the moving coil and digital volt meters, _________s were used in measuring voltage, hence the '-meter' part of their name. The method was described by Johann Christian Poggendorff around 1841 and became a standard laboratory measuring technique.

   a. Digital voltmeter
   b. Bifluoride
   c. Bismuthide
   d. Potentiometer

3. In electronics or EET, a _________ is a linear circuit that produces an output voltage (V_{out}) that is a fraction of its input voltage (V_{in}). Voltage division refers to the partitioning of a voltage among the components of the divider.

   An example of a _________ consists of two resistors in series or a potentiometer.

   a. Balancing network
   b. Voltage divider
   c. Capacitor-input filter
   d. Composite image filter

4. In the context of telecommunications, a _________ is a device which ends a telecommunications link and is the point at which a signal enters and/or leaves a network. Examples of equipment containing network terminations are telephones, fax machines, computer _________s and network devices, printers and workstations.

   a. Broadcast and Multicast Service
   b. Broadcasting
   c. Terminal
   d. Data transmission

5. . _________, also called emf, is the voltage developed by any source of electrical energy such as a battery or dynamo.

   The word 'force' in this case is not used to mean mechanical force, measured in newtons, but a potential, or energy per unit of charge, measured in volts.

   In electromagnetic induction, emf can be defined around a closed loop as the electromagnetic work that would be transferred to a unit of charge if it travels once around that loop.

a. Catapult effect
b. Cathode ray
c. Cavity perturbation theory
d. Electromotive force

ANSWER KEY
18. DC CIRCUITS

---

1. a
2. d
3. b
4. c
5. d

---

19. MAGNETISM

CHAPTER OUTLINE: KEY TERMS, PEOPLE, PLACES, CONCEPTS

Magnetic field

Magnetism

Magnetic monopole

True north

Gauss

Drift velocity

Ampere

Coulomb

Electromagnet

Solenoid

Superconducting magnet

Magnetic moment

Ammeter

Galvanometer

Ohmmeter

Voltmeter

Armature

Electric motor

Isotope

Velocity selector

Curie

19. MAGNETISM

CHAPTER OUTLINE: KEY TERMS, PEOPLE, PLACES, CONCEPTS

	Curie temperature
	Magnetic domain
	Electron
	Paramagnetism
	Saturation
	Toroid
	Torus
	Hysteresis
	Coaxial cable

CHAPTER HIGHLIGHTS & NOTES: KEY TERMS, PEOPLE, PLACES, CONCEPTS

Magnetic field	A magnetic field is a mathematical description of the magnetic influence of electric currents and magnetic materials. The magnetic field at any given point is specified by both a direction and a magnitude (or strength); as such it is a vector field. The term is used for two distinct but closely related fields denoted by the symbols B and H.
Magnetism	Magnetism is a class of physical phenomena that includes forces exerted by magnets on other magnets. It has its origin in electric currents and the fundamental magnetic moments of elementary particles. These give rise to a magnetic field that acts on other currents and moments.
Magnetic monopole	A magnetic monopole is a hypothetical particle in particle physics that is an isolated magnet with only one magnetic pole . In more technical terms, a magnetic monopole would have a net 'magnetic charge'. Modern interest in the concept stems from particle theories, notably the grand unified and superstring theories, which predict their existence.
True north	True north is the direction along the earth's surface towards the geographic North Pole.

True geodetic north usually differs from magnetic north (the direction a compass points toward the magnetic north pole), and from grid north (the direction northwards along the grid lines of a map projection). Geodetic true north also differs very slightly from Astronomical true north because the local gravity may not point at the exact rotational axis of the earth.

Gauss

The gauss, abbreviated as G or Gs, is the cgs unit of measurement of a magnetic field B, which is also known as the 'magnetic flux density' or the 'magnetic induction'. It is named after German mathematician and physicist Carl Friedrich Gauss. One gauss is defined as one maxwell per square centimeter.

Drift velocity

The drift velocity is the average velocity that a particle, such as an electron, attains due to an electric field. It can also be referred to as axial drift velocity since particles defined are assumed to be moving along a plane. In general, an electron will 'rattle around' in a conductor at the Fermi velocity randomly.

Ampere

The ampere, often shortened to amp, is the SI unit of electric current (quantity symbol: I, i) and is one of the seven SI base units. It is named after André-Marie Ampère (1775-1836), French mathematician and physicist, considered the father of electrodynamics.

In practical terms, the ampere is a measure of the amount of electric charge passing a point in an electric circuit per unit time, with 6.241×10^{18} electrons (or one coulomb) per second, constituting one ampere.

Coulomb

The coulomb is the SI derived unit of electric charge (symbol: Q or q). It is defined as the charge transported by a constant current of one ampere in one second: $1\ \mathrm{C} = 1\ \mathrm{A} \times 1\ \mathrm{s}$

One coulomb is also the amount of excess charge on the positive side of a capacitor of one farad charged to a potential difference of one volt: $1\ \mathrm{C} = 1\ \mathrm{F} \times 1\ \mathrm{V}$

Electromagnet

An electromagnet is a type of magnet in which the magnetic field is produced by electric current. The magnetic field disappears when the current is turned off. Electromagnets are widely used as components of other electrical devices, such as motors, generators, relays, loudspeakers, hard disks, MRI machines, scientific instruments, and magnetic separation equipment, as well as being employed as industrial lifting electromagnets for picking up and moving heavy iron objects like scrap iron.

Solenoid

A solenoid is a coil wound into a tightly packed helix. The term was invented by French physicist André-Marie Ampère to designate a helical coil.

19. MAGNETISM

CHAPTER HIGHLIGHTS & NOTES: KEY TERMS, PEOPLE, PLACES, CONCEPTS

Superconducting magnet	A superconducting magnet is an electromagnet made from coils of superconducting wire. They must be cooled to cryogenic temperatures during operation. In its superconducting state the wire can conduct much larger electric currents than ordinary wire, creating intense magnetic fields.
Magnetic moment	The magnetic moment of a magnet is a quantity that determines the force that the magnet can exert on electric currents and the torque that a magnetic field will exert on it. A loop of electric current, a bar magnet, an electron, a molecule, and a planet all have magnetic moments. Both the magnetic moment and magnetic field may be considered to be vectors having a magnitude and direction.
Ammeter	An ammeter is a measuring instrument used to measure the electric current in a circuit. Electric currents are measured in amperes (A), hence the name. Instruments used to measure smaller currents, in the milliampere or microampere range, are designated as milliammeters or microammeters.
Galvanometer	A galvanometer is a type of sensitive ammeter: an instrument for detecting electric current. It is an analog electromechanical actuator that produces a rotary deflection of some type of pointer in response to electric current flowing through its coil in a magnetic field. Galvanometers were the first instruments used to detect and measure electric currents.
Ohmmeter	An ohmmeter is an electrical instrument that measures electrical resistance, the opposition to an electric current. Micro-ohmmeters (microhmmeter or microohmmeter) make low resistance measurements. Megohmmeters (aka megaohmmeter or in the case of a trademarked device Megger) measure large values of resistance.
Voltmeter	A voltmeter is an instrument used for measuring electrical potential difference between two points in an electric circuit. Analog voltmeters move a pointer across a scale in proportion to the voltage of the circuit; digital voltmeters give a numerical display of voltage by use of an analog to digital converter. Voltmeters are made in a wide range of styles.
Armature	In electrical engineering, an armature generally refers to one of the two principal electrical components of an electromechanical machine -- generally in a motor or generator -- but it may also mean the pole piece of a permanent magnet or electromagnet, or the moving iron part of a solenoid or relay. The other component is the field winding or field magnet.

Electric motor	An electric motor is an electric machine that converts electrical energy into mechanical energy. In normal motoring mode, most electric motors operate through the interaction between an electric motor's magnetic field and winding currents to generate force within the motor. In certain applications, such as in the transportation industry with traction motors, electric motors can operate in both motoring and generating or braking modes to also produce electrical energy from mechanical energy.
Isotope	Isotopes are variants of a particular chemical element such that, while all isotopes of a given element have the same number of protons in each atom, they differ in neutron number. The term isotope is formed from the Greek roots isos (?s?? 'equal') and topos (t?p?? 'place'), meaning 'the same place'. Thus, different isotopes of a single element occupy the same position on the periodic table.
Velocity selector	A velocity selector is used in accelerator mass spectrometry to select particles based on their speed. The velocity selector is composed of orthogonal electric and magnetic fields, such that particles with the correct charge to mass ratio and speed will be unaffected, and other particles will be deflected.
Curie	The curie is a non-SI unit of radioactivity the curie is widely used throughout the US government and industry. One curie is roughly the activity of 1 gram of the radium isotope ^{226}Ra, a substance studied by the Curies. The SI derived unit of radioactivity is the becquerel (Bq), which equates to one decay per second.
Curie temperature	In physics and materials science, the Curie temperature, or Curie point, is the temperature where a material's permanent magnetism changes to induced magnetism. The force of magnetism is determined by magnetic moments. The Curie Temperature is the critical point where a material's intrinsic magnetic moments change direction.
Magnetic domain	A magnetic domain is a region within a magnetic material which has uniform magnetization. This means that the individual magnetic moments of the atoms are aligned with one another and they point in the same direction. When cooled below a temperature called the Curie temperature, the magnetization of a piece of ferromagnetic material spontaneously divides into many small regions called magnetic domains.
Electron	The electron is a subatomic particle with a negative elementary electric charge.

19. MAGNETISM

Electrons belong to the first generation of the lepton particle family, and are generally thought to be elementary particles because they have no known components or substructure. The electron has a mass that is approximately 1/1836 that of the proton.

Paramagnetism

Paramagnetism is a form of magnetism whereby certain materials are attracted by an externally applied magnetic field. In contrast with this behavior, diamagnetic materials are repelled by magnetic fields. Paramagnetic materials include most chemical elements and some compounds; they have a relative magnetic permeability greater than or equal to 1 (i.e., a positive magnetic susceptibility) and hence are attracted to magnetic fields.

Saturation

Seen in some magnetic materials, saturation is the state reached when an increase in applied external magnetic field H cannot increase the magnetization of the material further, so the total magnetic flux density B levels off. It is a characteristic particularly of ferromagnetic materials, such as iron, nickel, cobalt and their alloys.

Toroid

In mathematics, a toroid is a doughnut-shaped object, such as an O-ring. It is a ring form of a solenoid. Its annular shape is generated by revolving a plane geometrical figure about an axis external to that figure which is parallel to the plane of the figure and does not intersect the figure.

Torus

In geometry, a torus is a surface of revolution generated by revolving a circle in three-dimensional space about an axis coplanar with the circle. If the axis of revolution does not touch the circle, the surface has a ring shape and is called a ring torus or simply torus if the ring shape is implicit.

When the axis is tangent to the circle, the resulting surface is called a horn torus; when the axis is a chord of the circle, it is called a spindle torus.

Hysteresis

Hysteresis is the dependence of a system not only on its current environment but also on its past environment. This dependence arises because the system can be in more than one internal state. To predict its future development, either its internal state or its history must be known.

Coaxial cable

Coaxial cable, or coax, is a type of cable that has an inner conductor surrounded by a tubular insulating layer, surrounded by a tubular conducting shield. Many coaxial cables also have an insulating outer sheath or jacket. The term coaxial comes from the inner conductor and the outer shield sharing a geometric axis.

1. A _________ is a mathematical description of the magnetic influence of electric currents and magnetic materials. The _________ at any given point is specified by both a direction and a magnitude (or strength); as such it is a vector field. The term is used for two distinct but closely related fields denoted by the symbols B and H.

   a. Catapult effect
   b. Cathode ray
   c. Magnetic field
   d. Charge conservation

2. In physics and materials science, the _________, or Curie point, is the temperature where a material's permanent magnetism changes to induced magnetism. The force of magnetism is determined by magnetic moments.

   The _________ is the critical point where a material's intrinsic magnetic moments change direction.

   a. Bancroft point
   b. Boiling
   c. Curie temperature
   d. Bubble point

3. The _________ is a subatomic particle with a negative elementary electric charge. _________s belong to the first generation of the lepton particle family, and are generally thought to be elementary particles because they have no known components or substructure. The _________ has a mass that is approximately 1/1836 that of the proton.

   a. Larmor formula
   b. Laplace expansion
   c. Electron
   d. K-beta

4. _________ is a class of physical phenomena that includes forces exerted by magnets on other magnets. It has its origin in electric currents and the fundamental magnetic moments of elementary particles. These give rise to a magnetic field that acts on other currents and moments.

   a. 3D printing
   b. 3Doodler
   c. Magnetism
   d. CandyFab

5. . The _________ is a non-SI unit of radioactivity the _________ is widely used throughout the US government and industry.

   One _________ is roughly the activity of 1 gram of the radium isotope ^{226}Ra, a substance studied by the _________s.

   The SI derived unit of radioactivity is the becquerel (Bq), which equates to one decay per second.

   a. 5 yen coin

b. Background radiation

c. Background radiation equivalent time

d. Curie

ANSWER KEY
19. MAGNETISM

1. c
2. c
3. c
4. c
5. d

---

20. ELECTROMAGNETIC INDUCTION AND FARADAY'S LAW

CHAPTER OUTLINE: KEY TERMS, PEOPLE, PLACES, CONCEPTS

- Electromagnetic induction
- Electromotive force
- Electromagnetic
- Magnetic field
- Magnetic flux
- Armature
- Dynamo
- Electric field
- Electric generator
- Turbine
- Alternator
- Eddy current
- Power transmission
- Transmission
- Tape recorder
- Cordless
- MOSFET
- Field-effect transistor
- Semiconductor
- Inductance
- Inductor

20. ELECTROMAGNETIC INDUCTION AND FARADAY`S LAW

CHAPTER OUTLINE: KEY TERMS, PEOPLE, PLACES, CONCEPTS

______ Solenoid

______ Time constant

______ Capacitor

______ High-pass filter

______ Low-pass filter

______ Phasor

______ Phase angle

______ Power factor

______ LC circuit

______ Shielded cable

______ Magnetic damping

______ Ballistic galvanometer

______ Galvanometer

20. ELECTROMAGNETIC INDUCTION AND FARADAY'S LAW

Electromagnetic induction	Electromagnetic induction is the production of a potential difference across a conductor when it is exposed to a varying magnetic field. Michael Faraday is generally credited with the discovery of induction in 1831 though it may have been anticipated by the work of Francesco Zantedeschi in 1829. Around 1830 to 1832, Joseph Henry made a similar discovery, but did not publish his findings until later. Faraday's law of induction is a basic law of electromagnetism predicting how a magnetic field will interact with an electric circuit to produce an electromotive force (EMF).
Electromotive force	Electromotive force, also called emf, is the voltage developed by any source of electrical energy such as a battery or dynamo. The word 'force' in this case is not used to mean mechanical force, measured in newtons, but a potential, or energy per unit of charge, measured in volts. In electromagnetic induction, emf can be defined around a closed loop as the electromagnetic work that would be transferred to a unit of charge if it travels once around that loop.
Electromagnetic	Electromagnetic is a prefix used to specialise many technical terms that involve electromagnetism.
Magnetic field	A magnetic field is a mathematical description of the magnetic influence of electric currents and magnetic materials. The magnetic field at any given point is specified by both a direction and a magnitude (or strength); as such it is a vector field. The term is used for two distinct but closely related fields denoted by the symbols B and H.
Magnetic flux	In physics, specifically electromagnetism, the magnetic flux through a surface is the component of the magnetic B field passing through that surface. The SI unit of magnetic flux is the weber (Wb) (in derived units: volt-seconds), and the CGS unit is the maxwell. Magnetic flux is usually measured with a fluxmeter, which contains measuring coils and electronics, that evaluates the change of voltage in the measuring coils to calculate the magnetic flux.
Armature	In electrical engineering, an armature generally refers to one of the two principal electrical components of an electromechanical machine -- generally in a motor or generator -- but it may also mean the pole piece of a permanent magnet or electromagnet, or the moving iron part of a solenoid or relay. The other component is the field winding or field magnet. The role of the 'field' component is simply to create a magnetic field (magnetic flux) for the armature to interact with, thus the field component can comprise either permanent magnets, or electromagnets formed by a conducting coil.
Dynamo	A dynamo is an electrical generator that produces direct current with the use of a commutator.

Dynamos were the first electrical generators capable of delivering power for industry, and the foundation upon which many other later electric-power conversion devices were based, including the electric motor, the alternating-current alternator, and the rotary converter. Today, the simpler alternator dominates large scale power generation, for efficiency, reliability and cost reasons.

Electric field — An electric field is generated by electrically charged particles and time-varying magnetic fields. The electric field describes the electric force experienced by a motionless positively electrically charged test particle at any point in space relative to the source(s) of the field. The concept of an electric field was introduced by Michael Faraday.

Electric generator — In electricity generation, an electric generator is a device that converts mechanical energy to electrical energy. A generator forces electric current to flow through an external circuit. The source of mechanical energy may be a reciprocating or turbine steam engine, water falling through a turbine or waterwheel, an internal combustion engine, a wind turbine, a hand crank, compressed air, or any other source of mechanical energy.

Turbine — A turbine is a rotary mechanical device that extracts energy from a fluid flow and converts it into useful work. A turbine is a turbomachine with at least one moving part called a rotor assembly, which is a shaft or drum with blades attached. Moving fluid acts on the blades so that they move and impart rotational energy to the rotor.

Alternator — An alternator is an electromechanical device that converts mechanical energy to electrical energy in the form of alternating current.

Most alternators use a rotating magnetic field with a stationary armature but occasionally, a rotating armature is used with a stationary magnetic field; or a linear alternator is used.

In principle, any AC electrical generator can be called an alternator, but usually the term refers to small rotating machines driven by automotive and other internal combustion engines.

Eddy current — Eddy currents are electric currents induced within conductors by a changing magnetic field in the conductor. These circulating eddies of current have inductance and thus induce magnetic fields. These fields can cause repulsive, attractive, propulsion, drag, and heating effects.

Power transmission — Power transmission is the movement of energy from its place of generation to a location where it is applied to performing useful work.

Power is defined formally as units of energy per unit time. In SI units:

$$\mathrm{watt} = \frac{\mathrm{joule}}{\mathrm{second}} = \frac{\mathrm{newton} \times \mathrm{meter}}{\mathrm{second}}$$

Transmission

A machine consists of a power source and a power transmission system, which provides controlled application of the power. Merriam-Webster defines transmission as an assembly of parts including the speed-changing gears and the propeller shaft by which the power is transmitted from an engine to a live axle. Often transmission refers simply to the gearbox that uses gears and gear trains to provide speed and torque conversions from a rotating power source to another device.

Tape recorder

An audio tape recorder, tape deck, reel-to-reel tape deck, cassette deck or tape machine is an audio storage device that records and plays back sounds, including articulated voices, usually using magnetic tape, either wound on a reel or in a cassette, for storage. In its present day form, it records a fluctuating signal by moving the tape across a tape head that polarizes the magnetic domains in the tape in proportion to the audio signal.

The use of magnetic tape for sound recording originated around 1930. Magnetizable tape revolutionized both the radio broadcast and music recording industries.

Cordless

The term cordless is generally used to refer to electrical or electronic devices that are powered by a battery or battery pack and can operate without a power cord or cable attached to a fixed electricity supply such as an outlet, generator, or other centralized power source, allowing greater mobility. The development of more powerful rechargeable batteries in recent years has allowed the production of battery-powered versions of tools and appliances that once required a power cord, and these are distinguished by the term 'cordless', as in cordless drills, cordless saws, and cordless irons.

The term 'cordless' should not be confused with the term 'wireless', although it often is in common usage, possibly because some cordless devices (e.g., cordless telephones) are also wireless.

MOSFET

The metal-oxide-semiconductor field-effect transistor (MOSFET, MOS-FET, or MOS FET) is a transistor used for amplifying or switching electronic signals. Although the MOSFET is a four-terminal device with source (S), gate (G), drain (D), and body (B) terminals, the body (or substrate) of the MOSFET often is connected to the source terminal, making it a three-terminal device like other field-effect transistors. Because these two terminals are normally connected to each other (short-circuited) internally, only three terminals appear in electrical diagrams.

Field-effect transistor

The field-effect transistor is a transistor that uses an electric field to control the shape and hence the conductivity of a channel of one type of charge carrier in a semiconductor material. Field effect transistors are unipolar transistors as they involve single-carrier-type operation. The concept of the Field effect transistor predates the bipolar junction transistor (BJT), though it was not physically implemented until after BJTs due to the limitations of semiconductor materials and the relative ease of manufacturing BJTs compared to Field effect transistors at the time.

Semiconductor

A semiconductor is a material which has electrical conductivity to a degree between that of a metal and that of an insulator (such as glass).

Semiconductors are the foundation of modern electronics, including transistors, solar cells, light-emitting diodes (LEDs), quantum dots and digital and analog integrated circuits.

A semiconductor may have a number of unique properties, one of which is the ability to change conductivity by the addition of impurities ('doping') or by interaction with another phenomenon, such as an electric field or light; this ability makes a semiconductor very useful for constructing a device that can amplify, switch, or convert an energy input.

Inductance

In electromagnetism and electronics, inductance is the property of a conductor by which a change in current in the conductor 'induces' a voltage (electromotive force) in both the conductor itself (self-inductance) and in any nearby conductors (mutual inductance). These effects are derived from two fundamental observations of physics: First, that a steady current creates a steady magnetic field (Oersted's law), and second, that a time-varying magnetic field induces voltage in nearby conductors (Faraday's law of induction). According to Lenz's law, a changing electric current through a circuit that contains inductance, induces a proportional voltage, which opposes the change in current (self-inductance).

Inductor

An inductor, also called a coil or reactor, is a passive two-terminal electrical component which resists changes in electric current passing through it. It consists of a conductor such as a wire, usually wound into a coil. When a current flows through it, energy is stored temporarily in a magnetic field in the coil.

Solenoid

A solenoid is a coil wound into a tightly packed helix. The term was invented by French physicist André-Marie Ampère to designate a helical coil.

In physics, the term refers specifically to a long, thin loop of wire, often wrapped around a metallic core, which produces a uniform magnetic field in a volume of space (where some experiment might be carried out) when an electric current is passed through it.

Time constant

In physics and engineering, the time constant, usually denoted by the Greek letter τ, is the parameter characterizing the response to a step input of a first-order, linear time-invariant (LTI) system. The time constant is the main characteristic unit of a first-order LTI (linear time-invariant) system.

In the time domain, the usual choice to explore the time response is through the step response to a step input, or the impulse response to a Dirac delta function input.

Capacitor

A capacitor is a passive two-terminal electrical component used to store energy electrostatically in an electric field. The forms of practical capacitors vary widely, but all contain at least two electrical conductors separated by a dielectric (insulator); for example, one common construction consists of metal foils separated by a thin layer of insulating film.

High-pass filter

A high-pass filter is an electronic filter that passes high-frequency signals but attenuates (reduces the amplitude of) signals with frequencies lower than the cutoff frequency. The actual amount of attenuation for each frequency varies from filter to filter. A high-pass filter is usually modeled as a linear time-invariant system.

Low-pass filter

A low-pass filter is a filter that passes low-frequency signals and attenuates signals with frequencies higher than the cutoff frequency. The actual amount of attenuation for each frequency varies depending on specific filter design. It is sometimes called a high-cut filter, or treble cut filter in audio applications.

Phasor

In physics and engineering, a phase vector, or phasor, is a representation of a sinusoidal function whose amplitude, frequency (?), and phase (?) are time-invariant. It is a subset of a more general concept called analytic representation. Phasors separate the dependencies on A, ?, and ? into three independent factors.

Phase angle

In the context of vectors and phasors, the term phase angle refers to the angular component of the polar coordinate representation. The notation $A\angle\theta$, for a vector with magnitude (or amplitude) A and phase angle ?, is called angle notation.

In the context of periodic phenomena, such as a wave, phase angle is synonymous with phase.

Power factor

The power factor of an AC electrical power system is defined as the ratio of the real power flowing to the load, to the apparent power in the circuit, and is a dimensionless number between -1 and 1. Real power is the capacity of the circuit for performing work in a particular time. Apparent power is the product of the current and voltage of the circuit. Due to energy stored in the load and returned to the source, or due to a non-linear load that distorts the wave shape of the current drawn from the source, the apparent power will be greater than the real power.

LC circuit

An LC circuit, also called a resonant circuit, tank circuit, or tuned circuit, consists of an inductor, represented by the letter L, and a capacitor, represented by the letter C. When connected together, they can act as an electrical resonator, an electrical analogue of a tuning fork, storing energy oscillating at the circuit's resonant frequency.

LC circuits are used either for generating signals at a particular frequency, or picking out a signal at a particular frequency from a more complex signal. They are key components in many electronic devices, particularly radio equipment, used in circuits such as oscillators, filters, tuners and frequency mixers.

Shielded cable

A shielded cable is an electrical cable of one or more insulated conductors enclosed by a common conductive layer. The shield may be composed of braided strands of copper (or other metal, such as aluminium), a non-braided spiral winding of copper tape, or a layer of conducting polymer.

20. ELECTROMAGNETIC INDUCTION AND FARADAY`S LAW

CHAPTER HIGHLIGHTS & NOTES: KEY TERMS, PEOPLE, PLACES, CONCEPTS

Magnetic damping	Magnetic Damping is a form of damping that occurs when a magnetic field moves through a conductor .
Ballistic galvanometer	The ballistic galvanometer is d'arsonval type. however,it does not show a steady state deflection owing to transistory nature of current passing through it, but it oscillates with decreasing amplitude, the amplitude of first swing or through being proportional to the charge passing. A ballistic galvanometer is a type of sensitive galvanometer, commonly a mirror galvanometer.
Galvanometer	A galvanometer is a type of sensitive ammeter: an instrument for detecting electric current. It is an analog electromechanical actuator that produces a rotary deflection of some type of pointer in response to electric current flowing through its coil in a magnetic field. Galvanometers were the first instruments used to detect and measure electric currents.

CHAPTER QUIZ: KEY TERMS, PEOPLE, PLACES, CONCEPTS

1. A _________ is an electrical cable of one or more insulated conductors enclosed by a common conductive layer. The shield may be composed of braided strands of copper (or other metal, such as aluminium), a non-braided spiral winding of copper tape, or a layer of conducting polymer. Usually, this shield is covered with a jacket.

    a. Cable lacing
    b. Category 2 cable
    c. Category 3 cable
    d. Shielded cable

2. _________ is the production of a potential difference across a conductor when it is exposed to a varying magnetic field.

    Michael Faraday is generally credited with the discovery of induction in 1831 though it may have been anticipated by the work of Francesco Zantedeschi in 1829. Around 1830 to 1832, Joseph Henry made a similar discovery, but did not publish his findings until later.

    Faraday's law of induction is a basic law of electromagnetism predicting how a magnetic field will interact with an electric circuit to produce an electromotive force (EMF).

    a. Coupled mode theory
    b. Electromagnetic induction
    c. Bismuthide
    d. Bisulfide

3. _________, also called emf, is the voltage developed by any source of electrical energy such as a battery or dynamo.

The word 'force' in this case is not used to mean mechanical force, measured in newtons, but a potential, or energy per unit of charge, measured in volts.

In electromagnetic induction, emf can be defined around a closed loop as the electromagnetic work that would be transferred to a unit of charge if it travels once around that loop.

a. Catapult effect
b. Cathode ray
c. Electromotive force
d. Charge conservation

4. A _________ is a passive two-terminal electrical component used to store energy electrostatically in an electric field. The forms of practical _________s vary widely, but all contain at least two electrical conductors separated by a dielectric (insulator); for example, one common construction consists of metal foils separated by a thin layer of insulating film. _________s are widely used as parts of electrical circuits in many common electrical devices.

a. Capacitor
b. Gander Automated Air Traffic System
c. Phoenix
d. RMCDE

5. A _________ is a rotary mechanical device that extracts energy from a fluid flow and converts it into useful work. A _________ is a turbomachine with at least one moving part called a rotor assembly, which is a shaft or drum with blades attached. Moving fluid acts on the blades so that they move and impart rotational energy to the rotor.

a. CINDACTA
b. Turbine
c. Phoenix
d. RMCDE

ANSWER KEY
20. ELECTROMAGNETIC INDUCTION AND FARADAY`S LAW

1. d
2. b
3. c
4. a
5. b

---

21. ELECTROMAGNETIC WAVES

CHAPTER OUTLINE: KEY TERMS, PEOPLE, PLACES, CONCEPTS

- Electromagnetic
- Electric field
- Antenna
- Displacement current
- Electric flux
- Displacement
- Plane wave
- Speed of light
- Velocity
- Electromagnetic spectrum
- Radar
- Radio wave
- Infrared
- Wavelength
- Magnetic field
- Poynting vector
- Intensity
- Momentum transfer
- Radiation pressure
- Optical tweezers
- Solar sail

21. ELECTROMAGNETIC WAVES

CHAPTER OUTLINE: KEY TERMS, PEOPLE, PLACES, CONCEPTS

	Amplitude modulation
	Frequency modulation
	Frequency
	Satellite dish
	Remote control
	Solar energy

CHAPTER HIGHLIGHTS & NOTES: KEY TERMS, PEOPLE, PLACES, CONCEPTS

Electromagnetic	Electromagnetic is a prefix used to specialise many technical terms that involve electromagnetism.
Electric field	An electric field is generated by electrically charged particles and time-varying magnetic fields. The electric field describes the electric force experienced by a motionless positively electrically charged test particle at any point in space relative to the source(s) of the field. The concept of an electric field was introduced by Michael Faraday.
Antenna	An antenna is an electrical device which converts electric power into radio waves, and vice versa. It is usually used with a radio transmitter or radio receiver. In transmission, a radio transmitter supplies an oscillating radio frequency electric current to the antenna's terminals, and the antenna radiates the energy from the current as electromagnetic waves (radio waves).
Displacement current	In electromagnetism, displacement current is a quantity appearing in Maxwell's equations that is defined in terms of the rate of change of electric displacement field. Displacement current has the units of electric current density, and it has an associated magnetic field just as actual currents do. However it is not an electric current of moving charges, but a time-varying electric field.
Electric flux	In electromagnetism, electric flux is the rate of flow of the electric field through a given area. Electric flux is proportional to the number of electric field lines going through a virtual surface. If the electric field is uniform, the electric flux passing through a surface of vector area S is $\Phi_E = \mathbf{E} \cdot \mathbf{S} = ES\cos\theta,$

where E is the electric field, E is its magnitude, S is the area of the surface, and ? is the angle between the electric field lines and the normal (perpendicular) to S.

Displacement

In fluid mechanics, displacement occurs when an object is immersed in a fluid, pushing it out of the way and taking its place. The volume of the fluid displaced can then be measured, and from this the volume of the immersed object can be deduced (the volume of the immersed object will be exactly equal to the volume of the displaced fluid).

An object that sinks displaces an amount of fluid equal to the object's volume.

Plane wave

In the physics of wave propagation, a plane wave is a constant-frequency wave whose wavefronts (surfaces of constant phase) are infinite parallel planes of constant peak-to-peak amplitude normal to the phase velocity vector.

It is not possible in practice to have a true plane wave; only a plane wave of infinite extent will propagate as a plane wave. However, many waves are approximately plane waves in a localized region of space.

Speed of light

The speed of light in vacuum, commonly denoted c, is a universal physical constant important in many areas of physics. Its value is exactly 299,792,458 metres per second, a figure that is exact because the length of the metre is defined from this constant and the international standard for time. This is approximately 186,282.4 miles per second, or about 671 million miles per hour.

Velocity

Velocity is the rate of change of the position of an object, equivalent to a specification of its speed and direction of motion, e.g. 60 km/h to the north. Velocity is an important concept in kinematics, the branch of classical mechanics which describes the motion of bodies.

Velocity is a vector physical quantity; both magnitude and direction are required to define it.

Electromagnetic spectrum

The electromagnetic spectrum is the range of all possible frequencies of electromagnetic radiation. The 'electromagnetic spectrum' of an object has a different meaning, and is instead the characteristic distribution of electromagnetic radiation emitted or absorbed by that particular object.

The electromagnetic spectrum extends from below the low frequencies used for modern radio communication to gamma radiation at the short-wavelength (high-frequency) end, thereby covering wavelengths from thousands of kilometers down to a fraction of the size of an atom.

Radar

Radar is an object detection system which uses radio waves to determine the range, altitude, direction, or speed of objects. It can be used to detect aircraft, ships, spacecraft, guided missiles, motor vehicles, weather formations, and terrain.

Radio wave

Radio waves are a type of electromagnetic radiation with wavelengths in the electromagnetic spectrum longer than infrared light. Radio waves have frequencies from 300 GHz to as low as 3 kHz, and corresponding wavelengths ranging from 1 millimeter (0.039 in) to 100 kilometers (62 mi). Like all other electromagnetic waves, they travel at the speed of light.

Infrared

Infrared light is electromagnetic radiation with longer wavelengths than those of visible light, extending from the nominal red edge of the visible spectrum at 700 nanometres (nm) to 1 mm. This range of wavelengths corresponds to a frequency range of approximately 430 THz down to 300 GHz. Most of the thermal radiation emitted by objects near room temperature is infrared.

Wavelength

In physics, the wavelength of a sinusoidal wave is the spatial period of the wave--the distance over which the wave's shape repeats. It is usually determined by considering the distance between consecutive corresponding points of the same phase, such as crests, troughs, or zero crossings, and is a characteristic of both traveling waves and standing waves, as well as other spatial wave patterns. Wavelength is commonly designated by the Greek letter lambda (?).

Magnetic field

A magnetic field is a mathematical description of the magnetic influence of electric currents and magnetic materials. The magnetic field at any given point is specified by both a direction and a magnitude (or strength); as such it is a vector field. The term is used for two distinct but closely related fields denoted by the symbols B and H.

Poynting vector

In physics, the Poynting vector represents the directional energy flux density (the rate of energy transfer per unit area, in watts per square metre) of an electromagnetic field. It is named after its inventor John Henry Poynting. Oliver Heaviside and Nikolay Umov independently co-invented the Poynting vector.

Intensity

In physics, intensity is the power transferred per unit area. In the SI system, it has units watts per metre squared (W/m^2). It is used most frequently with waves (e.g. sound or light), in which case the average power transfer over one period of the wave is used.

Momentum transfer

In particle physics, wave mechanics and optics, momentum transfer is the amount of momentum that one particle gives to another particle.

In the simplest example of scattering of two colliding particles with initial momenta $\vec{p}_{i1}, \vec{p}_{i2}$, resulting in final momenta $\vec{p}_{f1}, \vec{p}_{f2}$, the momentum transfer is given by $\vec{q} = \vec{p}_{i1} - \vec{p}_{f1} = \vec{p}_{f2} - \vec{p}_{i2}$

where the last identity expresses momentum conservation. Momentum transfer is an important quantity because $\Delta x = \hbar/|q|$ is a better measure for the typical distance resolution of the reaction than the momenta themselves.

21. ELECTROMAGNETIC WAVES

CHAPTER HIGHLIGHTS & NOTES: KEY TERMS, PEOPLE, PLACES, CONCEPTS

Radiation pressure	Radiation pressure is the pressure exerted upon any surface exposed to electromagnetic radiation. Radiation pressure implies an interaction between electromagnetic radiation and bodies of various types, including clouds of particles or gases. The interactions can be absorption, reflection, or some of both (the common case).
Optical tweezers	Optical tweezers are scientific instruments that use a highly focused laser beam to provide an attractive or repulsive force (typically on the order of piconewtons), depending on the refractive index mismatch to physically hold and move microscopic dielectric objects. Optical tweezers have been particularly successful in studying a variety of biological systems in recent years.
Solar sail	Solar sails are a form of spacecraft propulsion using the radiation pressure (also called solar pressure) from stars to push large ultra-thin mirrors to high speeds. Light sails could also be driven by energy beams to extend their range of operations, which is strictly beam sailing rather than solar sailing. Solar sail craft offer the possibility of low-cost operations combined with long operating lifetimes.
Amplitude modulation	Amplitude modulation is a modulation technique used in electronic communication, most commonly for transmitting information via a radio carrier wave. AM works by varying the strength (amplitude) of the transmitted signal in relation to the information being sent. For example, changes in signal strength may be used to specify the sounds to be reproduced by a loudspeaker, or the light intensity of television pixels.
Frequency modulation	In telecommunications and signal processing, frequency modulation is the encoding of information in a carrier wave by varying the instantaneous frequency of the wave. (Compare with amplitude modulation, in which the amplitude of the carrier wave varies, while the frequency remains constant). In analog signal applications, the difference between the instantaneous and the base frequency of the carrier is directly proportional to the instantaneous value of the input-signal amplitude.
Frequency	Frequency is the number of occurrences of a repeating event per unit time. It is also referred to as temporal frequency, which emphasizes the contrast to spatial frequency and angular frequency. The period is the duration of one cycle in a repeating event, so the period is the reciprocal of the frequency.
Satellite dish	A satellite dish is a dish-shaped type of parabolic antenna designed to receive microwaves from communications satellites, which transmit data transmissions or broadcasts, such as satellite television.

CHAPTER HIGHLIGHTS & NOTES: KEY TERMS, PEOPLE, PLACES, CONCEPTS

Remote control

A remote control is a component of an electronics device, most commonly a television set, DVD player and home theater systems originally used for operating the device wirelessly from a short line-of-sight distance. Remote control has continually evolved and advanced over recent years to include Bluetooth connectivity, motion sensor-enabled capabilities and voice control.

Commonly, remote controls are Consumer IR devices used to issue commands from a distance to televisions or other consumer electronics such as stereo systems, DVD players and dimmers.

Solar energy

Solar energy, radiant light and heat from the sun, is harnessed using a range of ever-evolving technologies such as solar heating, solar photovoltaics, solar thermal electricity, solar architecture and artificial photosynthesis.

Solar technologies are broadly characterized as either passive solar or active solar depending on the way they capture, convert and distribute solar energy. Active solar techniques include the use of photovoltaic panels and solar thermal collectors to harness the energy.

CHAPTER QUIZ: KEY TERMS, PEOPLE, PLACES, CONCEPTS

1. In electromagnetism, _________ is the rate of flow of the electric field through a given area. _________ is proportional to the number of electric field lines going through a virtual surface. If the electric field is uniform, the _________ passing through a surface of vector area S is $\Phi_E = \mathbf{E} \cdot \mathbf{S} = ES\cos\theta,$

   where E is the electric field, E is its magnitude, S is the area of the surface, and ? is the angle between the electric field lines and the normal (perpendicular) to S.

   a. Electric flux
   b. Charge density
   c. Coefficients of potential
   d. Conductive textile

2. _________ is a prefix used to specialise many technical terms that involve electromagnetism.

   a. Aneroid
   b. Algebraic topology
   c. Arithmetic hyperbolic 3-manifold
   d. Electromagnetic

3. . An _________ is generated by electrically charged particles and time-varying magnetic fields.

The _________ describes the electric force experienced by a motionless positively electrically charged test particle at any point in space relative to the source(s) of the field. The concept of an _________ was introduced by Michael Faraday.

a. Catapult effect
b. Cathode ray
c. Electric field
d. Charge conservation

4. _________ light is electromagnetic radiation with longer wavelengths than those of visible light, extending from the nominal red edge of the visible spectrum at 700 nanometres (nm) to 1 mm. This range of wavelengths corresponds to a frequency range of approximately 430 THz down to 300 GHz. Most of the thermal radiation emitted by objects near room temperature is _________.

a. Infrared
b. Gamma ray
c. Background noise
d. 3D sound localization

5. In physics, the _________ of a sinusoidal wave is the spatial period of the wave--the distance over which the wave's shape repeats. It is usually determined by considering the distance between consecutive corresponding points of the same phase, such as crests, troughs, or zero crossings, and is a characteristic of both traveling waves and standing waves, as well as other spatial wave patterns. _________ is commonly designated by the Greek letter lambda (?).

a. 1s Slater-type function
b. Bloch wave
c. Bohr magneton
d. Wavelength

ANSWER KEY
21. ELECTROMAGNETIC WAVES

1. a
2. d
3. c
4. a
5. d

---

22. LIGHT: GEOMETRIC OPTICS

CHAPTER OUTLINE: KEY TERMS, PEOPLE, PLACES, CONCEPTS

- Reflection
- Diffuse reflection
- Specular reflection
- Real image
- Virtual image
- Focal length
- Parabolic reflector
- Satellite dish
- Spherical aberration
- Image formation
- Sign convention
- Index of refraction
- Refraction
- Speed of light
- Velocity
- Optical illusions
- Binoculars
- PRISM
- Lens
- Magnification

22. LIGHT: GEOMETRIC OPTICS

CHAPTER HIGHLIGHTS & NOTES: KEY TERMS, PEOPLE, PLACES, CONCEPTS

Reflection	Reflection is the change in direction of a wavefront at an interface between two different media so that the wavefront returns into the medium from which it originated. Common examples include the reflection of light, sound and water waves. The law of reflection says that for specular reflection the angle at which the wave is incident on the surface equals the angle at which it is reflected.
Diffuse reflection	Diffuse reflection is the reflection of light from a surface such that an incident ray is reflected at many angles rather than at just one angle as in the case of specular reflection. An illuminated ideal diffuse reflecting surface will have equal luminance from all directions which lie in the half-space adjacent to the surface (Lambertian reflectance). A surface built from a non-absorbing powder such as plaster, or from fibers such as paper, or from a polycrystalline material such as white marble, reflects light diffusely with great efficiency.
Specular reflection	Specular reflection is the mirror-like reflection of light from a surface, in which light from a single incoming direction (a ray) is reflected into a single outgoing direction. Such behavior is described by the law of reflection, which states that the direction of incoming light (the incident ray), and the direction of outgoing light reflected (the reflected ray) make the same angle with respect to the surface normal, thus the angle of incidence equals the angle of reflection ($\theta_i = \theta_r$ in the figure), and that the incident, normal, and reflected directions are coplanar. This behavior was first discovered through careful observation and measurement by Hero of Alexandria (AD c. 10-70).
Real image	In optics, a real image is an image which is located in the plane of convergence for the light rays that originate from a given object. If a screen is placed in the plane of a real image the image will generally become visible on the screen. Examples of real images include the image seen on a cinema screen (the source being the projector), the image produced on a detector in the rear of a camera, and the image produced on an eyeball retina (the camera and eye focus light through an internal convex lens).
Virtual image	In optics, a virtual image is an image in which the outgoing rays from a point on the object always diverge. It will appear to converge in or behind the optical device (e.g., a mirror). A simple example is a flat mirror where the image of oneself is perceived at twice the distance from oneself to the mirror.
Focal length	The focal length of an optical system is a measure of how strongly the system converges or diverges light. For an optical system in air, it is the distance over which initially collimated rays are brought to a focus. A system with a shorter focal length has greater optical power than one with a long focal length; that is, it bends the rays more strongly, bringing them to a focus in a shorter distance.
Parabolic reflector	A parabolic reflector is a reflective surface used to collect or project energy such as light, sound, or radio waves. Its shape is part of a circular paraboloid, that is, the surface generated by a parabola revolving around its axis.

Satellite dish

A satellite dish is a dish-shaped type of parabolic antenna designed to receive microwaves from communications satellites, which transmit data transmissions or broadcasts, such as satellite television.

Spherical aberration

Spherical aberration is an optical effect observed in an optical device that occurs due to the increased refraction of light rays when they strike a lens or a reflection of light rays when they strike a mirror near its edge, in comparison with those that strike nearer the centre. It signifies a deviation of the device from the norm, i.e., it results in an imperfection of the produced image.

A spherical lens has an aplanatic point (i.e., no spherical aberration) only at a radius that equals the radius of the sphere divided by the index of refraction of the lens material.

Image formation

The study of image formation encompasses the radiometric and geometric processes by which 2D images of 3D objects are formed. In the case of digital images, the image formation process also includes analog to digital conversion and sampling.

Image Formation in Eye

The principal difference between the lens of the eye and an ordinary optical lens is that the former is flexible.

Sign convention

In physics, a sign convention is a choice of the physical significance of signs for a set of quantities, in a case where the choice of sign is arbitrary. 'Arbitrary' here means that the same physical system can be correctly described using different choices for the signs, as long as one set of definitions is used consistently. The choices made may differ between authors.

Index of refraction

In optics the refractive index or index of refraction n of a substance is a dimensionless number that describes how light, or any other radiation, propagates through that medium. It is defined as $n = \frac{c}{v}$,

where c is the speed of light in vacuum and v is the speed of light in the substance. For example, the refractive index of water is 1.33, meaning that light travels 1.33 times slower in water than it does in vacuum.

Refraction

Refraction is the change in direction of a wave due to a change in its transmission medium.

Refraction is essentially a surface phenomenon. The phenomenon is mainly in governance to the law of conservation of energy and momentum.

Speed of light

The speed of light in vacuum, commonly denoted c, is a universal physical constant important in many areas of physics.

Its value is exactly 299,792,458 metres per second, a figure that is exact because the length of the metre is defined from this constant and the international standard for time. This is approximately 186,282.4 miles per second, or about 671 million miles per hour.

Velocity

Velocity is the rate of change of the position of an object, equivalent to a specification of its speed and direction of motion, e.g. 60 km/h to the north. Velocity is an important concept in kinematics, the branch of classical mechanics which describes the motion of bodies.

Velocity is a vector physical quantity; both magnitude and direction are required to define it.

Optical illusions

An optical illusion is characterized by visually perceived images that differ from objective reality. The information gathered by the eye is processed in the brain to give a perception that does not tally with a physical measurement of the stimulus source. There are three main types: literal optical illusions that create images that are different from the objects that make them, physiological ones that are the effects on the eyes and brain of excessive stimulation of a specific type (brightness, colour, size, position, tilt, movement), and cognitive illusions, the result of unconscious inferences.

Binoculars

Binoculars, field glasses or binocular telescopes are a pair of identical or mirror-symmetrical telescopes mounted side-by-side and aligned to point accurately in the same direction, allowing the viewer to use both eyes when viewing distant objects. Most are sized to be held using both hands, although sizes vary widely from opera glasses to large pedestal mounted military models. Many different abbreviations are used for binoculars, including glasses, nocs, binocs, noculars, binos and bins.

PRISM

PRISM is the name of a nuclear power plant design by GE Hitachi Nuclear Energy .

The S-PRISM represents GEH's Generation IV reactor solution to closing the nuclear fuel cycle and is also part of its Advanced Recycling Center (ARC) proposition to U.S. Congress to deal with nuclear waste.

It is based on a sodium-cooled fast breeder reactor called integral fast reactor.

Lens

A lens is an optical device which transmits and refracts light, converging or diverging the beam. A simple lens consists of a single optical element. A compound lens is an array of simple lenses (elements) with a common axis; the use of multiple elements allows more optical aberrations to be corrected than is possible with a single element.

Magnification

Magnification is the process of enlarging something only in appearance, not in physical size. This enlargement is quantified by a calculated number also called 'magnification'. When this number is less than one it refers to a reduction in size, sometimes called 'minification' or 'de-magnification'.

1. _________ is the name of a nuclear power plant design by GE Hitachi Nuclear Energy .

The S-_________ represents GEH's Generation IV reactor solution to closing the nuclear fuel cycle and is also part of its Advanced Recycling Center (ARC) proposition to U.S. Congress to deal with nuclear waste.

It is based on a sodium-cooled fast breeder reactor called integral fast reactor.

a. Bailly Nuclear Power Plant
b. Bataan Nuclear Power Plant
c. Bellefonte Nuclear Generating Station
d. PRISM

2. _________ is the change in direction of a wave due to a change in its transmission medium.

_________ is essentially a surface phenomenon. The phenomenon is mainly in governance to the law of conservation of energy and momentum.

a. Cardinal point
b. Caustic
c. Chromatic aberration
d. Refraction

3. _________ is the reflection of light from a surface such that an incident ray is reflected at many angles rather than at just one angle as in the case of specular reflection. An illuminated ideal diffuse reflecting surface will have equal luminance from all directions which lie in the half-space adjacent to the surface (Lambertian reflectance).

A surface built from a non-absorbing powder such as plaster, or from fibers such as paper, or from a polycrystalline material such as white marble, reflects light diffusely with great efficiency.

a. Bahtinov mask
b. Bandwidth-limited pulse
c. Diffuse reflection
d. Beam divergence

4. . An _________(s) is characterized by visually perceived images that differ from objective reality. The information gathered by the eye is processed in the brain to give a perception that does not tally with a physical measurement of the stimulus source. There are three main types: literal _________ that create images that are different from the objects that make them, physiological ones that are the effects on the eyes and brain of excessive stimulation of a specific type (brightness, colour, size, position, tilt, movement), and cognitive illusions, the result of unconscious inferences.

a. Optical illusions
b. Cell Transmission Model
c. Centrode

22. LIGHT: GEOMETRIC OPTICS

5. _________ is the change in direction of a wavefront at an interface between two different media so that the wavefront returns into the medium from which it originated. Common examples include the _________ of light, sound and water waves. The law of _________ says that for specular _________ the angle at which the wave is incident on the surface equals the angle at which it is reflected.

   a. Cardinal point
   b. Reflection
   c. Chromatic aberration
   d. Circle of confusion

ANSWER KEY
22. LIGHT: GEOMETRIC OPTICS

1. d
2. d
3. c
4. a
5. b

---

23. THE WAVE NATURE OF LIGHT

CHAPTER OUTLINE: KEY TERMS, PEOPLE, PLACES, CONCEPTS

Soap bubble

Diffraction

Refraction

Speed of light

Particle

Velocity

Double-slit experiment

Mirage

Optical illusions

Interference

Monochromatic

Plane wave

Wavelength

Coherence

Electromagnetic spectrum

Visible spectrum

Electromagnetic

Visible light

PRISM

Rainbow

Dispersion

23. THE WAVE NATURE OF LIGHT

CHAPTER OUTLINE: KEY TERMS, PEOPLE, PLACES, CONCEPTS

- Infrared
- Fresnel
- Intensity
- Diffraction grating
- Grating
- Spectrum
- Continuous spectrum
- Absorption
- Spectrometer
- Thin-film interference
- Thin film
- Air gap
- Optical coating
- Optical instrument
- Beam splitter
- Interferometer
- Polaroid
- Polarizer
- Polarization
- Reflection
- Liquid crystal

23. THE WAVE NATURE OF LIGHT

CHAPTER OUTLINE: KEY TERMS, PEOPLE, PLACES, CONCEPTS

______________	Pixel
______________	Laser

CHAPTER HIGHLIGHTS & NOTES: KEY TERMS, PEOPLE, PLACES, CONCEPTS

Soap bubble	A soap bubble is an extremely thin film of soapy water enclosing air that forms a hollow sphere with an iridescent surface. Soap bubbles usually last for only a few seconds before bursting, either on their own or on contact with another object. They are often used for children's enjoyment, but they are also used in artistic performances.
Diffraction	Diffraction refers to various phenomena which occur when a wave encounters an obstacle. In classical physics, the diffraction phenomenon is described as the apparent bending of waves around small obstacles and the spreading out of waves past small openings. Similar effects occur when a light wave travels through a medium with a varying refractive index, or a sound wave travels through one with varying acoustic impedance.
Refraction	Refraction is the change in direction of a wave due to a change in its transmission medium. Refraction is essentially a surface phenomenon. The phenomenon is mainly in governance to the law of conservation of energy and momentum.
Speed of light	The speed of light in vacuum, commonly denoted c, is a universal physical constant important in many areas of physics. Its value is exactly 299,792,458 metres per second, a figure that is exact because the length of the metre is defined from this constant and the international standard for time. This is approximately 186,282.4 miles per second, or about 671 million miles per hour.
Particle	In the physical sciences, a particle is a small localized object to which can be ascribed several physical or chemical properties such as volume or mass. The word is rather general in meaning, and is refined as needed by various scientific fields. Something that is composed of particles may be referred to as particulate, although this term is generally used to refer to a suspension of unconnected particles, rather than a connected particle aggregation.
Velocity	Velocity is the rate of change of the position of an object, equivalent to a specification of its speed and direction of motion, e.g. 60 km/h to the north. Velocity is an important concept in kinematics, the branch of classical mechanics which describes the motion of bodies.

23. THE WAVE NATURE OF LIGHT

CHAPTER HIGHLIGHTS & NOTES: KEY TERMS, PEOPLE, PLACES, CONCEPTS

Double-slit experiment	The double-slit experiment, sometimes called Young's experiment, is a demonstration that matter and energy can display characteristics of both classically defined waves and particles, and demonstrates the fundamentally probabilistic nature of quantum mechanical phenomena. In the basic version of this experiment, a coherent light source such as a laser beam illuminates a plate pierced by two parallel slits, and the light passing through the slits is observed on a screen behind the plate. The wave nature of light causes the light waves passing through the two slits to interfere, producing bright and dark bands on the screen--a result that would not be expected if light consisted of classical particles (i.e., small chunks of matter).
Mirage	A mirage is a naturally occurring optical phenomenon in which light rays are bent to produce a displaced image of distant objects or the sky. The word comes to English via the French mirage, from the Latin mirari, meaning 'to look at, to wonder at'. This is the same root as for 'mirror' and 'to admire'.
Optical illusions	An optical illusion is characterized by visually perceived images that differ from objective reality. The information gathered by the eye is processed in the brain to give a perception that does not tally with a physical measurement of the stimulus source. There are three main types: literal optical illusions that create images that are different from the objects that make them, physiological ones that are the effects on the eyes and brain of excessive stimulation of a specific type (brightness, colour, size, position, tilt, movement), and cognitive illusions, the result of unconscious inferences.
Interference	In physics, interference is a phenomenon in which two waves superimpose to form a resultant wave of greater or lower amplitude. Interference usually refers to the interaction of waves that are correlated or coherent with each other, either because they come from the same source or because they have the same or nearly the same frequency. Interference effects can be observed with all types of waves, for example, light, radio, acoustic and surface water waves.
Monochromatic	Monochrome describes paintings, drawings, design, or photographs in one color or shades of one color. A monochromatic object or image has colors in shades of limited colors or hues. Images using only shades of grey (with or without black and/or white) are called grayscale or black-and-white.
Plane wave	In the physics of wave propagation, a plane wave is a constant-frequency wave whose wavefronts (surfaces of constant phase) are infinite parallel planes of constant peak-to-peak amplitude normal to the phase velocity vector. It is not possible in practice to have a true plane wave; only a plane wave of infinite extent will propagate as a plane wave. However, many waves are approximately plane waves in a localized region of space.

23. THE WAVE NATURE OF LIGHT

CHAPTER HIGHLIGHTS & NOTES: KEY TERMS, PEOPLE, PLACES, CONCEPTS

Wavelength

In physics, the wavelength of a sinusoidal wave is the spatial period of the wave--the distance over which the wave's shape repeats. It is usually determined by considering the distance between consecutive corresponding points of the same phase, such as crests, troughs, or zero crossings, and is a characteristic of both traveling waves and standing waves, as well as other spatial wave patterns. Wavelength is commonly designated by the Greek letter lambda (?).

Coherence

In physics, coherence is an ideal property of waves that enables stationary interference. It contains several distinct concepts, which are limit cases that never occur in reality but allow an understanding of the physics of waves, and has become a very important concept in quantum physics. More generally, coherence describes all properties of the correlation between physical quantities of a single wave, or between several waves or wave packets.

Electromagnetic spectrum

The electromagnetic spectrum is the range of all possible frequencies of electromagnetic radiation. The 'electromagnetic spectrum' of an object has a different meaning, and is instead the characteristic distribution of electromagnetic radiation emitted or absorbed by that particular object.

The electromagnetic spectrum extends from below the low frequencies used for modern radio communication to gamma radiation at the short-wavelength (high-frequency) end, thereby covering wavelengths from thousands of kilometers down to a fraction of the size of an atom.

Visible spectrum

The visible spectrum is the portion of the electromagnetic spectrum that is visible to the human eye. Electromagnetic radiation in this range of wavelengths is called visible light or simply light. A typical human eye will respond to wavelengths from about 390 to 700 nm.

Electromagnetic

Electromagnetic is a prefix used to specialise many technical terms that involve electromagnetism.

Visible light

Visible light is electromagnetic radiation that is visible to the human eye, and is responsible for the sense of sight. Visible light is usually defined as having a wavelength in the range of 400 nanometres (nm), or 400×10^{-9} m, to 700 nanometres - between the infrared, with longer wavelengths and the ultraviolet, with shorter wavelengths. These numbers do not represent the absolute limits of human vision, but the approximate range within which most people can see reasonably well under most circumstances.

PRISM

PRISM is the name of a nuclear power plant design by GE Hitachi Nuclear Energy .

The S-PRISM represents GEH's Generation IV reactor solution to closing the nuclear fuel cycle and is also part of its Advanced Recycling Center (ARC) proposition to U.S. Congress to deal with nuclear waste.

It is based on a sodium-cooled fast breeder reactor called integral fast reactor.

23. THE WAVE NATURE OF LIGHT

CHAPTER HIGHLIGHTS & NOTES: KEY TERMS, PEOPLE, PLACES, CONCEPTS

Rainbow	A rainbow is an optical and meteorological phenomenon that is caused by both reflection and refraction of light in water droplets in the Earth's atmosphere, resulting in a spectrum of light appearing in the sky. It takes the form of a multicoloured arc. Rainbows caused by sunlight always appear in the section of sky directly opposite the sun.
Dispersion	In fluid dynamics, dispersion of water waves generally refers to frequency dispersion, which means that waves of different wavelengths travel at different phase speeds. Water waves, in this context, are waves propagating on the water surface, and forced by gravity and surface tension. As a result, water with a free surface is generally considered to be a dispersive medium.
Infrared	Infrared light is electromagnetic radiation with longer wavelengths than those of visible light, extending from the nominal red edge of the visible spectrum at 700 nanometres (nm) to 1 mm. This range of wavelengths corresponds to a frequency range of approximately 430 THz down to 300 GHz. Most of the thermal radiation emitted by objects near room temperature is infrared.
Fresnel	A Fresnel is a unit of frequency equal to 10^{12} s^{-1}. It was occasionally used in the field of spectroscopy, but its use has been superseded by terahertz (with the identical value 10^{12} hertz).
Intensity	In physics, intensity is the power transferred per unit area. In the SI system, it has units watts per metre squared (W/m^2). It is used most frequently with waves (e.g. sound or light), in which case the average power transfer over one period of the wave is used.
Diffraction grating	In optics, a diffraction grating is an optical component with a periodic structure, which splits and diffracts light into several beams travelling in different directions. The directions of these beams depend on the spacing of the grating and the wavelength of the light so that the grating acts as the dispersive element. Because of this, gratings are commonly used in monochromators and spectrometers.
Grating	A grating is any regularly spaced collection of essentially identical, parallel, elongated elements. Gratings usually consist of a single set of elongated elements, but can consist of two sets, in which case the second set is usually perpendicular to the first (as Illustrated). When the two sets are perpendicular, this is also known as a grid or a mesh.
Spectrum	A spectrum is a condition that is not limited to a specific set of values but can vary infinitely within a continuum. The word was first used scientifically within the field of optics to describe the rainbow of colors in visible light when separated using a prism; it has since been applied by analogy to many fields other than optics. Thus, one might talk about the spectrum of political opinion, or the spectrum of activity of a drug, or the autism spectrum.
Continuous spectrum	In physics, a continuous spectrum usually means a set of values for some physical quantity that is best described as an interval of real numbers.

It is opposed to discrete spectrum, a set of values that is discrete in the mathematical sense, where there is a positive gap between each value and the next one.

The classical example of a continuous spectrum, from which the name is derived, is the part of the spectrum of the light emitted by excited atoms of hydrogen that is due to free electrons becoming bound to an hydrogen ion, which is smoothly spread over a wide range of wavelengths; in contrast to the discrete lines due to electrons falling from some bound quantum state to a state of lower energy.

Absorption

Acoustic absorption refers to a material, structure or object absorbing sound energy when sound waves collide with it, as opposed to reflecting the energy. Part of the absorbed energy is transformed into heat and part is transmitted. The energy transformed into heat is said to have been 'lost'.When sound from a loudspeaker collides with the walls of a room part of the sound's energy is reflected and part is absorbed into the walls.

Spectrometer

A spectrometer is an instrument used to measure properties of light over a specific portion of the electromagnetic spectrum, typically used in spectroscopic analysis to identify materials. The variable measured is most often the light's intensity but could also, for instance, be the polarization state. The independent variable is usually the wavelength of the light or a unit directly proportional to the photon energy, such as wavenumber or electron volts, which has a reciprocal relationship to wavelength.

Thin-film interference

Thin-film interference is the phenomenon that occurs when incident light waves reflected by the upper and lower boundaries of a thin film interfere with one another to form a new wave. Studying this new wave can reveal information about the surfaces from which its components reflected, including the thickness of the film or the effective refractive index of the film medium. Thin films have many commercial applications including anti-reflection coatings, mirrors, and optical filters.

Thin film

A thin film is a layer of material ranging from fractions of a nanometer to several micrometers in thickness. Electronic semiconductor devices and optical coatings are the main applications benefiting from thin-film construction.

A familiar application of thin films is the household mirror, which typically has a thin metal coating on the back of a sheet of glass to form a reflective interface.

Air gap

An air gap, as it relates to the plumbing trade, is the unobstructed vertical space between the water outlet and the flood level of a fixture.

A simple example is the space between a wall mounted faucet and the sink rim (this space is the air gap). Water can easily flow from the faucet into the sink, but there is no way that water can flow from the sink into the faucet without modifying the system.

23. THE WAVE NATURE OF LIGHT

CHAPTER HIGHLIGHTS & NOTES: KEY TERMS, PEOPLE, PLACES, CONCEPTS

Optical coating	An optical coating is one or more thin layers of material deposited on an optical component such as a lens or mirror, which alters the way in which the optic reflects and transmits light. One type of optical coating is an antireflection coating, which reduces unwanted reflections from surfaces, and is commonly used on spectacle and photographic lenses. Another type is the high-reflector coating which can be used to produce mirrors which reflect greater than 99.99% of the light which falls on them.
Optical instrument	An optical instrument either processes light waves to enhance an image for viewing, or analyzes light waves to determine one of a number of characteristic properties.
Beam splitter	A beam splitter is an optical device that splits a beam of light in two. It is the crucial part of most interferometers. In its most common form, a cube, it is made from two triangular glass prisms which are glued together at their base using polyester, epoxy, or urethane-based adhesives.
Interferometer	Interferometry is a family of techniques in which waves, usually electromagnetic, are superimposed in order to extract information about the waves. Interferometry is an important investigative technique in the fields of astronomy, fiber optics, engineering metrology, optical metrology, oceanography, seismology, spectroscopy (and its applications to chemistry), quantum mechanics, nuclear and particle physics, plasma physics, remote sensing, biomolecular interactions, surface profiling, microfluidics, mechanical stress/strain measurement, and velocimetry. Interferometers are widely used in science and industry for the measurement of small displacements, refractive index changes and surface irregularities.
Polaroid	Polaroid is the trademark for a type of synthetic plastic sheet which is used as a polarizer or polarizing filter, made by Polaroid Corporation.
Polarizer	A polarizer or polariser is an optical filter that passes light of a specific polarization and blocks waves of other polarizations. It can convert a beam of light of undefined or mixed polarization into a beam with well-defined polarization. The common types of polarizers are linear polarizers and circular polarizers.
Polarization	In electrochemistry, polarization is an effect that counteracts and lowers the efficiency of electrochemical processes. The mechanism is typically depletion of reagents causing concentration gradients in boundary layers or the formation of compounds partly passivating the electrode surfaces and having the effect (depending on conditions) of decreasing the output voltage of batteries, increasing the voltage required by electrolysis cells or lowering currents. It is a type of kinetic deviation from equilibrium conditions.

23. THE WAVE NATURE OF LIGHT

CHAPTER HIGHLIGHTS & NOTES: KEY TERMS, PEOPLE, PLACES, CONCEPTS

Reflection

Reflection is the change in direction of a wavefront at an interface between two different media so that the wavefront returns into the medium from which it originated. Common examples include the reflection of light, sound and water waves. The law of reflection says that for specular reflection the angle at which the wave is incident on the surface equals the angle at which it is reflected.

Liquid crystal

Liquid crystals are matter in a state that has properties between those of conventional liquid and those of solid crystal. For instance, a liquid crystal may flow like a liquid, but its molecules may be oriented in a crystal-like way. There are many different types of liquid-crystal phases, which can be distinguished by their different optical properties (such as birefringence).

Pixel

In digital imaging, a pixel, or pel, is a physical point in a raster image, or the smallest addressable element in a display device; so it is the smallest controllable element of a picture represented on the screen. The address of a pixel corresponds to its physical coordinates. LCD pixels are manufactured in a two-dimensional grid, and are often represented using dots or squares, but CRT pixels correspond to their timing mechanisms and sweep rates.

Laser

A laser is a device that emits light through a process of optical amplification based on the stimulated emission of electromagnetic radiation. The term 'laser' originated as an acronym for Light Amplification by Stimulated Emission of Radiation. Lasers differ from other sources of light because they emit light coherently.

CHAPTER QUIZ: KEY TERMS, PEOPLE, PLACES, CONCEPTS

1. An _________ either processes light waves to enhance an image for viewing, or analyzes light waves to determine one of a number of characteristic properties.

   a. Optical instrument
   b. Beam splitter
   c. Binoviewer
   d. Blazed grating

2. . The _________ is the portion of the electromagnetic spectrum that is visible to the human eye. Electromagnetic radiation in this range of wavelengths is called visible light or simply light. A typical human eye will respond to wavelengths from about 390 to 700 nm.

   a. Visible spectrum
   b. Gamma ray
   c. Microwave

3. In fluid dynamics, _________ of water waves generally refers to frequency _________, which means that waves of different wavelengths travel at different phase speeds. Water waves, in this context, are waves propagating on the water surface, and forced by gravity and surface tension. As a result, water with a free surface is generally considered to be a dispersive medium.

   a. Baroclinity
   b. Barotropic fluid
   c. Basset force
   d. Dispersion

4. In physics, _________ is an ideal property of waves that enables stationary interference. It contains several distinct concepts, which are limit cases that never occur in reality but allow an understanding of the physics of waves, and has become a very important concept in quantum physics. More generally, _________ describes all properties of the correlation between physical quantities of a single wave, or between several waves or wave packets.

   a. 6-j symbol
   b. 9-j symbol
   c. Coherence
   d. Bloch sphere

5. A _________ is an instrument used to measure properties of light over a specific portion of the electromagnetic spectrum, typically used in spectroscopic analysis to identify materials. The variable measured is most often the light's intensity but could also, for instance, be the polarization state. The independent variable is usually the wavelength of the light or a unit directly proportional to the photon energy, such as wavenumber or electron volts, which has a reciprocal relationship to wavelength.

   a. Spectrometer
   b. Blueshift
   c. Collisional excitation
   d. Doppler spectroscopy

ANSWER KEY
23. THE WAVE NATURE OF LIGHT

1. a

2. a

3. d

4. c

5. a

---

24. OPTICAL INSTRUMENTS

CHAPTER OUTLINE: KEY TERMS, PEOPLE, PLACES, CONCEPTS

- Optical instrument
- CMOS
- Charge-coupled device
- Digital artifact
- Digital camera
- Pixel
- Film speed
- Shutter speed
- Circle of confusion
- Depth of field
- Lens
- Resolution
- Digital zoom
- Fovea
- Pupil
- Retina
- Eyeglasses
- Astigmatism
- Eyepiece
- Magnification
- Binoculars

24. OPTICAL INSTRUMENTS

CHAPTER OUTLINE: KEY TERMS, PEOPLE, PLACES, CONCEPTS

- Chromatic aberration
- Microscope
- Coma
- Spherical aberration
- Achromatic Lens
- Airy disk
- Radio wave
- Interference
- Crystallography
- X-ray crystallography
- Tomography
- Image formation

CHAPTER HIGHLIGHTS & NOTES: KEY TERMS, PEOPLE, PLACES, CONCEPTS

Optical instrument	An optical instrument either processes light waves to enhance an image for viewing, or analyzes light waves to determine one of a number of characteristic properties.
CMOS	Complementary metal-oxide-semiconductor (CMOS) is a technology for constructing integrated circuits. CMOS technology is used in microprocessors, microcontrollers, static RAM, and other digital logic circuits. CMOS technology is also used for several analog circuits such as image sensors (CMOS sensor), data converters, and highly integrated transceivers for many types of communication.

Charge-coupled device	A charge-coupled device is a device for the movement of electrical charge, usually from within the device to an area where the charge can be manipulated, for example conversion into a digital value. This is achieved by 'shifting' the signals between stages within the device one at a time. Charge coupled devices move charge between capacitive bins in the device, with the shift allowing for the transfer of charge between bins.
Digital artifact	A digital artifact is any undesired alteration in data introduced in a digital process by an involved technique and/or technology.
Digital camera	A digital camera is a camera that encodes digital images and videos digitally and stores them for later reproduction. Most cameras sold today are digital, and digital cameras are incorporated into many devices ranging from PDAs and mobile phones (called camera phones) to vehicles. Digital and film cameras share an optical system, typically using a lens with a variable diaphragm to focus light onto an image pickup device.
Pixel	In digital imaging, a pixel, or pel, is a physical point in a raster image, or the smallest addressable element in a display device; so it is the smallest controllable element of a picture represented on the screen. The address of a pixel corresponds to its physical coordinates. LCD pixels are manufactured in a two-dimensional grid, and are often represented using dots or squares, but CRT pixels correspond to their timing mechanisms and sweep rates.
Film speed	Film speed is the measure of a photographic film's sensitivity to light, determined by sensitometry and measured on various numerical scales, the most recent being the ISO system. A closely related ISO system is used to measure the sensitivity of digital imaging systems. Relatively insensitive film, with a correspondingly lower speed index requires more exposure to light to produce the same image density as a more sensitive film, and is thus commonly termed a slow film.
Shutter speed	In photography, shutter speed or exposure time is the length of time a camera's shutter is open when taking a photograph. The amount of light that reaches the film or image sensor is proportional to the exposure time.
Circle of confusion	In optics, a circle of confusion is an optical spot caused by a cone of light rays from a lens not coming to a perfect focus when imaging a point source. It is also known as disk of confusion, circle of indistinctness, blur circle, or blur spot. In photography, the circle of confusion is used to determine the depth of field, the part of an image that is acceptably sharp.

24. OPTICAL INSTRUMENTS

CHAPTER HIGHLIGHTS & NOTES: KEY TERMS, PEOPLE, PLACES, CONCEPTS

Depth of field	In optics, particularly as it relates to film and photography, depth of field is the distance between the nearest and farthest objects in a scene that appear acceptably sharp in an image. Although a lens can precisely focus at only one distance at a time, the decrease in sharpness is gradual on each side of the focused distance, so that within the Depth of field, the unsharpness is imperceptible under normal viewing conditions. In some cases, it may be desirable to have the entire image sharp, and a large Depth of field is appropriate.
Lens	A lens is an optical device which transmits and refracts light, converging or diverging the beam. A simple lens consists of a single optical element. A compound lens is an array of simple lenses (elements) with a common axis; the use of multiple elements allows more optical aberrations to be corrected than is possible with a single element.
Resolution	Resolution in terms of electron density is a measure of the resolvability in the electron density map of a molecule. In X-ray crystallography, resolution is the highest resolvable peak in the diffraction pattern. While cryo-electron microscopy is a frequency space comparison of two halves of the data, which strives to correlate with the X-ray definition.
Digital zoom	Digital zoom is a method of decreasing the apparent angle of view of a digital photographic or video image, quality is reduced except for optical zoom. Digital zoom is accomplished by cropping an image down to a centered area with the same aspect ratio as the original, and usually also interpolating the result back up to the pixel dimensions of the original. It is accomplished electronically, with no adjustment of the camera's optics, and no optical resolution is gained in the process.
Fovea	The fovea centralis, also generally known as the fovea is a part of the eye, located in the center of the macula region of the retina. The fovea is responsible for sharp central vision (also called foveal vision), which is necessary in humans for reading, driving, and any activity where visual detail is of primary importance. The fovea is surrounded by the parafovea belt, and the perifovea outer region.
Pupil	The pupil is a hole located in the center of the iris of the eye that allows light to enter the retina. It appears black because light rays entering the pupil are either absorbed by the tissues inside the eye directly, or absorbed after diffuse reflections within the eye that mostly miss exiting the narrow pupil. In humans the pupil is round, but other species, such as some cats, have vertical slit pupils, goats have horizontally oriented pupils, and some catfish have annular types.
Retina	Retina can also refer to the Kodak Retina camera and the Apple Retina Display. The vertebrate retina is a light-sensitive layer of tissue, lining the inner surface of the eye.

Eyeglasses	Glasses, also known as eyeglasses or spectacles, are frames bearing lenses worn in front of the eyes. They are normally used for vision correction or eye protection. Safety glasses are a kind of eye protection against flying debris or against visible and near visible light or radiation.
Astigmatism	An optical system with astigmatism is one where rays that propagate in two perpendicular planes have different foci. If an optical system with astigmatism is used to form an image of a cross, the vertical and horizontal lines will be in sharp focus at two different distances. The term comes from the Greek a- (a-) meaning 'without' and st??μa (stigma), 'a mark, spot, puncture'.
Eyepiece	An eyepiece, or ocular lens, is a type of lens that is attached to a variety of optical devices such as telescopes and microscopes. It is so named because it is usually the lens that is closest to the eye when someone looks through the device. The objective lens or mirror collects light and brings it to focus creating an image.
Magnification	Magnification is the process of enlarging something only in appearance, not in physical size. This enlargement is quantified by a calculated number also called 'magnification'. When this number is less than one it refers to a reduction in size, sometimes called 'minification' or 'de-magnification'.
Binoculars	Binoculars, field glasses or binocular telescopes are a pair of identical or mirror-symmetrical telescopes mounted side-by-side and aligned to point accurately in the same direction, allowing the viewer to use both eyes when viewing distant objects. Most are sized to be held using both hands, although sizes vary widely from opera glasses to large pedestal mounted military models. Many different abbreviations are used for binoculars, including glasses, nocs, binocs, noculars, binos and bins.
Chromatic aberration	In optics, chromatic aberration is a type of distortion in which there is a failure of a lens to focus all colors to the same convergence point. It occurs because lenses have a different refractive index for different wavelengths of light (the dispersion of the lens). The refractive index decreases with increasing wavelength.
Microscope	A microscope is an instrument used to see objects that are too small for the naked eye. The science of investigating small objects using such an instrument is called microscopy. Microscopic means invisible to the eye unless aided by a microscope.
Coma	In optics, the coma in an optical system refers to aberration inherent to certain optical designs or due to imperfection in the lens or other components that results in off-axis point sources such as stars appearing distorted, appearing to have a tail (coma) like a comet. Specifically, coma is defined as a variation in magnification over the entrance pupil. In refractive or diffractive optical systems, especially those imaging a wide spectral range, coma can be a function of wavelength, in which case it is a form of chromatic aberration.

24. OPTICAL INSTRUMENTS

CHAPTER HIGHLIGHTS & NOTES: KEY TERMS, PEOPLE, PLACES, CONCEPTS

Spherical aberration	Spherical aberration is an optical effect observed in an optical device that occurs due to the increased refraction of light rays when they strike a lens or a reflection of light rays when they strike a mirror near its edge, in comparison with those that strike nearer the centre. It signifies a deviation of the device from the norm, i.e., it results in an imperfection of the produced image. A spherical lens has an aplanatic point (i.e., no spherical aberration) only at a radius that equals the radius of the sphere divided by the index of refraction of the lens material.
Achromatic Lens	An achromatic lens or achromat is a lens that is designed to limit the effects of chromatic and spherical aberration. Achromatic lenses are corrected to bring two wavelengths (typically red and blue) into focus in the same plane. The most common type of achromat is the achromatic doublet, which is composed of two individual lenses made from glasses with different amounts of dispersion.
Airy disk	In optics, the Airy disk and Airy pattern are descriptions of the best focused spot of light that a perfect lens with a circular aperture can make, limited by the diffraction of light. The diffraction pattern resulting from a uniformly-illuminated circular aperture has a bright region in the center, known as the Airy disk which together with the series of concentric bright rings around is called the Airy pattern. Both are named after George Biddell Airy.
Radio wave	Radio waves are a type of electromagnetic radiation with wavelengths in the electromagnetic spectrum longer than infrared light. Radio waves have frequencies from 300 GHz to as low as 3 kHz, and corresponding wavelengths ranging from 1 millimeter (0.039 in) to 100 kilometers (62 mi). Like all other electromagnetic waves, they travel at the speed of light.
Interference	In physics, interference is a phenomenon in which two waves superimpose to form a resultant wave of greater or lower amplitude. Interference usually refers to the interaction of waves that are correlated or coherent with each other, either because they come from the same source or because they have the same or nearly the same frequency. Interference effects can be observed with all types of waves, for example, light, radio, acoustic and surface water waves.
Crystallography	Crystallography is the science that examines the arrangement of atoms in solids. The word 'crystallography' derives from the Greek words crystallon = cold drop / frozen drop, with its meaning extending to all solids with some degree of transparency, and grapho = write. A more comprehensive definition is: 'Crystallography is the science of condensed matter with emphasis on the atomic or molecular structure and its relation to physical and chemical properties.' Before the development of X-ray diffraction crystallography, the study of crystals was based on their geometry.

CHAPTER HIGHLIGHTS & NOTES: KEY TERMS, PEOPLE, PLACES, CONCEPTS

X-ray crystallography	X-ray crystallography is a method used for determining the atomic and molecular structure of a crystal, in which the crystalline atoms cause a beam of X-rays to diffract into many specific directions. By measuring the angles and intensities of these diffracted beams, a crystallographer can produce a three-dimensional picture of the density of electrons within the crystal. From this electron density, the mean positions of the atoms in the crystal can be determined, as well as their chemical bonds, their disorder and various other information.
Tomography	Tomography refers to imaging by sections or sectioning, through the use of any kind of penetrating wave. A device used in tomography is called a tomograph, while the image produced is a tomogram. Tomography as the computed tomographic (CT) scanner was invented by Sir Godfrey Hounsfield, and thereby made an exceptional contribution to medicine.
Image formation	The study of image formation encompasses the radiometric and geometric processes by which 2D images of 3D objects are formed. In the case of digital images, the image formation process also includes analog to digital conversion and sampling. Image Formation in Eye The principal difference between the lens of the eye and an ordinary optical lens is that the former is flexible.

CHAPTER QUIZ: KEY TERMS, PEOPLE, PLACES, CONCEPTS

1. A _________ is an instrument used to see objects that are too small for the naked eye. The science of investigating small objects using such an instrument is called microscopy. Microscopic means invisible to the eye unless aided by a _________.

   a. Microscope
   b. Bitplane
   c. Bright-field microscopy
   d. CellCognition

2. . An _________ either processes light waves to enhance an image for viewing, or analyzes light waves to determine one of a number of characteristic properties.

   a. Beam dump
   b. Beam splitter
   c. Binoviewer

3. In optics, a _________ is an optical spot caused by a cone of light rays from a lens not coming to a perfect focus when imaging a point source. It is also known as disk of confusion, circle of indistinctness, blur circle, or blur spot.

   In photography, the _________ is used to determine the depth of field, the part of an image that is acceptably sharp.

   a. Cardinal point
   b. Caustic
   c. Chromatic aberration
   d. Circle of confusion

4. An optical system with _________ is one where rays that propagate in two perpendicular planes have different foci. If an optical system with _________ is used to form an image of a cross, the vertical and horizontal lines will be in sharp focus at two different distances. The term comes from the Greek a- (a-) meaning 'without' and st??μa (stigma), 'a mark, spot, puncture'.

   a. Bifluoride
   b. Astigmatism
   c. Bisulfide
   d. Borohydride

5. _________, field glasses or _________(s) telescopes are a pair of identical or mirror-symmetrical telescopes mounted side-by-side and aligned to point accurately in the same direction, allowing the viewer to use both eyes when viewing distant objects. Most are sized to be held using both hands, although sizes vary widely from opera glasses to large pedestal mounted military models. Many different abbreviations are used for _________, including glasses, nocs, binocs, noculars, binos and bins.

   a. Beam dump
   b. Binoculars
   c. Bifluoride
   d. Bismuthide

ANSWER KEY
24. OPTICAL INSTRUMENTS

1. a
2. d
3. d
4. b
5. b

---

25. THE SPECIAL THEORY OF RELATIVITY

CHAPTER OUTLINE: KEY TERMS, PEOPLE, PLACES, CONCEPTS

- Special theory of relativity
- Interferometer
- Null result
- Speed of light
- Velocity
- Event
- Relative velocity
- Thought experiment
- Time dilation
- Elementary particle
- Proper time
- Twin paradox
- Length contraction
- Proper length
- Momentum
- Kinetics
- Kinetic energy
- Fermilab
- Proton
- Tevatron
- Correspondence principle

25. THE SPECIAL THEORY OF RELATIVITY

CHAPTER OUTLINE: KEY TERMS, PEOPLE, PLACES, CONCEPTS

______________ | Binding energy

CHAPTER HIGHLIGHTS & NOTES: KEY TERMS, PEOPLE, PLACES, CONCEPTS

Special theory of relativity	In physics, special relativity (SR, also known as the special theory of relativity or STR) is the accepted physical theory regarding the relationship between space and time. It is based on two postulates: (1) that the laws of physics are invariant (i.e., identical) in all inertial systems (non-accelerating frames of reference); and (2) that the speed of light in a vacuum is the same for all observers, regardless of the motion of the light source. It was originally proposed in 1905 by Albert Einstein in the paper 'On the Electrodynamics of Moving Bodies'.
Interferometer	Interferometry is a family of techniques in which waves, usually electromagnetic, are superimposed in order to extract information about the waves. Interferometry is an important investigative technique in the fields of astronomy, fiber optics, engineering metrology, optical metrology, oceanography, seismology, spectroscopy (and its applications to chemistry), quantum mechanics, nuclear and particle physics, plasma physics, remote sensing, biomolecular interactions, surface profiling, microfluidics, mechanical stress/strain measurement, and velocimetry. Interferometers are widely used in science and industry for the measurement of small displacements, refractive index changes and surface irregularities.
Null result	In science, a null result is a result without the expected content: that is, the proposed result is absent. It is an experimental outcome which does not show an otherwise expected effect. This does not imply a result of zero or nothing, simply a result that does not support the hypothesis.
Speed of light	The speed of light in vacuum, commonly denoted c, is a universal physical constant important in many areas of physics. Its value is exactly 299,792,458 metres per second, a figure that is exact because the length of the metre is defined from this constant and the international standard for time. This is approximately 186,282.4 miles per second, or about 671 million miles per hour.
Velocity	Velocity is the rate of change of the position of an object, equivalent to a specification of its speed and direction of motion, e.g. 60 km/h to the north. Velocity is an important concept in kinematics, the branch of classical mechanics which describes the motion of bodies. Velocity is a vector physical quantity; both magnitude and direction are required to define it.

Event

In computer science, an event is a type of synchronization mechanism that is used to indicate to waiting processes when a particular condition has become true.

An event is an abstract data type with a boolean state and the following operations:•wait - when executed, causes the executing process to suspend until the event's state is set to true. If the state is already set to true has no effect.•set - sets the event's state to true, release all waiting processes.•clear - sets the event's state to false.

Different implementations of events may provide different subsets of these possible operations; for example, the implementation provided by Microsoft Windows provides the operations wait (WaitForObject and related functions), set (SetEvent), and clear (ResetEvent).

Relative velocity

The relative velocity $\vec{v}_{\mathrm{BA}}$ is the velocity of an object or observer B in the rest frame of another object or observer A, if it is constant, $\vec{v}_{\mathrm{BA}} = -\vec{v}_{\mathrm{AB}}$

where $\vec{v}_{\mathrm{AB}}$ is A's velocity in the rest frame of B.

Thought experiment

A thought experiment or Gedankenexperiment considers some hypothesis, theory, or principle for the purpose of thinking through its consequences. Given the structure of the experiment, it may or may not be possible to actually perform it, and, in the case that it is possible for it to be performed, there need be no intention of any kind to actually perform the experiment in question. The common goal of a thought experiment is to explore the potential consequences of the principle in question.

Time dilation

In the theory of relativity, time dilation is an actual difference of elapsed time between two events as measured by observers either moving relative to each other or differently situated from gravitational masses.

An accurate clock at rest with respect to one observer may be measured to tick at a different rate when compared to a second observer's own equally accurate clocks. This effect arises neither from technical aspects of the clocks nor from the fact that signals need time to propagate, but from the nature of spacetime itself.

Elementary particle

In particle physics, an elementary particle or fundamental particle is a particle whose substructure is unknown, thus it is not known to be composed of other particles. Known elementary particles include the fundamental fermions (quarks, leptons, antiquarks, and antileptons), which generally are 'matter particles' and 'antimatter particles', as well as the fundamental bosons (gauge bosons and Higgs boson), which generally are 'force particles' that mediate interactions among fermions. A particle containing two or more elementary particles is a composite particle.

Proper time

In relativity, proper time is the elapsed time between two events as measured by a clock that passes through both events.

The proper time depends not only on the events but also on the motion of the clock between the events. An accelerated clock will measure a smaller elapsed time between two events than that measured by a non-accelerated (inertial) clock between the same two events.

Twin paradox

In physics, the twin paradox is a thought experiment in special relativity involving identical twins, one of whom makes a journey into space in a high-speed rocket and returns home to find that the twin who remained on Earth has aged more. This result appears puzzling because each twin sees the other twin as traveling, and so, according to an incorrect naive application of time dilation, each should paradoxically find the other to have aged more slowly. However, this scenario can be resolved within the standard framework of special relativity (because the twins are not equivalent; the space twin experienced additional, asymmetrical acceleration when switching direction to return home), and therefore is not a paradox in the sense of a logical contradiction.

Length contraction

In physics, length contraction is the phenomenon of a decrease in length measured by an observer of objects which are traveling at any non-zero velocity relative to the observer. This contraction, the contracted length is 99.9% of the length at rest; at a speed of 42,300,000 m/s, the length is still 99%. As the magnitude of the velocity approaches the speed of light, the effect becomes dominant, as can be seen from the formula:

$$L = \frac{L_0}{\gamma(v)} = L_0\sqrt{1 - v^2/c^2}$$

whereL₀ is the proper length (the length of the object in its rest frame),L is the length observed by an observer in relative motion with respect to the object,v is the relative velocity between the observer and the moving object,c is the speed of light,

and the Lorentz factor, ?(v), is defined as

$$\gamma(v) \equiv \frac{1}{\sqrt{1 - v^2/c^2}}.$$

In this equation it is assumed that the object is parallel with its line of movement.

Proper length

In relativistic physics, proper distance is an invariant measure of the distance between two spacelike-separated events, or of the length of a spacelike path within a spacetime. In contrast, proper length or rest length refer to the length of an object in the object's rest frame, which is not necessarily the same as the proper distance between two events.

The measurement of lengths is more complicated in the theory of relativity than in classical mechanics.

Momentum

In classical mechanics, linear momentum or translational momentum is the product of the mass and velocity of an object.

For example, a heavy truck moving fast has a large momentum--it takes a large and prolonged force to get the truck up to this speed, and it takes a large and prolonged force to bring it to a stop afterwards. If the truck were lighter, or moving more slowly, then it would have less momentum.

Kinetics

In physics and engineering, kinetics is a term for the branch of classical mechanics that is concerned with the relationship between the motion of bodies and its causes, namely forces and torques. Since the mid-20th century, the term 'dynamics' (or 'analytical dynamics') has largely superseded 'kinetics' in physics text books; the term 'kinetics' is still used in engineering.

In mechanics, the Kinetics is deduced from Kinematics by the introduction of the concept of mass.

Kinetic energy

In physics, the kinetic energy of an object is the energy which it possesses due to its motion. It is defined as the work needed to accelerate a body of a given mass from rest to its stated velocity. Having gained this energy during its acceleration, the body maintains this kinetic energy unless its speed changes.

Fermilab

Fermi National Accelerator Laboratory (Fermilab), located just outside Batavia, Illinois, near Chicago, is a US Department of Energy national laboratory specializing in high-energy particle physics. As of January 1, 2007, Fermilab is operated by the Fermi Research Alliance, a joint venture of the University of Chicago, Illinois Institute of Technology and the Universities Research Association (URA). Fermilab is a part of the Illinois Technology and Research Corridor.

Proton

The proton is a subatomic particle with the symbol p or p+ and a positive electric charge of 1 elementary charge. One or more protons are present in the nucleus of each atom. The number of protons in each atom is its atomic number.

Tevatron

The Tevatron was a circular particle accelerator in the United States, at the Fermi National Accelerator Laboratory, just east of Batavia, Illinois, and holds the title of the second highest energy particle collider in the world after the Large Hadron Collider (LHC) near Geneva, Switzerland. The Tevatron was a synchrotron that accelerated protons and antiprotons in a 6.86 km, or 4.26 mi, ring to energies of up to 1 TeV, hence its name. The Tevatron was completed in 1983 at a cost of $120 million and significant upgrade investments were made in 1983-2011.

Correspondence principle

In physics, the correspondence principle states that the behavior of systems described by the theory of quantum mechanics reproduces classical physics in the limit of large quantum numbers. In other words, it says that for large orbits and for large energies, quantum calculations must agree with classical calculations.

The principle was formulated by Niels Bohr in 1920, though he had previously made use of it as early as 1913 in developing his model of the atom.

25. THE SPECIAL THEORY OF RELATIVITY

CHAPTER HIGHLIGHTS & NOTES: KEY TERMS, PEOPLE, PLACES, CONCEPTS

Binding energy	Binding energy is the mechanical energy required to disassemble a whole entity into separate parts. A bound system typically has a lower potential energy than the sum of its constituent parts -- this is what keeps the system together. Often this means that energy is released upon the creation of a bound state.

CHAPTER QUIZ: KEY TERMS, PEOPLE, PLACES, CONCEPTS

1. The _________ $\vec{v}_{\mathrm{BA}}$ is the velocity of an object or observer B in the rest frame of another object or observer A, if it is constant, $\vec{v}_{\mathrm{BA}} = -\vec{v}_{\mathrm{AB}}$

   where $\vec{v}_{\mathrm{AB}}$ is A's velocity in the rest frame of B.

   a. Binet equation
   b. Bucket argument
   c. Center-of-momentum frame
   d. Relative velocity

2. In physics, the _________ states that the behavior of systems described by the theory of quantum mechanics reproduces classical physics in the limit of large quantum numbers. In other words, it says that for large orbits and for large energies, quantum calculations must agree with classical calculations.

   The principle was formulated by Niels Bohr in 1920, though he had previously made use of it as early as 1913 in developing his model of the atom.

   a. 6-j symbol
   b. 9-j symbol
   c. Bloch spectrum
   d. Correspondence principle

3. In science, a _________ is a result without the expected content: that is, the proposed result is absent. It is an experimental outcome which does not show an otherwise expected effect. This does not imply a result of zero or nothing, simply a result that does not support the hypothesis.

   a. Null result
   b. Black
   c. dev/null
   d. From the Acting to the Seeing

4. The _________ is a subatomic particle with the symbol p or p+ and a positive electric charge of 1 elementary charge. One or more _________s are present in the nucleus of each atom. The number of _________s in each atom is its atomic number.

   a. Nucleon
   b. Proton
   c. Panel edge staining
   d. Sibplaz

5. In physics, the _________ is a thought experiment in special relativity involving identical twins, one of whom makes a journey into space in a high-speed rocket and returns home to find that the twin who remained on Earth has aged more. This result appears puzzling because each twin sees the other twin as traveling, and so, according to an incorrect naive application of time dilation, each should paradoxically find the other to have aged more slowly. However, this scenario can be resolved within the standard framework of special relativity (because the twins are not equivalent; the space twin experienced additional, asymmetrical acceleration when switching direction to return home), and therefore is not a paradox in the sense of a logical contradiction.

   a. Twin paradox
   b. Cherenkov radiation
   c. Covariant formulation of classical electromagnetism
   d. Doubly special relativity

ANSWER KEY
25. THE SPECIAL THEORY OF RELATIVITY

---

1. d
2. d
3. a
4. b
5. a

---

26. EARLY QUANTUM THEORY AND MODELS OF THE ATOM

CHAPTER OUTLINE: KEY TERMS, PEOPLE, PLACES, CONCEPTS

	Electron microscope
	Electron
	Continuous spectrum
	Photon
	Quantum number
	Particle
	Quantization
	Conservation of energy
	Energy conservation
	Photoelectric effect
	Work function
	Light meter
	Photodiode
	Photosynthesis
	Momentum
	Compton wavelength
	Pair production
	Positron
	Matter wave
	De Broglie
	Electron diffraction

26. EARLY QUANTUM THEORY AND MODELS OF THE ATOM

CHAPTER OUTLINE: KEY TERMS, PEOPLE, PLACES, CONCEPTS

- Wavelength
- Magnetic lens
- Retina
- Magnification
- Microscope
- Alpha particle
- Atom
- Absorption
- Hydrogen
- Spectrum
- Balmer series
- Lyman series
- Rydberg constant
- Angular momentum
- Bohr model
- Principal quantum number
- Energy level
- Bohr radius
- Ionization energy
- Binding energy
- Ionization

26. EARLY QUANTUM THEORY AND MODELS OF THE ATOM

CHAPTER OUTLINE: KEY TERMS, PEOPLE, PLACES, CONCEPTS

______________	Spectral line
______________	Correspondence principle
______________	Quantum mechanics
______________	Big Bang theory

CHAPTER HIGHLIGHTS & NOTES: KEY TERMS, PEOPLE, PLACES, CONCEPTS

Electron microscope

An electron microscope is a type of microscope that uses an electron beam to illuminate a specimen and produce a magnified image.

An EM has greater resolving power than a light microscope and can reveal the structure of smaller objects because electrons have wavelengths about 100,000 times shorter than visible light photons. They can achieve better than 50 pm resolution and magnifications of up to about 10,000,000x whereas ordinary, non-confocal light microscopes are limited by diffraction to about 200 nm resolution and useful magnifications below 2000x.

Electron

The electron is a subatomic particle with a negative elementary electric charge. Electrons belong to the first generation of the lepton particle family, and are generally thought to be elementary particles because they have no known components or substructure. The electron has a mass that is approximately 1/1836 that of the proton.

Continuous spectrum

In physics, a continuous spectrum usually means a set of values for some physical quantity that is best described as an interval of real numbers. It is opposed to discrete spectrum, a set of values that is discrete in the mathematical sense, where there is a positive gap between each value and the next one.

The classical example of a continuous spectrum, from which the name is derived, is the part of the spectrum of the light emitted by excited atoms of hydrogen that is due to free electrons becoming bound to an hydrogen ion, which is smoothly spread over a wide range of wavelengths; in contrast to the discrete lines due to electrons falling from some bound quantum state to a state of lower energy.

Photon

A photon is an elementary particle, the quantum of light and all other forms of electromagnetic radiation, and the force carrier for the electromagnetic force, even when static via virtual photons.

The effects of this force are easily observable at both the microscopic and macroscopic level, because the photon has zero rest mass; this allows long distance interactions. Like all elementary particles, photons are currently best explained by quantum mechanics and exhibit wave-particle duality, exhibiting properties of both waves and particles.

Quantum number

Quantum numbers describe values of conserved quantities in the dynamics of a quantum system. Perhaps the most peculiar aspect of quantum mechanics is the quantization of observable quantities, since quantum numbers are discrete sets of integers or half-integers. This is distinguished from classical mechanics where the values can range continuously.

Particle

In the physical sciences, a particle is a small localized object to which can be ascribed several physical or chemical properties such as volume or mass. The word is rather general in meaning, and is refined as needed by various scientific fields. Something that is composed of particles may be referred to as particulate, although this term is generally used to refer to a suspension of unconnected particles, rather than a connected particle aggregation.

Quantization

In physics, quantization is the process of transition from a classical understanding of physical phenomena to a newer understanding known as 'quantum mechanics'. It is a procedure for constructing a quantum field theory starting from a classical field theory. This is a generalization of the procedure for building quantum mechanics from classical mechanics.

Conservation of energy

In physics, the law of conservation of energy states that the total energy of an isolated system cannot change--it is said to be conserved over time. Energy can be neither created nor destroyed, but can change form, for instance chemical energy can be converted to kinetic energy in the explosion of a stick of dynamite.

A consequence of the law of conservation of energy is that a perpetual motion machine of the first kind cannot exist.

Energy conservation

Energy conservation refers to reducing energy through using less of an energy service. Energy conservation differs from efficient energy use, which refers to using less energy for a constant service. For example, driving less is an example of energy conservation.

Photoelectric effect

In the photoelectric effect, electrons are emitted from solids, liquids or gases when they absorb energy from light. Electrons emitted in this manner may be called photoelectrons.

In 1887, Heinrich Hertz discovered that electrodes illuminated with ultraviolet light create electric sparks more easily.

Work function

In solid-state physics, the work function is the minimum thermodynamic work (i.e. energy) needed to remove an electron from a solid to a point in the vacuum immediately outside the solid surface.

Here 'immediately' means that the final electron position is far from the surface on the atomic scale, but still too close to the solid to be influenced by ambient electric fields in the vacuum. The work function is not a characteristic of a bulk material, but rather a property of the surface of the material (depending on crystal face and contamination).

Light meter

A light meter is a device used to measure the amount of light. In photography, a light meter is often used to determine the proper exposure for a photograph. Typically a light meter will include a computer, either digital or analog, which allows the photographer to determine which shutter speed and f-number should be selected for an optimum exposure, given a certain lighting situation and film speed.

Photodiode

A photodiode is a type of photodetector capable of converting light into either current or voltage, depending upon the mode of operation. The common, traditional solar cell used to generate electric solar power is a large area photodiode.

Photodiodes are similar to regular semiconductor diodes except that they may be either exposed (to detect vacuum UV or X-rays) or packaged with a window or optical fiber connection to allow light to reach the sensitive part of the device.

Photosynthesis

Photosynthesis is a process used by plants and other organisms to convert light energy, normally from the sun, into chemical energy that can be used to fuel the organisms' activities. Carbohydrates, such as sugars, are synthesized from carbon dioxide and water (hence the name photosynthesis, from the Greek f??, phos, 'light', and s???es??, synthesis, 'putting together'). Oxygen is also released, mostly as a waste product.

Momentum

In classical mechanics, linear momentum or translational momentum is the product of the mass and velocity of an object. For example, a heavy truck moving fast has a large momentum--it takes a large and prolonged force to get the truck up to this speed, and it takes a large and prolonged force to bring it to a stop afterwards. If the truck were lighter, or moving more slowly, then it would have less momentum.

Compton wavelength

The Compton wavelength is a quantum mechanical property of a particle. It was introduced by Arthur Compton in his explanation of the scattering of photons by electrons (a process known as Compton scattering). The Compton wavelength of a particle is equivalent to the wavelength of a photon whose energy is the same as the rest-mass energy of the particle.

Pair production

Pair production refers to the creation of an elementary particle and its antiparticle, usually when a photon interacts with a nucleus or another boson. For example an electron and its antiparticle, the positron, may be created. This is allowed, provided there is enough energy available to create the pair - at least the total rest mass energy of the two particles - and that the situation allows both energy and momentum to be conserved.

Positron	The positron or antielectron is the antiparticle or the antimatter counterpart of the electron. The positron has an electric charge of +1e, a spin of ½, and has the same mass as an electron. When a low-energy positron collides with a low-energy electron, annihilation occurs, resulting in the production of two or more gamma ray photons .
Matter wave	In quantum mechanics, the concept of matter waves or de Broglie waves reflects the wave-particle duality of matter. The theory was proposed by Louis de Broglie in 1924 in his PhD thesis. The de Broglie relations show that the wavelength is inversely proportional to the momentum of a particle and is also called de Broglie wavelength.
De Broglie	Louis-Victor-Pierre-Raymond, 7th duc de Broglie, was a French physicist who made groundbreaking contributions to quantum theory. In his 1924 PhD thesis he postulated the wave nature of electrons and suggested that all matter has wave properties. This concept is known as wave-particle duality or the de Broglie hypothesis.
Electron diffraction	Electron diffraction refers to the wave nature of electrons. However, from a technical or practical point of view, it may be regarded as a technique used to study matter by firing electrons at a sample and observing the resulting interference pattern. This phenomenon is commonly known as the wave-particle duality, which states that the behavior of a particle of matter (in this case the incident electron) can be described by a wave.
Wavelength	In physics, the wavelength of a sinusoidal wave is the spatial period of the wave--the distance over which the wave's shape repeats. It is usually determined by considering the distance between consecutive corresponding points of the same phase, such as crests, troughs, or zero crossings, and is a characteristic of both traveling waves and standing waves, as well as other spatial wave patterns. Wavelength is commonly designated by the Greek letter lambda (?).
Magnetic lens	A magnetic lens is a device for the focusing or deflection of moving charged particles, such as electrons or ions, by use of the magnetic Lorentz force. Its strength can often be varied by usage of electromagnets. Magnetic lenses are used in diverse applications, from cathode ray tubes over electron microscopy to particle accelerators.
Retina	Retina can also refer to the Kodak Retina camera and the Apple Retina Display. The vertebrate retina is a light-sensitive layer of tissue, lining the inner surface of the eye. The optics of the eye create an image of the visual world on the retina which serves much the same function as the film in a camera.
Magnification	Magnification is the process of enlarging something only in appearance, not in physical size. This enlargement is quantified by a calculated number also called 'magnification'. When this number is less than one it refers to a reduction in size, sometimes called 'minification' or 'de-magnification'.
Microscope	A microscope is an instrument used to see objects that are too small for the naked eye.

The science of investigating small objects using such an instrument is called microscopy. Microscopic means invisible to the eye unless aided by a microscope.

Alpha particle

Alpha particles consist of two protons and two neutrons bound together into a particle identical to a helium nucleus. They are generally produced in the process of alpha decay, but may also be produced in other ways. Alpha particles are named after the first letter in the Greek alphabet, a.

Atom

The atom is a basic unit of matter that consists of a dense central nucleus surrounded by a cloud of negatively charged electrons. The atomic nucleus contains a mix of positively charged protons and electrically neutral neutrons, which means 'uncuttable' or 'the smallest indivisible particle of matter'. Although the Indian and Greek concepts of the atom were based purely on philosophy, modern science has retained the name coined by Democritus.

Absorption

Acoustic absorption refers to a material, structure or object absorbing sound energy when sound waves collide with it, as opposed to reflecting the energy. Part of the absorbed energy is transformed into heat and part is transmitted. The energy transformed into heat is said to have been 'lost'.When sound from a loudspeaker collides with the walls of a room part of the sound's energy is reflected and part is absorbed into the walls.

Hydrogen

Hydrogen is a chemical element with chemical symbol H and atomic number 1. With an atomic weight of 1.00794 u, hydrogen is the lightest element and its monatomic form (H) is the most abundant chemical substance, constituting roughly 75% of the Universe's baryonic mass. Non-remnant stars are mainly composed of hydrogen in its plasma state.

At standard temperature and pressure, hydrogen is a colorless, odorless, tasteless, non-toxic, nonmetallic, highly combustible diatomic gas with the molecular formula H_2.

Spectrum

A spectrum is a condition that is not limited to a specific set of values but can vary infinitely within a continuum. The word was first used scientifically within the field of optics to describe the rainbow of colors in visible light when separated using a prism; it has since been applied by analogy to many fields other than optics. Thus, one might talk about the spectrum of political opinion, or the spectrum of activity of a drug, or the autism spectrum.

Balmer series

The Balmer series or Balmer lines in atomic physics, is the designation of one of a set of six different named series describing the spectral line emissions of the hydrogen atom. The Balmer series is calculated using the Balmer formula, an empirical equation discovered by Johann Balmer in 1885.

The visible spectrum of light from hydrogen displays four wavelengths, 410 nm, 434 nm, 486 nm, and 656 nm, that correspond to emissions of photons by electrons in excited states transitioning to the quantum level described by the principal quantum number n equals 2.

Lyman series

In physics and chemistry, the Lyman series is the series of transitions and resulting ultraviolet emission lines of the hydrogen atom as an electron goes from n = 2 to n = 1 the lowest energy level of the electron. The transitions are named sequentially by Greek letters: from n = 2 to n = 1 is called Lyman-alpha, 3 to 1 is Lyman-beta, 4 to 1 is Lyman-gamma, etc. The series is named after its discoverer, Theodore Lyman.

Rydberg constant

The Rydberg constant, symbol R_8 or R_H is a physical constant relating to atomic spectra, in the science of spectroscopy. The constant first arose as an empirical fitting parameter in the Rydberg formula for the hydrogen spectral series, but Niels Bohr later showed that its value could be calculated from more fundamental constants, explaining the relationship via his 'Bohr model'. As of 2012, R_8 is the most accurately measured fundamental physical constant.

Angular momentum

In physics, angular momentum, moment of momentum, or rotational momentum is the amount of rotation an object has, taking into account its mass and shape. It is a vector quantity that represents the product of a body's rotational inertia and rotational velocity about a particular axis. The angular momentum of a system of particles (e.g. a rigid body) is the sum of angular momenta of the individual particles.

Bohr model

In atomic physics, the Bohr model, introduced by Niels Bohr in 1913, depicts the atom as small, positively charged nucleus surrounded by electrons that travel in circular orbits around the nucleus--similar in structure to the solar system, but with attraction provided by electrostatic forces rather than gravity. After the cubic model .•Quantum ruleThe angular momentum $L = m_e vr$ is an integer multiple of h: $m_e vr = n\hbar$ Substituting the expression for the velocity gives an equation for r in terms of n: $\sqrt{Zk_e e^2 m_e r} = n\hbar$ so that the allowed orbit radius at any n is: $r_n = \frac{n^2\hbar^2}{Zk_e e^2 m_e}$ The smallest possible value of r in the hydrogen atom is called the Bohr radius and is equal to: $r_1 = \frac{\hbar^2}{k_e e^2 m_e} \approx 5.29 \times 10^{-11}\mathrm{m}$ The energy of the n-th level for any atom is determined by the radius and quantum number:

$$E = -\frac{Zk_e e^2}{2r_n} = -\frac{Z^2(k_e e^2)^2 m_e}{2\hbar^2 n^2} \approx \frac{-13.6Z^2}{n^2}\mathrm{eV}$$

An electron in the lowest energy level of hydrogen therefore has about 13.6 eV less energy than a motionless electron infinitely far from the nucleus. The next energy level is -3.4 eV. The third (n = 3) is -1.51 eV, and so on.

26. EARLY QUANTUM THEORY AND MODELS OF THE ATOM

CHAPTER HIGHLIGHTS & NOTES: KEY TERMS, PEOPLE, PLACES, CONCEPTS

Principal quantum number

The principal quantum number, symbolized as n, is the first of a set of quantum numbers (which includes: the principal quantum number, the azimuthal quantum number, the magnetic quantum number, and the spin quantum number) of an atomic orbital. The principal quantum number can only have positive integer values. As n increases, the orbital becomes larger and the electron spends more time farther from the nucleus.

Energy level

A quantum mechanical system or particle that is bound--that is, confined spatially--can only take on certain discrete values of energy. This contrasts with classical particles, which can have any energy. These discrete values are called energy levels.

Bohr radius

The Bohr radius is a physical constant, approximately equal to the most probable distance between the proton and electron in a hydrogen atom in its ground state. It is named after Niels Bohr, due to its role in the Bohr model of an atom. The precise definition of the Bohr radius is:

$$a_0 = \frac{4\pi\varepsilon_0\hbar^2}{m_e e^2} = \frac{\hbar}{m_e c \alpha}$$

where: ε_0 is the permittivity of free space $\hbar$ is the reduced Planck's constant m_e is the electron rest mass e is the elementary charge c is the speed of light in vacuum α is the fine structure constant.

Or, in Gaussian units the Bohr radius is simply

$$a_0 = \frac{\hbar^2}{m_e e^2}$$

According to 2010 CODATA the Bohr radius has a value of $5.2917721092(17)\times10^{-11}$ m (i.e., approximately 53 pm or 0.53 angstroms).

Ionization energy

The ionization energy of an atom or molecule describes the amount of energy required to remove an electron from the atom or molecule in the gaseous state. X + energy ? $X^+ + e^-$

The term ionization potential has been used in the past but is not recommended.

The units for ionization energy vary from discipline to discipline.

Binding energy

Binding energy is the mechanical energy required to disassemble a whole entity into separate parts. A bound system typically has a lower potential energy than the sum of its constituent parts -- this is what keeps the system together. Often this means that energy is released upon the creation of a bound state.

Ionization

Ionization is the process by which an atom or a molecule acquires a negative or positive charge by gaining or losing electrons.

26. EARLY QUANTUM THEORY AND MODELS OF THE ATOM

CHAPTER HIGHLIGHTS & NOTES: KEY TERMS, PEOPLE, PLACES, CONCEPTS

Spectral line	A spectral line is a dark or bright line in an otherwise uniform and continuous spectrum, resulting from a deficiency or excess of photons in a narrow frequency range, compared with the nearby frequencies. Spectral lines are often used as a sort of 'atomic fingerprint,' as gases emit light at very specific frequencies when exposed to electromagnetic waves, which are displayed in the form of spectral lines. These 'fingerprints' can be compared to the previously collected fingerprints of elements, and are thus used to identify the molecular construct of stars and planets which would otherwise be impossible.
Correspondence principle	In physics, the correspondence principle states that the behavior of systems described by the theory of quantum mechanics reproduces classical physics in the limit of large quantum numbers. In other words, it says that for large orbits and for large energies, quantum calculations must agree with classical calculations. The principle was formulated by Niels Bohr in 1920, though he had previously made use of it as early as 1913 in developing his model of the atom.
Quantum mechanics	Quantum mechanics is a branch of physics which deals with physical phenomena at microscopic scales, where the action is on the order of the Planck constant. It departs from classical mechanics primarily at the quantum realm of atomic and subatomic length scales. Quantum mechanics provides a mathematical description of much of the dual particle-like and wave-like behavior and interactions of energy and matter.
Big Bang theory	The Big Bang theory is the prevailing cosmological model for the early development of the Universe. According to the theory, the Big Bang occurred approximately 13.798 ± 0.037 billion years ago, which is thus considered the age of the universe. At this time, the Universe was in an extremely hot and dense state and began expanding rapidly.

CHAPTER QUIZ: KEY TERMS, PEOPLE, PLACES, CONCEPTS

1. In the _________, electrons are emitted from solids, liquids or gases when they absorb energy from light. Electrons emitted in this manner may be called photoelectrons.

   In 1887, Heinrich Hertz discovered that electrodes illuminated with ultraviolet light create electric sparks more easily.

   a. Photoelectric effect
   b. Friedrich Oskar Giesel
   c. Panel edge staining
   d. Sibplaz

2. In the physical sciences, a _________ is a small localized object to which can be ascribed several physical or chemical properties such as volume or mass. The word is rather general in meaning, and is refined as needed by various scientific fields. Something that is composed of _________s may be referred to as particulate, although this term is generally used to refer to a suspension of unconnected _________s, rather than a connected _________ aggregation.

   a. 3D printing
   b. Particle
   c. Building printing
   d. CandyFab

3. _________ refers to reducing energy through using less of an energy service. _________ differs from efficient energy use, which refers to using less energy for a constant service. For example, driving less is an example of _________.

   a. Energy conservation
   b. Buffer solution
   c. Buffering agent
   d. Carbonate alkalinity

4. An _________ is a type of microscope that uses an electron beam to illuminate a specimen and produce a magnified image.

   An EM has greater resolving power than a light microscope and can reveal the structure of smaller objects because electrons have wavelengths about 100,000 times shorter than visible light photons. They can achieve better than 50 pm resolution and magnifications of up to about 10,000,000x whereas ordinary, non-confocal light microscopes are limited by diffraction to about 200 nm resolution and useful magnifications below 2000x.

   a. Charge contrast imaging
   b. Electron microscope
   c. Cryo-electron microscopy
   d. Durcupan

5. The _________, symbol R_8 or R_H is a physical constant relating to atomic spectra, in the science of spectroscopy. The constant first arose as an empirical fitting parameter in the Rydberg formula for the hydrogen spectral series, but Niels Bohr later showed that its value could be calculated from more fundamental constants, explaining the relationship via his 'Bohr model'. As of 2012, R_8 is the most accurately measured fundamental physical constant.

   a. Broad iron K line
   b. Rydberg constant
   c. Hydrogen line
   d. Lyc photon

ANSWER KEY
26. EARLY QUANTUM THEORY AND MODELS OF THE ATOM

1. a
2. b
3. a
4. b
5. b

---

27. QUANTUM MECHANICS OF ATOMS

CHAPTER OUTLINE: KEY TERMS, PEOPLE, PLACES, CONCEPTS

- Fine structure
- Atom
- Quantum mechanics
- Correspondence principle
- Matter wave
- Photon
- Wave function
- Amplitude
- Double-slit experiment
- De Broglie
- Electron
- Uncertainty principle
- Wave Motion
- Electron microscope
- Determinism
- Bohr radius
- Copenhagen interpretation
- Magnetic quantum number
- Quantum number
- Spin quantum number
- Zeeman effect

27. QUANTUM MECHANICS OF ATOMS

CHAPTER OUTLINE: KEY TERMS, PEOPLE, PLACES, CONCEPTS

Angular momentum

Energy level

Hydrogen

Hydrogen atom

Selection rule

Atomic number

Exclusion principle

Helium

Lithium

Pauli exclusion principle

Ground state

Boson

Electron configuration

Fermion

Meson

Periodic table

Actinide

Halogen

Lanthanide

Lyman series

Valence

27. QUANTUM MECHANICS OF ATOMS

CHAPTER OUTLINE: KEY TERMS, PEOPLE, PLACES, CONCEPTS

Molybdenum

Cutoff

Bremsstrahlung

Fluorescence

Stimulated emission

Absorption

Diffraction

Optical pumping

Ruby laser

Chemical laser

DVD player

Dye laser

Gas laser

27. QUANTUM MECHANICS OF ATOMS

CHAPTER HIGHLIGHTS & NOTES: KEY TERMS, PEOPLE, PLACES, CONCEPTS

Fine structure

In atomic physics, the fine structure describes the splitting of the spectral lines of atoms due to quantum mechanical and relativistic corrections.

The gross structure of line spectra is the line spectra predicted by the quantum mechanics of non-relativistic electrons with no spin. For a hydrogenic atom, the gross structure energy levels only depend on the principal quantum number n.

Atom

The atom is a basic unit of matter that consists of a dense central nucleus surrounded by a cloud of negatively charged electrons. The atomic nucleus contains a mix of positively charged protons and electrically neutral neutrons, which means 'uncuttable' or 'the smallest indivisible particle of matter'. Although the Indian and Greek concepts of the atom were based purely on philosophy, modern science has retained the name coined by Democritus.

Quantum mechanics

Quantum mechanics is a branch of physics which deals with physical phenomena at microscopic scales, where the action is on the order of the Planck constant. It departs from classical mechanics primarily at the quantum realm of atomic and subatomic length scales. Quantum mechanics provides a mathematical description of much of the dual particle-like and wave-like behavior and interactions of energy and matter.

Correspondence principle

In physics, the correspondence principle states that the behavior of systems described by the theory of quantum mechanics reproduces classical physics in the limit of large quantum numbers. In other words, it says that for large orbits and for large energies, quantum calculations must agree with classical calculations.

The principle was formulated by Niels Bohr in 1920, though he had previously made use of it as early as 1913 in developing his model of the atom.

Matter wave

In quantum mechanics, the concept of matter waves or de Broglie waves reflects the wave-particle duality of matter. The theory was proposed by Louis de Broglie in 1924 in his PhD thesis. The de Broglie relations show that the wavelength is inversely proportional to the momentum of a particle and is also called de Broglie wavelength.

Photon

A photon is an elementary particle, the quantum of light and all other forms of electromagnetic radiation, and the force carrier for the electromagnetic force, even when static via virtual photons. The effects of this force are easily observable at both the microscopic and macroscopic level, because the photon has zero rest mass; this allows long distance interactions. Like all elementary particles, photons are currently best explained by quantum mechanics and exhibit wave-particle duality, exhibiting properties of both waves and particles.

Wave function

A wave function or wavefunction in quantum mechanics describes the quantum state of a particle and how it behaves. Typically, its values are complex numbers and, for a single particle, it is a function of space and time.

Amplitude	The amplitude of a periodic variable is a measure of its change over a single period . There are various definitions of amplitude, which are all functions of the magnitude of the difference between the variable's extreme values. In older texts the phase is sometimes called the amplitude.
Double-slit experiment	The double-slit experiment, sometimes called Young's experiment, is a demonstration that matter and energy can display characteristics of both classically defined waves and particles, and demonstrates the fundamentally probabilistic nature of quantum mechanical phenomena. In the basic version of this experiment, a coherent light source such as a laser beam illuminates a plate pierced by two parallel slits, and the light passing through the slits is observed on a screen behind the plate. The wave nature of light causes the light waves passing through the two slits to interfere, producing bright and dark bands on the screen--a result that would not be expected if light consisted of classical particles (i.e., small chunks of matter).
De Broglie	Louis-Victor-Pierre-Raymond, 7th duc de Broglie, was a French physicist who made groundbreaking contributions to quantum theory. In his 1924 PhD thesis he postulated the wave nature of electrons and suggested that all matter has wave properties. This concept is known as wave-particle duality or the de Broglie hypothesis.
Electron	The electron is a subatomic particle with a negative elementary electric charge. Electrons belong to the first generation of the lepton particle family, and are generally thought to be elementary particles because they have no known components or substructure. The electron has a mass that is approximately 1/1836 that of the proton.
Uncertainty principle	In quantum mechanics, the uncertainty principle is any of a variety of mathematical inequalities asserting a fundamental limit to the precision with which certain pairs of physical properties of a particle known as complementary variables, such as position x and momentum p, can be known simultaneously. For instance, the more precisely the position of some particle is determined, the less precisely its momentum can be known, and vice versa.. The formal inequality relating the standard deviation of position s_x and the standard deviation of momentum s_p was derived by Earle Hesse Kennard later that year and by Hermann Weyl in 1928, where h is the reduced Planck constant.
Wave Motion	Wave Motion is a peer-reviewed scientific journal publishing papers on the physics of waves - with emphasis on the areas of acoustics, optics, geophysics, seismology, electromagnetic theory, solid and fluid mechanics. Original research articles on analytical, numerical and experimental aspects of wave motion are covered. Since the journal's establishment in 1979, the editor in chief has been Jan D. Achenbach.

27. QUANTUM MECHANICS OF ATOMS

CHAPTER HIGHLIGHTS & NOTES: KEY TERMS, PEOPLE, PLACES, CONCEPTS

Electron microscope

An electron microscope is a type of microscope that uses an electron beam to illuminate a specimen and produce a magnified image.

An EM has greater resolving power than a light microscope and can reveal the structure of smaller objects because electrons have wavelengths about 100,000 times shorter than visible light photons. They can achieve better than 50 pm resolution and magnifications of up to about 10,000,000x whereas ordinary, non-confocal light microscopes are limited by diffraction to about 200 nm resolution and useful magnifications below 2000x.

Determinism

Determinism is a philosophical position stating that for everything that happens there are conditions such that, given those conditions, nothing else could happen. 'There are many determinisms, depending upon what pre-conditions are considered to be determinative of an event.' Deterministic theories throughout the history of philosophy have sprung from diverse motives and considerations, some of which overlap. Some forms of determinism can be tested empirically with ideas stemming from physics and the philosophy of physics.

Bohr radius

The Bohr radius is a physical constant, approximately equal to the most probable distance between the proton and electron in a hydrogen atom in its ground state. It is named after Niels Bohr, due to its role in the Bohr model of an atom. The precise definition of the Bohr radius is:

$$a_0 = \frac{4\pi\varepsilon_0\hbar^2}{m_e e^2} = \frac{\hbar}{m_e\, c\, \alpha}$$

where: ε_0 is the permittivity of free space $\hbar$ is the reduced Planck's constant m_e is the electron rest mass e is the elementary charge c is the speed of light in vacuum α is the fine structure constant.

Or, in Gaussian units the Bohr radius is simply $a_0 = \frac{\hbar^2}{m_e e^2}$

According to 2010 CODATA the Bohr radius has a value of $5.2917721092(17)\times10^{-11}$ m (i.e., approximately 53 pm or 0.53 angstroms).

Copenhagen interpretation

The Copenhagen interpretation is one of the earliest and most commonly taught interpretations of quantum mechanics. It holds that quantum mechanics does not yield a description of an objective reality but deals only with probabilities of observing, or measuring, various aspects of energy quanta, entities that fit neither the classical idea of particles nor the classical idea of waves. The act of measurement causes the set of probabilities to immediately and randomly assume only one of the possible values.

Magnetic quantum number	In atomic physics, the magnetic quantum number is the third of a set of quantum numbers (the principal quantum number, the azimuthal quantum number, the magnetic quantum number, and the spin quantum number) which describe the unique quantum state of an electron and is designated by the letter m. The magnetic quantum number denotes the energy levels available within a subshell.
Quantum number	Quantum numbers describe values of conserved quantities in the dynamics of a quantum system. Perhaps the most peculiar aspect of quantum mechanics is the quantization of observable quantities, since quantum numbers are discrete sets of integers or half-integers. This is distinguished from classical mechanics where the values can range continuously.
Spin quantum number	In atomic physics, the spin quantum number is a quantum number that parameterizes the intrinsic angular momentum of a given particle. The spin quantum number is the fourth of a set of quantum numbers (the principal quantum number, the azimuthal quantum number, the magnetic quantum number, and the spin quantum number), which describe the unique quantum state of an electron and is designated by the letter s.
Zeeman effect	The Zeeman effect is the effect of splitting a spectral line into several components in the presence of a static magnetic field. It is analogous to the Stark effect, the splitting of a spectral line into several components in the presence of an electric field. Also similar to the Stark effect, transitions between different components have, in general, different intensities, with some being entirely forbidden (in the dipole approximation), as governed by the selection rules.
Angular momentum	In physics, angular momentum, moment of momentum, or rotational momentum is the amount of rotation an object has, taking into account its mass and shape. It is a vector quantity that represents the product of a body's rotational inertia and rotational velocity about a particular axis. The angular momentum of a system of particles (e.g. a rigid body) is the sum of angular momenta of the individual particles.
Energy level	A quantum mechanical system or particle that is bound--that is, confined spatially--can only take on certain discrete values of energy. This contrasts with classical particles, which can have any energy. These discrete values are called energy levels.
Hydrogen	Hydrogen is a chemical element with chemical symbol H and atomic number 1. With an atomic weight of 1.00794 u, hydrogen is the lightest element and its monatomic form (H) is the most abundant chemical substance, constituting roughly 75% of the Universe's baryonic mass. Non-remnant stars are mainly composed of hydrogen in its plasma state. At standard temperature and pressure, hydrogen is a colorless, odorless, tasteless, non-toxic, nonmetallic, highly combustible diatomic gas with the molecular formula H_2.
Hydrogen atom	A hydrogen atom is an atom of the chemical element hydrogen.

27. QUANTUM MECHANICS OF ATOMS

The electrically neutral atom contains a single positively charged proton and a single negatively charged electron bound to the nucleus by the Coulomb force. Atomic hydrogen constitutes about 75% of the elemental mass of the universe.

Selection rule

In physics and chemistry a selection rule, or transition rule, formally constrains the possible transitions of a system from one state to another. Selection rules have been derived for electronic, vibrational, and rotational transitions. The selection rules may differ according to the technique used to observe the transition.

Atomic number

In chemistry and physics, the atomic number is the number of protons found in the nucleus of an atom and therefore identical to the charge number of the nucleus. It is conventionally represented by the symbol Z. The atomic number uniquely identifies a chemical element. In an atom of neutral charge, the atomic number is also equal to the number of electrons.

Exclusion principle

The Exclusion principle is a philosophical principle that states:If an event e causes event e*, then there is no event e# such that e# is non-supervenient on e and e# causes e*..

Helium

Helium is a chemical element with symbol He and atomic number 2. It is a colorless, odorless, tasteless, non-toxic, inert, monatomic gas that heads the noble gas group in the periodic table. Its boiling and melting points are the lowest among the elements and it exists only as a gas except in extreme conditions.

Helium is the second lightest element and is the second most abundant element in the observable universe, being present at about 24% of the total elemental mass, which is more than 12 times the mass of all the heavier elements combined.

Lithium

Lithium is a chemical element with symbol Li and atomic number 3. It is a soft, silver-white metal belonging to the alkali metal group of chemical elements. Under standard conditions it is the lightest metal and the least dense solid element. Like all alkali metals, lithium is highly reactive and flammable.

Pauli exclusion principle

The Pauli exclusion principle is the quantum mechanical principle that no two identical fermions may occupy the same quantum state simultaneously. A more rigorous statement is that the total wave function for two identical fermions is anti-symmetric with respect to exchange of the particles. The principle was formulated by Austrian physicist Wolfgang Pauli in 1925.

Ground state

The ground state of a quantum mechanical system is its lowest-energy state; the energy of the ground state is known as the zero-point energy of the system. An excited state is any state with energy greater than the ground state. The ground state of a quantum field theory is usually called the vacuum state or the vacuum.

Boson

In particle physics, the bosons comprise one of two classes of elementary particles, the other being fermions.

The name boson was coined by Paul Dirac to commemorate the contribution of Satyendra Nath Bose in developing, with Einstein, Bose-Einstein statistics--which theorizes the characteristics of elementary particles. Examples of bosons include fundamental particles (e.g., the Higgs boson, the four force-carrying gauge bosons of the Standard Model, and the still-theoretical graviton of quantum gravity); composite particles (e.g., mesons and stable nuclei of even mass number such as deuterium, helium-4, or lead-208); and quasiparticles (e.g. Cooper pairs, plasmons, and phonons).

Electron configuration	In atomic physics and quantum chemistry, the electron configuration is the distribution of electrons of an atom or molecule in atomic or molecular orbitals. For example, the electron configuration of the neon atom is $1s^2\ 2s^2\ 2p^6$. Electronic configurations describe electrons as each moving independently in an orbital, in an average field created by all other orbitals.
Fermion	In particle physics, a fermion is any particle characterized by Fermi-Dirac statistics and following the Pauli exclusion principle; fermions include all quarks and leptons, as well as any composite particle made of an odd number of these, such as all baryons and many atoms and nuclei. Fermions contrast with bosons which obey Bose-Einstein statistics. A fermion can be an elementary particle, such as the electron; or it can be a composite particle, such as the proton.
Meson	In particle physics, mesons are hadronic subatomic particles composed of one quark and one antiquark, bound together by the strong interaction. Because mesons are composed of sub-particles, they have a physical size, with a radius roughly one femtometre, which is about $^2/_3$ the size of a proton or neutron. All mesons are unstable, with the longest-lived lasting for only a few hundredths of a microsecond.
Periodic table	The periodic table is a tabular arrangement of the chemical elements, organized on the basis of their atomic numbers, electron configurations, and recurring chemical properties. Elements are presented in order of increasing atomic number (the number of protons in the nucleus). The standard form of the table consists of a grid of elements laid out in 18 columns and 7 rows, with a double row of elements below that.
Actinide	The actinide or actinoid series encompasses the 15 metallic chemical elements with atomic numbers from 89 to 103, actinium through lawrencium. The actinide series derives its name from the group 3 element actinium. The informal chemical symbol An is used in general discussions of actinide chemistry to refer to any actinide.

27. QUANTUM MECHANICS OF ATOMS

Halogen

The halogens or halogen elements are a group in the periodic table consisting of five chemically related elements, fluorine, chlorine (Cl), bromine (Br), iodine (I), and astatine (At). The artificially created element 117 (ununseptium) may also be a halogen. In the modern IUPAC nomenclature, this group is known as group 17.

Lanthanide

The lanthanide or lanthanoid series of chemical elements comprises the fifteen metallic chemical elements with atomic numbers 57 through 71, from lanthanum through lutetium. These fifteen lanthanide elements, along with the chemically similar elements scandium and yttrium, are often collectively known as the rare earth elements.

The informal chemical symbol Ln is used in general discussions of lanthanide chemistry to refer to any lanthanide.

Lyman series

In physics and chemistry, the Lyman series is the series of transitions and resulting ultraviolet emission lines of the hydrogen atom as an electron goes from n = 2 to n = 1 the lowest energy level of the electron. The transitions are named sequentially by Greek letters: from n = 2 to n = 1 is called Lyman-alpha, 3 to 1 is Lyman-beta, 4 to 1 is Lyman-gamma, etc. The series is named after its discoverer, Theodore Lyman.

Valence

In chemistry, valence, also known as valency or valence number, is the number of valence bonds a given atom has formed, or can form, with one or more other atoms. For most elements the number of bonds can vary. The IUPAC definition limits valence to the maximum number of univalent atoms that may combine with the atom, that is the maximum number of valence bonds that is possible for the given element.

Molybdenum

Molybdenum is a Group 6 chemical element with the symbol Mo and atomic number 42. The name is from Neo-Latin Molybdaenum, from Ancient Greek ????ßd?? molybdos, meaning lead, since its ores were confused with lead ores. Molybdenum minerals have been known into prehistory, but the element was discovered (in the sense of differentiating it as a new entity from the mineral salts of other metals) in 1778 by Carl Wilhelm Scheele. The metal was first isolated in 1781 by Peter Jacob Hjelm.

Cutoff

In theoretical physics, cutoff is an arbitrary maximal or minimal value of energy, momentum, or length, used in order that objects with larger or smaller values than these physical quantities are ignored in some calculation. It is usually represented within a particular energy or length scale, such as Planck units.

When used in this context, the traditional terms 'infrared' and 'ultraviolet' are not literal references to specific regions of the spectrum.

Bremsstrahlung

Bremsstrahlung is electromagnetic radiation produced by the deceleration of a charged particle when deflected by another charged particle, typically an electron by an atomic nucleus.

The moving particle loses kinetic energy, which is converted into a photon because energy is conserved. The term is also used to refer to the process of producing the radiation.

Fluorescence — Fluorescence is the emission of light by a substance that has absorbed light or other electromagnetic radiation. It is a form of luminescence. In most cases, the emitted light has a longer wavelength, and therefore lower energy, than the absorbed radiation.

Stimulated emission — Stimulated emission is the process by which an atomic electron interacting with an electromagnetic wave of a certain frequency may drop to a lower energy level, transferring its energy to that field. A new photon created in this manner has the same phase, frequency, polarization, and direction of travel as the photons of the incident wave. This is in contrast to spontaneous emission which occurs without regard to the ambient electromagnetic field.

Absorption — Acoustic absorption refers to a material, structure or object absorbing sound energy when sound waves collide with it, as opposed to reflecting the energy. Part of the absorbed energy is transformed into heat and part is transmitted. The energy transformed into heat is said to have been 'lost'.When sound from a loudspeaker collides with the walls of a room part of the sound's energy is reflected and part is absorbed into the walls.

Diffraction — Diffraction refers to various phenomena which occur when a wave encounters an obstacle. In classical physics, the diffraction phenomenon is described as the apparent bending of waves around small obstacles and the spreading out of waves past small openings. Similar effects occur when a light wave travels through a medium with a varying refractive index, or a sound wave travels through one with varying acoustic impedance.

Optical pumping — Optical pumping is a process in which light is used to raise electrons from a lower energy level in an atom or molecule to a higher one. It is commonly used in laser construction, to pump the active laser medium so as to achieve population inversion. The technique was developed by 1966 Nobel Prize winner Alfred Kastler in the early 1950s.

Ruby laser — A ruby laser is a solid-state laser that uses a synthetic ruby crystal as its gain medium. The first working laser was a ruby laser made by Theodore H. 'Ted' Maiman at Hughes Research Laboratories on May 16, 1960.

Ruby lasers produce pulses of visible light at a wavelength of 694.3 nm, which is a deep red color.

Chemical laser — A chemical laser is a laser that obtains its energy from a chemical reaction. Chemical lasers can reach continuous wave output with power reaching to megawatt levels. They are used in industry for cutting and drilling.

DVD player — A DVD player is a device that plays discs produced under both the DVD-Video and DVD-Audio technical standards, two different and incompatible standards.

27. QUANTUM MECHANICS OF ATOMS

CHAPTER HIGHLIGHTS & NOTES: KEY TERMS, PEOPLE, PLACES, CONCEPTS

The first DVD player ever made was created by Tatung Company in Taiwan in collaboration with Pacific Digital Company from the United States in 1994. Some manufacturers originally announced that DVD players would be available as early as the middle of 1996. These predictions were woefully optimistic. Delivery was initially held up for 'political' reasons of copy protection demanded by movie studios, but was later delayed by lack of titles.

Dye laser

A dye laser is a laser which uses an organic dye as the lasing medium, usually as a liquid solution. Compared to gases and most solid state lasing media, a dye can usually be used for a much wider range of wavelengths. The wide bandwidth makes them particularly suitable for tunable lasers and pulsed lasers.

Gas laser

A gas laser is a laser in which an electric current is discharged through a gas to produce coherent light. The gas laser was the first continuous-light laser and the first laser to operate on the principle of converting electrical energy to a laser light output. The first gas laser, the Helium-neon laser (HeNe), was co-invented by Iranian physicist Ali Javan and American physicist William R. Bennett, Jr.

CHAPTER QUIZ: KEY TERMS, PEOPLE, PLACES, CONCEPTS

1. _________ refers to various phenomena which occur when a wave encounters an obstacle. In classical physics, the _________ phenomenon is described as the apparent bending of waves around small obstacles and the spreading out of waves past small openings. Similar effects occur when a light wave travels through a medium with a varying refractive index, or a sound wave travels through one with varying acoustic impedance.

   a. Diffraction
   b. Collisional excitation
   c. Doppler spectroscopy
   d. K-line

2. In physics and chemistry, the _________ is the series of transitions and resulting ultraviolet emission lines of the hydrogen atom as an electron goes from n = 2 to n = 1 the lowest energy level of the electron. The transitions are named sequentially by Greek letters: from n = 2 to n = 1 is called Lyman-alpha, 3 to 1 is Lyman-beta, 4 to 1 is Lyman-gamma, etc. The series is named after its discoverer, Theodore Lyman.

   a. Broad iron K line
   b. Gaussian broadening
   c. Hydrogen line
   d. Lyman series

3. The _________ is a physical constant, approximately equal to the most probable distance between the proton and electron in a hydrogen atom in its ground state. It is named after Niels Bohr, due to its role in the Bohr model of an atom. The precise definition of the _________ is: $a_0 = \frac{4\pi\varepsilon_0\hbar^2}{m_e e^2} = \frac{\hbar}{m_e\, c\, \alpha}$

   where: ε_0 is the permittivity of free space $\hbar$ is the reduced Planck's constant m_e is the electron rest mass e is the elementary charge c is the speed of light in vacuum α is the fine structure constant.

   Or, in Gaussian units the _________ is simply $a_0 = \frac{\hbar^2}{m_e e^2}$

   According to 2010 CODATA the _________ has a value of 5.2917721092(17)×10^{-11} m (i.e., approximately 53 pm or 0.53 angstroms).

   a. Bohr magneton
   b. Bohr model
   c. Potential well
   d. Bohr radius

4. A _________ is an elementary particle, the quantum of light and all other forms of electromagnetic radiation, and the force carrier for the electromagnetic force, even when static via virtual _________s. The effects of this force are easily observable at both the microscopic and macroscopic level, because the _________ has zero rest mass; this allows long distance interactions. Like all elementary particles, _________s are currently best explained by quantum mechanics and exhibit wave-particle duality, exhibiting properties of both waves and particles.

   a. Photon
   b. Cathode ray
   c. Cavity perturbation theory
   d. Charge conservation

5. _________ is a philosophical position stating that for everything that happens there are conditions such that, given those conditions, nothing else could happen. 'There are many _________s, depending upon what pre-conditions are considered to be determinative of an event.' Deterministic theories throughout the history of philosophy have sprung from diverse motives and considerations, some of which overlap. Some forms of _________ can be tested empirically with ideas stemming from physics and the philosophy of physics.

   a. Bootstrap paradox
   b. Borussian myth
   c. Determinism
   d. Causal chain

ANSWER KEY
27. QUANTUM MECHANICS OF ATOMS

---

1. a

2. d

3. d

4. a

5. c

---

28. MOLECULES AND SOLIDS

CHAPTER OUTLINE: KEY TERMS, PEOPLE, PLACES, CONCEPTS

- Chemical bond
- Molecule
- Bond energy
- Covalent bond
- Exclusion principle
- Pauli exclusion principle
- Uncertainty principle
- Dissociation
- Electron
- Quantum mechanics
- Hydrogen bond
- Electrostatics
- Hydrogen
- Amino acid
- Quantum number
- Diatomic molecule
- Selection rule
- Zero-point energy
- Molecular vibration
- Amorphous solid
- Solid-state physics

28. MOLECULES AND SOLIDS

CHAPTER OUTLINE: KEY TERMS, PEOPLE, PLACES, CONCEPTS

- Fermi energy
- Fermi gas
- Fermi level
- Fermion
- Kinetic theory
- Band gap
- Conduction band
- Valence band
- Energy level
- Thermal
- Intrinsic semiconductor
- Semiconductor
- Silicon
- Transparency
- Germanium
- Diode
- Transistor
- Donor
- Electronic circuit
- Rectifier
- Zener diode

28. MOLECULES AND SOLIDS

CHAPTER OUTLINE: KEY TERMS, PEOPLE, PLACES, CONCEPTS

Capacitor

Compound semiconductor

Light-emitting diode

Particle detector

Phonon

Photodiode

Solid-state lighting

OLED

Organic compounds

Amplifier

Bipolar junction transistor

Exciton

Field-effect transistor

Inductor

Integrated circuit

MOSFET

Bond length

Chemical bond

A chemical bond is an attraction between atoms that allows the formation of chemical substances that contain two or more atoms. The bond is caused by the electrostatic force of attraction between opposite charges, either between electrons and nuclei, or as the result of a dipole attraction. The strength of chemical bonds varies considerably; there are 'strong bonds' such as covalent or ionic bonds and 'weak bonds' such as dipole-dipole interactions, the London dispersion force and hydrogen bonding.

Molecule

A molecule is an electrically neutral group of two or more atoms held together by chemical bonds. Molecules are distinguished from ions by their lack of electrical charge. However, in quantum physics, organic chemistry, and biochemistry, the term molecule is often used less strictly, also being applied to polyatomic ions.

Bond energy

In chemistry, bond energy is the measure of bond strength in a chemical bond. It is the heat required to break one Mole (unit) of molecules into their individual atoms. For example, the carbon-hydrogen bond energy in methane E(C-H) is the enthalpy change involved with breaking up one molecule of methane into a carbon atom and 4 hydrogen radicals divided by 4.Bond energy should not be confused with bond-dissociation energy.

Covalent bond

A covalent bond is a chemical bond that involves the sharing of electron pairs between atoms. The stable balance of attractive and repulsive forces between atoms when they share electrons is known as covalent bonding. For many molecules, the sharing of electrons allows each atom to attain the equivalent of a full outer shell, corresponding to a stable electronic configuration.

Exclusion principle

The Exclusion principle is a philosophical principle that states:If an event e causes event e*, then there is no event e# such that e# is non-supervenient on e and e# causes e*..

Pauli exclusion principle

The Pauli exclusion principle is the quantum mechanical principle that no two identical fermions may occupy the same quantum state simultaneously. A more rigorous statement is that the total wave function for two identical fermions is anti-symmetric with respect to exchange of the particles. The principle was formulated by Austrian physicist Wolfgang Pauli in 1925.

Uncertainty principle

In quantum mechanics, the uncertainty principle is any of a variety of mathematical inequalities asserting a fundamental limit to the precision with which certain pairs of physical properties of a particle known as complementary variables, such as position x and momentum p, can be known simultaneously. For instance, the more precisely the position of some particle is determined, the less precisely its momentum can be known, and vice versa.. The formal inequality relating the standard deviation of position s_x and the standard deviation of momentum s_p was derived by Earle Hesse Kennard later that year and by Hermann Weyl in 1928,

where h is the reduced Planck constant.

28. MOLECULES AND SOLIDS

CHAPTER HIGHLIGHTS & NOTES: KEY TERMS, PEOPLE, PLACES, CONCEPTS

Dissociation	Dissociation in chemistry and biochemistry is a general process in which ionic compounds separate or split into smaller particles, ions, or radicals, usually in a reversible manner. For instance, when a Brønsted-Lowry acid is put in water, a covalent bond between an electronegative atom and a hydrogen atom is broken by heterolytic fission, which gives a proton and a negative ion. Dissociation is the opposite of association and recombination.
Electron	The electron is a subatomic particle with a negative elementary electric charge. Electrons belong to the first generation of the lepton particle family, and are generally thought to be elementary particles because they have no known components or substructure. The electron has a mass that is approximately 1/1836 that of the proton.
Quantum mechanics	Quantum mechanics is a branch of physics which deals with physical phenomena at microscopic scales, where the action is on the order of the Planck constant. It departs from classical mechanics primarily at the quantum realm of atomic and subatomic length scales. Quantum mechanics provides a mathematical description of much of the dual particle-like and wave-like behavior and interactions of energy and matter.
Hydrogen bond	A hydrogen bond is the electromagnetic attractive interaction between polar molecules in which hydrogen is bound to a highly electronegative atom, such as nitrogen (N), oxygen (O) or fluorine (F). The name hydrogen bond is something of a misnomer, as it is not a true bond but a particularly strong dipole-dipole attraction, and should not be confused with a covalent bond. These hydrogen-bond attractions can occur between molecules (intermolecular) or within different parts of a single molecule (intramolecular).
Electrostatics	Electrostatics is a branch of physics that deals with the phenomena and properties of stationary or slow-moving electric charges with no acceleration. Since classical antiquity, it has been known that some materials such as amber attract lightweight particles after rubbing. The Greek word for amber, ??e?t??? electron, was the source of the word 'electricity'.
Hydrogen	Hydrogen is a chemical element with chemical symbol H and atomic number 1. With an atomic weight of 1.00794 u, hydrogen is the lightest element and its monatomic form (H) is the most abundant chemical substance, constituting roughly 75% of the Universe's baryonic mass. Non-remnant stars are mainly composed of hydrogen in its plasma state. At standard temperature and pressure, hydrogen is a colorless, odorless, tasteless, non-toxic, nonmetallic, highly combustible diatomic gas with the molecular formula H_2.
Amino acid	Amino acids are biologically important organic compounds composed of amine ($-NH_2$) and carboxylic acid (-COOH) functional groups, along with a side-chain specific to each amino acid.

The key elements of an amino acid are carbon, hydrogen, oxygen, and nitrogen, though other elements are found in the side-chains of certain amino acids. About 500 amino acids are known and can be classified in many ways.

Quantum number

Quantum numbers describe values of conserved quantities in the dynamics of a quantum system. Perhaps the most peculiar aspect of quantum mechanics is the quantization of observable quantities, since quantum numbers are discrete sets of integers or half-integers. This is distinguished from classical mechanics where the values can range continuously.

Diatomic molecule

Diatomic molecules are molecules composed only of two atoms, of either the same or different chemical elements. The prefix di- is of Greek origin, meaning two.

Selection rule

In physics and chemistry a selection rule, or transition rule, formally constrains the possible transitions of a system from one state to another. Selection rules have been derived for electronic, vibrational, and rotational transitions. The selection rules may differ according to the technique used to observe the transition.

Zero-point energy

Zero-point energy, also called quantum vacuum zero-point energy, is the lowest possible energy that a quantum mechanical physical system may have; it is the energy of its ground state. All quantum mechanical systems undergo fluctuations even in their ground state and have an associated zero-point energy, a consequence of their wave-like nature. The uncertainty principle requires every physical system to have a zero-point energy greater than the minimum of its classical potential well.

Molecular vibration

A molecular vibration occurs when atoms in a molecule are in periodic motion while the molecule as a whole has constant translational and rotational motion. The frequency of the periodic motion is known as a vibration frequency, and the typical frequencies of molecular vibrations range from less than 10^{12} to approximately 10^{14} Hz.

In general, a molecule with N atoms has 3N - 6 normal modes of vibration, but a linear molecule has 3N - 5 such modes, as rotation about its molecular axis cannot be observed.

Amorphous solid

In condensed matter physics, an amorphous or non-crystalline solid is a solid that lacks the long-range order characteristic of a crystal.

In some older books, the term has been used synonymously with glass. Nowadays, 'amorphous solid' is considered to be the overarching concept, and glass the more special case: A glass is an amorphous solid that exhibits a glass transition.

Solid-state physics

Solid-state physics is the study of rigid matter, or solids, through methods such as quantum mechanics, crystallography, electromagnetism, and metallurgy. It is the largest branch of condensed matter physics.

28. MOLECULES AND SOLIDS

Fermi energy

The Fermi energy is a concept in quantum mechanics usually referring to the energy difference between the highest and lowest occupied single-particle states, in a quantum system of non-interacting fermions at absolute zero temperature. In a Fermi gas the lowest occupied state is taken to have zero kinetic energy, whereas in a metal the lowest occupied state is typically taken to mean the bottom of the conduction band.

Confusingly, the term 'Fermi energy' is often used to refer to a different but closely related concept, the Fermi level (also called electrochemical potential).

Fermi gas

A Fermi gas is an ensemble of a large number of fermions. Fermions are particles that obey Fermi-Dirac statistics. These statistics determine the energy distribution of fermions in a Fermi gas in thermal equilibrium, and is characterized by their number density, temperature, and the set of available energy states.

Fermi level

The Fermi level is the total chemical potential for electrons and is usually denoted by μ or E_F. The Fermi level of a body is a thermodynamic quantity, and its significance is the thermodynamic work required to add one electron to the body (not counting the work required to remove the electron from wherever it came from). A precise understanding of the Fermi level--how it relates to electronic band structure in determining electronic properties, how it relates to the voltage and flow of charge in an electronic circuit--is essential to an understanding of solid-state physics.

Fermion

In particle physics, a fermion is any particle characterized by Fermi-Dirac statistics and following the Pauli exclusion principle; fermions include all quarks and leptons, as well as any composite particle made of an odd number of these, such as all baryons and many atoms and nuclei. Fermions contrast with bosons which obey Bose-Einstein statistics.

A fermion can be an elementary particle, such as the electron; or it can be a composite particle, such as the proton.

Kinetic theory

The kinetic theory of gases describes a gas as a large number of small particles, all of which are in constant, random motion. The rapidly moving particles constantly collide with each other and with the walls of the container. Kinetic theory explains macroscopic properties of gases, such as pressure, temperature, viscosity, thermal conductivity, and volume, by considering their molecular composition and motion.

Band gap

In solid-state physics, a band gap, also called an energy gap or bandgap, is an energy range in a solid where no electron states can exist. In graphs of the electronic band structure of solids, the band gap generally refers to the energy difference (in electron volts) between the top of the valence band and the bottom of the conduction band in insulators and semiconductors.

Conduction band

The conduction band is the range of electron energies enough to free an electron from binding with its atom to move freely within the atomic lattice of the material as a 'delocalized electron'. Various materials may be classified by their band gap: this is defined as the difference between the valence and conduction bands. •In non-conductors, commonly known as insulators, the conduction band is higher than that of the valence band, so it takes infeasibly high energies to delocalize their valence electrons.

Valence band

In solids, the valence band is the highest range of electron energies in which electrons are normally present at absolute zero temperature.

The valence electrons are bound to individual atoms, as opposed to conduction electrons, which can move freely within the atomic lattice of the material. On a graph of the electronic band structure of a material, the valence band is located below the conduction band, separated from it in insulators and semiconductors by a band gap.

Energy level

A quantum mechanical system or particle that is bound--that is, confined spatially--can only take on certain discrete values of energy. This contrasts with classical particles, which can have any energy. These discrete values are called energy levels.

Thermal

A thermal column (or thermal) is a column of rising air in the lower altitudes of the Earth's atmosphere. Thermals are created by the uneven heating of the Earth's surface from solar radiation, and are an example of convection, specifically atmospheric convection. The Sun warms the ground, which in turn warms the air directly above it.

Intrinsic semiconductor

An intrinsic semiconductor, also called an undoped semiconductor or i-type semiconductor, is a pure semiconductor without any significant dopant species present. The number of charge carriers is therefore determined by the properties of the material itself instead of the amount of impurities. In intrinsic semiconductors the number of excited electrons and the number of holes are equal: $n = p$.

Semiconductor

A semiconductor is a material which has electrical conductivity to a degree between that of a metal and that of an insulator (such as glass). Semiconductors are the foundation of modern electronics, including transistors, solar cells, light-emitting diodes (LEDs), quantum dots and digital and analog integrated circuits.

A semiconductor may have a number of unique properties, one of which is the ability to change conductivity by the addition of impurities ('doping') or by interaction with another phenomenon, such as an electric field or light; this ability makes a semiconductor very useful for constructing a device that can amplify, switch, or convert an energy input.

Silicon

Silicon, a tetravalent metalloid, is a chemical element with the symbol Si and atomic number 14. It is less reactive than its chemical analog carbon, the nonmetal directly above it in the periodic table, but more reactive than germanium, the metalloid directly below it in the table.

Controversy about silicon's character dates to its discovery; it was first prepared and characterized in pure form in 1823. In 1808, it was given the name silicium (from Latin: silex, hard stone or flint), with an -ium word-ending to suggest a metal, a name which the element retains in several non-English languages. However, its final English name, first suggested in 1817, reflects the more physically similar elements carbon and boron.

Transparency

A transparency, also known in industrial settings as a 'viewfoil' or 'foil', is a thin sheet of transparent flexible material, typically cellulose acetate, onto which figures can be drawn. These are then placed on an overhead projector for display to an audience. Many companies and small organizations use a system of projectors and transparencies in meetings and other groupings of people, though this system is being largely replaced by video projectors and interactive whiteboards.

Germanium

Germanium is a chemical element with symbol Ge and atomic number 32. It is a lustrous, hard, grayish-white metalloid in the carbon group, chemically similar to its group neighbors tin and silicon. Purified germanium is a semiconductor, with an appearance most similar to elemental silicon. Like silicon, germanium naturally reacts and forms complexes with oxygen in nature.

Diode

In electronics, a diode is a two-terminal electronic component with asymmetric conductance, it has low resistance to current flow in one direction, and high (ideally infinite) resistance in the other. Diodes were the first semiconductor electronic devices. The discovery of crystals' rectifying abilities was made by German physicist Ferdinand Braun in 1874. The first semiconductor diodes, called cat's whisker diodes, developed around 1906, were made of mineral crystals such as galena.

Transistor

A transistor is a semiconductor device used to amplify and switch electronic signals and electrical power. It is composed of semiconductor material with at least three terminals for connection to an external circuit. A voltage or current applied to one pair of the transistor's terminals changes the current through another pair of terminals.

Donor

In semiconductor physics, a donor is a dopant atom that, when added to a semiconductor, can form a n-type region.

For example, when silicon, having four valence electrons, needs to be doped as an n-type semiconductor, elements from group V like phosphorus (P) or arsenic (As) can be used because they have five valence electrons. A dopant with five valence electrons is also called a pentavalent impurity.

Electronic circuit

An electronic circuit is composed of individual electronic components, such as resistors, transistors, capacitors, inductors and diodes, connected by conductive wires or traces through which electric current can flow. The combination of components and wires allows various simple and complex operations to be performed: signals can be amplified, computations can be performed, and data can be moved from one place to another.

Rectifier

A rectifier is an electrical device that converts alternating current, which periodically reverses direction, to direct current (DC), which flows in only one direction. The process is known as rectification. Physically, rectifiers take a number of forms, including vacuum tube diodes, mercury-arc valves, copper and selenium oxide rectifiers, semiconductor diodes, silicon-controlled rectifiers and other silicon-based semiconductor switches.

Zener diode

A Zener diode is a diode which allows current to flow in the forward direction in the same manner as an ideal diode, but also permits it to flow in the reverse direction when the voltage is above a certain value known as the breakdown voltage, 'zener knee voltage', 'zener voltage', 'avalanche point', or 'peak inverse voltage'.

The device was named after Clarence Zener, who discovered this electrical property. Many diodes described as 'zener' diodes rely instead on avalanche breakdown as the mechanism.

Capacitor

A capacitor is a passive two-terminal electrical component used to store energy electrostatically in an electric field. The forms of practical capacitors vary widely, but all contain at least two electrical conductors separated by a dielectric (insulator); for example, one common construction consists of metal foils separated by a thin layer of insulating film. Capacitors are widely used as parts of electrical circuits in many common electrical devices.

Compound semiconductor

A compound semiconductor is a semiconductor compound composed of elements from two or more different groups of the periodic table. These semiconductors typically form in groups 13-15 (old groups III-V), for example of elements from group 13 (old group III, boron, aluminium, gallium, indium) and from group 15 (old group V, nitrogen, phosphorus, arsenic, antimony, bismuth). The range of possible formulae is quite broad because these elements can form binary (two elements, e.g. gallium(III) arsenide (GaAs)), ternary (three elements, e.g. indium gallium arsenide (InGaAs)) and quaternary (four elements, e.g. aluminium gallium indium phosphide (AlInGaP)) alloys.

Light-emitting diode

A light-emitting diode is a semiconductor light source. Light emitting diodes are used as indicator lamps in many devices and are increasingly used for general lighting. Appearing as practical electronic components in 1962, early Light emitting diodes emitted low-intensity red light, but modern versions are available across the visible, ultraviolet, and infrared wavelengths, with very high brightness.

Particle detector

In experimental and applied particle physics, nuclear physics, and nuclear engineering, a particle detector, also known as a radiation detector, is a device used to detect, track, and/or identify high-energy particles, such as those produced by nuclear decay, cosmic radiation, or reactions in a particle accelerator. Modern detectors are also used as calorimeters to measure the energy of the detected radiation. They may also be used to measure other attributes such as momentum, spin, charge etc.

28. MOLECULES AND SOLIDS

Phonon

In physics, a phonon is a collective excitation in a periodic, elastic arrangement of atoms or molecules in condensed matter, such as solids and some liquids. Often referred to as a quasiparticle, it represents an excited state in the quantum mechanical quantization of the modes of vibrations of elastic structures of interacting particles.

Phonons play a major role in many of the physical properties of condensed matter, such as thermal conductivity and electrical conductivity.

Photodiode

A photodiode is a type of photodetector capable of converting light into either current or voltage, depending upon the mode of operation. The common, traditional solar cell used to generate electric solar power is a large area photodiode.

Photodiodes are similar to regular semiconductor diodes except that they may be either exposed (to detect vacuum UV or X-rays) or packaged with a window or optical fiber connection to allow light to reach the sensitive part of the device.

Solid-state lighting

Solid-state lighting refers to a type of lighting that uses semiconductor light-emitting diodes (LEDs), organic light-emitting diodes (OLED), or polymer light-emitting diodes (PLED) as sources of illumination rather than electrical filaments, plasma (used in arc lamps such as fluorescent lamps), or gas.

The term 'solid state' refers commonly to light emitted by solid-state electroluminescence, as opposed to incandescent bulbs (which use thermal radiation) or fluorescent tubes. Compared to incandescent lighting, Solid state lighting creates visible light with reduced heat generation or parasitic energy dissipation.

OLED

An OLED is a light-emitting diode (LED) in which the emissive electroluminescent layer is a film of organic compound which emits light in response to an electric current. This layer of organic semiconductor is situated between two electrodes. Generally, at least one of these electrodes is transparent.

Organic compounds

Some organic compounds are valid minerals, recognized by the CNMNC .

Amplifier

An electronic amplifier, amplifier, or amp is an electronic device that increases the power of a signal. It does this by taking energy from a power supply and controlling the output to match the input signal shape but with a larger amplitude. In this sense, an amplifier modulates the output of the power supply.

Bipolar junction transistor

A bipolar junction transistor is a type of transistor that relies on the contact of two types of semiconductor for its operation. Bipolar junction transistors can be used as amplifiers, switches, or in oscillators.

Exciton	An exciton is a bound state of an electron and an electron hole which are attracted to each other by the electrostatic Coulomb force. It is an electrically neutral quasiparticle that exists in insulators, semiconductors and in some liquids. The exciton is regarded as an elementary excitation of condensed matter that can transport energy without transporting net electric charge.
Field-effect transistor	The field-effect transistor is a transistor that uses an electric field to control the shape and hence the conductivity of a channel of one type of charge carrier in a semiconductor material. Field effect transistors are unipolar transistors as they involve single-carrier-type operation. The concept of the Field effect transistor predates the bipolar junction transistor (BJT), though it was not physically implemented until after BJTs due to the limitations of semiconductor materials and the relative ease of manufacturing BJTs compared to Field effect transistors at the time.
Inductor	An inductor, also called a coil or reactor, is a passive two-terminal electrical component which resists changes in electric current passing through it. It consists of a conductor such as a wire, usually wound into a coil. When a current flows through it, energy is stored temporarily in a magnetic field in the coil.
Integrated circuit	An integrated circuit or monolithic integrated circuit is a set of electronic circuits on one small plate ('chip') of semiconductor material, normally silicon. This can be made much smaller than a discrete circuit made from independent components. Integrated circuits are used in virtually all electronic equipment today and have revolutionized the world of electronics.
MOSFET	The metal-oxide-semiconductor field-effect transistor (MOSFET, MOS-FET, or MOS FET) is a transistor used for amplifying or switching electronic signals. Although the MOSFET is a four-terminal device with source (S), gate (G), drain (D), and body (B) terminals, the body (or substrate) of the MOSFET often is connected to the source terminal, making it a three-terminal device like other field-effect transistors. Because these two terminals are normally connected to each other (short-circuited) internally, only three terminals appear in electrical diagrams.
Bond length	In molecular geometry, bond length or bond distance is the average distance between nuclei of two bonded atoms in a molecule. It is a transferable property of a bond between atoms of fixed types, relatively independent of the rest of the molecule.

28. MOLECULES AND SOLIDS

CHAPTER QUIZ: KEY TERMS, PEOPLE, PLACES, CONCEPTS

1. A _________ is an ensemble of a large number of fermions. Fermions are particles that obey Fermi-Dirac statistics. These statistics determine the energy distribution of fermions in a _________ in thermal equilibrium, and is characterized by their number density, temperature, and the set of available energy states.

   a. Fermi energy
   b. Four-acceleration
   c. Jounce
   d. Fermi gas

2. A _________ occurs when atoms in a molecule are in periodic motion while the molecule as a whole has constant translational and rotational motion. The frequency of the periodic motion is known as a vibration frequency, and the typical frequencies of _________s range from less than 10^{12} to approximately 10^{14} Hz.

   In general, a molecule with N atoms has 3N - 6 normal modes of vibration, but a linear molecule has 3N - 5 such modes, as rotation about its molecular axis cannot be observed.

   a. Molecular vibration
   b. Bathochromic shift
   c. Benchtop NMR spectrometer
   d. Breathalyzer

3. A _________ is an attraction between atoms that allows the formation of chemical substances that contain two or more atoms. The bond is caused by the electrostatic force of attraction between opposite charges, either between electrons and nuclei, or as the result of a dipole attraction. The strength of _________s varies considerably; there are 'strong bonds' such as covalent or ionic bonds and 'weak bonds' such as dipole-dipole interactions, the London dispersion force and hydrogen bonding.

   a. Basis set
   b. Basis set superposition error
   c. Bond hardening
   d. Chemical bond

4. The _________ of gases describes a gas as a large number of small particles, all of which are in constant, random motion. The rapidly moving particles constantly collide with each other and with the walls of the container. _________ explains macroscopic properties of gases, such as pressure, temperature, viscosity, thermal conductivity, and volume, by considering their molecular composition and motion.

   a. Backdraft
   b. Batteryless radio
   c. Bennett acceptance ratio
   d. Kinetic theory

5. . A _________ is a chemical bond that involves the sharing of electron pairs between atoms.

The stable balance of attractive and repulsive forces between atoms when they share electrons is known as covalent bonding. For many molecules, the sharing of electrons allows each atom to attain the equivalent of a full outer shell, corresponding to a stable electronic configuration.

a. 18-Electron rule
b. Bartell mechanism
c. Bent bond
d. Covalent bond

ANSWER KEY
28. MOLECULES AND SOLIDS

---

1. d
2. a
3. d
4. d
5. d

---

29. NUCLEAR PHYSICS AND RADIOACTIVITY

CHAPTER OUTLINE: KEY TERMS, PEOPLE, PLACES, CONCEPTS

Nuclear physics

Atomic mass number

Atomic number

Deuterium

Isotope

Natural abundance

Neutron

Neutron number

Nucleon

Nuclide

Proton

Tritium

Nuclear density

Helium

Nuclear binding energy

Neutral

Nuclear force

Strong nuclear force

Beta decay

Polonium

Radioactive decay

29. NUCLEAR PHYSICS AND RADIOACTIVITY

CHAPTER OUTLINE: KEY TERMS, PEOPLE, PLACES, CONCEPTS

- Radionuclide
- Radium
- Unstable
- Alpha decay
- Alpha particle
- Beta particle
- Radon
- Conservation of energy
- Energy conservation
- Exclusion principle
- Pauli exclusion principle
- Antiparticle
- Electron capture
- Positron
- Internal conversion
- Angular momentum
- Electric charge
- Linear momentum
- Half-life
- Time constant
- Coulomb barrier

29. NUCLEAR PHYSICS AND RADIOACTIVITY

CHAPTER OUTLINE: KEY TERMS, PEOPLE, PLACES, CONCEPTS

- ______ Dynode
- ______ Geiger counter
- ______ Particle detector
- ______ Phosphor
- ______ Photocathode
- ______ Scintillation counter
- ______ Scintillator
- ______ Bubble chamber
- ______ Cloud chamber
- ______ Diode
- ______ Photographic emulsion
- ______ Semiconductor detector
- ______ Rubidium-strontium dating
- ______ Mass excess
- ______ Potassium
- ______ Strontium

29. NUCLEAR PHYSICS AND RADIOACTIVITY

CHAPTER HIGHLIGHTS & NOTES: KEY TERMS, PEOPLE, PLACES, CONCEPTS

Nuclear physics

Nuclear physics is the field of physics that studies the constituents and interactions of atomic nuclei. The most commonly known applications of nuclear physics are nuclear power generation and nuclear weapons technology, but the research has provided application in many fields, including those in nuclear medicine and magnetic resonance imaging, ion implantation in materials engineering, and radiocarbon dating in geology and archaeology.

The field of particle physics evolved out of nuclear physics and is typically taught in close association with nuclear physics.

Atomic mass number

The mass number, also called atomic mass number or nucleon number, is the total number of protons and neutrons (together known as nucleons) in an atomic nucleus. Because protons and neutrons both are baryons, the mass number A is identical with the baryon number B as of the nucleus as of the whole atom or ion. The mass number is different for each different isotope of a chemical element.

Atomic number

In chemistry and physics, the atomic number is the number of protons found in the nucleus of an atom and therefore identical to the charge number of the nucleus. It is conventionally represented by the symbol Z. The atomic number uniquely identifies a chemical element. In an atom of neutral charge, the atomic number is also equal to the number of electrons.

Deuterium

Deuterium is one of two stable isotopes of hydrogen. It has a natural abundance in Earth's oceans of about one atom in 6,420 of hydrogen. Thus deuterium accounts for approximately 0.0156% (or on a mass basis: 0.0312%) of all the naturally occurring hydrogen in the oceans, while the most common isotope (hydrogen-1 or protium) accounts for more than 99.98%.

Isotope

Isotopes are variants of a particular chemical element such that, while all isotopes of a given element have the same number of protons in each atom, they differ in neutron number. The term isotope is formed from the Greek roots isos (?s?? 'equal') and topos (t?p?? 'place'), meaning 'the same place'. Thus, different isotopes of a single element occupy the same position on the periodic table.

Natural abundance

In chemistry, natural abundance refers to the abundance of isotopes of a chemical element as naturally found on a planet. The relative atomic mass (a weighted average) of these isotopes is the atomic weight listed for the element in the periodic table. The abundance of an isotope varies from planet to planet, and even from place to place on the Earth, but remains relatively constant in time.

Neutron

The neutron is a subatomic hadron particle that has the symbol n or n0, no net electric charge and a mass slightly larger than that of a proton. With the exception of hydrogen-1, nuclei of atoms consist of protons and neutrons, which are therefore collectively referred to as nucleons. The number of protons in a nucleus is the atomic number and defines the type of element the atom forms.

Neutron number

The neutron number, symbol N, is the number of neutrons in a nuclide.

Atomic number plus neutron number equals mass number: Z+N=A. The difference between the neutron number and the atomic number is known as the neutron excess: D = N - Z = A - 2Z.

Neutron number is rarely written explicitly in nuclide symbol notation, but appears as a subscript to the right of the element symbol. In order of increasing explicitness and decreasing frequency of usage:

Nuclides that have the same neutron number but a different proton number are called isotones.

Nucleon

In chemistry and physics, a nucleon is one of the particles that makes up the atomic nucleus. Each atomic nucleus consists of one or more nucleons, and each atom in turn consists of a cluster of nucleons surrounded by one or more electrons. There are two known kinds of nucleon: the neutron and the proton.

Nuclide

A nuclide is an atomic species characterized by the specific constitution of its nucleus, i.e., by its number of protons Z, its number of neutrons N, and its nuclear energy state.

The word nuclide was proposed by Truman P. Kohman in 1947. Doctor Kohman originally suggested nuclide as referring to a 'species of nucleus' defined by containing a certain number of neutrons and protons. The word thus was originally intended to focus on the nucleus.

Proton

The proton is a subatomic particle with the symbol p or p+ and a positive electric charge of 1 elementary charge. One or more protons are present in the nucleus of each atom. The number of protons in each atom is its atomic number.

Tritium

Tritium is a radioactive isotope of hydrogen. The nucleus of tritium contains one proton and two neutrons, whereas the nucleus of protium (by far the most abundant hydrogen isotope) contains one proton and no neutrons. Naturally occurring tritium is extremely rare on Earth, where trace amounts are formed by the interaction of the atmosphere with cosmic rays.

Nuclear density

Nuclear density is the density of the nucleus of an atom, averaging about 2.3×10^{17} kg/m^3. The descriptive term nuclear density is also applied to situations where similarly high densities occur, such as within neutron stars.

The nuclear density for a typical nucleus can be approximately calculated from the size of the nucleus, which itself can be approximated based on the number of protons and neutrons in it.

Helium

Helium is a chemical element with symbol He and atomic number 2. It is a colorless, odorless, tasteless, non-toxic, inert, monatomic gas that heads the noble gas group in the periodic table.

Its boiling and melting points are the lowest among the elements and it exists only as a gas except in extreme conditions.

Helium is the second lightest element and is the second most abundant element in the observable universe, being present at about 24% of the total elemental mass, which is more than 12 times the mass of all the heavier elements combined.

Nuclear binding energy

Nuclear binding energy is the energy required to split a nucleus of an atom into its component parts. The component parts are neutrons and protons, which are collectively called nucleons. The binding energy of nuclei is always a positive number, since all nuclei require net energy to separate them into individual protons and neutrons.

Neutral

Neutral and neutrality may mean the following:

Nuclear force

The nuclear force is the force between two or more nucleons. Its fundamental laws and constants are unknown unlike the Coulomb and Newton laws. It is responsible for binding protons and neutrons into atomic nuclei.

Strong nuclear force

In particle physics, the strong interaction (also called the strong force, strong nuclear force, nuclear strong force or color force) is one of the four fundamental interactions of nature, the others being electromagnetism, the weak interaction and gravitation. At atomic scale, it is about 100 times stronger than electromagnetism, which in turn is orders of magnitude stronger than the weak force interaction and gravitation. It ensures the stability of ordinary matter, in confining the elementary particles quarks into hadrons such as the proton and neutron, the largest components of the mass of ordinary matter.

Beta decay

In nuclear physics, beta decay is a type of radioactive decay in which a beta particle (an electron or a positron) is emitted from an atomic nucleus. Beta decay is a process which allows the atom to obtain the optimal ratio of protons and neutrons.

Beta decay is mediated by the weak force.

Polonium

Polonium is a chemical element with the symbol Po and atomic number 84, discovered in 1898 by Marie Curie and Pierre Curie. A rare and highly radioactive element with no stable isotopes, polonium is chemically similar to bismuth and tellurium, and it occurs in uranium ores. Applications of polonium are few, and include heaters in space probes, antistatic devices, and sources of neutrons and alpha particles.

Radioactive decay

Radioactive decay, also known as nuclear decay or radioactivity, is the process by which a nucleus of an unstable atom loses energy by emitting particles of ionizing radiation. A material that spontaneously emits this kind of radiation--which includes the emission of energetic alpha particles, beta particles, and gamma rays--is considered radioactive.

Radionuclide

A radionuclide, or a radioactive nuclide, is an atom with an unstable nucleus, characterized by excess energy available to be imparted either to a newly created radiation particle within the nucleus or via internal conversion. During this process, the radionuclide is said to undergo radioactive decay, resulting in the emission of gamma ray(s) and/or subatomic particles such as alpha or beta particles. These emissions constitute ionizing radiation.

Radium

Radium is a chemical element with symbol Ra and atomic number 88. Radium is an almost pure-white alkaline earth metal, but it readily oxidizes on exposure to air, becoming black in color. All isotopes of radium are highly radioactive, with the most stable isotope being radium-226, which has a half-life of 1601 years and decays into radon gas. Because of such instability, radium is luminescent, glowing a faint blue.

Unstable

In numerous fields of study, the component of instability within a system is generally characterized by some of the outputs or internal states growing without bounds. Not all systems that are not stable are unstable; systems can also be marginally stable or exhibit limit cycle behavior.

In control theory, a system is unstable if any of the roots of its characteristic equation has real part greater than zero (or if zero is a repeated root).

Alpha decay

Alpha decay, or a-decay, is a type of radioactive decay in which an atomic nucleus emits an alpha particle and thereby transforms into an atom with a mass number 4 less and atomic number 2 less. For example, uranium-238 decaying through a-particle emission to form thorium-234 can be expressed as: ${}^{238}_{92}\mathrm{U} \rightarrow {}^{234}_{90}\mathrm{Th} + \alpha$

Because an alpha particle is the same as the nucleus of a helium-4 atom - consisting of two protons and two neutrons and thus having mass number 4 and atomic number 2 - this can also be written as: ${}^{238}_{92}\mathrm{U} \rightarrow {}^{234}_{90}\mathrm{Th} + {}^{4}_{2}\mathrm{He}$

Notice how, on either side of the nuclear equation, both the mass number and the atomic number are conserved: the mass number is 238 on the right side and (234 + 4) on the left side, and the atomic number is 92 on the right side and (90 + 2) on the left side.

The alpha particle also has a charge +2, but the charge is usually not written in nuclear equations, which describe nuclear reactions without considering the electrons.

Alpha particle

Alpha particles consist of two protons and two neutrons bound together into a particle identical to a helium nucleus. They are generally produced in the process of alpha decay, but may also be produced in other ways. Alpha particles are named after the first letter in the Greek alphabet, a.

Beta particle

Beta particles are high-energy, high-speed electrons or positrons emitted by certain types of radioactive nuclei such as potassium-40.

The beta particles emitted are a form of ionizing radiation also known as beta rays. The production of beta particles is termed beta decay. They are designated by the Greek letter beta (ß).

Radon

Radon is a chemical element with symbol Rn and atomic number 86. It is a radioactive, colorless, odorless, tasteless noble gas, occurring naturally as an indirect decay product of uranium or thorium. Its most stable isotope, ^{222}Rn, has a half-life of 3.8 days. Radon is one of the densest substances that remains a gas under normal conditions.

Conservation of energy

In physics, the law of conservation of energy states that the total energy of an isolated system cannot change--it is said to be conserved over time. Energy can be neither created nor destroyed, but can change form, for instance chemical energy can be converted to kinetic energy in the explosion of a stick of dynamite.

A consequence of the law of conservation of energy is that a perpetual motion machine of the first kind cannot exist.

Energy conservation

Energy conservation refers to reducing energy through using less of an energy service. Energy conservation differs from efficient energy use, which refers to using less energy for a constant service. For example, driving less is an example of energy conservation.

Exclusion principle

The Exclusion principle is a philosophical principle that states:If an event e causes event e*, then there is no event e# such that e# is non-supervenient on e and e# causes e*..

Pauli exclusion principle

The Pauli exclusion principle is the quantum mechanical principle that no two identical fermions may occupy the same quantum state simultaneously. A more rigorous statement is that the total wave function for two identical fermions is anti-symmetric with respect to exchange of the particles. The principle was formulated by Austrian physicist Wolfgang Pauli in 1925.

Antiparticle

Corresponding to most kinds of particles, there is an associated antiparticle with the same mass and opposite charge . For example, the antiparticle of the electron is the positively charged antielectron, or positron, which is produced naturally in certain types of radioactive decay.

The laws of nature are very nearly symmetrical with respect to particles and antiparticles.

Electron capture

Electron capture is a process in which a proton-rich nuclide absorbs an inner atomic electron, thereby changing a nuclear proton to a neutron and simultaneously causing the emission of an electron neutrino. Various photon emissions follow, as the energy of the atom falls to the ground state of the new nuclide.

Positron	The positron or antielectron is the antiparticle or the antimatter counterpart of the electron. The positron has an electric charge of +1e, a spin of ½, and has the same mass as an electron. When a low-energy positron collides with a low-energy electron, annihilation occurs, resulting in the production of two or more gamma ray photons .
Internal conversion	Internal conversion is a radioactive decay process where an excited nucleus interacts electromagnetically with an electron in one of the lower atomic orbitals, causing the electron to be emitted from the atom. Thus, in an internal conversion process, a high-energy electron is emitted from the radioactive atom, but not from a nucleon in the nucleus. Instead, the electron is ejected as a result of an interaction between the entire nucleus and an outside electron that interacts with it.
Angular momentum	In physics, angular momentum, moment of momentum, or rotational momentum is the amount of rotation an object has, taking into account its mass and shape. It is a vector quantity that represents the product of a body's rotational inertia and rotational velocity about a particular axis. The angular momentum of a system of particles (e.g. a rigid body) is the sum of angular momenta of the individual particles.
Electric charge	Electric charge is the physical property of matter that causes it to experience a force when close to other electrically charged matter. There are two types of electric charges - positive and negative. Positively charged substances are repelled from other positively charged substances, but attracted to negatively charged substances; negatively charged substances are repelled from negative and attracted to positive.
Linear momentum	In classical mechanics, linear momentum or translational momentum is the product of the mass and velocity of an object. For example, a heavy truck moving fast has a large momentum--it takes a large and prolonged force to get the truck up to this speed, and it takes a large and prolonged force to bring it to a stop afterwards. If the truck were lighter, or moving more slowly, then it would have less momentum.
Half-life	Half-life is the amount of time required for a quantity to fall to half its value as measured at the beginning of the time period. While the term 'half-life' can be used to describe any quantity which follows an exponential decay, it is most often used within the context of nuclear physics and nuclear chemistry--that is, the time required, probabilistically, for half of the unstable, radioactive atoms in a sample to undergo radioactive decay. The original term, dating to Ernest Rutherford's discovery of the principle in 1907, was 'half-life period', which was shortened to 'half-life' in the early 1950s.
Time constant	In physics and engineering, the time constant, usually denoted by the Greek letter τ , is the parameter characterizing the response to a step input of a first-order, linear time-invariant (LTI) system. The time constant is the main characteristic unit of a first-order LTI (linear time-invariant) system.

29. NUCLEAR PHYSICS AND RADIOACTIVITY

Coulomb barrier

The Coulomb barrier which is named after physicist Charles-Augustin de Coulomb, is the energy barrier due to electrostatic interaction that two nuclei need to overcome so they can get close enough to undergo a nuclear reaction. This energy barrier is given by the electrostatic potential energy:

$$U_{coul} = k\frac{q_1 q_2}{r} = \frac{1}{4\pi\epsilon_0}\frac{q_1 q_2}{r}$$

wherek is the Coulomb's constant = 8.9876×10^9 N m² C^{-2};e_0 is the permittivity of free space;q_1, q_2 are the charges of the interacting particles;r is the interaction radius.

A positive value of U is due to a repulsive force, so interacting particles are at higher energy levels as they get closer. A negative potential energy indicates a bound state (due to an attractive force).

Dynode

A dynode is one of a series of electrodes within a photomultiplier tube. Each dynode is at a more positive electrical potential than its predecessor. Secondary emission occurs at the surface of each dynode.

Geiger counter

A Geiger-Müller counter, also called a Geiger counter, is a type of particle detector that measures ionizing radiation. It detects the emission of nuclear radiation -- alpha particles, beta particles, and gamma rays -- by the ionization produced in a low-pressure gas in a Geiger-Müller tube, which gives its name to the instrument. In wide and prominent use as a hand-held radiation survey instrument, it is perhaps one of the world's best-known radiation instruments.

Particle detector

In experimental and applied particle physics, nuclear physics, and nuclear engineering, a particle detector, also known as a radiation detector, is a device used to detect, track, and/or identify high-energy particles, such as those produced by nuclear decay, cosmic radiation, or reactions in a particle accelerator. Modern detectors are also used as calorimeters to measure the energy of the detected radiation. They may also be used to measure other attributes such as momentum, spin, charge etc.

Phosphor

A phosphor, most generally, is a substance that exhibits the phenomenon of luminescence. Somewhat confusingly, this includes both phosphorescent materials, which show a slow decay in brightness (> 1 ms), and fluorescent materials, where the emission decay takes place over tens of nanoseconds. Phosphorescent materials are known for their use in radar screens and glow-in-the-dark toys, whereas fluorescent materials are common in cathode ray tube (CRT) and plasma video display screens, sensors, and white LEDs.

Photocathode

A photocathode is a negatively charged electrode in a light detection device such as a photomultiplier or phototube that is coated with a photosensitive compound. When this is struck by a quantum of light (photon), the absorbed energy causes electron emission due to the photoelectric effect.

Scintillation counter	A scintillation counter is an instrument for detecting and measuring ionizing radiation. It consists of a scintillator which generates photons of light in response to incident radiation, a sensitive photomultiplier tube which converts the light to an electrical signal, and the necessary electronics to process the photomultiplier tube output. Scintillation counters are widely used because they can be made inexpensively yet with good quantum efficiency and can measure both the intensity and the energy of incident radiation.
Scintillator	A scintillator is a material that exhibits scintillation -- the property of luminescence when excited by ionizing radiation. Luminescent materials, when struck by an incoming particle, absorb its energy and scintillate, (i.e., re-emit the absorbed energy in the form of light). Sometimes, the excited state is metastable, so the relaxation back down from the excited state to lower states is delayed (necessitating anywhere from a few microseconds to hours depending on the material): the process then corresponds to either one of two phenomena, depending on the type of transition and hence the wavelength of the emitted optical photon: delayed fluorescence or phosphorescence, also called after-glow.
Bubble chamber	A bubble chamber is a vessel filled with a superheated transparent liquid used to detect electrically charged particles moving through it. It was invented in 1952 by Donald A. Glaser, for which he was awarded the 1960 Nobel Prize in Physics. Supposedly, Glaser was inspired by the bubbles in a glass of beer; however, in a 2006 talk, he refuted this story, saying that although beer was not the inspiration for the bubble chamber, he did experiments using beer to fill early prototypes.
Cloud chamber	The cloud chamber, also known as the Wilson chamber, is a particle detector used for detecting ionizing radiation. In its most basic form, a cloud chamber is a sealed environment containing a supersaturated vapor of water or alcohol. When a charged particle (for example, an alpha or beta particle) interacts with the mixture, it ionizes it.
Diode	In electronics, a diode is a two-terminal electronic component with asymmetric conductance, it has low resistance to current flow in one direction, and high (ideally infinite) resistance in the other. Diodes were the first semiconductor electronic devices. The discovery of crystals' rectifying abilities was made by German physicist Ferdinand Braun in 1874. The first semiconductor diodes, called cat's whisker diodes, developed around 1906, were made of mineral crystals such as galena.
Photographic emulsion	Photographic emulsion is a light-sensitive colloid. Most commonly, in silver-gelatin photography it consists of silver halide crystals dispersed in gelatin. The emulsion is usually coated onto a substrate of glass, films of cellulose nitrate, cellulose acetate or polyester, paper or fabric.

29. NUCLEAR PHYSICS AND RADIOACTIVITY

CHAPTER HIGHLIGHTS & NOTES: KEY TERMS, PEOPLE, PLACES, CONCEPTS

Semiconductor detector	A semiconductor detector is a device that uses a semiconductor to detect traversing charged particles or the absorption of photons. In the field of particle physics, these detectors are usually known as silicon detectors. When their sensitive structures are based on a single diode, they are called semiconductor diode detectors.
Rubidium-strontium dating	The rubidium-strontium dating method is a radiometric dating technique used by scientists to determine the age of rocks and minerals from the quantities they contain of specific isotopes of rubidium and strontium (^{87}Sr, ^{86}Sr). Development of this process was aided by German chemist Fritz Strassmann, who later went on to discover nuclear fission with German chemist Otto Hahn and Swedish physicist Lise Meitner. The utility of the rubidium-strontium isotope system results from the fact that ^{87}Rb (one of two naturally occurring isotopes of rubidium) decays to ^{87}Sr with a half life of 48.8 billion years.
Mass excess	The mass excess of a nuclide is the difference between its actual mass and its mass number in atomic mass units. It is one of the predominant methods for tabulating nuclear mass. The mass of an atomic nucleus is well approximated (less than 0.1 difference for most nuclides) by its mass number, which indicates that most of the mass of a nucleus arises from mass of its constituent protons and neutrons.
Potassium	Potassium is a chemical element with symbol K and atomic number 19. Elemental potassium is a soft silvery-white alkali metal that oxidizes rapidly in air and is very reactive with water, generating sufficient heat to ignite the hydrogen emitted in the reaction and burning with a lilac flame. Naturally occurring potassium is composed of three isotopes, one of which, ^{40}K, is radioactive. Traces, (0.01%), of this isotope is found in all potassium making it the most common radioactive element in the Human body and in many biological materials, as well as in common building materials such as concrete.
Strontium	Strontium is a chemical element with symbol Sr and atomic number 38. An alkaline earth metal, strontium is a soft silver-white or yellowish metallic element that is highly reactive chemically. The metal turns yellow when it is exposed to air. Strontium has physical and chemical properties similar to those of its two neighbors calcium and barium.

1. Corresponding to most kinds of particles, there is an associated _________ with the same mass and opposite charge . For example, the _________ of the electron is the positively charged antielectron, or positron, which is produced naturally in certain types of radioactive decay.

   The laws of nature are very nearly symmetrical with respect to particles and _________s.

   a. Friedrich Oskar Giesel
   b. Kuznetsov NK-14
   c. Panel edge staining
   d. Antiparticle

2. _________ is the field of physics that studies the constituents and interactions of atomic nuclei. The most commonly known applications of _________ are nuclear power generation and nuclear weapons technology, but the research has provided application in many fields, including those in nuclear medicine and magnetic resonance imaging, ion implantation in materials engineering, and radiocarbon dating in geology and archaeology.

   The field of particle physics evolved out of _________ and is typically taught in close association with _________.

   a. Friedrich Oskar Giesel
   b. Nuclear physics
   c. Sibplaz
   d. The Aluminum Association

3. The mass number, also called _________ or nucleon number, is the total number of protons and neutrons (together known as nucleons) in an atomic nucleus. Because protons and neutrons both are baryons, the mass number A is identical with the baryon number B as of the nucleus as of the whole atom or ion. The mass number is different for each different isotope of a chemical element.

   a. Atomic mass number
   b. Panel edge staining
   c. Sibplaz
   d. The Aluminum Association

4. The _________ is the force between two or more nucleons. Its fundamental laws and constants are unknown unlike the Coulomb and Newton laws. It is responsible for binding protons and neutrons into atomic nuclei.

   a. Baryon number
   b. Beta decay
   c. Binary collision approximation
   d. Nuclear force

5. . In chemistry and physics, the _________ is the number of protons found in the nucleus of an atom and therefore identical to the charge number of the nucleus. It is conventionally represented by the symbol Z.

The _________ uniquely identifies a chemical element. In an atom of neutral charge, the _________ is also equal to the number of electrons.

a. 1s Slater-type function
b. Boson
c. Bohr model
d. Atomic number

ANSWER KEY
29. NUCLEAR PHYSICS AND RADIOACTIVITY

1. d

2. b

3. a

4. d

5. d

---

30. NUCLEAR ENERGY; EFFECTS AND USES OF RADIATION

CHAPTER OUTLINE: KEY TERMS, PEOPLE, PLACES, CONCEPTS

- Nuclear reaction
- Exothermic reaction
- Helium
- Endothermic
- Cross section
- Neptunium
- Plutonium
- Strong nuclear force
- Nuclear fission
- Reactor
- Nuclear reactor
- Control rod
- Critical mass
- Enriched uranium
- Graphite
- Heat engine
- Heavy water
- Nuclear power
- Research reactor
- Delayed neutron
- Breeder reactor

30. NUCLEAR ENERGY; EFFECTS AND USES OF RADIATION

CHAPTER OUTLINE: KEY TERMS, PEOPLE, PLACES, CONCEPTS

- Radioactive waste
- Nuclear fusion
- Energy source
- Plasma
- Hydrogen
- ITER
- Inertial confinement fusion
- Ionizing radiation
- Joint European Torus
- Lawson criterion
- National Ignition Facility
- Tokamak
- Tokamak Fusion Test Reactor
- Torus
- Dosimetry
- Mutation
- Photoelectric effect
- Radiation damage
- Ionization
- Radiation
- Absorbed dose

30. NUCLEAR ENERGY; EFFECTS AND USES OF RADIATION

CHAPTER OUTLINE: KEY TERMS, PEOPLE, PLACES, CONCEPTS

- Becquerel
- Curie
- Radionuclide
- Roentgen
- Effective dose
- Radon
- Relative biological effectiveness
- Radiation therapy
- Bragg peak
- Radioactive tracer
- Sterilization
- TRACER
- Gamma camera
- Medical imaging
- Positron
- Scintillator
- Technetium
- Nuclear magnetic resonance
- Chemical shift
- Magnetic resonance imaging

30. NUCLEAR ENERGY; EFFECTS AND USES OF RADIATION

CHAPTER HIGHLIGHTS & NOTES: KEY TERMS, PEOPLE, PLACES, CONCEPTS

Nuclear reaction	In nuclear physics and nuclear chemistry, a nuclear reaction is semantically considered to be the process in which two nuclei, or else a nucleus of an atom and a subatomic particle from outside the atom, collide to produce one or more nuclides that are different from the nuclide(s) that began the process. Thus, a nuclear reaction must cause a transformation of at least one nuclide to another. If a nucleus interacts with another nucleus or particle and they then separate without changing the nature of any nuclide, the process is simply referred to as a type of nuclear scattering, rather than a nuclear reaction.
Exothermic reaction	An exothermic reaction is a chemical reaction that releases energy in the form of light or heat. It is the opposite of an endothermic reaction. Expressed in a chemical equation: reactants ? products + energy
Helium	Helium is a chemical element with symbol He and atomic number 2. It is a colorless, odorless, tasteless, non-toxic, inert, monatomic gas that heads the noble gas group in the periodic table. Its boiling and melting points are the lowest among the elements and it exists only as a gas except in extreme conditions. Helium is the second lightest element and is the second most abundant element in the observable universe, being present at about 24% of the total elemental mass, which is more than 12 times the mass of all the heavier elements combined.
Endothermic	In thermodynamics, the term endothermic describes a process or reaction in which the system absorbs energy from its surroundings in the form of heat. It is a modern coinage from Greek roots. The prefix endo- derives from the Greek word 'endon' (??d??) meaning 'within,' and the latter part of the word comes from the Greek word root 'therm' (?e?µ-) meaning 'hot.' The intended sense is that of a reaction that depends on taking in heat if it is to proceed.
Cross section	A cross section is the effective area that governs the probability of some scattering or absorption event. Together with particle density and path length, it can be used to predict the total scattering probability via the Beer-Lambert law. In nuclear and particle physics, the concept of a cross section is used to express the likelihood of interaction between particles.
Neptunium	Neptunium is a chemical element with the symbol Np and atomic number 93. A radioactive actinide metal, neptunium is the first transuranic element. Its position in the periodic table just after uranium led to its being named after Neptune, the next planet beyond Uranus. A neptunium atom has 93 protons and 93 electrons, of which seven are valence electrons.
Plutonium	Plutonium is a transuranic radioactive chemical element with the symbol Pu and atomic number 94.

It is an actinide metal of silvery-gray appearance that tarnishes when exposed to air, and forms a dull coating when oxidized. The element normally exhibits six allotropes and four oxidation states. It reacts with carbon, halogens, nitrogen, silicon and hydrogen.

Strong nuclear force

In particle physics, the strong interaction (also called the strong force, strong nuclear force, nuclear strong force or color force) is one of the four fundamental interactions of nature, the others being electromagnetism, the weak interaction and gravitation. At atomic scale, it is about 100 times stronger than electromagnetism, which in turn is orders of magnitude stronger than the weak force interaction and gravitation. It ensures the stability of ordinary matter, in confining the elementary particles quarks into hadrons such as the proton and neutron, the largest components of the mass of ordinary matter.

Nuclear fission

In nuclear physics and nuclear chemistry, nuclear fission is either a nuclear reaction or a radioactive decay process in which the nucleus of a particle splits into smaller parts . The fission process often produces free neutrons and photons (in the form of gamma rays), and releases a very large amount of energy even by the energetic standards of radioactive decay.

Nuclear fission of heavy elements was discovered on December 17, 1938 by Otto Hahn and his assistant Fritz Strassmann, and explained theoretically in January 1939 by Lise Meitner and her nephew Otto Robert Frisch.

Reactor

Reactor can mean:In science•Nuclear reactor, a device for containing and controlling a nuclear reaction•Reactor a physics simulation engine•The reactor pattern, a design pattern used in concurrent programmingIn entertainment•Reactor an alternative title for the 1978 Italian film War of the Robots directed by Alfonso Brescia•Re-ac-tor, a 1981 album by Neil Young and Crazy Horse•Reactor an arcade game created by Gottlieb•Reactor, Inc., a defunct interactive entertainment company founded by Mike Saenz.

Nuclear reactor

A nuclear reactor is a device to initiate and control a sustained nuclear chain reaction. Nuclear reactors are used at nuclear power plants for electricity generation and in propulsion of ships. Heat from nuclear fission is passed to a working fluid (water or gas), which runs through turbines.

Control rod

A control rod is a rod used in nuclear reactors to control the rate of fission of uranium and plutonium. They are made of chemical elements capable of absorbing many neutrons without fissioning themselves, such as silver, indium and cadmium. Because these elements have different capture cross sections for neutrons of varying energies, the compositions of the control rods must be designed for the neutron spectrum of the reactor it is supposed to control.

Critical mass

A critical mass is the smallest amount of fissile material needed for a sustained nuclear chain reaction. The critical mass of a fissionable material depends upon its nuclear properties (specifically, the nuclear fission cross-section), its density, its shape, its enrichment, its purity, its temperature, and its surroundings.

30. NUCLEAR ENERGY; EFFECTS AND USES OF RADIATION

CHAPTER HIGHLIGHTS & NOTES: KEY TERMS, PEOPLE, PLACES, CONCEPTS

Enriched uranium	Enriched uranium is a type of uranium in which the percent composition of uranium-235 has been increased through the process of isotope separation. Natural uranium is 99.284% U^{238} isotope, with U^{235} only constituting about 0.711% of its weight. U^{235} is the only nuclide existing in nature (in any appreciable amount) that is fissile with thermal neutrons.
Graphite	The mineral graphite is an allotrope of carbon. It was named by Abraham Gottlob Werner in 1789 from the Ancient Greek ???f? (grapho), 'to draw/write', for its use in pencils, where it is commonly called lead (not to be confused with the metallic element lead). Unlike diamond (another carbon allotrope), graphite is an electrical conductor, a semimetal.
Heat engine	In thermodynamics, a heat engine is a system that performs the conversion of heat or thermal energy to mechanical work. It does this by bringing a working substance from a higher state temperature to a lower state temperature. A heat 'source' generates thermal energy that brings the working substance to the high temperature state.
Heavy water	Heavy water, formally called deuterium oxide or 2H2O or D_2O, is a form of water that contains a larger than normal amount of the hydrogen isotope deuterium, rather than the common hydrogen-1 isotope that makes up most of the hydrogen in normal water.
Nuclear power	Nuclear power, or nuclear energy, is the use of exothermic nuclear processes, to generate useful heat and electricity. The term includes nuclear fission, nuclear decay and nuclear fusion. Presently the nuclear fission of elements in the actinide series of the periodic table produce the vast majority of nuclear energy in the direct service of humankind, with nuclear decay processes, primarily in the form of geothermal energy, and radioisotope thermoelectric generators, in niche uses making up the rest.
Research reactor	Research reactors are nuclear reactors that serve primarily as a neutron source. They are also called non-power reactors, in contrast to power reactors that are used for electricity production, heat generation, or maritime propulsion.
Delayed neutron	In nuclear engineering, a delayed neutron is a neutron emitted after a nuclear fission event, by one of the fission products, any time from a few milliseconds to a few minutes after the fission event. Neutrons born within 10^{-14} seconds of the fission are termed 'prompt neutrons'. In a nuclear reactor large nuclides fission in two neutron-rich fission products (i.e. unstable nuclides).
Breeder reactor	A breeder reactor is a nuclear reactor capable of generating more fissile material than it consumes. These devices are able to achieve this feat because their neutron economy is high enough to breed more fissile fuel than they use from fertile material like uranium-238 or thorium-232.

Breeders were at first considered attractive because of their superior fuel economy compared to light water reactors. Interest in breeders declined after the 1960s as more uranium reserves were found, and new methods of uranium enrichment reduced fuel costs.

Radioactive waste

Radioactive wastes are wastes that contain radioactive material. Radioactive wastes are usually by -products of nuclear power generation and other applications of nuclear fission or nuclear technology, such as research and medicine. Radioactive waste is hazardous to most forms of life and the environment, and is regulated by government agencies in order to protect human health and the environment.

Nuclear fusion

In nuclear physics, nuclear fusion is a nuclear reaction in which two or more atomic nuclei collide at a very high speed and join to form a new type of atomic nucleus. During this process, matter is not conserved because some of the mass of the fusing nuclei is converted to photons (energy). Fusion is the process that powers active or 'main sequence' stars.

Energy source

Energy development is a field of endeavor focused on making available sufficient primary energy sources and secondary energy forms to meet the needs of society. These endeavors encompass those which provide for the production of conventional, alternative and renewable sources of energy, and for the recovery and reuse of energy that would otherwise be wasted. Energy conservation and efficiency measures reduce the impact of energy development, and can have benefits to society with changes in economic cost and with changes in the environmental effects.

Plasma

Plasma is one of the four fundamental states of matter (the others being solid, liquid, and gas). It comprises the major component of the Sun. Heating a gas may ionize its molecules or atoms (reducing or increasing the number of electrons in them), thus turning it into a plasma, which contains charged particles: positive ions and negative electrons or ions.

Hydrogen

Hydrogen is a chemical element with chemical symbol H and atomic number 1. With an atomic weight of 1.00794 u, hydrogen is the lightest element and its monatomic form (H) is the most abundant chemical substance, constituting roughly 75% of the Universe's baryonic mass. Non-remnant stars are mainly composed of hydrogen in its plasma state.

At standard temperature and pressure, hydrogen is a colorless, odorless, tasteless, non-toxic, nonmetallic, highly combustible diatomic gas with the molecular formula H_2.

ITER

ITER is an international nuclear fusion research and engineering project, which is currently building the world's largest experimental tokamak nuclear fusion reactor adjacent to the Cadarache facility in the south of France. The ITER project aims to make the long-awaited transition from experimental studies of plasma physics to full-scale electricity-producing fusion power plants. The project is funded and run by seven member entities -- the European Union (EU), India, Japan, China, Russia, South Korea and the United States.

30. NUCLEAR ENERGY; EFFECTS AND USES OF RADIATION

CHAPTER HIGHLIGHTS & NOTES: KEY TERMS, PEOPLE, PLACES, CONCEPTS

Inertial confinement fusion	Inertial confinement fusion is a type of fusion energy research that attempts to initiate nuclear fusion reactions by heating and compressing a fuel target, typically in the form of a pellet that most often contains a mixture of deuterium and tritium. To compress and heat the fuel, energy is delivered to the outer layer of the target using high-energy beams of laser light, electrons or ions, although for a variety of reasons, almost all Inertial confinement fusion devices to date have used lasers. The heated outer layer explodes outward, producing a reaction force against the remainder of the target, accelerating it inwards, compressing the target.
Ionizing radiation	Ionizing radiation is radiation composed of particles that individually carry enough kinetic energy to liberate an electron from an atom or molecule, ionizing it. Ionizing radiation is generated through nuclear reactions, either artificial or natural, by very high temperature (e.g. plasma discharge or the corona of the Sun), via production of high energy particles in particle accelerators, or due to acceleration of charged particles by the electromagnetic fields produced by natural processes, from lightning to supernova explosions. When ionizing radiation is emitted by or absorbed by an atom, it can liberate an atomic particle (typically an electron, proton, or neutron, but sometimes an entire nucleus) from the atom.
Joint European Torus	Joint European Torus, the Joint European Torus, is a magnetic confinement plasma physics experiment located in Oxfordshire, UK. It is currently the largest facility of its kind in operation. Its main purpose is to open the way to future nuclear fusion experimental tokamak reactors such as ITER and DEMO.
Lawson criterion	In nuclear fusion research, the Lawson criterion, first derived on fusion reactors by John D. Lawson in 1955 and published in 1957, is an important general measure of a system that defines the conditions needed for a fusion reactor to reach ignition, that is, that the heating of the plasma by the products of the fusion reactions is sufficient to maintain the temperature of the plasma against all losses without external power input. As originally formulated the Lawson criterion gives a minimum required value for the product of the plasma (electron) density n_e and the 'energy confinement time' τ_E . Later analyses suggested that a more useful figure of merit is the 'triple product' of density, confinement time, and plasma temperature T. The triple product also has a minimum required value, and the name 'Lawson criterion' often refers to this inequality.
National Ignition Facility	The National Ignition Facility, or National Ignition Facility, is a large, laser-based inertial confinement fusion research device located at the Lawrence Livermore National Laboratory in Livermore, California, USA. National Ignition Facility uses powerful lasers to heat and compress a small amount of hydrogen fuel to the point where nuclear fusion reactions take place. National Ignition Facility's mission is to achieve fusion ignition with high energy gain, and to support nuclear weapon maintenance and design by studying the behavior of matter under the conditions found within nuclear weapons.

Tokamak	A tokamak is a device using a magnetic field to confine a plasma in the shape of a torus. Achieving a stable plasma equilibrium requires magnetic field lines that move around the torus in a helical shape. Such a helical field can be generated by adding a toroidal field (traveling around the torus in circles) and a poloidal field (traveling in circles orthogonal to the toroidal field).
Tokamak Fusion Test Reactor	The Tokamak Fusion Test Reactor was an experimental tokamak built at Princeton Plasma Physics Laboratory (in Princeton, New Jersey) circa 1980. Following on from the PDX (Poloidal Diverter Experiment) and PLT (Princeton Large Torus) devices, it was hoped that Tokamak Fusion Test Reactor would finally achieve fusion energy break-even. Unfortunately, the Tokamak Fusion Test Reactor never achieved this goal. However it did produce major advances in confinement time and energy density, which ultimately contributed to the knowledge base necessary to build ITER. Tokamak Fusion Test Reactor operated from 1982 to 1997.
Torus	In geometry, a torus is a surface of revolution generated by revolving a circle in three-dimensional space about an axis coplanar with the circle. If the axis of revolution does not touch the circle, the surface has a ring shape and is called a ring torus or simply torus if the ring shape is implicit. When the axis is tangent to the circle, the resulting surface is called a horn torus; when the axis is a chord of the circle, it is called a spindle torus.
Dosimetry	Radiation dosimetry is the measurement and calculation of the radiation dose received by matter and tissue resulting from the exposure to indirect and direct ionizing radiation. It is a scientific sub-specialty in the fields of health physics and medical physics that is focused on the calculation and analysis of internal and external dose. Internal dose is calculated from a variety of physiological techniques, whilst external dose is measured with a dosimeter or inferred from other radiation instruments.
Mutation	In genetics, a mutation is a change of the nucleotide sequence of the genome of an organism, virus, or extrachromosomal genetic element. Mutations result from unrepaired damage to DNA or to RNA genomes (typically caused by radiation or chemical mutagens), errors in the process of replication, or from the insertion or deletion of segments of DNA by mobile genetic elements. Mutations may or may not produce discernible changes in the observable characteristics (phenotype) of an organism.
Photoelectric effect	In the photoelectric effect, electrons are emitted from solids, liquids or gases when they absorb energy from light. Electrons emitted in this manner may be called photoelectrons. In 1887, Heinrich Hertz discovered that electrodes illuminated with ultraviolet light create electric sparks more easily.
Radiation damage	Radiation damage is a term associated with ionizing radiation.

30. NUCLEAR ENERGY; EFFECTS AND USES OF RADIATION

CHAPTER HIGHLIGHTS & NOTES: KEY TERMS, PEOPLE, PLACES, CONCEPTS

Ionization	Ionization is the process by which an atom or a molecule acquires a negative or positive charge by gaining or losing electrons.
Radiation	In physics, radiation is a process in which energetic particles or energetic waves travel through a vacuum, or through matter-containing media that are not required for their propagation. Waves of a mass filled medium itself, such as water waves or sound waves, are usually not considered to be forms of 'radiation' in this sense. Radiation can be classified as either ionizing or non-ionizing according to whether it ionizes or does not ionize ordinary chemical matter.
Absorbed dose	Absorbed dose is a measure of the energy deposited in a medium by ionizing radiation per unit mass, which may be measured as joules per kilogram when it is represented by the equivalent SI unit, gray (Gy). The CGS units, rad and rep are also used. The absorbed dose from a given level of incident radiation depends on the absorbing medium.
Becquerel	The becquerel is the SI-derived unit of radioactivity. One Bq is defined as the activity of a quantity of radioactive material in which one nucleus decays per second. The Bq unit is therefore equivalent to an inverse second, s^{-1}.
Curie	The curie is a non-SI unit of radioactivity the curie is widely used throughout the US government and industry. One curie is roughly the activity of 1 gram of the radium isotope ^{226}Ra, a substance studied by the Curies. The SI derived unit of radioactivity is the becquerel (Bq), which equates to one decay per second.
Radionuclide	A radionuclide, or a radioactive nuclide, is an atom with an unstable nucleus, characterized by excess energy available to be imparted either to a newly created radiation particle within the nucleus or via internal conversion. During this process, the radionuclide is said to undergo radioactive decay, resulting in the emission of gamma ray(s) and/or subatomic particles such as alpha or beta particles. These emissions constitute ionizing radiation.
Roentgen	The roentgen is a legacy unit of measurement for the kerma of X-rays and gamma rays up to 3 MeV. The unit is still used in the United States Navy nuclear propulsion program. It is named after the German physicist Wilhelm Röntgen, who discovered X-rays. Originating in 1908, this unit has been redefined and renamed over the years.
Effective dose	The effective dose in radiation protection and radiology is a measure of the cancer risk to a whole organism due to ionizing radiation delivered non-uniformly to part of its body.

It takes into account both the type of radiation and the nature of each organ being irradiated. The SI unit for effective dose is the sievert (Sv) which is one joule/kilogram (J/kg).

Radon

Radon is a chemical element with symbol Rn and atomic number 86. It is a radioactive, colorless, odorless, tasteless noble gas, occurring naturally as an indirect decay product of uranium or thorium. Its most stable isotope, ^{222}Rn, has a half-life of 3.8 days. Radon is one of the densest substances that remains a gas under normal conditions.

Relative biological effectiveness

In radiology, the relative biological effectiveness is the ratio of biological effectiveness of one type of ionizing radiation relative to another, given the same amount of absorbed energy. The Relative biological effectiveness is an empirical value that varies depending on the particles, energies involved, and which biological effects are deemed relevant. It is a set of experimental measurements.

Radiation therapy

Radiation therapy, radiation oncology, or radiotherapy (in the UK, and Australia), sometimes abbreviated to XRT or DXT, is the medical use of ionizing radiation, generally as part of cancer treatment to control or kill malignant cells. Radiation therapy may be curative in a number of types of cancer if they are localized to one area of the body. It may also be used as part of adjuvant therapy, to prevent tumor recurrence after surgery to remove a primary malignant tumor (for example, early stages of breast cancer).

Bragg peak

The Bragg peak is a pronounced peak on the Bragg curve which plots the energy loss of ionizing radiation during its travel through matter. For protons, a-rays, and other ion rays, the peak occurs immediately before the particles come to rest. This is called Bragg peak, for William Henry Bragg who discovered it in 1903.

Radioactive tracer

A radioactive tracer, or radioactive label, is a chemical compound in which one or more atoms have been replaced by a radioisotope so by virtue of its radioactive decay it can be used to explore the mechanism of chemical reactions by tracing the path that the radioisotope follows from reactants to products.

Radioisotopes of hydrogen, carbon, phosphorus, sulphur, and iodine have been used extensively to trace the path of biochemical reactions. A radioactive tracer can also be used to track the distribution of a substance within a natural system such as a cell or tissue.

Sterilization

Sterilization is a term referring to any process that eliminates (removes) or kills all forms of microbial life, including transmissible agents (such as fungi, bacteria, viruses, spore forms, etc). present on a surface, contained in a fluid, in medication, or in a compound such as biological culture media. Sterilization can be achieved by applying heat, chemicals, irradiation, high pressure, and filtration or combinations thereof.

30. NUCLEAR ENERGY; EFFECTS AND USES OF RADIATION

CHAPTER HIGHLIGHTS & NOTES: KEY TERMS, PEOPLE, PLACES, CONCEPTS

TRACER	Transition Radiation Array for Cosmic Energetic Radiation (TRACER) is a balloon flown cosmic ray detector built and designed at the University of Chicago. The detector is designed to measure the energy spectra of cosmic ray nuclei with atomic numbers between five and twenty-six (boron to iron).
Gamma camera	A gamma camera, also called a scintillation camera or Anger camera, is a device used to image gamma radiation emitting radioisotopes, a technique known as scintigraphy. The applications of scintigraphy include early drug development and nuclear medical imaging to view and analyse images of the human body or the distribution of medically injected, inhaled, or ingested radionuclides emitting gamma rays.
Medical imaging	Medical imaging is the technique and process used to create images of the human body for clinical purposes (medical procedures seeking to reveal, diagnose, or examine disease) or medical science (including the study of normal anatomy and physiology). Although imaging of removed organs and tissues can be performed for medical reasons, such procedures are not usually referred to as medical imaging, but rather are a part of pathology. As a discipline and in its widest sense, it is part of biological imaging and incorporates Radiology, Magnetic Resonance Imaging, Nuclear medicine, medical Ultrasonography or Ultrasound, Endoscopy, Elastography, Tactile Imaging, Thermography and medical photography.
Positron	The positron or antielectron is the antiparticle or the antimatter counterpart of the electron. The positron has an electric charge of +1e, a spin of ½, and has the same mass as an electron. When a low-energy positron collides with a low-energy electron, annihilation occurs, resulting in the production of two or more gamma ray photons .
Scintillator	A scintillator is a material that exhibits scintillation -- the property of luminescence when excited by ionizing radiation. Luminescent materials, when struck by an incoming particle, absorb its energy and scintillate, (i.e., re-emit the absorbed energy in the form of light). Sometimes, the excited state is metastable, so the relaxation back down from the excited state to lower states is delayed (necessitating anywhere from a few microseconds to hours depending on the material): the process then corresponds to either one of two phenomena, depending on the type of transition and hence the wavelength of the emitted optical photon: delayed fluorescence or phosphorescence, also called after-glow.
Technetium	Technetium is the chemical element with atomic number 43 and the symbol Tc. It is the lowest atomic number element without any stable isotopes; every form of it is radioactive. Nearly all technetium is produced synthetically, and only minute amounts are found in nature.
Nuclear magnetic resonance	Nuclear magnetic resonance is a physical phenomenon in which nuclei in a magnetic field absorb and re-emit electromagnetic radiation.

This energy is at a specific resonance frequency which depends on the strength of the magnetic field and the magnetic properties of the isotope of the atoms; in practical applications, the frequency is similar to VHF and UHF television broadcasts (60-1000 MHz). Nuclear magnetic resonance allows the observation of specific quantum mechanical magnetic properties of the atomic nucleus.

Chemical shift — In nuclear magnetic resonance spectroscopy, the chemical shift is the resonant frequency of a nucleus relative to a standard. Often the position and number of chemical shifts are diagnostic of the structure of a molecule. Chemical shifts are also used to describe signals in other forms of spectroscopy such as photoemission spectroscopy.

Magnetic resonance imaging — Magnetic resonance imaging, nuclear magnetic resonance imaging or magnetic resonance tomography (MRT) is a medical imaging technique used in radiology to investigate the anatomy and function of the body in both health and disease. Magnetic resonance imaging scanners use strong magnetic fields and radiowaves to form images of the body. The technique is widely used in hospitals for medical diagnosis, staging of disease and for follow-up without exposure to ionizing radiation.

CHAPTER QUIZ: KEY TERMS, PEOPLE, PLACES, CONCEPTS

1. A _________ is the smallest amount of fissile material needed for a sustained nuclear chain reaction. The _________ of a fissionable material depends upon its nuclear properties (specifically, the nuclear fission cross-section), its density, its shape, its enrichment, its purity, its temperature, and its surroundings. The concept is important in nuclear weapon design.

   a. Critical mass
   b. Background radiation
   c. Background radiation equivalent time
   d. Bateman Equation

2. In thermodynamics, the term _________ describes a process or reaction in which the system absorbs energy from its surroundings in the form of heat. It is a modern coinage from Greek roots. The prefix endo- derives from the Greek word 'endon' (??d??) meaning 'within,' and the latter part of the word comes from the Greek word root 'therm' (?e?µ-) meaning 'hot.' The intended sense is that of a reaction that depends on taking in heat if it is to proceed.

   a. Endothermic
   b. Davies equation
   c. Bisulfide
   d. Buffer solution

3. _________ is the technique and process used to create images of the human body for clinical purposes (medical procedures seeking to reveal, diagnose, or examine disease) or medical science (including the study of normal anatomy and physiology). Although imaging of removed organs and tissues can be performed for medical reasons, such procedures are not usually referred to as _________, but rather are a part of pathology.

   As a discipline and in its widest sense, it is part of biological imaging and incorporates Radiology, Magnetic Resonance Imaging, Nuclear medicine, medical Ultrasonography or Ultrasound, Endoscopy, Elastography, Tactile Imaging, Thermography and medical photography.

   a. Background subtraction
   b. Bicubic interpolation
   c. Medical imaging
   d. Black balance

4. In nuclear magnetic resonance spectroscopy, the _________ is the resonant frequency of a nucleus relative to a standard. Often the position and number of _________s are diagnostic of the structure of a molecule. _________s are also used to describe signals in other forms of spectroscopy such as photoemission spectroscopy.

   a. Band emission
   b. Bathochromic shift
   c. Benchtop NMR spectrometer
   d. Chemical shift

5. _________ is a type of fusion energy research that attempts to initiate nuclear fusion reactions by heating and compressing a fuel target, typically in the form of a pellet that most often contains a mixture of deuterium and tritium.

   To compress and heat the fuel, energy is delivered to the outer layer of the target using high-energy beams of laser light, electrons or ions, although for a variety of reasons, almost all _________ devices to date have used lasers. The heated outer layer explodes outward, producing a reaction force against the remainder of the target, accelerating it inwards, compressing the target.

   a. Bootstrap current
   b. Bubble fusion
   c. Inertial confinement fusion
   d. Compact toroid

ANSWER KEY
30. NUCLEAR ENERGY; EFFECTS AND USES OF RADIATION

1. a
2. a
3. c
4. d
5. c

---

31. ELEMENTARY PARTICLES

CHAPTER OUTLINE: KEY TERMS, PEOPLE, PLACES, CONCEPTS

- Elementary particle
- Higgs boson
- Large Hadron Collider
- Atom
- Dark energy
- Dark matter
- Gauge boson
- Lepton
- Meson
- Neutron
- Nucleon
- Particle accelerator
- Photon
- Positron
- De Broglie
- De Broglie wavelength
- Fermilab
- Synchrotron radiation
- Tevatron
- Storage ring
- Super Proton Synchrotron

31. ELEMENTARY PARTICLES

CHAPTER OUTLINE: KEY TERMS, PEOPLE, PLACES, CONCEPTS

- CMOS
- International Linear Collider
- Particle detector
- Electromagnetic force
- Feynman diagram
- Nuclear force
- Quantum electrodynamics
- Virtual particle
- Electromagnetic
- Gluon
- Pion
- Antiparticle
- Antiproton
- Gravitational force
- Graviton
- Gravity
- Antineutron
- Bubble chamber
- Dirac equation
- Vacuum state
- Baryon number

31. ELEMENTARY PARTICLES

CHAPTER OUTLINE: KEY TERMS, PEOPLE, PLACES, CONCEPTS

- Conservation of energy
- Energy conservation
- Pair production
- Electric charge
- Lepton number
- Muon
- Solar neutrino problem
- Neutrino
- Baryon
- Boson
- Electron neutrino
- Hadron
- Muon neutrino
- Proton decay
- Tau neutrino
- Proton
- Bottom quark
- Kaon
- Strangeness
- Charm quark
- Down quark

31. ELEMENTARY PARTICLES

CHAPTER OUTLINE: KEY TERMS, PEOPLE, PLACES, CONCEPTS

- ______ Strange quark
- ______ Top quark
- ______ Up quark
- ______ Color charge
- ______ Exclusion principle
- ______ Fermion
- ______ Pauli exclusion principle
- ______ Quark
- ______ Glueball
- ______ Beta decay
- ______ Gauge theory
- ______ Grand Unified Theory
- ______ Higgs field
- ______ Supersymmetry
- ______ Symmetry breaking
- ______ Big Bang theory
- ______ Cosmology
- ______ Planck
- ______ Planck time
- ______ Brane
- ______ Gluino

31. ELEMENTARY PARTICLES

CHAPTER OUTLINE: KEY TERMS, PEOPLE, PLACES, CONCEPTS

______	M-theory
______	Photino
______	Superstring theory
______	Proper time

CHAPTER HIGHLIGHTS & NOTES: KEY TERMS, PEOPLE, PLACES, CONCEPTS

Elementary particle	In particle physics, an elementary particle or fundamental particle is a particle whose substructure is unknown, thus it is not known to be composed of other particles. Known elementary particles include the fundamental fermions (quarks, leptons, antiquarks, and antileptons), which generally are 'matter particles' and 'antimatter particles', as well as the fundamental bosons (gauge bosons and Higgs boson), which generally are 'force particles' that mediate interactions among fermions. A particle containing two or more elementary particles is a composite particle.
Higgs boson	The Higgs boson or Higgs particle is an elementary particle initially theorised in 1964, and tentatively confirmed to exist on 14 March 2013. The discovery has been called 'monumental' because it appears to confirm the existence of the Higgs field, which is pivotal to the Standard Model and other theories within particle physics. It would explain why some fundamental particles have mass when the symmetries controlling their interactions should require them to be massless, and--linked to this--why the weak force has a much shorter range than the electromagnetic force. The discovery of a Higgs boson should allow physicists to finally validate the last untested area of the Standard Model's approach to fundamental particles and forces, guide other theories and discoveries in particle physics, and potentially lead to developments in 'new' physics.
Large Hadron Collider	The Large Hadron Collider is the highest-energy particle collider ever made and is considered as 'one of the great engineering milestones of mankind.' It was built by the European Organization for Nuclear Research (CERN) from 1998 to 2008, with the aim of allowing physicists to test the predictions of different theories of particle physics and high-energy physics, and particularly prove or disprove the existence of the theorized Higgs particle and of the large family of new particles predicted by supersymmetric theories. The Higgs particle was confirmed by data from the Large Hadron Collider in 2013. The Large Hadron Collider is expected to address some of the unsolved questions of physics, advancing human understanding of physical laws. It contains seven detectors each designed for specific kinds of exploration.

31. ELEMENTARY PARTICLES

CHAPTER HIGHLIGHTS & NOTES: KEY TERMS, PEOPLE, PLACES, CONCEPTS

Atom

The atom is a basic unit of matter that consists of a dense central nucleus surrounded by a cloud of negatively charged electrons. The atomic nucleus contains a mix of positively charged protons and electrically neutral neutrons, which means 'uncuttable' or 'the smallest indivisible particle of matter'. Although the Indian and Greek concepts of the atom were based purely on philosophy, modern science has retained the name coined by Democritus.

Dark energy

In physical cosmology and astronomy, dark energy is a hypothetical form of energy that permeates all of space and tends to accelerate the expansion of the universe. Dark energy is the most accepted hypothesis to explain observations since the 1990s that indicate that the universe is expanding at an accelerating rate. According to the Planck mission team, and based on the standard model of cosmology, the total mass-energy of the universe contains 4.9% ordinary matter, 26.8% dark matter and 68.3% dark energy.

Dark matter

Dark matter is a type of matter hypothesized in astronomy and cosmology to account for a large part of the mass that appears to be missing from the universe. Dark matter cannot be seen directly with telescopes; evidently it neither emits nor absorbs light or other electromagnetic radiation at any significant level. Instead, the existence and properties of dark matter are inferred from its gravitational effects on visible matter, radiation, and the large-scale structure of the universe.

Gauge boson

In particle physics, a gauge boson is a force carrier, a bosonic particle that carries any of the fundamental interactions of nature. Elementary particles, whose interactions are described by a gauge theory, interact with each other by the exchange of gauge bosons--usually as virtual particles.

Lepton

A lepton is an elementary, spin-$^1/_2$ particle that does not undergo strong interactions, but is subject to the Pauli exclusion principle. The best known of all leptons is the electron, which governs nearly all of chemistry as it is found in atoms and is directly tied to all chemical properties. Two main classes of leptons exist: charged leptons (also known as the electron-like leptons), and neutral leptons (better known as neutrinos).

Meson

In particle physics, mesons are hadronic subatomic particles composed of one quark and one antiquark, bound together by the strong interaction. Because mesons are composed of sub-particles, they have a physical size, with a radius roughly one femtometre, which is about $^2/_3$ the size of a proton or neutron. All mesons are unstable, with the longest-lived lasting for only a few hundredths of a microsecond.

Neutron

The neutron is a subatomic hadron particle that has the symbol n or n0, no net electric charge and a mass slightly larger than that of a proton. With the exception of hydrogen-1, nuclei of atoms consist of protons and neutrons, which are therefore collectively referred to as nucleons. The number of protons in a nucleus is the atomic number and defines the type of element the atom forms.

Nucleon	In chemistry and physics, a nucleon is one of the particles that makes up the atomic nucleus. Each atomic nucleus consists of one or more nucleons, and each atom in turn consists of a cluster of nucleons surrounded by one or more electrons. There are two known kinds of nucleon: the neutron and the proton.
Particle accelerator	A particle accelerator is a device that uses electromagnetic fields to propel charged particles to high speeds and to contain them in well-defined beams. There are two basic classes of accelerators, known as electrostatic and oscillating field accelerators. Electrostatic accelerators use static electric fields to accelerate particles.
Photon	A photon is an elementary particle, the quantum of light and all other forms of electromagnetic radiation, and the force carrier for the electromagnetic force, even when static via virtual photons. The effects of this force are easily observable at both the microscopic and macroscopic level, because the photon has zero rest mass; this allows long distance interactions. Like all elementary particles, photons are currently best explained by quantum mechanics and exhibit wave-particle duality, exhibiting properties of both waves and particles.
Positron	The positron or antielectron is the antiparticle or the antimatter counterpart of the electron. The positron has an electric charge of +1e, a spin of ½, and has the same mass as an electron. When a low-energy positron collides with a low-energy electron, annihilation occurs, resulting in the production of two or more gamma ray photons .
De Broglie	Louis-Victor-Pierre-Raymond, 7th duc de Broglie, was a French physicist who made groundbreaking contributions to quantum theory. In his 1924 PhD thesis he postulated the wave nature of electrons and suggested that all matter has wave properties. This concept is known as wave-particle duality or the de Broglie hypothesis.
De Broglie wavelength	In quantum mechanics, the concept of matter waves or de Broglie waves reflects the wave-particle duality of matter. The theory was proposed by Louis de Broglie in 1924 in his PhD thesis. The de Broglie relations show that the wavelength is inversely proportional to the momentum of a particle and is also called de Broglie wavelength.
Fermilab	Fermi National Accelerator Laboratory (Fermilab), located just outside Batavia, Illinois, near Chicago, is a US Department of Energy national laboratory specializing in high-energy particle physics. As of January 1, 2007, Fermilab is operated by the Fermi Research Alliance, a joint venture of the University of Chicago, Illinois Institute of Technology and the Universities Research Association (URA). Fermilab is a part of the Illinois Technology and Research Corridor.
Synchrotron radiation	The electromagnetic radiation emitted when charged particles are accelerated radially is called synchrotron radiation. It is produced in synchrotrons using bending magnets, undulators and/or wigglers.

31. ELEMENTARY PARTICLES

CHAPTER HIGHLIGHTS & NOTES: KEY TERMS, PEOPLE, PLACES, CONCEPTS

Tevatron	The Tevatron was a circular particle accelerator in the United States, at the Fermi National Accelerator Laboratory, just east of Batavia, Illinois, and holds the title of the second highest energy particle collider in the world after the Large Hadron Collider (LHC) near Geneva, Switzerland. The Tevatron was a synchrotron that accelerated protons and antiprotons in a 6.86 km, or 4.26 mi, ring to energies of up to 1 TeV, hence its name. The Tevatron was completed in 1983 at a cost of $120 million and significant upgrade investments were made in 1983-2011.
Storage ring	A storage ring is a type of circular particle accelerator in which a continuous or pulsed particle beam may be kept circulating for a long period of time, up to many hours. Storage of a particular particle depends upon the mass, energy and usually charge of the particle being stored. Most commonly, storage rings are to store electrons, positrons, or protons.
Super Proton Synchrotron	The Super Proton Synchrotron is a particle accelerator of the synchrotron type at CERN. It is housed in a circular tunnel, 6.9 kilometres (4.3 mi) in circumference, straddling the border of France and Switzerland near Geneva, Switzerland.
CMOS	Complementary metal-oxide-semiconductor (CMOS) is a technology for constructing integrated circuits. CMOS technology is used in microprocessors, microcontrollers, static RAM, and other digital logic circuits. CMOS technology is also used for several analog circuits such as image sensors (CMOS sensor), data converters, and highly integrated transceivers for many types of communication.
International Linear Collider	The International Linear Collider is a proposed linear particle accelerator. It is planned to have a collision energy of 500 GeV initially, with the possibility for a later upgrade to 1000 GeV (1 TeV). The host country for the accelerator has not yet been chosen and proposed locations are Japan, Europe (CERN) and the USA (Fermilab).
Particle detector	In experimental and applied particle physics, nuclear physics, and nuclear engineering, a particle detector, also known as a radiation detector, is a device used to detect, track, and/or identify high-energy particles, such as those produced by nuclear decay, cosmic radiation, or reactions in a particle accelerator. Modern detectors are also used as calorimeters to measure the energy of the detected radiation. They may also be used to measure other attributes such as momentum, spin, charge etc.
Electromagnetic force	Electromagnetism, or the electromagnetic force is one of the four fundamental interactions in nature, the other three being the strong interaction, the weak interaction, and gravitation. This force is described by electromagnetic fields, and has innumerable physical instances including the interaction of electrically charged particles and the interaction of uncharged magnetic force fields with electrical conductors.

31. ELEMENTARY PARTICLES

Feynman diagram	In theoretical physics, Feynman diagrams are pictorial representations of the mathematical expressions governing the behavior of subatomic particles. The scheme is named for its inventor, Nobel Prize-winning American physicist Richard Feynman, and was first introduced in 1948. The interaction of sub-atomic particles can be complex and difficult to understand intuitively, and the Feynman diagrams allow for a simple visualization of what would otherwise be a rather arcane and abstract formula. As David Kaiser writes, 'since the middle of the 20th century, theoretical physicists have increasingly turned to this tool to help them undertake critical calculations,' and as such 'Feynman diagrams have revolutionized nearly every aspect of theoretical physics'.
Nuclear force	The nuclear force is the force between two or more nucleons. Its fundamental laws and constants are unknown unlike the Coulomb and Newton laws. It is responsible for binding protons and neutrons into atomic nuclei.
Quantum electrodynamics	In particle physics, quantum electrodynamics is the relativistic quantum field theory of electrodynamics. In essence, it describes how light and matter interact and is the first theory where full agreement between quantum mechanics and special relativity is achieved. QED mathematically describes all phenomena involving electrically charged particles interacting by means of exchange of photons and represents the quantum counterpart of classical electromagnetism giving a complete account of matter and light interaction.
Virtual particle	In physics, a virtual particle is a transient fluctuation that exhibits many of the characteristics of an ordinary particle, but that exists for a limited time. The concept of virtual particles arises in perturbation theory of quantum field theory where interactions between ordinary particles are described in terms of exchanges of virtual particles. Any process involving virtual particles admits a schematic representation known as a Feynman diagram, in which virtual particles are represented by internal lines.
Electromagnetic	Electromagnetic is a prefix used to specialise many technical terms that involve electromagnetism.
Gluon	Gluons are elementary particles that act as the exchange particles for the strong force between quarks, analogous to the exchange of photons in the electromagnetic force between two charged particles. In technical terms, gluons are vector gauge bosons that mediate strong interactions of quarks in quantum chromodynamics (QCD). Gluons themselves carry the color charge of the strong interaction.
Pion	In particle physics, a pion is any of three subatomic particles: p0, p+, and p-. Each pion consists of a quark and an antiquark and is therefore a meson. Pions are the lightest mesons and they play an important role in explaining the low-energy properties of the strong nuclear force.

31. ELEMENTARY PARTICLES

CHAPTER HIGHLIGHTS & NOTES: KEY TERMS, PEOPLE, PLACES, CONCEPTS

Antiparticle	Corresponding to most kinds of particles, there is an associated antiparticle with the same mass and opposite charge . For example, the antiparticle of the electron is the positively charged antielectron, or positron, which is produced naturally in certain types of radioactive decay. The laws of nature are very nearly symmetrical with respect to particles and antiparticles.
Antiproton	The antiproton, p, pronounced p-bar) is the antiparticle of the proton. Antiprotons are stable, but they are typically short-lived since any collision with a proton will cause both particles to be annihilated in a burst of energy. The existence of the antiproton with -1 electric charge, opposite to the +1 electric charge of the proton, was predicted by Paul Dirac in his 1933 Nobel Prize lecture.
Gravitational force	Gravitation, or gravity, is a natural phenomenon by which all physical bodies attract each other. It is most commonly recognized and experienced as the agent that gives weight to physical objects, and causes physical objects to fall toward the ground when dropped from a height. It is hypothesized that the gravitational force is mediated by a massless spin-2 particle called the graviton.
Graviton	In physics, the graviton is a hypothetical elementary particle that mediates the force of gravitation in the framework of quantum field theory. If it exists, the graviton is expected to be massless (because the gravitational force appears to have unlimited range) and must be a spin-2 boson. The spin follows from the fact that the source of gravitation is the stress-energy tensor, a second-rank tensor (compared to electromagnetism's spin-1 photon, the source of which is the four-current, a first-rank tensor).
Gravity	In chemistry, gravity is the density of a fluid, particularly a fuel. It is expressed in degrees, with lower numbers indicating heavier liquids and higher numbers indicating lighter liquids. See specific gravity and API gravity.
Antineutron	The antineutron is the antiparticle of the neutron with symbol n. It differs from the neutron only in that some of its properties have equal magnitude but opposite sign. It has the same mass as the neutron, and no net electric charge, but has opposite baryon number (+1 for neutron, -1 for the antineutron).
Bubble chamber	A bubble chamber is a vessel filled with a superheated transparent liquid used to detect electrically charged particles moving through it. It was invented in 1952 by Donald A. Glaser, for which he was awarded the 1960 Nobel Prize in Physics. Supposedly, Glaser was inspired by the bubbles in a glass of beer; however, in a 2006 talk, he refuted this story, saying that although beer was not the inspiration for the bubble chamber, he did experiments using beer to fill early prototypes.

Dirac equation

In particle physics, the Dirac equation is a relativistic wave equation derived by British physicist Paul Dirac in 1928 and later seen to be an elaboration of the work of Wolfgang Pauli. In its free form, or including electromagnetic interactions, it describes all spin-½ particles, such as electrons and quarks, and is consistent with both the principles of quantum mechanics and the theory of special relativity, and was the first theory to account fully for special relativity in the context of quantum mechanics.

It accounted for the fine details of the hydrogen spectrum in a completely rigorous way.

Vacuum state

In quantum field theory, the vacuum state is the quantum state with the lowest possible energy. Generally, it contains no physical particles. Zero-point field is sometimes used as a synonym for the vacuum state of an individual quantized field.

Baryon number

In particle physics, the baryon number is an approximate conserved quantum number of a system.

It is defined as $$B = \frac{1}{3}\left(n_{\mathrm{q}} - n_{\bar{\mathrm{q}}}\right),$$

where n_q is the number of quarks, and n_q is the number of antiquarks. Baryons (three quarks) have a baryon number of +1, mesons (one quark, one antiquark) a baryon number of 0, and antibaryons (three antiquarks) have a baryon number of -1. Exotic hadrons like pentaquarks (four quarks, one antiquark) and tetraquarks (two quarks, two antiquarks) are also classified as baryons and mesons depending on their baryon number.

Conservation of energy

In physics, the law of conservation of energy states that the total energy of an isolated system cannot change--it is said to be conserved over time. Energy can be neither created nor destroyed, but can change form, for instance chemical energy can be converted to kinetic energy in the explosion of a stick of dynamite.

A consequence of the law of conservation of energy is that a perpetual motion machine of the first kind cannot exist.

Energy conservation

Energy conservation refers to reducing energy through using less of an energy service. Energy conservation differs from efficient energy use, which refers to using less energy for a constant service. For example, driving less is an example of energy conservation.

Pair production

Pair production refers to the creation of an elementary particle and its antiparticle, usually when a photon interacts with a nucleus or another boson. For example an electron and its antiparticle, the positron, may be created. This is allowed, provided there is enough energy available to create the pair - at least the total rest mass energy of the two particles - and that the situation allows both energy and momentum to be conserved.

31. ELEMENTARY PARTICLES

CHAPTER HIGHLIGHTS & NOTES: KEY TERMS, PEOPLE, PLACES, CONCEPTS

Electric charge	Electric charge is the physical property of matter that causes it to experience a force when close to other electrically charged matter. There are two types of electric charges - positive and negative. Positively charged substances are repelled from other positively charged substances, but attracted to negatively charged substances; negatively charged substances are repelled from negative and attracted to positive.
Lepton number	In particle physics, the lepton number is the number of leptons minus the number of antileptons. In equation form, $L = n_\ell - n_{\overline{\ell}}$ so all leptons have assigned a value of +1, antileptons -1, and non-leptonic particles 0. Lepton number is an additive quantum number, which means that its sum is preserved in interactions (as opposed to multiplicative quantum numbers such as parity, where the product is preserved instead). Beside the leptonic number, leptonic family numbers are also defined:•L_e?, the electronic number for the electron and the electron neutrino;•L_μ?, the muonic number for the muon and the muon neutrino;•L_t?, the tauonic number for the tau and the tau neutrino; with the same assigning scheme as the leptonic number: +1 for particles of the corresponding family, -1 for the antiparticles, and 0 for leptons of other families or non-leptonic particles.
Muon	The muon is an elementary particle similar to the electron, with unitary negative electric charge of roughly -1 and a spin of $^1/_2$, but with much more mass (105.7 MeV/c2). Together with the electron (mass 0.511 MeV/c2), the tau (mass 1,777.8 MeV/c2), and the three neutrinos, it is classified as a lepton. As is the case with other leptons, the muon is not believed to have any sub-structure at all (i.e., is not thought to be composed of any simpler particles), except possibly at the string scale.
Solar neutrino problem	The solar neutrino problem was a major discrepancy between measurements of the numbers of neutrinos flowing through the Earth and theoretical models of the solar interior, lasting from the mid -1960s to about 2002. The discrepancy has since been resolved by new understanding of neutrino physics, requiring a modification of the Standard Model of particle physics - specifically, neutrino oscillation. Essentially, as neutrinos have mass, they can change from the type that had been expected to be produced in the Sun's interior into two types that would not be caught by the detectors in use at the time.
Neutrino	A neutrino is an electrically neutral, weakly interacting elementary subatomic particle with half-integer spin. The neutrino is denoted by the Greek letter ? (nu). All evidence suggests that neutrinos have mass but that their mass is tiny even by the standards of subatomic particles.
Baryon	A baryon is a composite subatomic particle made up of three quarks .

Baryons and mesons belong to the hadron family, which are the quark-based particles. The name 'baryon' comes from the Greek word for 'heavy' (ßa???, barys), because, at the time of their naming, most known elementary particles had lower masses than the baryons.

Boson

In particle physics, the bosons comprise one of two classes of elementary particles, the other being fermions. The name boson was coined by Paul Dirac to commemorate the contribution of Satyendra Nath Bose in developing, with Einstein, Bose-Einstein statistics--which theorizes the characteristics of elementary particles. Examples of bosons include fundamental particles (e.g., the Higgs boson, the four force-carrying gauge bosons of the Standard Model, and the still-theoretical graviton of quantum gravity); composite particles (e.g., mesons and stable nuclei of even mass number such as deuterium, helium-4, or lead-208); and quasiparticles (e.g. Cooper pairs, plasmons, and phonons).

Electron neutrino

The electron neutrino is a subatomic lepton elementary particle which has no net electric charge. Together with the electron it forms the first generation of leptons, hence its name electron neutrino. It was first hypothesized by Wolfgang Pauli in 1930, to account for missing momentum and missing energy in beta decay, and was discovered in 1956 by a team led by Clyde Cowan and Frederick Reines .

Hadron

In particle physics, a hadron is a composite particle made of quarks held together by the strong force (in a similar way as atoms and molecules are held together by the electromagnetic force).

Hadrons are categorized into two families: baryons (such as protons and neutrons, made of three quarks) and mesons (such as pions, made of one quark and one antiquark). Other types of hadron may exist, such as tetraquarks (or, more generally, exotic mesons) and pentaquarks (exotic baryons), but no current evidence conclusively suggests their existence.

Muon neutrino

The muon neutrino is a subatomic lepton elementary particle which has the symbol ?µ and no net electric charge. Together with the muon it forms the second generation of leptons, hence its name muon neutrino. It was first hypothesized in the early 1940s by several people, and was discovered in 1962 by Leon Lederman, Melvin Schwartz and Jack Steinberger.

Proton decay

In particle physics, proton decay is a hypothetical form of radioactive decay in which the proton decays into lighter subatomic particles, such as a neutral pion and a positron. There is currently no experimental evidence that proton decay occurs.

In the Standard Model, protons, a type of baryon, are theoretically stable because baryon number (quark number) is conserved .

Tau neutrino

The tau neutrino or tauon neutrino is a subatomic elementary particle which has the symbol ?t and no net electric charge. Together with the tau, it forms the third generation of leptons, hence its name tau neutrino.

31. ELEMENTARY PARTICLES

CHAPTER HIGHLIGHTS & NOTES: KEY TERMS, PEOPLE, PLACES, CONCEPTS

Proton

The proton is a subatomic particle with the symbol p or p+ and a positive electric charge of 1 elementary charge. One or more protons are present in the nucleus of each atom. The number of protons in each atom is its atomic number.

Bottom quark

The bottom quark or b quark, also known as the beauty quark, is a third-generation quark with a charge of $-^{1}/_{3}$ e. Although all quarks are described in a similar way by the quantum chromodynamics, the bottom quark's large bare mass (around 4,200 MeV/c^2, a bit more than four times the mass of a proton), combined with low values of the CKM matrix elements V_{ub} and V_{cb}, gives it a distinctive signature that makes it relatively easy to identify experimentally (using a technique called B-tagging). Because three generations of quark are required for CP violation, mesons containing the bottom quark are the easiest particles to use to investigate the phenomenon; such experiments are being performed at the BaBar and Belle experiments.

Kaon

In particle physics, a kaon, also called a K meson and denoted K, is any of a group of four mesons distinguished by a quantum number called strangeness. In the quark model they are understood to be bound states of a strange quark (or antiquark) and an up or down antiquark (or quark).

Kaons have proved to be a copious source of information on the nature of fundamental interactions since their discovery in cosmic rays in 1947. They were essential in establishing the foundations of the Standard Model of particle physics, such as the quark model of hadrons and the theory of quark mixing (the latter was acknowledged by a Nobel Prize in Physics in 2008).

Strangeness

In particle physics, strangeness S is a property of particles, expressed as a quantum number, for describing decay of particles in strong and electromagnetic reactions, which occur in a short period of time. The strangeness of a particle is defined as: $S = -(n_s - n_{\bar{s}})$

where n_s represents the number of strange quarks and n_s represents the number of strange antiquarks (s).

The terms strange and strangeness predate the discovery of the quark, and were adopted after its discovery in order to preserve the continuity of the phrase; strangeness of anti-particles being referred to as +1, and particles as -1 as per the original definition.

Charm quark

The charm quark or c quark is the third most massive of all quarks, a type of elementary particle. Charm quarks are found in hadrons, which are subatomic particles made of quarks. Example of hadrons containing charm quarks include the J/? meson, D mesons, charmed Sigma baryons (Sc), and other charmed particles.

Down quark

The down quark or d quark is the second-lightest of all quarks, a type of elementary particle, and a major constituent of matter. Together with the up quark, it forms the neutrons (one up quark, two down quarks) and protons (two up quarks, one down quark) of atomic nuclei.

It is part of the first generation of matter, has an electric charge of $-^{1}/_{3}$ e and a bare mass of 4.8+0.5 -0.3 MeV/c^2.

Strange quark	The strange quark or s quark is the third-lightest of all quarks, a type of elementary particle. Strange quarks are found in subatomic particles called hadrons. Example of hadrons containing strange quarks include kaons, strange D mesons (Ds), Sigma baryons, and other strange particles.
Top quark	The top quark, also known as the t quark or truth quark, is an elementary particle and a fundamental constituent of matter. Like all quarks, the top quark is an elementary fermion with spin-$^{1}/_{2}$, and experiences all four fundamental interactions: gravitation, electromagnetism, weak interactions, and strong interactions. It has an electric charge of $+^{2}/_{3}$ e, and is the most massive of all observed elementary particles.
Up quark	The up quark or u quark is the lightest of all quarks, a type of elementary particle, and a major constituent of matter. It, along with the down quark, forms the neutrons (one up quark, two down quarks) and protons (two up quarks, one down quark) of atomic nuclei. It is part of the first generation of matter, has an electric charge of $+^{2}/_{3}$ e and a bare mass of 1.8-3.0 MeV/c^2.
Color charge	In particle physics, color charge is a property of quarks and gluons that is related to the particles' strong interactions in the theory of quantum chromodynamics . Color charge has analogies with the notion of electric charge of particles, but because of the mathematical complications of QCD, there are many technical differences. The 'color' of quarks and gluons is completely unrelated to visual perception of color.
Exclusion principle	The Exclusion principle is a philosophical principle that states:If an event e causes event e*, then there is no event e# such that e# is non-supervenient on e and e# causes e*..
Fermion	In particle physics, a fermion is any particle characterized by Fermi-Dirac statistics and following the Pauli exclusion principle; fermions include all quarks and leptons, as well as any composite particle made of an odd number of these, such as all baryons and many atoms and nuclei. Fermions contrast with bosons which obey Bose-Einstein statistics. A fermion can be an elementary particle, such as the electron; or it can be a composite particle, such as the proton.
Pauli exclusion principle	The Pauli exclusion principle is the quantum mechanical principle that no two identical fermions may occupy the same quantum state simultaneously. A more rigorous statement is that the total wave function for two identical fermions is anti-symmetric with respect to exchange of the particles. The principle was formulated by Austrian physicist Wolfgang Pauli in 1925.
Quark	A quark is an elementary particle and a fundamental constituent of matter.

Quarks combine to form composite particles called hadrons, the most stable of which are protons and neutrons, the components of atomic nuclei. Due to a phenomenon known as color confinement, quarks are never directly observed or found in isolation; they can be found only within hadrons, such as baryons, named up, down, strange, charm, bottom, and top .

Glueball

In particle physics, a glueball is a hypothetical composite particle. It consists solely of gluon particles, without valence quarks. Such a state is possible because gluons carry color charge and experience the strong interaction.

Beta decay

In nuclear physics, beta decay is a type of radioactive decay in which a beta particle (an electron or a positron) is emitted from an atomic nucleus. Beta decay is a process which allows the atom to obtain the optimal ratio of protons and neutrons.

Beta decay is mediated by the weak force.

Gauge theory

In physics, a gauge theory is a type of field theory in which the Lagrangian is invariant under a continuous group of local transformations.

The term gauge refers to redundant degrees of freedom in the Lagrangian. The transformations between possible gauges, called gauge transformations, form a Lie group--referred to as the symmetry group or the gauge group of the theory.

Grand Unified Theory

A Grand Unified Theory is a model in particle physics in which at high energy, the three gauge interactions of the Standard Model which define the electromagnetic, weak, and strong interactions, are merged into one single interaction characterized by one larger gauge symmetry and thus one unified coupling constant. In contrast, the experimentally supported Standard Model of particle physics is based on three independent interactions, symmetries and coupling constants.

Models that do not unify all interactions using one simple Lie group as the gauge symmetry, but do so using semisimple groups, can exhibit similar properties and are sometimes referred to as Grand Unified Theories as well.

Higgs field

Spontaneous symmetry breaking, a vacuum Higgs field, a Higgs boson are quantum phenomena. A vacuum Higgs field is responsible for spontaneous symmetry breaking the gauge symmetries of fundamental interactions and provides the Higgs mechanism of generating mass of elementary particles. However, no adequate mathematical model of this Higgs vacuum has been suggested in the framework of quantum gauge theory, though somebody treats it as sui generis a condensate by analogy with that of Cooper pairs in condensed matter physics.

Supersymmetry

In particle physics, supersymmetry, SUSY, is a proposed extension of spacetime symmetry that relates two basic classes of elementary particles: bosons, which have an integer-valued spin, and fermions, which have a half-integer spin.

Each particle from one group is associated with a particle from the other, called its superpartner, whose spin differs by a half-integer. In a theory with unbroken supersymmetry each pair of superpartners shares the same mass and internal quantum numbers besides spin, but since no superpartners have been observed yet, supersymmetry must be a spontaneously broken symmetry.

Symmetry breaking

Symmetry breaking in physics describes a phenomenon where small fluctuations acting on a system which is crossing a critical point decide the system's fate, by determining which branch of a bifurcation is taken. To an outside observer unaware of the fluctuations (or 'noise'), the choice will appear arbitrary. This process is called symmetry 'breaking', because such transitions usually bring the system from a symmetric but disorderly state into one or more definite states.

Big Bang theory

The Big Bang theory is the prevailing cosmological model for the early development of the Universe. According to the theory, the Big Bang occurred approximately 13.798 ± 0.037 billion years ago, which is thus considered the age of the universe. At this time, the Universe was in an extremely hot and dense state and began expanding rapidly.

Cosmology

Cosmology is the study of the origins and eventual fate of the universe. Physical cosmology is the scholarly and scientific study of the origin, evolution, structure, dynamics, and ultimate fate of the universe, as well as the natural laws that keep it in order. Religious cosmology is a body of beliefs based on the historical, mythological, religious, and esoteric literature and traditions of creation and eschatology.

Planck

Max Karl Ernst Ludwig Planck, FRS was a German theoretical physicist who originated quantum theory, which won him the Nobel Prize in Physics in 1918.

Planck made many contributions to theoretical physics, but his fame rests primarily on his role as originator of the quantum theory. This theory revolutionized human understanding of atomic and subatomic processes, just as Albert Einstein's theory of relativity revolutionized the understanding of space and time.

Planck time

In physics, the Planck time is the unit of time in the system of natural units known as Planck units. It is the time required for light to travel, in a vacuum, a distance of 1 Planck length. The unit is named after Max Planck, who was the first to propose it.

Brane

A brane, in string theory and related theories such as supergravity theories, is a physical object that generalizes the notion of a point particle to higher dimensions. For example, a point particle can be viewed as a brane of dimension zero, while a string can be viewed as a brane of dimension one. It is also possible to consider higher dimensional branes.

Gluino

A gluino is the hypothetical supersymmetric partner of a gluon.

31. ELEMENTARY PARTICLES

Gluinos are expected by supersymmetry theorists to be pair produced in particle accelerators such as the Large Hadron Collider if they exist.

In supersymmetric theories, gluinos are Majorana fermions and interact via the strong force as a color octet.

M-theory

In theoretical physics, M-theory is an extension of string theory in which 11 dimensions of spacetime are identified as seven higher-dimensions plus the four common dimensions . Proponents believe that the 11-dimensional theory unites all five 10 dimensional string theories and supersedes them. Though a full description of the theory is not known, the low-entropy dynamics are known to be supergravity interacting with 2- and 5-dimensional membranes.

Photino

A photino is a subatomic particle, the fermion WIMP superpartner of the photon predicted by supersymmetry. It is an example of a gaugino. Photinos have a lepton number 0, baryon number 0, and spin 1/2. With an R-parity of -1 it is a possible candidate for dark matter.

Superstring theory

Superstring theory is an attempt to explain all of the particles and fundamental forces of nature in one theory by modelling them as vibrations of tiny supersymmetric strings.

'Superstring theory' is a shorthand for supersymmetric string theory because unlike bosonic string theory, it is the version of string theory that incorporates fermions and supersymmetry.

Since the second superstring revolution the five superstring theories are regarded as different limits of a single theory tentatively called M-theory, or simply string theory.

Proper time

In relativity, proper time is the elapsed time between two events as measured by a clock that passes through both events. The proper time depends not only on the events but also on the motion of the clock between the events. An accelerated clock will measure a smaller elapsed time between two events than that measured by a non-accelerated (inertial) clock between the same two events.

1. In particle physics, a _________ is any of three subatomic particles: p0, p+, and p-. Each _________ consists of a quark and an antiquark and is therefore a meson. _________s are the lightest mesons and they play an important role in explaining the low-energy properties of the strong nuclear force.

   a. B meson
   b. Bottom eta meson
   c. Pion
   d. Kaon

2. In chemistry, _________ is the density of a fluid, particularly a fuel. It is expressed in degrees, with lower numbers indicating heavier liquids and higher numbers indicating lighter liquids. See specific _________ and API _________.

   a. Bollard pull
   b. Carcel
   c. Characteristic admittance
   d. Gravity

3. _________ is a prefix used to specialise many technical terms that involve electromagnetism.

   a. Aneroid
   b. Electromagnetic
   c. Arithmetic hyperbolic 3-manifold
   d. BF model

4. A _________ is a device that uses electromagnetic fields to propel charged particles to high speeds and to contain them in well-defined beams.

   There are two basic classes of accelerators, known as electrostatic and oscillating field accelerators. Electrostatic accelerators use static electric fields to accelerate particles.

   a. Particle accelerator
   b. Hadron collider
   c. KALI
   d. LHC Accelerator Research Program

5. . The _________ is a subatomic hadron particle that has the symbol n or n0, no net electric charge and a mass slightly larger than that of a proton. With the exception of hydrogen-1, nuclei of atoms consist of protons and _________s, which are therefore collectively referred to as nucleons. The number of protons in a nucleus is the atomic number and defines the type of element the atom forms.

   a. Baryon
   b. Baryonic dark matter
   c. Neutron

ANSWER KEY
31. ELEMENTARY PARTICLES

1. c
2. d
3. b
4. a
5. c

---

32. ASTROPHYSICS AND COSMOLOGY

CHAPTER OUTLINE: KEY TERMS, PEOPLE, PLACES, CONCEPTS

- Cosmology
- General theory of relativity
- Gravitational force
- Gravity
- Galaxy
- Orion
- Spiral galaxy
- Supercluster
- Luminosity
- Neutron star
- Quasar
- Red giant
- White dwarf
- Neutron
- Coulomb barrier
- Nuclear fusion
- Nucleosynthesis
- Energy source
- Evolution
- Exclusion principle
- Pauli exclusion principle

32. ASTROPHYSICS AND COSMOLOGY

CHAPTER OUTLINE: KEY TERMS, PEOPLE, PLACES, CONCEPTS

- Binary system
- Neutron capture
- Beta decay
- Inverse Beta Decay
- Parallax
- Triangulation
- PARSEC
- Electromagnetic force
- Gravitational field
- Nuclear force
- Redshift
- Special theory of relativity
- Electromagnetic
- Einstein Cross
- Einstein ring
- Geodesic
- Curvature
- Event horizon
- Gravitational collapse
- Schwarzschild radius
- Singularity

32. ASTROPHYSICS AND COSMOLOGY

CHAPTER OUTLINE: KEY TERMS, PEOPLE, PLACES, CONCEPTS

Event

Universe

Blueshift

Gravitational redshift

Big Bang theory

Observable universe

Observable

Horizon

Lepton

Planck

Standard Model

Baryon number

Hadron

Nucleon

Photon

Symmetry breaking

Lepton number

Quark

Dark energy

Dark matter

Flatness

32. ASTROPHYSICS AND COSMOLOGY

CHAPTER OUTLINE: KEY TERMS, PEOPLE, PLACES, CONCEPTS

	Quantum fluctuation
	Vacuum state
	Magnetic monopole
	Baryon
	Cosmological constant
	Vacuum energy
	Gravity wave

CHAPTER HIGHLIGHTS & NOTES: KEY TERMS, PEOPLE, PLACES, CONCEPTS

Cosmology	Cosmology is the study of the origins and eventual fate of the universe. Physical cosmology is the scholarly and scientific study of the origin, evolution, structure, dynamics, and ultimate fate of the universe, as well as the natural laws that keep it in order. Religious cosmology is a body of beliefs based on the historical, mythological, religious, and esoteric literature and traditions of creation and eschatology.
General theory of relativity	General relativity, or the general theory of relativity, is the geometric theory of gravitation published by Albert Einstein in 1916 and the current description of gravitation in modern physics. General relativity generalizes special relativity and Newton's law of universal gravitation, providing a unified description of gravity as a geometric property of space and time, or spacetime. In particular, the curvature of spacetime is directly related to the energy and momentum of whatever matter and radiation are present.
Gravitational force	Gravitation, or gravity, is a natural phenomenon by which all physical bodies attract each other. It is most commonly recognized and experienced as the agent that gives weight to physical objects, and causes physical objects to fall toward the ground when dropped from a height. It is hypothesized that the gravitational force is mediated by a massless spin-2 particle called the graviton.
Gravity	In chemistry, gravity is the density of a fluid, particularly a fuel.

It is expressed in degrees, with lower numbers indicating heavier liquids and higher numbers indicating lighter liquids. See specific gravity and API gravity.

Galaxy

A galaxy is a massive, gravitationally bound system consisting of stars, stellar remnants, an interstellar medium of gas and dust, and dark matter, an important but poorly understood component. The word galaxy is derived from the Greek galaxias, literally 'milky', a reference to the Milky Way. Examples of galaxies range from dwarfs with as few as ten million galaxies in the observable universe.

Orion

Orion is a system-on-a-chip manufactured by Marvell Technology Group and used in network-attached storage. Based on the ARM architecture, it has on-chip support for Ethernet, SATA and USB, and is used in hardware made by Hewlett-Packard and D-Link among others. It is supported by the Lenny release of Debian GNU/Linux.

Spiral galaxy

A spiral galaxy is a certain kind of galaxy originally described by Edwin Hubble in his 1936 work The Realm of the Nebulae and, as such, forms part of the Hubble sequence. Spiral galaxies consist of a flat, rotating disk containing stars, gas and dust, and a central concentration of stars known as the bulge. These are surrounded by a much fainter halo of stars, many of which reside in globular clusters.

Supercluster

Superclusters are large groups of smaller galaxy groups and galaxy clusters and are among the largest known structures of the cosmos.

Luminosity

Luminosity is generally understood as a measurement of brightness. Each discipline, however, defines the term differently, depending on what is being measured.

In astronomy, luminosity measures the total amount of energy emitted by a star or other astronomical object per unit time.

Neutron star

A neutron star is a type of stellar remnant that can result from the gravitational collapse of a massive star during a Type II, Type Ib or Type Ic supernova event. Such stars are composed almost entirely of neutrons, which are subatomic particles without net electrical charge and with slightly larger mass than protons. Neutron stars are very hot and are supported against further collapse by quantum degeneracy pressure due to the phenomenon described by the Pauli exclusion principle.

Quasar

A quasi-stellar radio source ('quasar',) is a very energetic and distant active galactic nucleus. Quasars are extremely luminous and were first identified as being high redshift sources of electromagnetic energy, including radio waves and visible light, that were point-like, similar to stars, rather than extended sources similar to galaxies.

32. ASTROPHYSICS AND COSMOLOGY

CHAPTER HIGHLIGHTS & NOTES: KEY TERMS, PEOPLE, PLACES, CONCEPTS

Red giant

A red giant is a luminous giant star of low or intermediate mass (roughly 0.3-8 solar masses) in a late phase of stellar evolution. The outer atmosphere is inflated and tenuous, making the radius immense and the surface temperature low, from 5,000 K and lower. The appearance of the red giant is from yellow-orange to red, including the spectral types K and M, but also class S stars and most carbon stars.

White dwarf

A white dwarf, also called a degenerate dwarf, is a stellar remnant composed mostly of electron-degenerate matter. They are very dense; a white dwarf's mass is comparable to that of the Sun, and its volume is comparable to that of the Earth. Its faint luminosity comes from the emission of stored thermal energy.

Neutron

The neutron is a subatomic hadron particle that has the symbol n or n0, no net electric charge and a mass slightly larger than that of a proton. With the exception of hydrogen-1, nuclei of atoms consist of protons and neutrons, which are therefore collectively referred to as nucleons. The number of protons in a nucleus is the atomic number and defines the type of element the atom forms.

Coulomb barrier

The Coulomb barrier which is named after physicist Charles-Augustin de Coulomb, is the energy barrier due to electrostatic interaction that two nuclei need to overcome so they can get close enough to undergo a nuclear reaction. This energy barrier is given by the electrostatic potential energy:

$$U_{coul} = k\frac{q_1 q_2}{r} = \frac{1}{4\pi\epsilon_0}\frac{q_1 q_2}{r}$$

wherek is the Coulomb's constant = 8.9876×10^9 N m² C^{-2};e_0 is the permittivity of free space;q_1, q_2 are the charges of the interacting particles;r is the interaction radius.

A positive value of U is due to a repulsive force, so interacting particles are at higher energy levels as they get closer. A negative potential energy indicates a bound state (due to an attractive force).

Nuclear fusion

In nuclear physics, nuclear fusion is a nuclear reaction in which two or more atomic nuclei collide at a very high speed and join to form a new type of atomic nucleus. During this process, matter is not conserved because some of the mass of the fusing nuclei is converted to photons (energy). Fusion is the process that powers active or 'main sequence' stars.

Nucleosynthesis

Nucleosynthesis is the process that creates new atomic nuclei from pre-existing nucleons, primarily protons and neutrons. The first nuclei were formed about three minutes after the Big Bang, through the process called Big Bang nucleosynthesis. It was then that hydrogen and helium formed that became the content of the first stars, and is responsible for the present hydrogen/helium ratio of the cosmos.

Energy source

Energy development is a field of endeavor focused on making available sufficient primary energy sources and secondary energy forms to meet the needs of society. These endeavors encompass those which provide for the production of conventional, alternative and renewable sources of energy, and for the recovery and reuse of energy that would otherwise be wasted. Energy conservation and efficiency measures reduce the impact of energy development, and can have benefits to society with changes in economic cost and with changes in the environmental effects.

Evolution

Evolution is the change in the inherited characteristics of biological populations over successive generations. Evolutionary processes give rise to diversity at every level of biological organisation, including species, individual organisms and molecules such as DNA and proteins.

All life on Earth is descended from a last universal ancestor that lived approximately 3.8 billion years ago.

Exclusion principle

The Exclusion principle is a philosophical principle that states:If an event e causes event e*, then there is no event e# such that e# is non-supervenient on e and e# causes e*..

Pauli exclusion principle

The Pauli exclusion principle is the quantum mechanical principle that no two identical fermions may occupy the same quantum state simultaneously. A more rigorous statement is that the total wave function for two identical fermions is anti-symmetric with respect to exchange of the particles. The principle was formulated by Austrian physicist Wolfgang Pauli in 1925.

Binary system

A binary system is a system of two objects in space which are so close that their gravitational interaction causes them to orbit about a common center of mass. Some definitions (e.g. that of double planet, but not that of binary star) require that this center of mass is not located within the interior of either object. A multiple system is like a binary system but consists of three or more objects.

Neutron capture

Neutron capture is a nuclear reaction in which an atomic nucleus and one or more neutrons collide and merge to form a heavier nucleus. Since neutrons have no electric charge they can enter a nucleus more easily than positively charged protons, which are repelled electrostatically.

Neutron capture plays an important role in the cosmic nucleosynthesis of heavy elements.

Beta decay

In nuclear physics, beta decay is a type of radioactive decay in which a beta particle (an electron or a positron) is emitted from an atomic nucleus. Beta decay is a process which allows the atom to obtain the optimal ratio of protons and neutrons.

Beta decay is mediated by the weak force.

Inverse Beta Decay

Inverse beta decay is a somewhat vague term referring to one of several processes related to beta decay.

Inverse beta decay originally referred to the process $\bar{\nu}_e + p \rightarrow e^+ + n$,

in which the existence of the antineutrino was decisively verified in the Cowan-Reines neutrino experiment. Understanding this process is important to our understanding of the mechanism of a supernova explosion.

Parallax

Parallax is a displacement or difference in the apparent position of an object viewed along two different lines of sight, and is measured by the angle or semi-angle of inclination between those two lines. The term is derived from the Greek pa????a??? (parallaxis), meaning 'alteration.' Nearby objects have a larger parallax than more distant objects when observed from different positions, so parallax can be used to determine distances.

Astronomers use the principle of parallax to measure distances to celestial objects including to the Moon, the Sun, and to stars beyond the Solar System.

Triangulation

In trigonometry and geometry, triangulation is the process of determining the location of a point by measuring angles to it from known points at either end of a fixed baseline, rather than measuring distances to the point directly . The point can then be fixed as the third point of a triangle with one known side and two known angles.

Triangulation can also refer to the accurate surveying of systems of very large triangles, called triangulation networks.

PARSEC

PARSEC is a package designed to perform electronic structure calculations of solids and molecules using density functional theory . The acronym stands for Pseudopotential Algorithm for Real-Space Electronic Calculations. It solves the Kohn-Sham equations in real space, without the use of explicit basis sets.

Electromagnetic force

Electromagnetism, or the electromagnetic force is one of the four fundamental interactions in nature, the other three being the strong interaction, the weak interaction, and gravitation. This force is described by electromagnetic fields, and has innumerable physical instances including the interaction of electrically charged particles and the interaction of uncharged magnetic force fields with electrical conductors.

The word electromagnetism is a compound form of two Greek terms, ??e?t???, elektron, 'amber', and μa???t??, magnetes, 'magnet'.

Gravitational field

In physics, a gravitational field is a model used to explain the influence that a massive body extends into the space around itself, producing a force on another massive body. Thus, a gravitational field is used to explain gravitational phenomena, and is measured in newtons per kilogram (N/kg).

Nuclear force	The nuclear force is the force between two or more nucleons. Its fundamental laws and constants are unknown unlike the Coulomb and Newton laws. It is responsible for binding protons and neutrons into atomic nuclei.
Redshift	In physics, redshift happens when light or other electromagnetic radiation from an object moving away from the observer is increased in wavelength, or shifted to the red end of the spectrum. In general, whether or not the radiation is within the visible spectrum, 'redder' means an increase in wavelength - equivalent to a lower frequency and a lower photon energy, in accordance with, respectively, the wave and quantum theories of light. Redshifts are an example of the Doppler effect, familiar in the change in the apparent pitches of sirens and frequency of the sound waves emitted by speeding vehicles.
Special theory of relativity	In physics, special relativity (SR, also known as the special theory of relativity or STR) is the accepted physical theory regarding the relationship between space and time. It is based on two postulates: (1) that the laws of physics are invariant (i.e., identical) in all inertial systems (non-accelerating frames of reference); and (2) that the speed of light in a vacuum is the same for all observers, regardless of the motion of the light source. It was originally proposed in 1905 by Albert Einstein in the paper 'On the Electrodynamics of Moving Bodies'.
Electromagnetic	Electromagnetic is a prefix used to specialise many technical terms that involve electromagnetism.
Einstein Cross	The Einstein Cross or Q2237+030 or QSO 2237+0305 is a gravitationally lensed quasar that sits directly behind ZW 2237+030, Huchra's Lens. Four images of the same distant quasar appear around a foreground galaxy due to strong gravitational lensing. According to current interpretations of redshift, the quasar is located about 8 billion light years from Earth, while the lensing galaxy is located at a distance of 400 million light years.
Einstein ring	In observational astronomy an Einstein ring is the deformation of the light from a source into a ring through gravitational lensing of the source's light by an object with an extremely large mass (such as another galaxy, or a black hole). This occurs when the source, lens and observer are all aligned. The first complete Einstein ring, designated B1938+666, was discovered by collaboration between astronomers at the University of Manchester and NASA's Hubble Space Telescope in 1998.
Geodesic	In mathematics, particularly differential geometry, a geodesic is a generalization of the notion of a 'straight line' to 'curved spaces'. In the presence of an affine connection, a geodesic is defined to be a curve whose tangent vectors remain parallel if they are transported along it. If this connection is the Levi-Civita connection induced by a Riemannian metric, then the geodesics are (locally) the shortest path between points in the space.

32. ASTROPHYSICS AND COSMOLOGY

Curvature	The canonical example of extrinsic curvature is that of a circle, which everywhere has curvature equal to the reciprocal of its radius. Smaller circles bend more sharply, and hence have higher curvature. The curvature of a smooth curve is defined as the curvature of its osculating circle at each point.
Event horizon	In general relativity, an event horizon is a boundary in spacetime beyond which events cannot affect an outside observer. In layman's terms, it is defined as 'the point of no return' i.e. the point at which the gravitational pull becomes so great as to make escape impossible. The most common case of an event horizon is that surrounding a black hole.
Gravitational collapse	Gravitational collapse is the inward fall of a body due to the influence of its own gravity. In any stable body, this gravitational force is counterbalanced by the internal pressure of the body, in the opposite direction to the force of gravity (gravity being generally orientated to the center of mass). If the inwards pointing gravitational force, however, is stronger than the total combination of the outward pointing forces, the equilibrium becomes unbalanced and a collapse occurs until the internal pressure increases above that of the gravitational force and an equilibrium is once again attained (the exception being black holes).
Schwarzschild radius	The Schwarzschild radius is the radius of a sphere such that, if all the mass of an object is compressed within that sphere, the escape speed from the surface of the sphere would equal the speed of light. An example of an object smaller than its Schwarzschild radius is a black hole. Once a stellar remnant collapses below this radius, light cannot escape and the object is no longer visible.
Singularity	Singularity is a novel by Bill DeSmedt published by Per Aspera Press on November 8, 2004. It is based on the theory that the Tunguska Event was caused by a micro black hole.
Event	In computer science, an event is a type of synchronization mechanism that is used to indicate to waiting processes when a particular condition has become true. An event is an abstract data type with a boolean state and the following operations:•wait - when executed, causes the executing process to suspend until the event's state is set to true. If the state is already set to true has no effect.•set - sets the event's state to true, release all waiting processes.•clear - sets the event's state to false. Different implementations of events may provide different subsets of these possible operations; for example, the implementation provided by Microsoft Windows provides the operations wait (WaitForObject and related functions), set (SetEvent), and clear (ResetEvent).
Universe	The Universe is commonly defined as the totality of existence, including planets, stars, galaxies, the contents of intergalactic space, and all matter and energy.

Similar terms include the cosmos, the world and nature.

The observable universe is about 46 billion light years in radius.

Blueshift

A blueshift is any decrease in wavelength ; the opposite effect is referred to as redshift. In visible light, this shifts the color from the red end of the spectrum to the blue end. The term also applies when photons outside the visible spectrum (e.g. x-rays and radio waves) are shifted toward shorter wavelengths, as well as to shifts in the de Broglie wavelength of particles.

Gravitational redshift

In astrophysics, gravitational redshift or Einstein shift is the process by which electromagnetic radiation originating from a source that is in gravitational field is reduced in frequency, or redshifted, when observed in a region of a weaker gravitational field. This is a direct result of Gravitational time dilation - as one moves away from a source of gravitational field, the rate at which time passes is increased relative to the case when one is near the source. As frequency is inverse of time (specifically, time required for completing one wave oscillation), frequency of the electromagnetic radiation is reduced in an area of a higher gravitational potential (i.e., equivalently, of lower gravitational field) .

Big Bang theory

The Big Bang theory is the prevailing cosmological model for the early development of the Universe. According to the theory, the Big Bang occurred approximately 13.798 ± 0.037 billion years ago, which is thus considered the age of the universe. At this time, the Universe was in an extremely hot and dense state and began expanding rapidly.

Observable universe

The observable universe consists of the galaxies and other matter that can, in principle, be observed from Earth in the present day because light from those objects has had time to reach the Earth since the beginning of the cosmological expansion, . Assuming the universe is isotropic, the distance to the edge of the observable universe is roughly the same in every direction. That is, the observable universe is a spherical volume (a ball) centered on the observer, regardless of the shape of the universe as a whole.

Observable

In physics, particularly in quantum physics, a system observable is a measurable operator, or gauge, where the property of the system state can be determined by some sequence of physical operations. For example, these operations might involve submitting the system to various electromagnetic fields and eventually reading a value off some gauge. In systems governed by classical mechanics, any experimentally observable value can be shown to be given by a real-valued function on the set of all possible system states.

Horizon

The horizon is the apparent line that separates earth from sky, the line that divides all visible directions into two categories: those that intersect the Earth's surface, and those that do not. At many locations, the true horizon is obscured by trees, buildings, mountains, etc., and the resulting intersection of earth and sky is called the visible horizon.

32. ASTROPHYSICS AND COSMOLOGY

CHAPTER HIGHLIGHTS & NOTES: KEY TERMS, PEOPLE, PLACES, CONCEPTS

Lepton

A lepton is an elementary, spin-$^1/_2$ particle that does not undergo strong interactions, but is subject to the Pauli exclusion principle. The best known of all leptons is the electron, which governs nearly all of chemistry as it is found in atoms and is directly tied to all chemical properties. Two main classes of leptons exist: charged leptons (also known as the electron-like leptons), and neutral leptons (better known as neutrinos).

Planck

Max Karl Ernst Ludwig Planck, FRS was a German theoretical physicist who originated quantum theory, which won him the Nobel Prize in Physics in 1918.

Planck made many contributions to theoretical physics, but his fame rests primarily on his role as originator of the quantum theory. This theory revolutionized human understanding of atomic and subatomic processes, just as Albert Einstein's theory of relativity revolutionized the understanding of space and time.

Standard Model

The Standard Model is renormalizable and mathematically self-consistent, however despite having huge and continued successes in providing experimental predictions it does leave some unexplained phenomena. In particular, although the physics of special relativity is incorporated, general relativity is not, and the Standard Model will fail at energies or distances where the graviton is expected to emerge. Therefore in a modern field theory context, it is seen as an effective field theory.

Baryon number

In particle physics, the baryon number is an approximate conserved quantum number of a system.

It is defined as

$$B = \frac{1}{3}\left(n_{\mathrm{q}} - n_{\bar{\mathrm{q}}}\right),$$

where n_q is the number of quarks, and n_q is the number of antiquarks. Baryons (three quarks) have a baryon number of +1, mesons (one quark, one antiquark) a baryon number of 0, and antibaryons (three antiquarks) have a baryon number of -1. Exotic hadrons like pentaquarks (four quarks, one antiquark) and tetraquarks (two quarks, two antiquarks) are also classified as baryons and mesons depending on their baryon number.

Hadron

In particle physics, a hadron is a composite particle made of quarks held together by the strong force (in a similar way as atoms and molecules are held together by the electromagnetic force).

Hadrons are categorized into two families: baryons (such as protons and neutrons, made of three quarks) and mesons (such as pions, made of one quark and one antiquark). Other types of hadron may exist, such as tetraquarks (or, more generally, exotic mesons) and pentaquarks (exotic baryons), but no current evidence conclusively suggests their existence.

Nucleon

In chemistry and physics, a nucleon is one of the particles that makes up the atomic nucleus.

Each atomic nucleus consists of one or more nucleons, and each atom in turn consists of a cluster of nucleons surrounded by one or more electrons. There are two known kinds of nucleon: the neutron and the proton.

Photon

A photon is an elementary particle, the quantum of light and all other forms of electromagnetic radiation, and the force carrier for the electromagnetic force, even when static via virtual photons. The effects of this force are easily observable at both the microscopic and macroscopic level, because the photon has zero rest mass; this allows long distance interactions. Like all elementary particles, photons are currently best explained by quantum mechanics and exhibit wave-particle duality, exhibiting properties of both waves and particles.

Symmetry breaking

Symmetry breaking in physics describes a phenomenon where small fluctuations acting on a system which is crossing a critical point decide the system's fate, by determining which branch of a bifurcation is taken. To an outside observer unaware of the fluctuations (or 'noise'), the choice will appear arbitrary. This process is called symmetry 'breaking', because such transitions usually bring the system from a symmetric but disorderly state into one or more definite states.

Lepton number

In particle physics, the lepton number is the number of leptons minus the number of antileptons.

In equation form, $L = n_\ell - n_{\overline{\ell}}$

so all leptons have assigned a value of +1, antileptons -1, and non-leptonic particles 0. Lepton number is an additive quantum number, which means that its sum is preserved in interactions (as opposed to multiplicative quantum numbers such as parity, where the product is preserved instead).

Beside the leptonic number, leptonic family numbers are also defined:•L_e?, the electronic number for the electron and the electron neutrino;•L_μ?, the muonic number for the muon and the muon neutrino;•L_t?, the tauonic number for the tau and the tau neutrino;

with the same assigning scheme as the leptonic number: +1 for particles of the corresponding family, -1 for the antiparticles, and 0 for leptons of other families or non-leptonic particles.

Quark

A quark is an elementary particle and a fundamental constituent of matter. Quarks combine to form composite particles called hadrons, the most stable of which are protons and neutrons, the components of atomic nuclei. Due to a phenomenon known as color confinement, quarks are never directly observed or found in isolation; they can be found only within hadrons, such as baryons, named up, down, strange, charm, bottom, and top .

Dark energy

In physical cosmology and astronomy, dark energy is a hypothetical form of energy that permeates all of space and tends to accelerate the expansion of the universe.

32. ASTROPHYSICS AND COSMOLOGY

Dark energy is the most accepted hypothesis to explain observations since the 1990s that indicate that the universe is expanding at an accelerating rate. According to the Planck mission team, and based on the standard model of cosmology, the total mass-energy of the universe contains 4.9% ordinary matter, 26.8% dark matter and 68.3% dark energy.

Dark matter

Dark matter is a type of matter hypothesized in astronomy and cosmology to account for a large part of the mass that appears to be missing from the universe. Dark matter cannot be seen directly with telescopes; evidently it neither emits nor absorbs light or other electromagnetic radiation at any significant level. Instead, the existence and properties of dark matter are inferred from its gravitational effects on visible matter, radiation, and the large-scale structure of the universe.

Flatness

Flatness refers to the shape of a liquid's free surface. On planet Earth, the flatness of a liquid is a function of the curvature of the Earth, and from trigonometry, can be found to deviate from true flatness by approximately 19.6 nanometers over an area of 1 square meter, a deviation which is dominated by the effects of surface tension. This calculation using the Earth's mean radius at sea level, however a liquid will be slightly flatter at the poles.

Quantum fluctuation

In quantum physics, a quantum vacuum fluctuation (or quantum fluctuation or vacuum fluctuation) is the temporary change in the amount of energy in a point in space, arising from Werner Heisenberg's uncertainty principle.

According to one formulation of the principle, energy and time can be related by the relation $\Delta E \Delta t \approx \frac{h}{2\pi}$

That means that conservation of energy can appear to be violated, but only for small times. This allows the creation of particle-antiparticle pairs of virtual particles.

Vacuum state

In quantum field theory, the vacuum state is the quantum state with the lowest possible energy. Generally, it contains no physical particles. Zero-point field is sometimes used as a synonym for the vacuum state of an individual quantized field.

Magnetic monopole

A magnetic monopole is a hypothetical particle in particle physics that is an isolated magnet with only one magnetic pole . In more technical terms, a magnetic monopole would have a net 'magnetic charge'. Modern interest in the concept stems from particle theories, notably the grand unified and superstring theories, which predict their existence.

Baryon

A baryon is a composite subatomic particle made up of three quarks . Baryons and mesons belong to the hadron family, which are the quark-based particles. The name 'baryon' comes from the Greek word for 'heavy' (ßa???, barys), because, at the time of their naming, most known elementary particles had lower masses than the baryons.

Cosmological constant

In cosmology, the cosmological constant is the value of the energy density of the vacuum of space. It was introduced by Albert Einstein as an addition to his theory of general relativity to 'hold back gravity' and achieve a static universe, which was the accepted view at the time. Einstein abandoned the concept as his 'greatest blunder' after Hubble's 1928 discovery that the distant galaxies are expanding away from each other, implying an overall expanding Universe (which is only detectable on the largest of scales).

Vacuum energy

Vacuum energy is an underlying background energy that exists in space throughout the entire Universe. One contribution to the vacuum energy may be from virtual particles which are thought to be particle pairs that blink into existence and then annihilate in a timespan too short to observe. They are expected to do this everywhere, throughout the Universe.

Gravity wave

In fluid dynamics, gravity waves are waves generated in a fluid medium or at the interface between two media which has the restoring force of gravity or buoyancy. An example of such an interface is that between the atmosphere and the ocean, which gives rise to wind waves.

When a fluid element is displaced on an interface or internally to a region with a different density, gravity will try to restore it toward equilibrium, resulting in an oscillation about the equilibrium state or wave orbit.

CHAPTER QUIZ: KEY TERMS, PEOPLE, PLACES, CONCEPTS

1. _________ is the study of the origins and eventual fate of the universe. Physical _________ is the scholarly and scientific study of the origin, evolution, structure, dynamics, and ultimate fate of the universe, as well as the natural laws that keep it in order. Religious _________ is a body of beliefs based on the historical, mythological, religious, and esoteric literature and traditions of creation and eschatology.

   a. Background noise
   b. 3D sound localization
   c. Bass trap
   d. Cosmology

2. . In quantum physics, a quantum vacuum fluctuation (or _________ or vacuum fluctuation) is the temporary change in the amount of energy in a point in space, arising from Werner Heisenberg's uncertainty principle.

   According to one formulation of the principle, energy and time can be related by the relation $\Delta E \Delta t \approx \frac{h}{2\pi}$

   That means that conservation of energy can appear to be violated, but only for small times.

This allows the creation of particle-antiparticle pairs of virtual particles.

a. Quantum fluctuation
b. 9-j symbol
c. Bloch spectrum
d. Bloch sphere

3. _________ is a nuclear reaction in which an atomic nucleus and one or more neutrons collide and merge to form a heavier nucleus. Since neutrons have no electric charge they can enter a nucleus more easily than positively charged protons, which are repelled electrostatically.

_________ plays an important role in the cosmic nucleosynthesis of heavy elements.

a. Neutron capture
b. Beta decay
c. Binary collision approximation
d. Binding energy

4. The _________ is the quantum mechanical principle that no two identical fermions may occupy the same quantum state simultaneously. A more rigorous statement is that the total wave function for two identical fermions is anti-symmetric with respect to exchange of the particles. The principle was formulated by Austrian physicist Wolfgang Pauli in 1925.

a. Friedrich Oskar Giesel
b. Pauli exclusion principle
c. Panel edge staining
d. Sibplaz

5. General relativity, or the _________, is the geometric theory of gravitation published by Albert Einstein in 1916 and the current description of gravitation in modern physics. General relativity generalizes special relativity and Newton's law of universal gravitation, providing a unified description of gravity as a geometric property of space and time, or spacetime. In particular, the curvature of spacetime is directly related to the energy and momentum of whatever matter and radiation are present.

a. General theory of relativity
b. 3-manifold
c. Berge conjecture
d. Beat

ANSWER KEY
32. ASTROPHYSICS AND COSMOLOGY

1. d
2. a
3. a
4. b
5. a

CPSIA information can be obtained at www.ICGtesting.com
Printed in the USA
BVOW06s1802200814

363538BV00002B/36/P

ULTIMATE

Christmas Music Collection

Alfred Publishing Co., Inc.
16320 Roscoe Blvd., Suite 100
P.O. Box 10003
Van Nuys, CA 91410-0003
alfred.com

ISBN-10: 0-7390-4315-3
ISBN-13: 978-0-7390-4315-8

CONTENTS

CONTENTS

AND SUDDENLY IT'S CHRISTMAS

Lyrics by
ERVIN DRAKE

Music by
BURTON LANE

C7
B♭6
E♭m
C7
Christ - mas!
F7
Cm7
When you speak my name, not
F7
B♭maj7
B♭6
B♭maj7
on - ly do I tin - gle,
B♭6
G13
G7#5
G13
sleigh - bells

G7#5
C9
C7♭9
jin - gle!
F
G13
My prac - ti - cal brain says
G7
Gm7
C7
E♭m6/G♭
mir - a - cles don't hap - pen.
C9
F
Cm7
Then who can ex - plain the

F7
B♭maj7
B♭6
B♭maj7
ma - gic when you're near?
B♭6
Gm7♭5
F7
You de - fy lo - gi - cal rea -
B♭m
F
sons. You are my love for all
Am7
D7
G7
sea - sons. 'Cause one look at

C9sus C7 F

you and, sud - den - ly, it's Christ -

B♭ F/A A♭dim7 To Coda C9

mas! One look
They

F♯dim7 C9 A♭dim7 C9 C7♭9 Fmaj7

that's all it takes for me

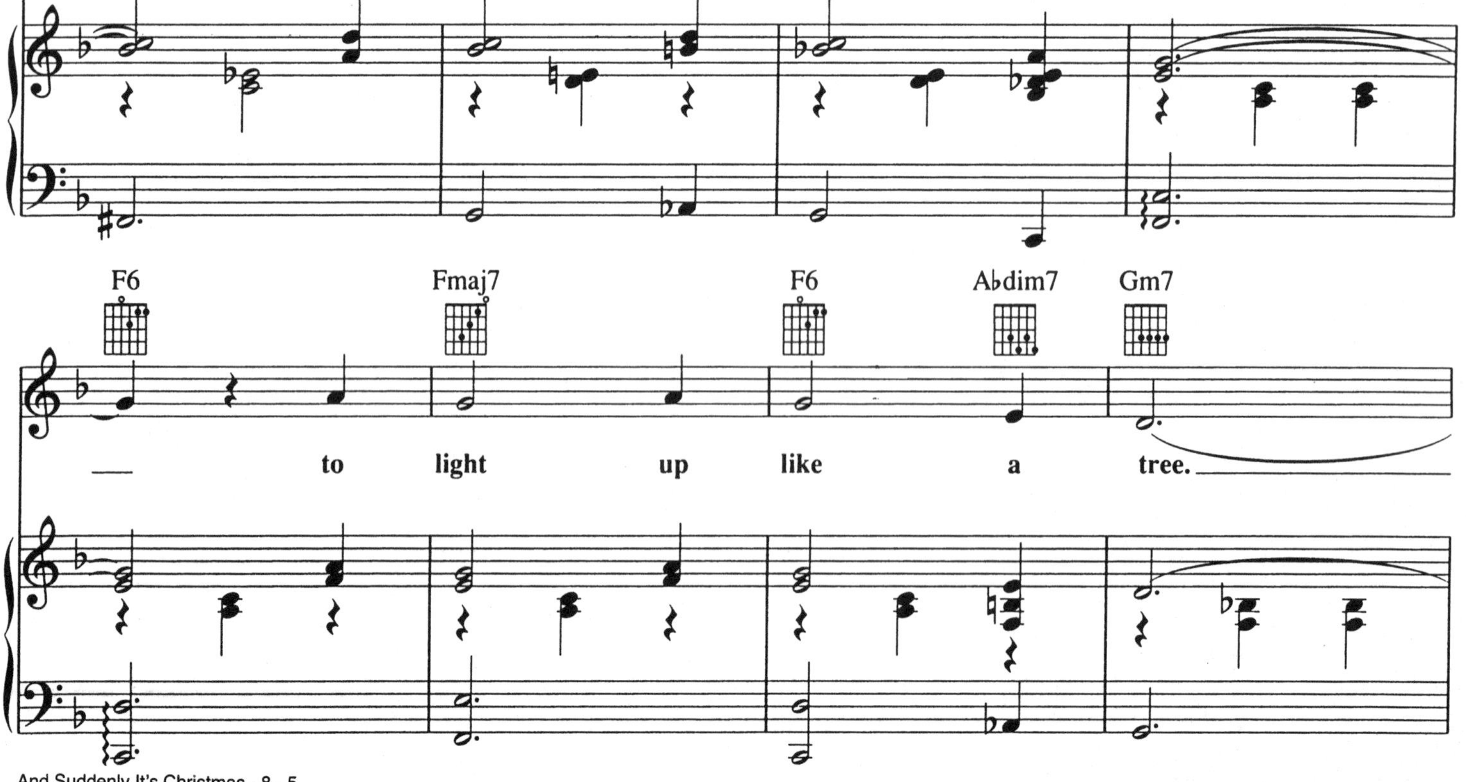

C9
F♯dim7
Gm7
C9
My hol - i - day be -
F
F+
Fmaj7
F6
G9/F
F
B♭7/A♭
gins!
One
Gm7
F♯dim7
Gm7
A♭dim7
Gm7
C7♭9
sigh that's all I have to
Fmaj7
F6
Fmaj7
hear a far ca -

F6
A/E
Bm/E
the - dral bell chimes No - ël
E13
A
C7
loud and clear.
D.S. al Coda
CODA
Gm7
F♯dim7
say it
Gm7
A♭dim7
Gm7
C7♭9
Fmaj7
comes but once a year,

F6
Fmaj7
F6
A♭dim7
Gm7
but Christ - mas comes my way
C9
F♯dim7
Gm7
C9
when - ev - er you are
rit.
F
C9sus
near!
a tempo
rit.
F

THE ANNUAL ANIMAL CHRISTMAS BALL

Words and Music by
GEORGE DAVID WEISS

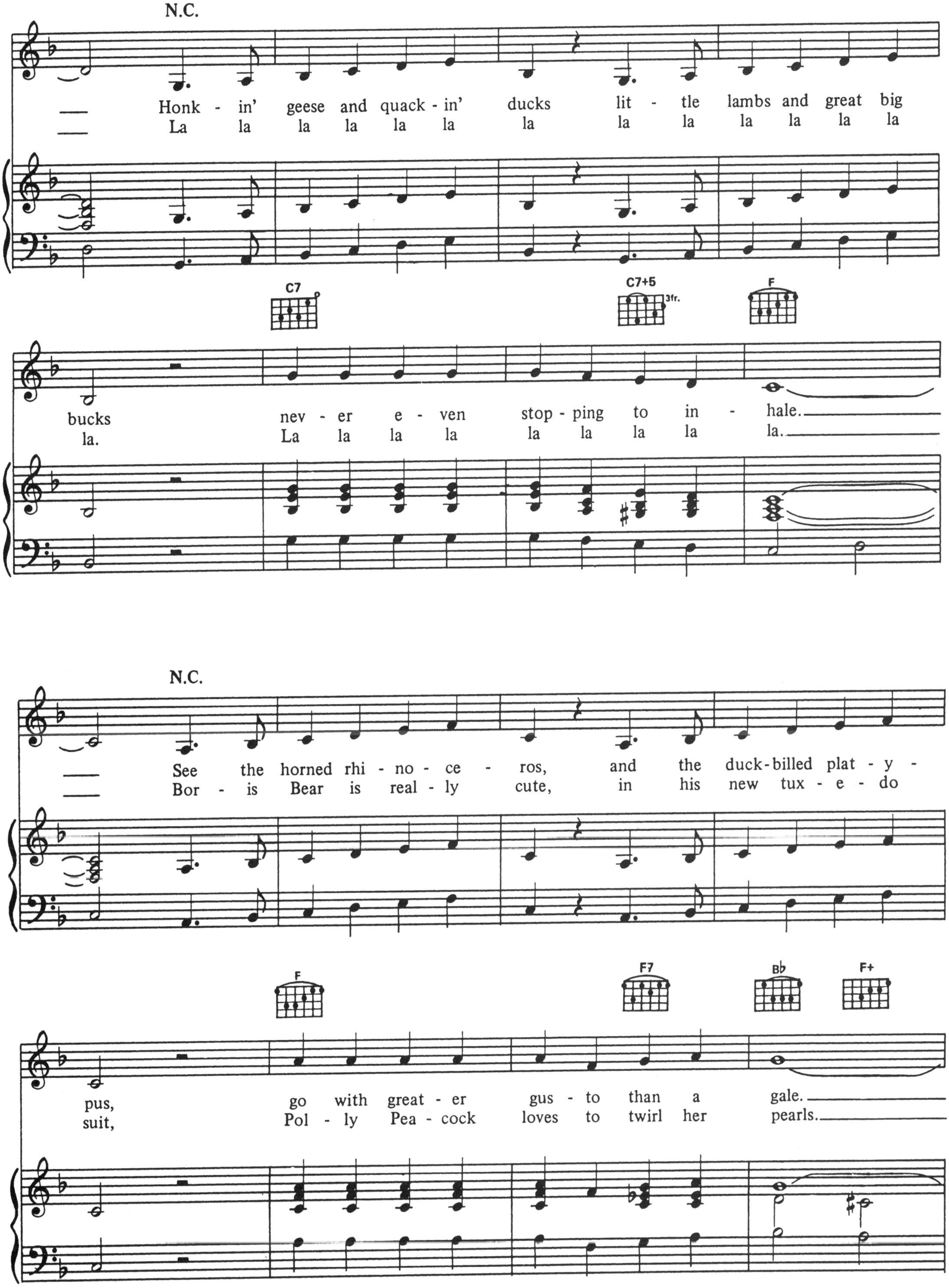
N.C.
Honk - in' geese and quack - in' ducks lit - tle lambs and great big
La la la la la la la la la la la la la
C7
C7+5
3fr.
F
bucks nev - er e - ven stop - ping to in - hale.
la. La la la la la la la la la.
N.C.
See the horned rhi - no - ce - ros, and the duck-billed plat - y -
Bor - is Bear is real - ly cute, in his new tux - e - do
F
F7
B♭
F+
pus, go with great - er gus - to than a gale.
suit, Pol - ly Pea - cock loves to twirl her pearls.

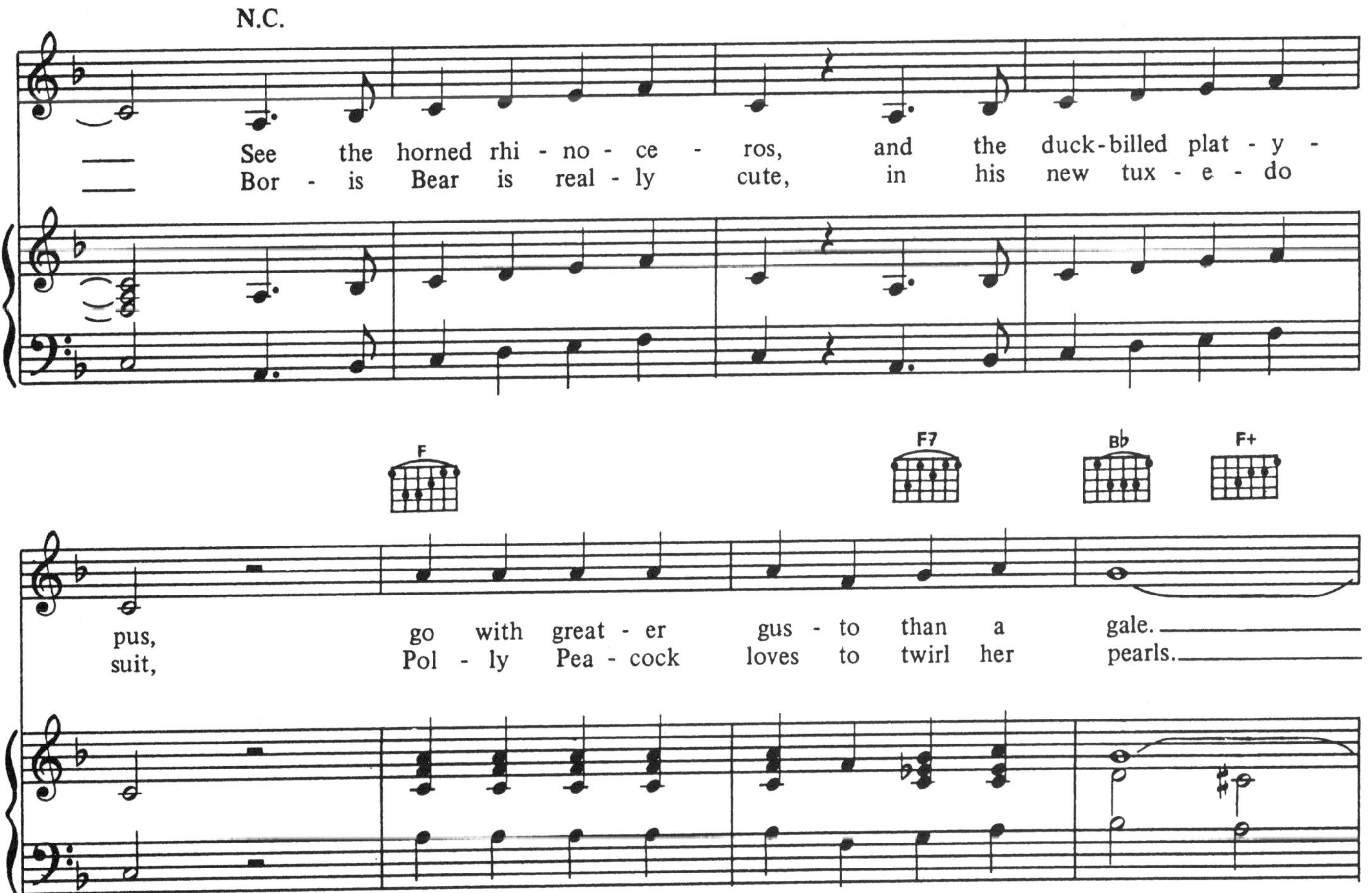

B♭
B♭m
Dm7/A
And it's not po - lite to laugh, when the ca - mel and gi -
Look at Ken - neth Croc - o - dile, see him flash his tooth - y
G7
Gm
C7
To Coda
F
raffe, stop to thumb their no - ses at the snail.
smile, Will - iam Wolf is scar - in' all the
N.C.
What's got - ten in - to all of them, what can it be that's
Dm
Em7-5
A7
Adim.
call - in' them; ev' - ry-bod - y who's an - y-bod - y is here.

A7
Gm7
3fr.
C7
F
Why it's the big - gest shin - dig of the year.
In 4, L'istesso
B♭
Bop, bop, bop. It's the
B♭
F7
AN - NU-AL AN - I-MAL CHRIST-MAS BALL, it's the AN - NU-AL AN - I-MAL
B♭
B♭7/A♭
E♭/G
E♭
CHRIST-MAS BALL and a ver - y good time will be had by all at the

Gm
3fr.
F7
Bb
In "4"
Bb
AN-NU-AL AN-I-MAL CHRIST-MAS BALL.
Nel - lie El - e-phant grace-ful-ly
F7
Bb
Bb7/Ab
taps her toe. Tes-sie Tur-key is search-in' for Ro-me-o and Pen - el - o - pe Por-cu-pine
Eb/G
Eb
Gm
3fr.
F7
N.C.
(In two)
D.S. al Coda
stops the show at the AN-NU-AL AN-I-MAL...
La la
(Hand claps)
Coda
(In 4) L'istesso
F
Bb
girls. Bri - an Li - on is roar - in' to start a fight, Eg - bert
AN - NU-AL AN - I-MAL CHRIST-MAS BALL, it's the

F7
Bb
Bb7/Ab
Eagle is fly-in' high out of sight, Terrence Tiger is los-in' his
AN-NU-AL AN-I-MAL CHRIST-MAS BALL, and a ver-y good time will be
Eb/G
Eb
Eb/G
Eb
1.
Gm
3fr.
F7
Bb
stripes to-night (stripes to-night) at the AN-NU-AL AN-I-MAL CHRIST-MAS BALL.
had by all, (had by all,) at the
2.
C9
F7
It's the AN-NU-AL AN-I-MAL
In "4"
Eb6
F7 -9 -5
Bb
Cb
Bb
CHRIST - MAS BALL.

AWAY IN A MANGER

Words by
MARTIN LUTHER

Music by
JONATHAN E. SPILLMAN

Away in a Manger - 2 - 1

D
Em
A7
D
cat - tle are low - ing, the poor ba - by wakes, But
way in a man - ger, no crib for His bed, The
mf
G
D
A7
D
D9
lit - tle Lord Je - sus, no cry - ing He makes. I
lit - tle Lord Je - sus lay down His sweet head. The
G
D7
G
C
G
love Thee, Lord Je - sus, look down from the sky And
stars in the heav - ens looked down where He lay, The
D
G
G7
C
G
D7
G
stay by my cra - dle to watch lul - la - by.
lit - tle Lord Je - sus a - sleep in the hay.

ALL I WANT FOR CHRISTMAS IS YOU

(A Christmas Love Song)

Words and Music by
ALAN and MARILYN BERGMAN
and JOHNNY MANDEL

B
E♭6/9
A♭Ma9
GMa7
Em7
All I need for Christ - mas is here. Find - ing
Ped.
sim.
Am7
A♭+/A
C/D
D13 D9(+5)
G6/D
Em7
ev - 'ry sweet sur - prise wrapped up in your eyes, wait - ing there for me
Fm7
B♭13
B♭7+(♯9/♭9)
C
B♭m9
E♭9
B♭m7
E♭13(♭9)
un - der - neath the tree. We'll spend the day ex - chang - ing
A♭Ma7
A♭6
A♭Ma7
Fm7
D♭13
B♭/C
C7(♭9/+5)
C7(♭9)
kiss - es. Smile and say "What a
8va

E♭/F F13
C♭7 A♭/B♭ F♭7/B♭
D
A♭Ma9
Christ - mas
this is!"
Long be - fore
the
snow - flakes
ap -
Gm7
Cm7
Fm7
C+/F
A♭/B♭
B♭13
pear,
with - out
bells or mis - tle - toe
or
the
Gm7
C13
Gm7
C9
E♭/F
F9
A♭/B♭
B♭13
tin - sel's sil - ver
glow,
you
just
look at me and oh,
Christ - mas
is
poco rall.
last x rall.
1.
Fm7
A♭/B♭
2.
here!
here!
8va
rall.

A BIG RED CHRISTMAS BOW

Words and Music by
SAMMY CAHN and JANIS GOTT

F
Am/E
Dm7
F/C
Gm7
3fr.
C7
never been on his sleigh. It's al - ways on my mind, a gift I'm
Gm7
3fr.
C7
Gm7
3fr.
C7
F
hop - ing to find when I o - pen my eyes on Christ - mas Day.
Moderate Country beat
Chorus:
B♭/C
F
I want you to wrap your love a - round me like a
mp
mf
Gm7
3fr.
C7
Gm7
3fr.
big red Christ-mas bow; I want to feel your love sur - round

C7
Fmaj7
F7
me
ev - 'ry - where I
go.
And when the
Bb
Bbm
F
Am/E
hol - i - days
are o - ver
no more tin - sel,
no more
not a trace of
mis - tle -
Dm7
F/C
Gm7
3fr.
C7
snow;
toe;
your love will
still be wrapped
a - round
me
like a
Gm7
3fr.
C7
To Coda
F
Bb/C
big
red Christ - mas
bow!!!
sfz

Verse:
F(add G)
Gm7
3fr.
2. Take the stock - ings from the fi - re - place but leave the an - gel on the tree,
C7
Gm7
C7
Gm7
C7
to watch, pro - tect, and to di - rect your
Fmaj7
F7
B♭
love straight down to me. Now close your eyes, here's
B♭m
F
Am/E
Dm7
F/C
my sur - prise, feel my heart if you need a clue. It is

Gm7
C7
Gm7
C7
Gm7
3fr.
yours a - lone, for you to keep and to own, in re - turn I ask,
D.S. al Coda
C7
F
Chorus:
B♭/C
one thing of you. I want you to
Coda
Dm
Dm(maj7)
Dm7
G7
Gm7
C7
bow!!! Your love will still be wrapped a - round me like a
Gm7
C7
F
big red Christ - mas bow!!!
sfz

From THE POLAR EXPRESS

BELIEVE

Words and Music by
GLEN BALLARD and ALAN SILVESTRI

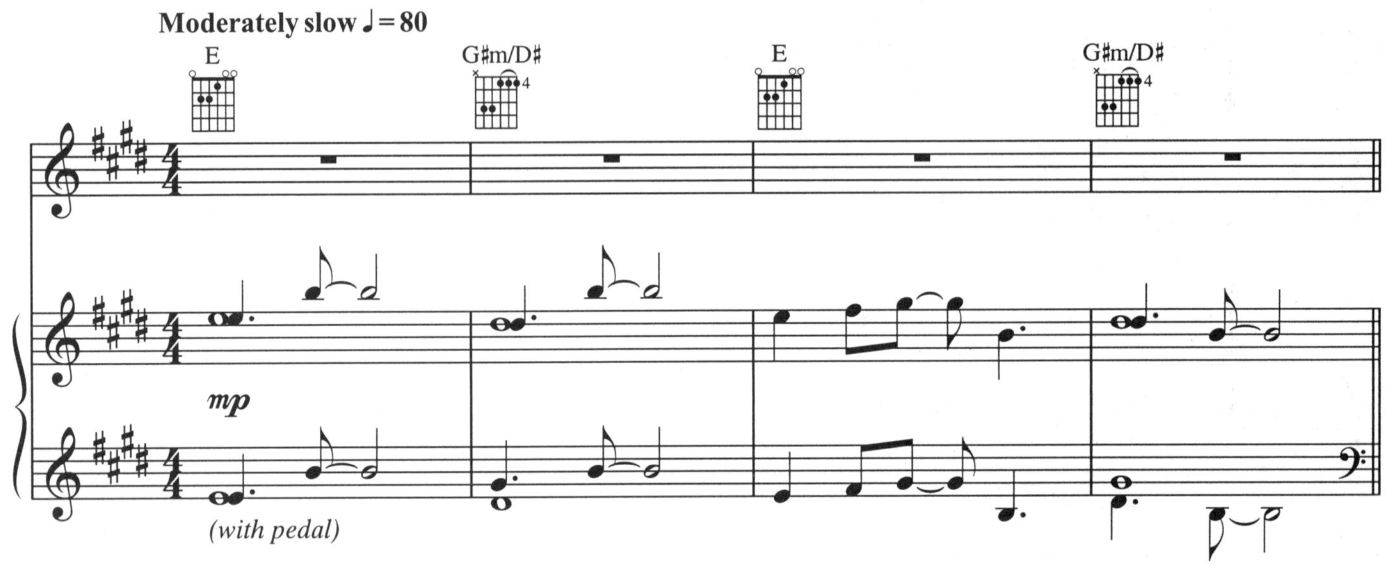

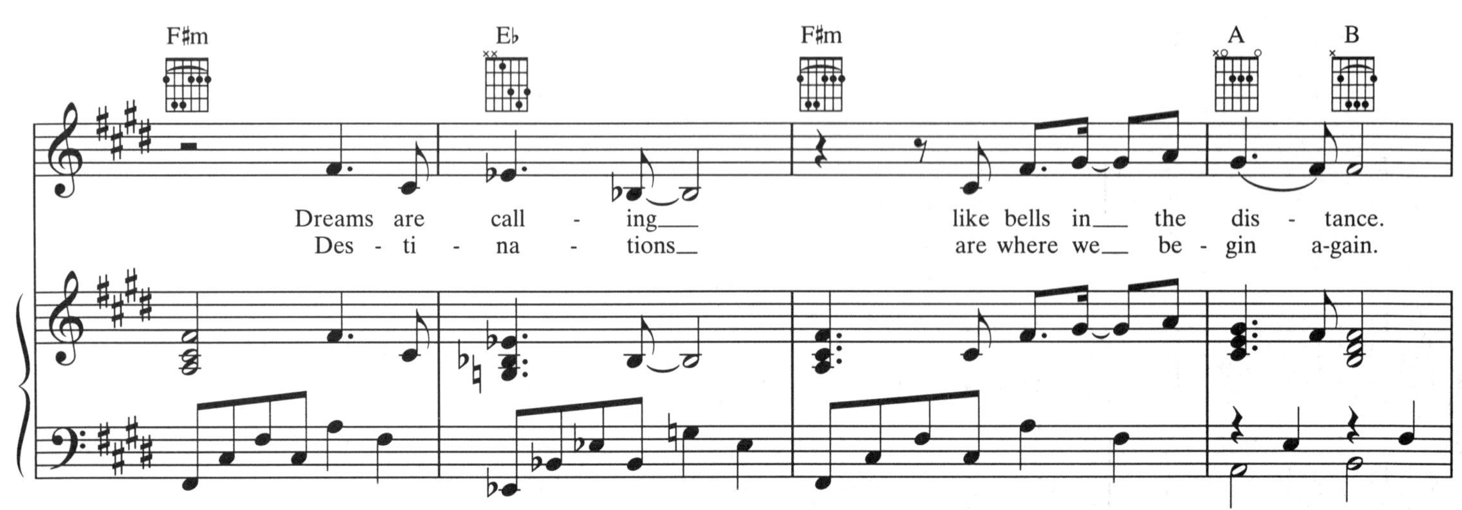

E G♯m/D♯ E G♯m/D♯
We were dream - ers, not so long a - go,
Ships go sail - ing far a - cross the sea,
F♯m E♭ F♯m A B
but one by one, we all had to grow up.
trust - ing star - light to get where they need to be.
G♯m A D/F♯
When it seems the mag - ic slipped a - way, we find it all a - gain on Christ-mas
When it seems that we have lost our way, we find our-selves a - gain on Christ-mas
mf
1. To Next Strain
2.
Chorus:
Bsus B Bsus B E F♯m11
Day. Be - Day.
Be - lieve in what your heart is say-ing,
cresc.

E(9)/G♯
A
E
B(4)/D♯
hear the mel - o - dy that's play-ing. There's no time to waste, there's so
F♯m7
E/B
Bsus
E
F♯m11
much to cel - e - brate. Be - lieve in what you feel in - side and
E(9)/G♯
G♯7(♯5)
C♯m
give your dreams the wings to fly.
1.
F♯m7
B7sus
E
G♯m/D♯
You have ev - 'ry-thing you need if you just be-lieve.
8va

2.
E
F♯m11
E(9)/G♯
A
E
B(4)/D♯
F♯m7
E/B
Bsus
__ be-lieve. If you just____ be-lieve, if you just__
__ be-lieve, if you just____ be-lieve. Just be-
lieve, just____ be-lieve.
Repeat ad lib. and fade

THE BELLS OF CHRISTMAS

(Hear the Bells)

Words and Music by
MARY STUART

Am7
D7
G
Em
Am7
Love was born to - day,
Peace was born to - day,
brought us love this day,
And
Love was
Peace was
brought us
D7
G
Em
G
1.2.
Em
3.
D.C. al Coda
Em
born to - day.
born to - day.
peace this day.
Coda
Am7
D7
G
Em
Love was born to - day,
Peace was born to - day,
Am7
D7
G
Em
Love and peace to - day,
Am7
D7
G
Love and peace this day.
rit.

CELEBRATE ME HOME

Words by
KENNY LOGGINS

Music by
KENNY LOGGINS and
BOB JAMES

G7sus4
G7
Bb/C
F
Am7
Dm7
Gm7
Oh, my friends.
Please celebrate me home.
C
C#o7
Dm
Am
Gm
C
Bbmaj7
Gimme a number. Please celebrate me home. Play me one more song that I'll
Am7
Dm
Dm(maj7)
F/G
G9
Bb/C
always remember; that I can recall whenever I find myself too all a-
C
Em7-5
F
Eb6/9/F
Bb6/9/F
Eb7
lone. I can sing me home.

F
Bb/F
C/E
F
Bb/F
C/E
Un-eas - y high - way, trav-'lin' where the west-er - ly winds can fly.
Dm
G7sus4
G7
Gm7/C
Bb/C
Am7/C
Bb/C
Some-bod- y tried to tell me. But the man for - got to tell me why.
F
Bb/F
C/E
F
Cm/Eb
I got to count on be-ing gone. Come on, Ma-ma. Come on, Dad-dy. And
cresc.
mf
Dm9
3fr.
Bm7-5
E7
Am
Cm7
3fr
F7-9
Bbm9
6fr.
please, what do you want from me? I'll be strong.

Fbmaj7
Abm7/Db
Bb/C
I'll be weak. I'll be weak.
cresc.
F
Am7
Dm7
Gm7
C
C#o7
Dm
Am
Please cel-e-brate me home. Gim-me a num-ber. Please cel-e-brate me
f
Gm
C
Bbmaj7
Am7
home. Play me one more song that I'll al-ways re-mem-ber;
Dm
Dm(maj7)
F/G
G9
Bb/C
that I can re-call when-ev-er I find my-self too all a - lone.

Cm7
C/E
I can make be-lieve I've nev-er gone. Lem-me, lem-me know where I be-long. Sing me
F Am7 Dm7 Gm7 C C#o7 Dm Am
Please
home. cel-e-brate me home. Gim-me a num-ber. Please cel-e-brate me
Gm C Bbmaj7 Am7 Gm7 Bb/C F Gm7 F/A
home. Play me one more song, y'all. Well, I'm
15ma
loco
sub. pp
mp
Repeat and fade
Bbmaj7 Am7 Gm7 Bb/C F Gm7 F/A
fi-n'lly here. But I'm bound to roam. Come on, cel-e-brate me home. Well, I'm

CHRISTMAS AIN'T CHRISTMAS, NEW YEAR'S AIN'T NEW YEAR'S WITHOUT THE ONE YOU LOVE

Words and Music by
KENNETH GAMBLE and LEON HUFF

C G/B Am C/G F C/E
Now I'm stay-ing home_ a - lone, and my house is not a home with - out that girl of mine,_
F/G G
Chorus: E♭ B♭/D Cm E♭/B♭ A♭ Fm7
oh! Christ - mas just ain't Christ - mas___ with-out the one you love.___
A♭/B♭ E♭ B♭/D Cm E♭/B♭
1. Fm A♭
And New Year's just ain't New Year's__ with-out the one you love.___
G7sus G7
2. Fm A♭ Dm7 G7
Interlude: Csus C F6 F
one you love.___

Verse 2:
Twelve o'clock and all is well,
And I was doing oh so swell,
Last year, this time.
Goin' shopping with friends together,
Making vows to leave each other never.
It was a waste of time.
(To Chorus:)

C-H-R-I-S-T-M-A-S

Words by
JENNY LOU CARSON

Music by
EDDIE ARNOLD

Moderato (with expression)

F
C
G7
C
born up - on this day,
"H" for her - ald an - gels in the night.
"R" means our Re -
F
G7
C
deem - er,
"I" means Is - ra - el,
"S" is for the star that shone so bright.
G7
C
D7
"T" is for three wise men,
They who trav - eled far,
"M," is for the man - ger where He
G7
C
F
lay.
"A"'s for all He stands for,
"S" means shep - herds came
And
G7
1 C
Dm7
G7
2 C
F
C
that's why there's a Christ - mas day.
day.

CHRISTMAS ALL ACROSS THE U.S.A.

Words and Music by
RITA ABRAMS

Em7
G/A
A
D
here's the an - swer that came through to me.
It's in the
rit.
Moderately, in 2 (𝅗𝅥 = 63)
Chorus:
G
G6
Gmaj7
G6
D
F♯m7
big Mon - tan - a sky,
it's in the Rock - y Moun - tains high,
it's in the
Em7
G/A
A
D
C/D
D
wide Ne - bras - ka plain,
and down the rug - ged coast of Maine,
the Mis - sis -
G
G6
Gmaj7
G6
F♯m7
Bm7
sip - pi run - nin' free,
the Blue Ridge hills of Ten - nes - see.
Yes, it is

To Coda
Em7 G/A A D C/D D
Christ - mas all a - cross the U. S. A. It's in the
G G6 Gmaj7 G6 D F♯m7
Car - o - li - na pines, and in the Penn - syl - va - nia mines, A - las - ka's
ah, ah, ah,
Em7 G/A A D C/D D
gla - ciers white with snow, the frost - ed fields of I - da - ho. It's in the
ah, ah, ah. Ah,
G G6 Gmaj7 G6 F♯m7
peo - ple ev - 'ry - where with lov - ing hearts and dreams to share.
ah, ah, ah,

Bm7 Em7 G/A A

Yes, it is Christ - mas all a - cross the U. S. A.
ah, ah, ah.

D

1. 2. *D.S.* 𝄋 *al Coda*

(Children:) Ah, It's in the
(with monologue)

𝄌 *Coda* D D♭/E♭ E♭ A♭ A♭6 A♭maj7 A♭6

(Children:) It's in the Car - o - li - na pines, and in the

E♭ Gm7 Fm7 A♭/B♭ B♭

Penn - syl - va - nia mines, A - las - ka's gla - ciers white with snow, the frost - ed

Monologue:
People, I know the world is changing
And things are moving fast,
And some folks are complaining
That the real Christmas is past.
But I've been all over this country
And one thing I know,
That there is a Christmas Spirit
Everywhere you go.
(To Chorus:)

THE CHRISTMAS CHILD

A French Noël
Harmonized and Set by
DOUGLAS MACLEAN

CHRISTMAS AULD LANG SYNE

Words and Music by
MANN CURTIS and FRANK MILITARY

F Dm Gm7 C7o F Dm7 Gm7 C7o F F7
SYNE. When sleigh-bells ring and choirs sing and the chil-dren's fac-es
B♭ Gm7 C9 F Am Dm Gm7 C7o A7 Dm B♭ Gm7 C7o
shine; With each new toy we share their joy, with a CHRIST-MAS AULD LANG
F Dm Gm7 C9 F Dm Gm7 C7o F F7
SYNE. We sing His praise this day of days and pray next year this
B♭ Gm7 C9 F Dm 1. Gm7 C7o A7 Dm B♭ Gm7 C7o
time, We'll all be near to share the cheer of a CHRIST-MAS AULD LANG
F Dm Gm7 C7o 2. Gm7 G9 F Dm Gm7 C7o F
SYNE. When share the cheer of a CHRIST-MAS AULD LANG SYNE.
rall.

CHRISTMAS EVE

Words and Music by
MARIA CHRISTENSEN
and CURT FRASCA

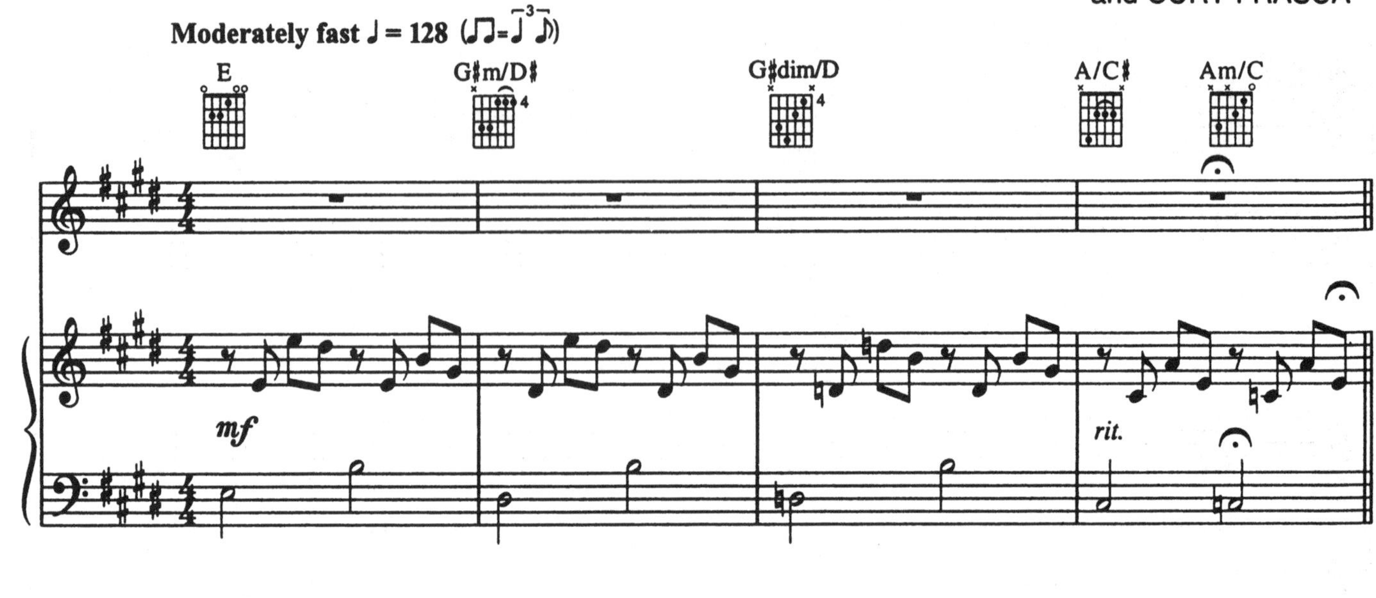

Verse:
E
G♯m/D♯
1. Snow fall - ing gent - ly to the ground.
2. We're stay - in' up late to - night, dec - o - rate the tree.
C♯m7
'Tis the night be - fore, and
Just look in - to my eyes and
Am/C
B7sus
B7/D♯
E
in my heart there is no doubt that this is
I will tell you truth - ful - ly that I don't
G♯m/D♯
gon - na be the bright - est hol - i - day,
need no San - ta Claus to hear my Christ - mas list.

C♯m7
Am/C
'cause here you are with me. Ba - by, ba - by, I
I got you in my arms and what could be a bet -
B7sus
B7
A
B
can't wait to spend the spe - cial time of year with some - one
ter gift then to spend my ve - ry fav - 'rite time of
A
B
N.C.
who makes me feel the spe - cial way that you do.
year with the one I real - ly love so dear?
Oh, yeah, yeah, yeah, yeah.
Chorus:
E
G♯m/D♯
Walk - ing with you in a win - ter's snow, kiss - ing un - der - neath the

G♯dim/D
mis - tle - toe. Peo - ple smil - ing ev - 'ry - where we go. It's Christ-
C♯m7
A
B
E
mas Eve___ and they___ can see___ we're in love.___ Ooh, you make the
G♯m/D♯
G♯dim/D
sea - son bright, with the lights re - flect - ed in your eyes. All my dreams are com - ing
C♯m7
1.
A
B
true to - night. It's Christ - mas Eve___ and I______ can see___ we're in love.__

2.
Bridge:
A
B
G♯m7
can see we're in love.
And there's a ring-ing when I
F♯m7
G♯m7
hear you say,
my ba-by,
we'll do it all a-gain on
A
Amaj7/B
B
N.C.
Christ-mas to-day.
Oh,
I can't wait.
F
Am/E
Walk-ing with you in a win-ter's snow,
kiss-ing un-der-neath the

A dim/E♭
mis - tle - toe. Peo - ple smil - ing ev - 'ry - where we go. It's Christ-
Dm7
B♭
C
F
mas Eve__ and they__ can see__ we're in love.__ Ooh, you make the sea - son bright,
Am/E
A dim/E♭
with the lights re - flect - ed in your eyes. All my dreams are com - ing
Repeat ad lib. and fade
Dm7
B♭
C
true to - night. It's Christ - mas Eve__ and I____ can see__ we're in love.__

CHRISTMAS IN KILLARNEY

Words and Music by
JOHN REDMOND, JAMES CAVANAUGH
and FRANK WELDON
A.S.C.A.P.

*Symbols for Guitar & Banjo, Frames for Ukulele

3588-2

F C F C
cud - dling un - der the mis - tle - toe, And San - ta Claus, you know of course, is
Dm G7 C Am Am7 Am6 Em
one of the boys from home. The door is al - ways o - pen, The neigh - bors pay a call and
G Am7 D7 G7 C
Fa-ther John, be-fore he's gone, Will bless the house and all. How grand it feels, to click your heels, And
F C F C C7 F A7 Dm
join in the fun of the jigs and reels. I'm hand-ing you no blar - ney, The likes you've nev - er known, Is
F F♯dim C Am 1. Dm G7 C 2. Dm G7 C
CHRIST-MAS IN KIL - LAR - NEY, With all of the folks at home. The all of the folks at home.
rit.

CHRISTMAS LULLABY

Words and Music by
ANN HAMPTON CALLAWAY

𝄋 *Bridge:*

Dm7 G11 G F/C Fm/C C G7sus G7 F/C C Dm/C C/E

I sing to you each pass-ing year. The world is wrapped in joy and won-der,

mp

G7sus G7 Cmaj7 G7sus G13 C(9) G/F F B♭13(♯11)

in si-lent mys-ter-y. And in this spell that we are un-der

Dm7 *To Coda* 𝄌 F/G G7(♭9) C C/E F(9) C/E

Verse:

bless-ings sur-round our hearts com-plete-ly. This is a Christ-mas lul-la-by

rit. *a tempo*

Dm(9) Dm Fmaj7 G7sus E7(♯5) Am(9) Am Cmaj7/G

for some-one love-ly as snow fall-ing. I sing your Christ-mas lul-la-

Interlude:
F C/E Dm7 Fmaj7/G G7(♭9) Fmaj7 C/E Dm7 G7 C C/E
by to cra - dle you with all my love.
mf
F C/E Dm F G7sus G7 C C/E
Let peace on earth be yours to - night
F C/E Dm7 F/C Fm/C C D.S. 𝄋 al Coda
un - der the star that shines so bright.
dim.
Coda
F/G G7(♭9)
Verse:
B B/D♯
hearts com - plete - ly. Now close your eyes and as you
rit.
mf
a tempo

E
B/D♯
C♯m
E
F♯7sus
F♯7
D♯/G
sigh, make up a Christ-mas wish to dream on.
G♯m
G♯m/F♯
E(9)
C♯m
D♯7sus
And like the moon that shines on high, send out your wish up to that
G♯m7
C♯9(♯11)
Freely
C♯m7
F♯7sus
F♯7
star in the sky blessed by this Christ - mas lul - la -
rit.
mp
B
B/D♯
E(9)
Em(maj7)
B(9)
by.
a tempo
molto rit. e dim.
p
L.H.

CHRISTMAS LULLABY

F7 B♭ Gm7 C9 C7 F F Fmaj7 F7
lov - ing you the way I do my lit - tle one, sleep well. An - gels bless you
B♭ C9 C7 F A Dm F G7
lit - tle one while you're fast a - sleep. You'll a - wake to danc - ing toys,
C7(sus4) C7 F Am Dm F7 B♭ C9 C7
can - dy canes, Christ - mas joys. And I pray your whole life through, An - gels will watch
F Fmaj7 F7 B♭ Gm7 C9 C7 F
o - ver you, lov - ing you the way I do my lit - tle one, sleep well.
rit.

CHRISTMAS MEM'RIES

Words and Music by
ALAN and MARILYN BERGMAN
and DON COSTA

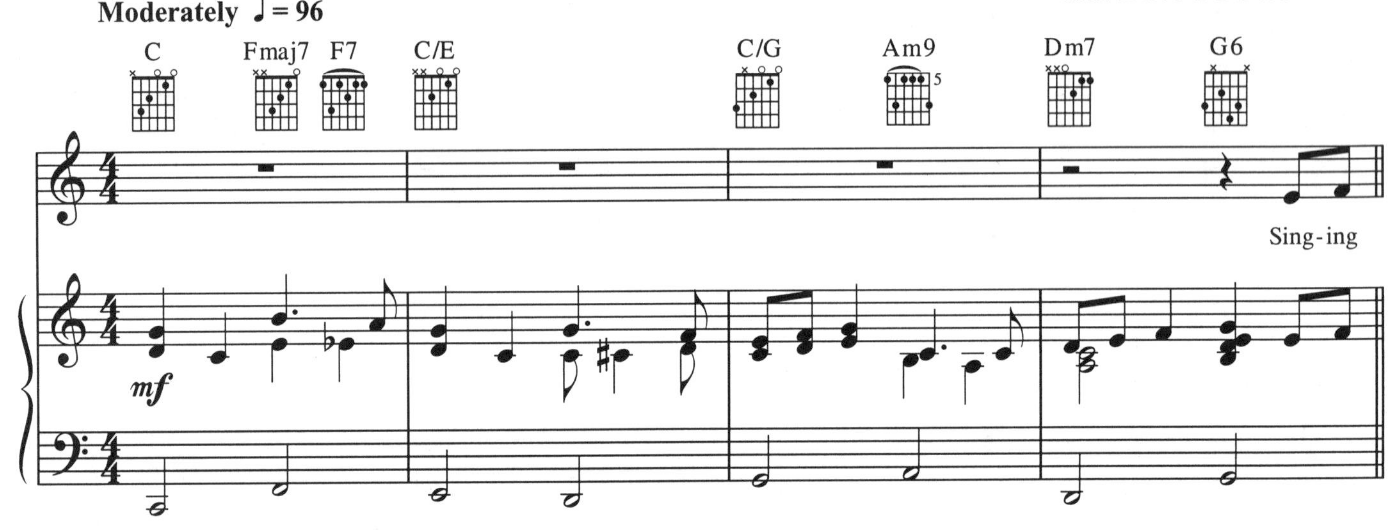

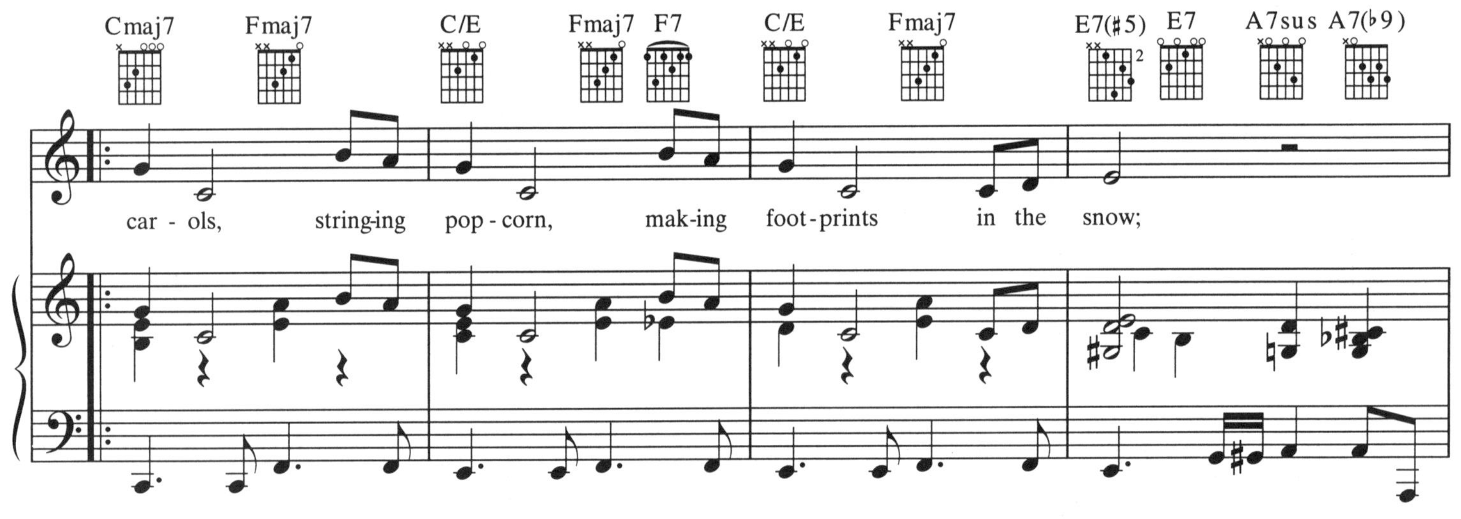

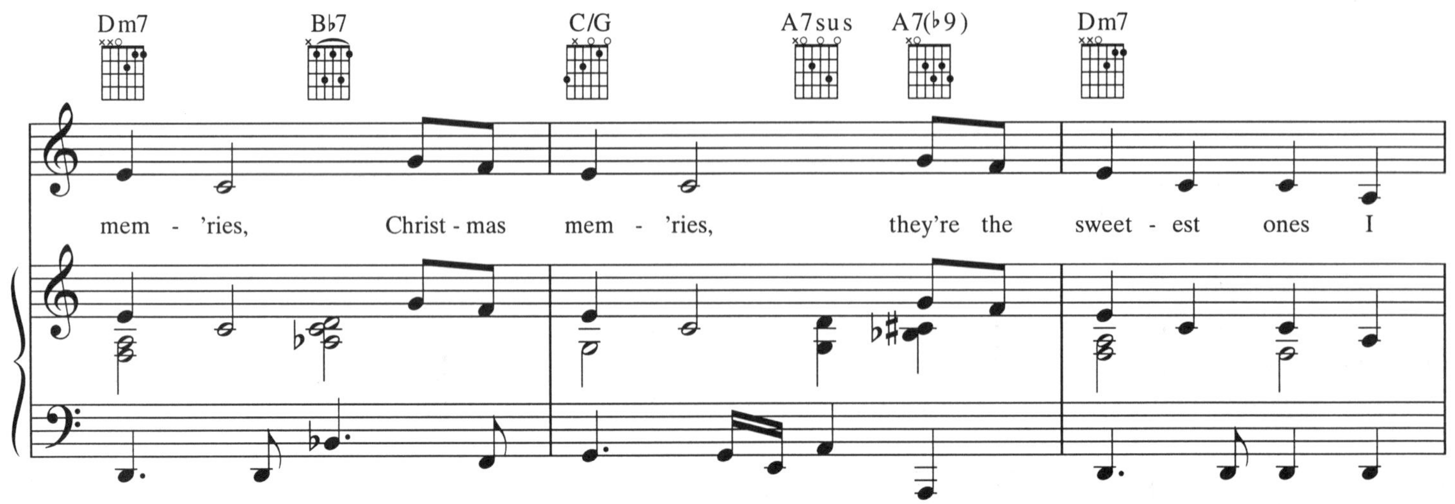

B♭
G11
Cmaj7
Fmaj7
C/E
Fmaj7
F7
know. Cook - ies bak - ing in the kitch - en, cards and
C/E
Fmaj7
E7(♯5)
E7
A7sus
A7(♭9)
Dm7
B♭7
rib - bons ev - 'ry - where; frost - y Christ - mas
C/G
A7sus
A7(♭9)
Dm7
G11
C
Am7
mem - 'ries float like snow - flakes in the air. And
Gm7
E♭/G
C7/G
C7sus
C13(♭9)
F
oh, the joy of wak - ing Christ-mas morn - ing, the fam - 'ly 'round the tree;

Am7
F/A
D7/A
D7sus
D13(♭9)
we had a way of mak - ing Christ - mas morn - ing as
G6
G9
Cmaj7
Fmaj7
mer - ry as can be. I close my eyes and see shin - y fac - es of all the
C/E
Fmaj7
C/E
Fmaj7
E7(♯5)
E7
A7sus
A7(♭9)
chil - dren who now have chil - dren of their own.
F♯m7(♭5)
Fm
C/E
Am7
A7(♭9)
D9
Fun - ny, but come De - cem - ber, I re - mem - ber ev - 'ry

1.
F/G
C
Fmaj7
F7
C/E
G11
2.
F/G
G/F
Christ - mas I've known.
Sing - ing
Christ - mas I've
Em7
B♭7(♯11)
G6/A
C13
C7(♯5)
Fmaj7
B♭7
Fm6/A♭
known.
Sing - ing car - ols, string - ing pop - corn, shin - y
C/G
A7sus
A13
A7(♯5)
Dm7
G7sus
G7
fac - es of all the chil - dren, pre - cious mem - 'ries of ev - 'ry Christ - mas I've
Fmaj7
C/E
Dm7/G
D♭maj7
C6/9
known.
a tempo
rit.

CHRISTMAS MUST BE TONIGHT

Words and Music by
ROBBIE ROBERTSON

D7
C
G
C
wrapped in swad - dling clothes, the Prince of Peace.
The wheels start
G
Am
turn - in', torch - es start burn - ing, and the old
D7
C
G
wise men jour - ney from the East.
How a
Chorus:
Em
Am
D
G
C
G/B
lit - tle ba - by boy bring the peo - ple so much joy.
Son of a car

Am G/B Am/C C G/B Am G/B Am/C C G/B
pen-ter, Mar - y car-ried the light, this must be Christ -
Am D G Em
mas, must be to - night.
1. 2.
G Em
2. A shep-herd on a
3.
G Em
Son of a car -
Am G/B Am/C C G/B Am G/B Am/C C G/B
pen-ter, Mar - y car-ried the light, this must be Christ -

Verse 2:
A shepherd on a hillside, while over my flock I 'bide,
On a cold winter night a band of angels sing.
In a dream I heard a voice saying, "Fear not, come rejoice!
It's the end of the beginning, praise the newborn King!"
(To Chorus:)

Verse 3:
I saw it with my own eyes, written up in the skies.
But why a simple herdsmen such as I?
And then it came to pass, he was born at last,
Right below the star that shines on high.
(To Chorus:)

THE CHRISTMAS SHOES

Words and Music by
LEONARD AHLSTROM and
EDDIE CARSWELL

G G/F♯ Em7 G/D

Stand-ing right in front of me was a lit-tle boy wait-ing anx-ious-ly,

C D7sus D7 Am7 D7sus D7

pac-ing 'round like lit-tle boys do and in his hands he held a pair of shoes.

G5 D/F♯ Em G/D

And his clothes were worn and old. He was

Em G/D C G/B

dirt-y from head to toe. And when it came his time to pay, I

G/C
D7sus
D7
couldn't believe what I heard him say. Sir, I wanna
Chorus:
A
E
F♯m7
E
buy these shoes for my Mama, please. It's
mf
D
E7sus
E7
A
F♯m
E
Christmas Eve and these shoes are just her size. Could you
A
E
F♯m7
E
hurry, Sir, Daddy says there's not much time. You see,

D
E7sus
E7
D
E7sus
E7
Mom's been sick for quite a while. And I know these shoes would make her smile. And I
D
E7sus
E7
Bm7
C♯m7
D2
E7sus
want her to look beau - ti - ful if Ma - ma meets Je - sus to -
A
E/G♯
F♯m7
D
E7sus
night.
2. He count - ed
Verse 2:
A
A/G♯
F♯m7
A/E
pen - nies for what seemed like years. Then the cash - ier said, "Son, there's not e - nough here."

D Esus E Bm7 Esus E
He searched his pock - ets fran - ti - c'lly, then he turned and he looked at me. He said,
A A/G♯ F♯m7 A/E
"Ma-ma made Christ-mas good at our house, though most years she just did with-out. Tell me,
D E7sus E7 Bm7 E7sus E7
sir, what am I gon - na do? Some-how I've got to buy her these Christ-mas
A F♯m7 A/E
shoes." So I laid the mon - ey down. I just

F♯m7 A/E D A/C♯

had to help him out. And I'll nev-er for-get the look on his face when he said,

A/D E7sus E7

"Ma-ma's gon-na look so great." Sir, I wan-na

𝄋 *Chorus:*

B F♯ G♯m7 F♯

buy these shoes for my Ma-ma, please. It's

a tempo

E F♯7sus F♯7 B G♯m F♯

Christ-mas Eve and these shoes are just her size. Could you

B
F♯
G♯m7
F♯
hur - ry, Sir, Dad - dy says there's not much time. You see,
E
F♯
E
F♯
Mom's been sick for quite a while. And I know these shoes would make her smile. And I
To Coda ⊕
E
F♯
C♯m7
D♯m7
E2
F♯7sus
want her to look beau - ti - ful if Ma - ma meets Je - sus to -
Bridge:
B
F♯/B
B
C♯m7
B/D♯
night. I knew I caught a glimpse of heav - en's love as he

F♯
G♯m7
A
E/G♯
thanked me and ran out. I knew that God had sent that lit-tle boy to re-
F♯sus
F♯
C♯m9
F♯sus
freely
D.S.𝄋 al Coda
mind me what Christ-mas is all a-bout. Sir, I want to
rit.
Coda
B2
E
F♯sus
F♯
C♯m7
D♯m7
B/E
F♯sus
night. I want her to look beau-ti-ful if Ma-ma meets Je-sus to-
B
F♯/A♯
G♯m7
E2
B(9)
night.
a tempo
rit.

CHRISTMAS TIME

Words and Music by
BENNIE BENJAMIN and
GEORGE DAVID WEISS

G7 G9 F C Dm G7
mer - ry, mer - ry crowds are Christ - mas shop - pin', They love to stop in ev - 'ry
mp
C G7 G9 F C
store, And when it's time for San - ta Claus to drop in, The kids are
D7 G7 C
watch - in' from ev - 'ry door. Christ - mas Eve, when the bells be -
p
Dm7 G7 Dm7 G7 G9 G7
gin to chime, Can't you hear them say, "A Hap - py Hol - i - day, it's
sfz sfz p
1 Fm C G7
CHRIST - MAS TIME." CHRIST - MAS
p p
2 Fm C F C G7 C
CHRIST - MAS TIME."
p rall. mp

83

THE CHRISTMAS WALTZ

Music by
JULE STYNE

The Christmas Waltz - 3 - 1

Gm7
C7-9
Fmaj7
Dm7
G9
G7-5
filled his sleigh with things, Things for you and for
C7
C7+5
F
D7sus4
D7
Gm7
me. It's that time of year, When the world falls in
C7
F
D7-9
love, Ev - 'ry song you hear seems to
Gm
C7-9
F
say: "Mer - ry Christ - mas, May your

Gm7
C7
Am7-5
D7
D+
D7
New Year dreams come true." And this
G9
C9
C7
F
song of mine, in three - quar - ter time,
D7
G7
Cm7
C7
Wish - es you and yours the same thing
F
Dm
Gm7
C9
F
too.
poco rall.

DANCE OF THE SUGAR-PLUM FAIRY

Music by
PETER I. TCHAIKOVSKY

DECK THE HALL

TRADITIONAL OLD WELSH

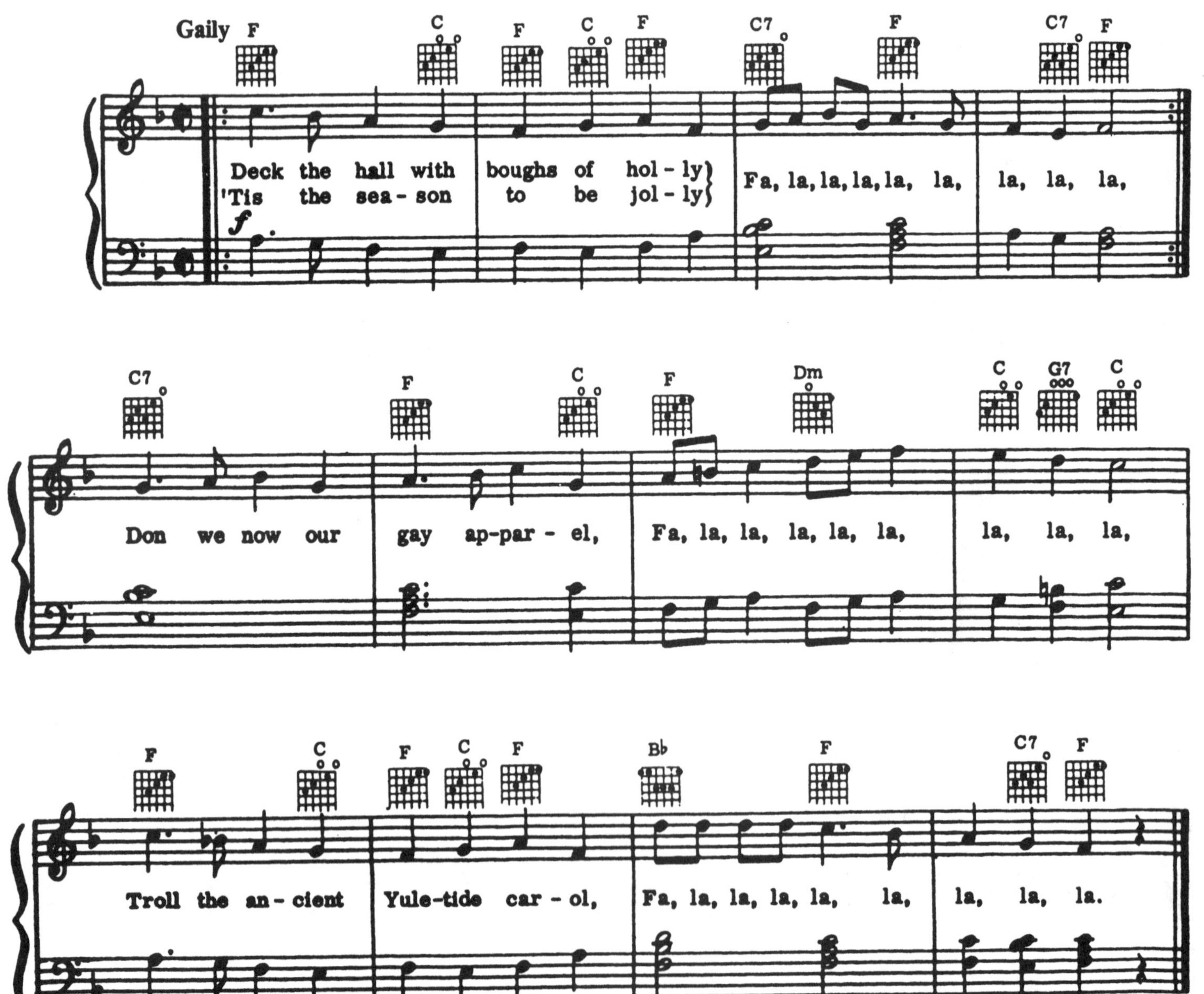

DO THEY KNOW IT'S CHRISTMAS?

Words and Music by
BOB GELDOF and MIDGE URE

F
Dm
G6
C
Throw your arms a - round the world at Christ - mas - time.
F
G
C
But say a prayer, to pray for the oth - er ones
F
G
C
at Christ - mas - time. It's hard, but when you're hav - ing fun
F
G
C
there's a world out - side your win - dow, and it's a world of dread and fear

F Dm7 G C
where the on - ly wa - ter flow - ing is the bit - ter sting of
F Dm7 G C
tears. And the Christ - mas bells that ring there are the clang - ing chimes of doom.
F Dm7 G C
Well, to - night thank God it's them in - stead of you.
Csus C F G C
And there won't be snow in Af - ri - ca this Christ - mas - time,

F G C
the great-est gift_ they'll get this year_ is life.__ Oh._
Dm/C C F G C
Where noth-ing ev-er grows,_ no rain or riv-ers flow,_
F Dm7 F/G C
do they know it's Christ-mas-time at_ all?
F C Am G Am G
Here's to you, raise a glass for ev'ry-one; here's to them un-der-neath that burn-ing sun.

F
F/G
C
F
C/E
F
C/E
Do they know it's Christ-mas-time at all?
Dm7
Dm7/G
C
F
C/E
F
C/E
Dm7
Dm7/G
Feed the world.
C
F
C/E
F
Am/E
Dm7
Dm7/G
Feed the world, let them know it's Christ-mas-time a-
C
F
C/E
F
Am/E
Dm7
Dm7/G
Feed the world,
Repeat and Fade
gain. let them know it's Christ-mas-time a-

DO YOUR CHRISTMAS LOVING EARLY

Words and Music by
PORTIA NELSON

Moderately bright swing

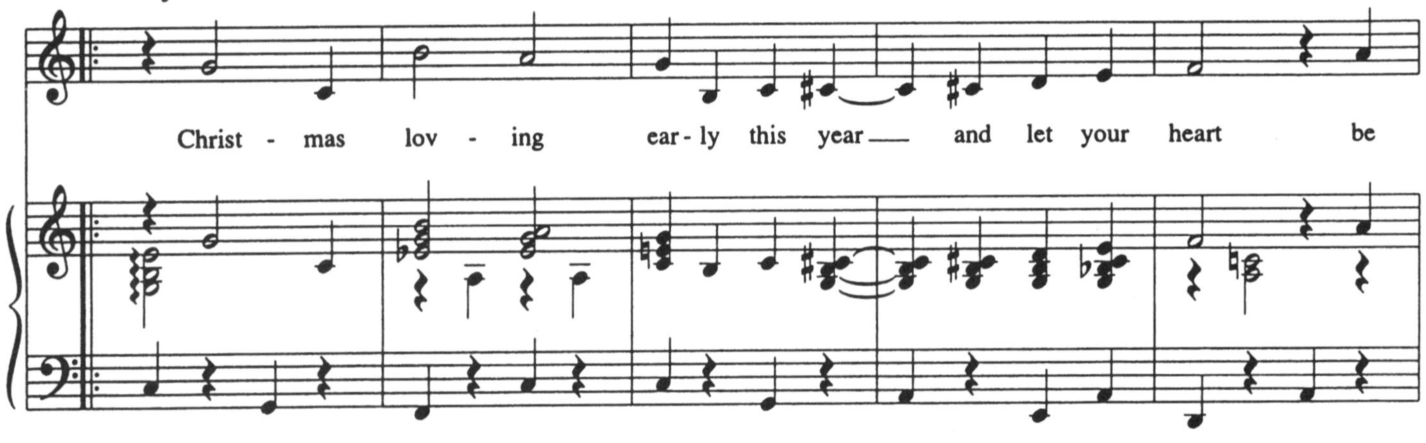

G9
Cmaj7
C6
Am7
a - long the miles to ev - 'ry
D9
G7sus4
G7
Gm9
girl and boy. Don't wait for trees and snow
C13
Fmaj9
E7-9
or mis - tle toe. Don't wait for those
A7-9
D9
A♭9
G9
Cmaj7
F9
yule - tide songs. Just do your Christ - mas lov - ing

1.
2.
Em7
Am7
D9
C/G
Dm9/G
G9
ear - ly and you'll have Christ - mas all year
C
Eb°
Dm7
G7
Db9
C/G
Am7/G
long. Do your Christ - mas
Dm7/G
Db9-5
C/G
all year long.
Gb7-5
Fmaj7
Bb7
G7
C

THE FIRST NOEL

TRADITIONAL

EVERYTIME YOU HEAR "AULD LANG SYNE"

(A counter melody to "Auld Lang Syne")

Words and Music by
ALAN and MARILYN BERGMAN
and MARVIN HAMLISCH

Am7
Am/G
Dm7
F/G
G7
friends who, through the years, will walk be - side you.
Cmaj7
A7(♭5 ♭9)
Dm7
G7
G7(♯5)
Friends who stand the test of time. Friends who make the best of time.
B♭/C
C9
Fmaj9
D(9)/F♯
F7
Em7
Am7
The friends you know will be near each and ev - 'ry year,

Dm7
Dm7/G
F/G
C (9)
F/G
ev - 'ry - time you hear "Auld Lang Syne." Should
cresc.
C (9)
Am7
Dm7
F/G
G/F
Gm7/C
C7
Time is for - ev - er pass - ing by,
auld ac - quain - tance be for - got, and nev - er brought to
mf
Fmaj7
F6
Em7
Am7
Dm7
F/G
Fm/A♭
an ev - er con - stant friend mov - ing on, just like the
mind? Should auld ac - quain - tance be for - got and

Am7
Am/G
Dm7
F/G
G7
friends who, through the years, will walk be - side you.
days of Auld Lang Syne? For
Cmaj7
A7(♭5 ♭9)
Dm7
G7
G7(♯5)
Friends who stand the test of time. Friends who make the best of time.
Auld Lang Syne, my dear, for
B♭/C
C9
Fmaj9
D(9)/F♯
F7
The friends you know will be near
Auld Lang Syne, we'll

Em7
Am7
Dm7
Dm7/G
each and ev - 'ry year, ev - 'ry - time you hear
take a cup o' kind - ness yet, for
F/G
C (9)
F/G
"Auld Lang Syne."
Auld Lang Syne. For
cresc.
Cmaj7
A7(♭5 ♭9)
Dm7
G7
G7(♯5)
Love, that stands the test of time, love, that makes the best of time.
Auld Lang Syne, my dear, for
f

B♭/C
C9
Fmaj9
D(9)/F♯
F7
Em7
Am7
The love you know will be near, each and ev - 'ry year,
Auld Lang Syne, we'll take a cup o'
Dm7
Dm7/G
F/G
C(9)
ev - 'ry - time you hear "Auld Lang Syne."
kind - ness yet, for Auld Lang Syne.
dim.
Em7
Am7
Dm7
Dm7/G
F/G
C(9)
Each and ev - 'ry year, ev - 'ry-time you hear "Auld Lang Syne."
rit. e dim.
mp

FLICKER LITTLE CANDLE

(Shine)

Words and Music by
LESSIA BONN

Chorus:
Bm7
D/E
E
D
and may - be peace can be found some - how.
Wish I knew all the things you know.
Shine for ev - 'ry - thing
cresc.
mf
A/C♯
Bm7
D/E
A
D
3
good.
Shine for what's right and fair.
Shine that there can be
C♯m7
F♯m7
Bm7
D/E
E
1.
D/E
E
peace on earth here and ev - 'ry - where.
2.
Half-verse:
D/E
E
A
D/E
E
A
Flick-er, lit - tle can - dle, burn - ing bright.
Fill up all our hearts with

Bridge:
D/E
E
D/E
E
F♯m
C♯m7
love to-night.
And as you flick-er, lit-tle can - dle now,
dim.
mp
Bm7
D/E
E
D/E
E
is there some way you can teach___ us how___ to shine___
cresc.
Chorus:
D
A/C♯
Bm7
D/E
A
___ for ev - 'ry-thing good?
Shine for what's right and fair.
mf
D
C♯m7
F♯m7
Bm7
D/E
F
Shine that there can be peace on earth here and ev - 'ry - where.___
cresc.

Chorus:
Eb
Bb/D
Cm7
Eb/F
Bb
Shine for ev - 'ry-thing good.
Shine for what's right and fair.
f
Eb
Dm7
Gm7
Cm7
1.
Eb/F
F
Shine that there can be peace on earth here and ev - 'ry - where.
2.
Eb/F
F
Eb/F
F
Bb
Eb/F
F
So shine,
dim.
mf
Bb
Eb/F
F
Eb
Bb
shine, so shine, lit - tle can - dle, shine.
mp
p

FROSTY THE SNOWMAN

Words and Music by
STEVE NELSON and JACK ROLLINS

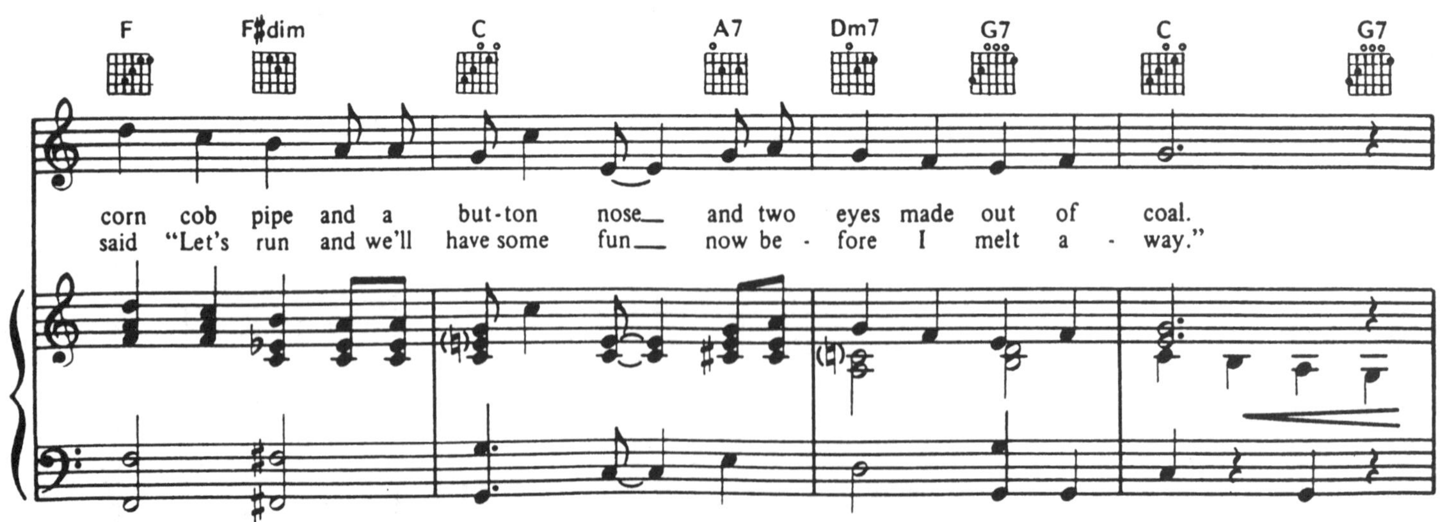

C C7 F F♯dim C
FROS - TY THE SNOW MAN is a fair - y tale they say, He was
Down to the vil - lage with a broom-stick in his hand, Run-ning
mf
F F♯dim C Am A7 Dm7 G7 C C7
made of snow but the chil-dren know how he came to life one day. There
here and there all a - round the square, say-in' "catch me if you can." He
F F♯dim C Dm7 G7 C Caug
must have been some mag - ic in that old silk hat they found. For
led them down the streets of town right to the traf - fic cop. And he
mp
G Ddim Am D7 G Gaug
when they placed it on his head he be - gan to dance a - round. Oh,
on - ly paused a mo - ment when he heard him hol - ler "stop"! For
cresc.

C
C7
F
F♯dim
C
FROS - TY THE SNOW MAN was a - live as he could be___ And the
FROS - TY THE SNOW MAN had to hur - ry on his way___ But he
f
F
F♯dim
C
Am
A7
Dm7
G7
C
G7
chil - dren say he could laugh and play__ just the same as you and me.
waved good - bye say - in', "Don't you cry,__ I'll be back a - gain some day."
C
G7
Thump-et - y thump thump, thump-et - y thump thump Look at Fros - ty go.
mf (lightly)
C
Thump-et - y thump thump, thump-et - y thump thump O - ver the hills of snow.
f
sfz

GATHER AROUND THE CHRISTMAS TREE

Words and Music by
JOHN HOPKINS

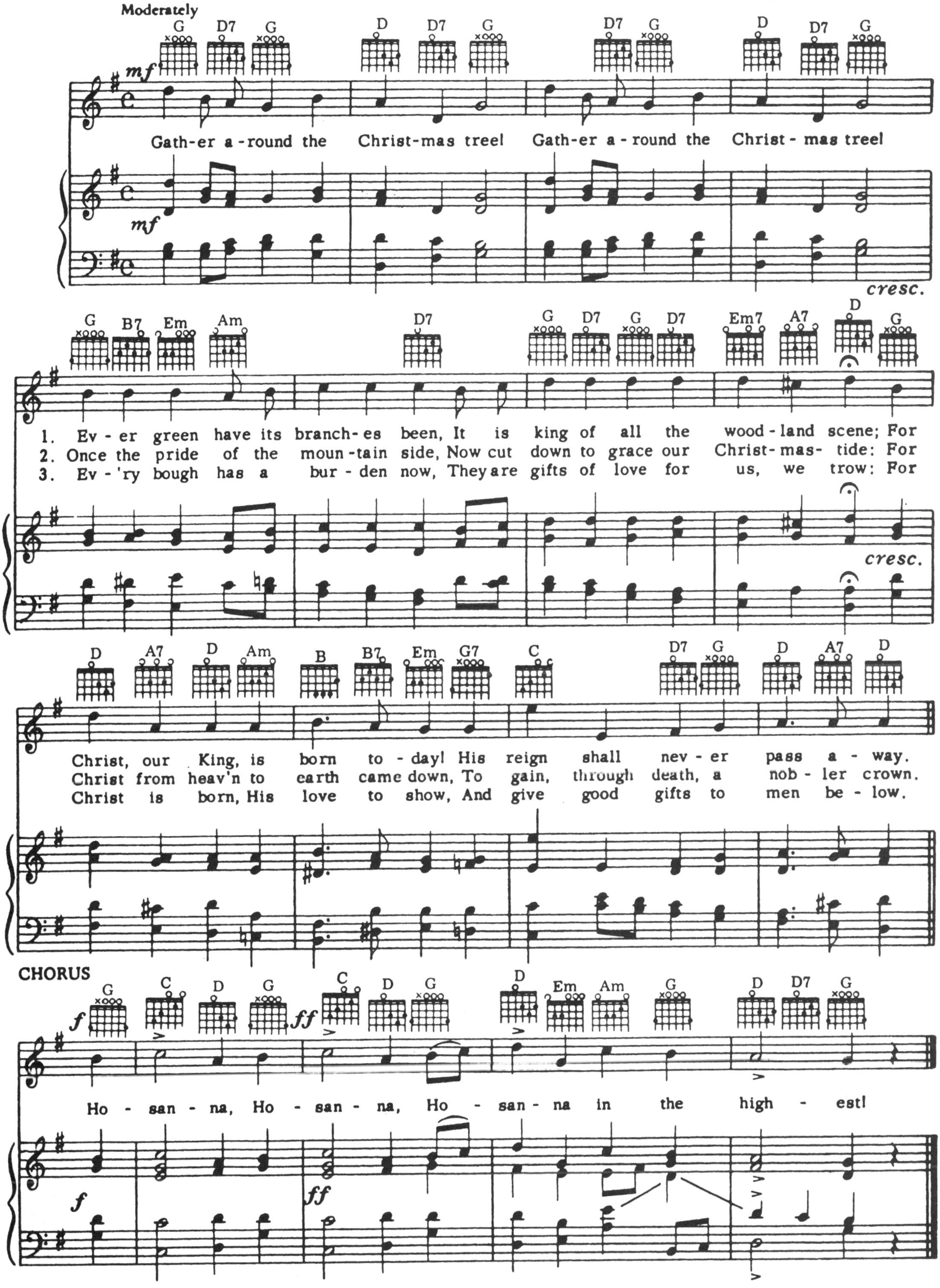

Moderately

Gath-er a-round the Christ-mas tree! Gath-er a-round the Christ-mas tree!

1. Ev-er green have its branch-es been, It is king of all the wood-land scene; For Christ, our King, is born to-day! His reign shall nev-er pass a-way.
2. Once the pride of the moun-tain side, Now cut down to grace our Christ-mas-tide: For Christ from heav'n to earth came down, To gain, through death, a nob-ler crown.
3. Ev-'ry bough has a bur-den now, They are gifts of love for us, we trow: For Christ is born, His love to show, And give good gifts to men be-low.

CHORUS

Ho-san-na, Ho-san-na, Ho-san-na in the high-est!

GESÙ BAMBINO

(The Infant Jesus)

Words by
FREDERICK H. MARTENS
Italian Version by
PIETRO A. YON

Music by
PIETRO A. YON

* In bars 3-6 and where passage is repeated the melody in the accompaniment may be played on chimes. The introduction may be treated in like manner.

an - gels sang, the shep-herds sang, The grate - ful earth re - joiced,
And at His bless - ed birth the stars Their ex - ul - ta - tion
voiced. O come let us a -
dore Him, O come let us a - dore Him, O
Non troppo lento
sentito
p
f
pp

rall.
a tempo
come let us a - dore Him, Christ the
rall.
a tempo
Lord.
A -
Tempo I
gain the heart with rap - ture glows To greet the ho - ly night That

a tempo
rall
gave the world its Christ-mas Rose, Its King of Love and Light. Let
a tempo
rall.
ev - 'ry voice ac-claim His name, The grate-ful cho - rus swell,
p
p
f
From par - a-dise to earth He came That we with Him might
f
f

Non troppo lento
pp
dwell. O come let us a - dore Him, O come let us a - dore Him, O come let us a - dore Him Christ the Lord. Ah!
pp
rall.
a tempo
rall.
a tempo

O come let us a - dore Him,
a - dore Him Christ the Lord. O come, O
come, O come let us a - dore Him,
let us a - dore Him. Christ the Lord.
f
p
rall.
a tempo
pp

THE GIFT

Words and Music by
JIM BRICKMAN and
TOM DOUGLAS

Gm7 B♭/F E♭(9) B♭/D Cm7
You're the an-swer when I prayed_ I would find some - one, and, ba-by, I___ found you._
Chorus:
F7sus F7 B♭/D E♭(9) F7sus F7
And all I want___ is to hold___ you for - ev-er.___ And all I need_
B♭/D E♭(9) F7sus F7 B♭/D D7
___ is you more___ ev-'ry day.___ You saved my heart___ from be-ing
Gm B♭/F Em7(♭5) Cm7 B♭/D F7sus
bro-ken a - part.___ You gave your love a-way, and I'm thank-ful ev-'ry day for the

Bb(9)
F/A
Gm7
Bb/F
Eb(9)
gift.
Verse 2:
F(9)
C/E
Dm7
F/C
Bb(9)
F/A
He:
2. Watch - ing as you soft - ly__ sleep. What I'd give if I__ could_ keep just this mo-ment. If
Gm7
F(9)
C/E
Dm7
F/C
on - ly time_ stood still. But the col - ors fade__ a-way and the years will make us__ gray.__
Bb(9)
F/A
Gm7
C7sus
C7
Both:
__ But, ba-by, in my eyes,__ you'll still be beau-ti - ful.__ And all I want_

Chorus:
F/A
B♭(9)
C7sus
C7
F/A
B♭(9)
___ is to hold___ you for - ev-er.
All I need___ is you more___ ev - 'ry
To Coda
C7sus
C7
F/A
A7
Dm
F/C
Bm7(♭5)
He:
She:
day.
You saved___ my heart from be-ing bro-ken a - part.___ You gave___ your
Gm7
F/A
C7sus
F
He:
Both:
love a - way,
and I'm thank - ful ev-'ry day for the gift.
B♭(9)
C7sus
Dm7
F/A
B♭(9)
F/A
Gm7
C7sus
C7

D.S. 𝄋 al Coda
B♭(9)/D C/E F B♭ Gm7 F/A C7sus C7
And all I want
Coda
Dm F/C Bm7(♭5) Gm7 F/A
She:
He:
bro - ken a - part.
You gave your love a-way.
I can't find the
B♭(9) C/D Dm7 Gm7 C7sus F(9) C/E
She:
Both:
words to say.
And I'm thank - ful ev - 'ry day
for the gift.
rit.
a tempo
Dm7 F/C B♭(9) C7sus F(9)
rit.

GRANDMA GOT RUN OVER BY A REINDEER

Words and Music by
RANDY BROOKS

B
To Coda
E
D
A
as for me and Grand - pa, we be - lieve.
Verse:
E
B
1. She'd been drink - ing too much egg - nog
mp
E
and we begged her not to go,
E7
A
but she for - got her med - i - ca - tion, and she

B
E
stag - gered out the door in - to the snow.
C#m
G#m
When we found her Christ - mas morn - ing
B7
E
at the scene of the at - tack,
E7
A
she had hoof - prints on her fore - head, and in -

B
E
1st and 2nd time D.S.
3rd time D.S. al Coda
crim - i - nat - ing Claus marks on her back.
Coda
E
C♯
F♯
lieve.
Grand-ma got run o - ver by a
rein - deer
walk - ing home from our house Christ -mas
B
Eve.
You can say there's no such thing as

Verse 2:
Now we're all so proud of Grandpa,
He's been taking this so well.
See him in there watching football,
Drinking beer and playing cards with Cousin Mel.
It's not Christmas without Grandma.
All the family's dressed in black,
And we just can't help but wonder:
Should we open up her gifts or send them back?

(To Chorus:)

Verse 3:
Now the goose is on the table,
And the pudding made of fig,
And the blue and silver candles,
That would just have matched the hair in Grandma's wig.
I've warned all my friends and neighbors,
Better watch out for yourselves.
They should never give a license
To a man who drives a sleigh and plays with elves.

(To Chorus:)

GOD REST YE MERRY, GENTLEMEN

TRADITIONAL ENGLISH CAROL

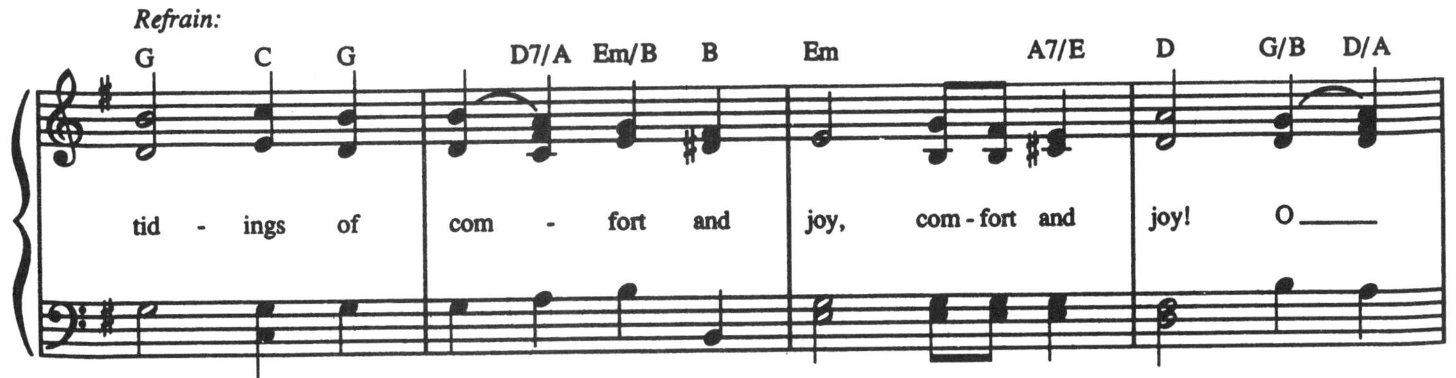

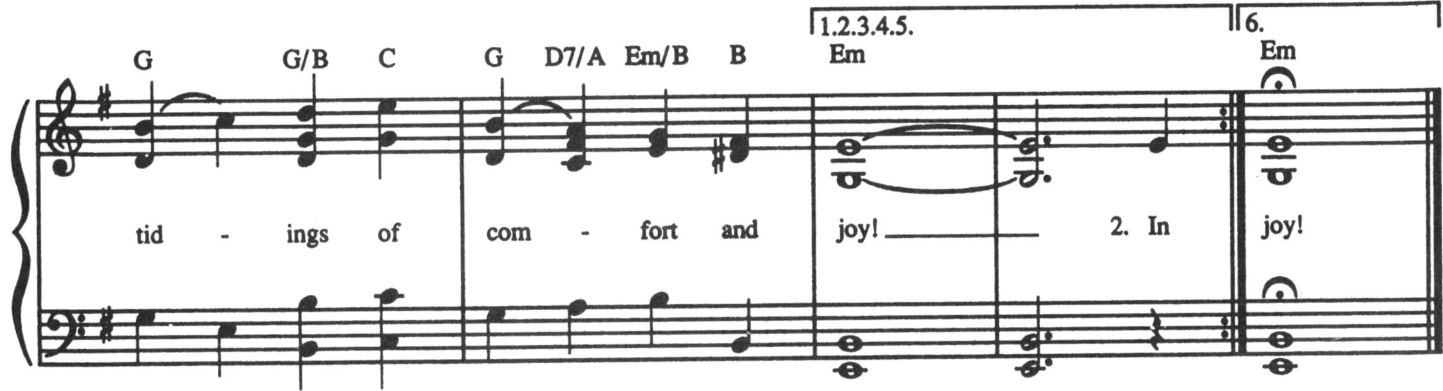

Verse 3:
From God, our Heav'nly Father,
A blessed Angel came,
And unto certain Shepherds
Brought tidings of the same;
How that in Bethlehem was born
The Son of God by Name.
(To Refrain:)

Verse 4:
"Fear not, then," said the Angel,
"Let nothing you affright,
This day is born a Saviour,
Of a pure Virgin bright,
To free all those who trust in Him
From Satan's power and might."
(To Refrain:)

Verse 5:
The Shepherds at those tidings
Rejoiced much in mind;
And left their flocks a-feeding,
In tempest, storm and wind;
And went to Bethlehem straight-way,
The Son of God to find.
(To Refrain:)

Verse 6:
Now to the Lord sing praises,
All you within this place,
And with true love and brotherhood
Each other now embrace;
This holy tide of Christmas
All other doth deface.
(To Refrain:)

GROWN-UP CHRISTMAS LIST

Words and Music by
DAVID FOSTER and
LINDA THOMPSON JENNER

Bbm7
Fm/Ab
Gb
Db/F
Ebm7
6fr.
you still help some - how?
I'm not a child _ but my heart still can
Ab7sus4
4fr.
Ab
Db
Bbm
dream.
So here's my life long wish,
my
grown - up Christ - mas list,
not for my - self _ but for a world _ in
Bb
Gm7
3fr.
need.
No more lives _ torn a - part, _
rall.
a tempo
f

E♭maj7 Cm7 F7sus4 Dm7 Gm7 F6 E♭maj7 E♭/F F7
3fr.
— and wars would nev - er start, and time would heal — all hearts.
B♭ Gm7 E♭maj7 Cm7 F7sus4 Dm7 Gm7 F6
Ev - 'ry man would have — a friend, — that right would al - ways win, and love would nev - er
Em7-5 A13-9 E♭7 Dm7 Gm7 Cm7 F7sus4 B♭
5fr.
end. This is my grown - up Christ - mas list.
rall.
a tempo
mp
Rubato
Fm7 B♭7sus4 B♭7 E♭ Gm7 C7sus4 C7
What is this il - lu - sion called, the in - no - cence of youth. May - be on - ly in our blind be - lief can we

F
A7sus4
A7
D
A
Bm
A
G
ev - er find the truth.
Oo.-
a tempo
rall.
D/F♯
Em7
A7sus4
A7
B
G♯m7
4fr.
There'd be
no more lives torn a - part,-
a tempo
rall.
f
Emaj7
C♯7
4fr.
F♯7
D♯m7
6fr.
G♯m7
4fr.
F♯6
Emaj7
E/F♯
F♯7
and wars would nev-er start,
and time would heal all hearts.
B
G♯m7
4fr.
Emaj7
C♯m7
4fr.
F♯7sus4
Ev - 'ry man would have a friend,
and right would al - ways

D♯m7
G♯m7
F♯6
Fm7-5
B♭13-9
E7
win, and love would nev - er end.
rall.
C♯m7
F♯7
This is my grown-up Christ-mas list. This is my on - ly life - long
a tempo
mp
F♯7sus4
B
F♯
G♯m
wish. This is my grown-up Christ-mas list.
Emaj7

HARK! THE HERALD ANGELS SING

Words by
CHARLES WESLEY

Music by
FELIX MENDELSSOHN

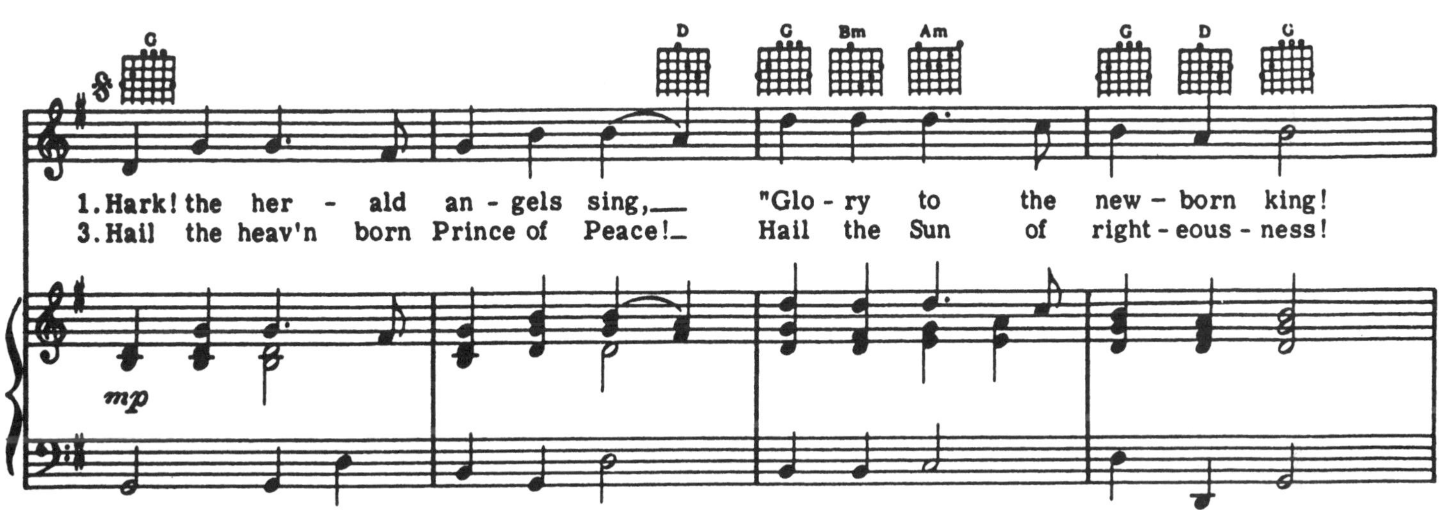

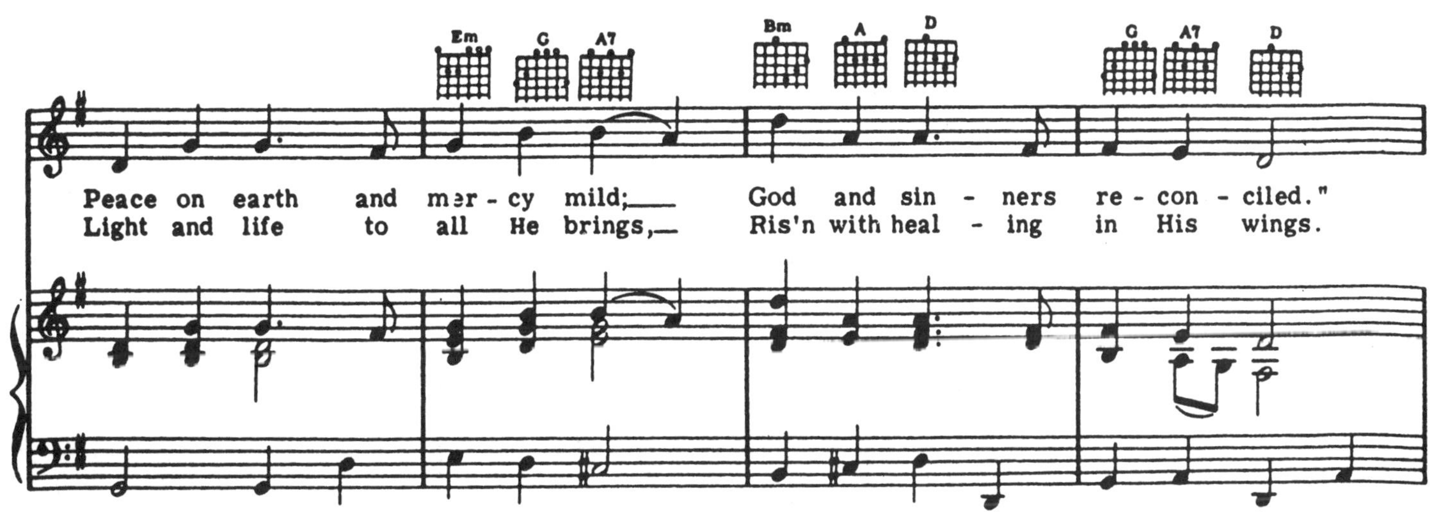

Hark! The Herald Angels Sing - 3 - 1

G
D7
D
Joy - ful, all ye na - tions rise, Join the tri - umph of the skies.
Mild, He lays His glo - ry by, Born that man no more may die,
mf
C
Am
E
With an - gel - ic host pro - claim "Christ is born in Beth - le - hem."
Born to raise the sons of earth, Born to give them sec - ond birth.
f
Fine
Hark! the her - ald an - gels sing, "Glo - ry to the new born king!"
Hark! the her - ald an - gels sing, "Glo - ry to the new born king!"
rit. last time
Bm
2. Christ, by high - est heav'n a - dored, Christ the ev - er - last - ing Lord,
mp lightly

Em
G
Em
A7
Bm
A
D
Bm
A7
D
Late in time be - hold Him come,
Off - spring of the Vir - gin's womb.
G
D7
G
D
G
D7
G
D
Veiled in flesh the God - head see,
Hail th' in - car - nate De - i - ty.
mf
C
G
Am
E
Am
D7
G
D7
G
Pleased as man with men ap - pear,
Je - sus, our Im - man - uel here.
f
C
G
Am
E
Am
D
D7
G
D7
G
D.S. al Fine
Hark! the her - ald an - gels sing,
"Glo - ry to the new - born king!"

HAVE YOURSELF A MERRY LITTLE CHRISTMAS

Words and Music by
HUGH MARTIN and RALPH BLANE

F Fm C Cdim Dm7 G+ Em
Here we are as in old-en days, hap-py gold-en days of yore,
Am6 B7 Em G+ G Am D7 Dm7 G7
Faith - ful friends who are dear to us gath-er near to us once more.
C Am7 Dm7 G7 C Am7 Dm7 G7
Through the years we all will be to-geth-er, if the Fates al - low,
C Am Dm7 E7 Am C+
Hang a shin-ing star up-on the high - est bough, And
F Am Dm7 G7-9 C
have your - self a mer-ry lit - tle Christ-mas now.
rit.

(There's No Place Like)

HOME FOR THE HOLIDAYS

F F♯dim C C♯dim
man who lives in Ten - nes - see and he was head - in' for Penn - syl -
G7 F♯7 G7 C C7 Gm7 C7
van - ia and some home - made pump - kin pie. From Penn - syl -
F F♯dim C Cm
van - ia folks are trav - 'lin' down to Dix - ie's sun - ny shore; From At -
G G♯dim Am7 D7 G7 C♯dim Dm7 G7
D. S. al Coda
lan - tic to Pa - cif - ic, gee, the traf - fic is ter - rif - ic. Oh, there's
Coda
G7 C♯dim Dm7 G9 G7-9 C F6 C
can't beat home, sweet home.
cresc.
f

HURRAY FOR CHRISTMAS

Words and Music by
DON SEBESKY

Chorus:
A♭7 N.C.
D♭
I'm as bright as a holy berry. I'm so merry;
B♭m7
Gm11
G♭(2)
E♭m7
G♭/A♭
A♭7
all I can think of to say is, "Hurray for Christmas
D♭(2)
D♭/A♭
E♭m/D♭
A♭
Day!" The
Bridge:
C7sus
F
B♭2
Gm/D
kids have been waiting and anticipating the happiest day of the
Gm7/B♭
D♭7sus
G♭
E♭m7
A♭m7
year. Wherever you go, folks are shouting "Hello!" and their

D♭7sus G♭9 C♭11 A♭
smiles go from ear to ear, and ev - 'ry - one's heart is so
D♭(2) E♭m/D♭ D2/A Em/A
full of hol - i - day cheer.
Verse:
D Bm7 Em7 A
Can-dles gleam-ing, fac - es beam-ing; hur - ray for Christ-mas!
E C♯m7
Hearts are glow - ing 'cause they're know - ing to - day is
F♯m7 D7 G2 G/D C♯7sus C♯7 F♯2 F♯/C♯
Christ-mas. So, make way for the man in the sleigh.

C7sus C7 F2 B♭maj7 A7sus
He ar-rived in the nick of time and chased all our trou-bles a-way.
A7 N.C.
Chorus:
D Bm7
I'm as bright as a hol-ly ber-ry. I'm so mer-ry; all I can think of to
G♯11(♯5) G(2) G/D G♯m7(♭5) D/A B♭7
say is, "Hur-ray, hur-ray, hur-
A11 A7 D2 Em/D D2
ray for Christ-mas Day!"
Em/D D2 Em/D D2 Em/D
Repeat and fade

I DON'T WANT TO BE ALONE FOR CHRISTMAS

(Unless I'm Alone With You)

Words and Music by
DIANE WARREN

Bb2
Bb
F(9)/A
put the smile on my face the way you used to do.
raise a glass to-geth-er to love that nev-er dies. And
Gm7(4)
F
Ebmaj7
D7sus
D7
All I want for Christ-mas is Christ-mas-time with you. I don't
I'll be spend-ing Christ-mas look-ing in your eyes. There's no
Gm9
Cm7
Gm9
Cm7
wan-na spend the time with-out you. I just
bet-ter time to be to-geth-er. There's no
Gm9
Gbmaj7
Cm7
Bb(9)/D
wan-na hold you close to me, kiss be-side the Christ-mas tree.
sad-der time to be a-lone, hur-ry back please come back home.

1st time only
E♭maj7
E♭maj7(♭5)
Cm7/F
Ba - by, say__ that you'll__ be com - ing home.
Stay with me__ and make__ my dreams_ come true.
Chorus:
Cm7/F
B♭(9)
Cm7
I don't wan-na be a-lone for Christ-mas un-less I'm a-lone__
a tempo
B♭(9)/D
E♭maj7
__ with you. 'Coz it won't be
Dm7
Gm7
Christ - mas, won't be Christ - mas__ un -

1.
Cm7
Cm7/F
less I'm a - lone,
a - lone
with you.
B♭(9)
E♭/B♭
2.
E♭maj7
less I'm hold - ing you.
Cm7/F
B♭(9)
Cm7
I just wan - na hold you close this Christ - mas
the way that I used to
B♭(9)/D
E♭maj7
Dm7
do.
I don't wan - na be a - lone
for Christ - mas
un-

Cm7
Cm7/F
less I'm a - lone,
a - lone
with
Gbmaj7
Ebm9
Fm7
Bbm7
Ab
Gbmaj7
Ebm9
you.
I don't wan-na be a-lone, ba-by.
(I don't wan-na be a - lone.)
Fm7
C#m7/F#
I just wan-na hold you
B(9)
C#m7
close this Christ - mas
the way that I used to

B(9)/D♯
Emaj7
do oh, ba - by, I don't wan - na be a - lone
D♯m7
G♯m7
for Christ - mas don't let me be a - lone for Christ - mas un -
C♯m7
B/D♯
G♯m7
G♯7(♯5)
C♯m7
less I'm a - lone, a - lone, un - less I'm a - lone, a -
Slowly
C♯m7/F♯
Bsus
C♯m7/F♯
B
lone with you.

I WANT AN OLD-FASHIONED CHRISTMAS

Words by
FLORENCE TARR

Music by
FAY FOSTER

C
G7
C
Am
Dm7
C
G7
C
home - folks cheer - i - ly
nod - ding a mer - ry
warm "Hel - lo!"
Eb7
Ab
4 fr.
Bbm7
I want to
hear the lit - tle
Db
Ab
4 fr.
Db
Dbm
Ab
4 fr.
Ab6
D7-5
chil - dren sing - ing the
Christ - mas car - ols I
used to know; And
C
G7
C
G7
Am7
hear the ev - 'ning
church - bells ring - ing out their
joy - ous wel - come of

Dm7
G7
C
Dm
E7
C
G7
long a - go.
I want an old - fash - ioned
rit.
a tempo
C
C7
F
G7
Christ - mas, To be a child a - gain, To make be - lieve that there's a
C
A7
Fm6
G7
C
G7
C
G7
San - ta, For I was hap - pi - est then. Mer - ry Christ - mas! Mer - ry
3
F+
A7
Dm7
C
Christ - mas! Mer - ry Christ - mas!
rit.

IT MUST HAVE BEEN THE MISTLETOE

Words and Music by
JUSTIN WILDE and DOUG KONECKY

Cmaj7
C/D
D7
Cmaj7
may-be just the stars so bright that shined a - bove you our first
f
Gmaj7
Am7
D7
Gmaj7
Christ - mas; more than we'd been dream - ing of.
Cm7
F
Dm7
Gm7
Csus
C
Old Saint Nich - 'las had his fin-gers crossed that
Dsus
D7
Gmaj7
we would fall in love. It could have been the hol - i - day, the
mf

Gmaj7/B
C
mid-night ride __ up - on the sleigh, _ the coun - try - side __ all dressed in white; _ that
C/D Bm/D C/D D Gmaj7
cra - zy snow - ball fight. It could have been __ the stee - ple bell __ that
Dm7 G7 Cmaj7
wrapped us up with - in its spell. _ It on - ly took one kiss to know _ it
C/D Bm/D D6 G Cmaj7
must have been the mis - tle - toe. Our first
f

Gmaj7
Am7
D7
Gmaj7
Christ - mas, more than we'd been dream - ing of.
Cm7
F
Dm7
Gm7
Csus
C
Old Saint Nich - 'las must have known that kiss would
E♭/F
F7
B♭maj7
lead to all of this. It must have been the mis - tle - toe, the
mf
B♭maj7/D
E♭
la - zy fire, the fall - ing snow, the mag - ic in the frost - y air that

Eb/F Dm/F Eb/F F7 Bbmaj7 Fm7 Bb7
made me love you. On Christ-mas Eve a wish came true that night I fell in love with you. It
Eb Cm7 Eb/F Dm/F F6
on - ly took one kiss to know it must have been the
Bb Eb/F Dm/F F6 Gm7
mis-tle-toe. It must have been the mis-tle-toe. It
Eb/F Dm/F F6 Bb Ebmaj7 Bbmaj7
must have been the mis-tle-toe.
8va
a tempo
p

L BE HOME FOR CHRISTMAS

Music by
WALTER KENT

G9 C♯dim Dm Dm7 G7 C Cdim Dm7 G7
tree. Christ - mas Eve will find me
Dm7 G7 C6 Gm6 A7 Dm
Where the love - light gleams.
Dm7 Fm6 G7 C G+ Gm6 A7 Dm Dm7
I'LL BE HOME FOR CHRIST - MAS, If on - ly
mf
rit.
Fm6 G7
1. C G7-9
2. C
in my dreams.
dreams.
rall.

IT CAME UPON THE MIDNIGHT CLEAR

Words by
EDMUND H. SEARS

Music by
RICHARD S. WILLIS

3. And ye beneath life's crushing load,
Whose forms are bending low,
Who toil along the climbing way
With painful steps and slow,
Look now! for glad and golden hours
Come swiftly on the wing.
O rest beside the weary road
And hear the angels sing.

4. For lo, the days are hast'ning on,
By prophet bards foretold,
When with the ever circling years
Comes round the age of gold,
When peace shall over all the earth
Its ancient splendor fling,
And the whole world give back the song
Which now the angels sing.

IT'S CHRISTMAS
(Yes Christmas)

Words and Music by
JUSTIN WILDE

Dreamily

F(2) Em7 A7(♭5) A7 Dm7

mf

G7(♯11 ♭13)

8va

Rubato

Cmaj7 B7(♯5) Gm/B♭ A7(♭5)

It's Christ-mas, yes Christ-mas, that spe - cial time of year, when

Dm9 B♭9(♯11) Em7 Fmaj9 F♯m7(♭5) E/G♯ Am9 E7(♭5) E7

in - no-cence and hap - pi - ness, can't wait to re - ap - pear; when all the world's en - light-ened by

Am9 Am9/G F♯m7(♭5) F9 Em7 D13(♯11) D9 Dm9 G7(♭5 ♭9)

one bright shin - ing star; re - mind-ing us that peace on earth can nev - er be too far. It's

Cmaj7
B7(♯5)
Gm/B♭
A7(♭5)
Dm9
B♭9(♯11)
Christ-mas, yes Christ-mas, and as the hol-ly's hung, sleigh bells ring, while chil-dren sing of
Em7
Fmaj9
F♯m7(♭5)
E/G♯
Am9
E7(♭5)
E7
Am9
Am9/G
F♯m7(♭5)
F9
hope for ev-'ry-one; with friends in-vit-ed o-ver to dec-o-rate the tree,
Em11(4)
D13(♯11)
D9
Dm9
F/G
G7(♭9)
C
once a-gain we all be-come one big fam-i-ly, at Christ-mas. With
Moderately (Relaxed Four)
Gm7
C9
Gm7
C13(♯11)
C9
Grand-ma in the kitch-en on hol-i-day pa-trol, the

Fmaj7 B♭9(♯11) Fmaj7 B♭9 Fmaj9
cook - ie pop - u - la - tion grows out of all con - trol. And
Am7 D9 Am7 D9
kids are writ - ing let - ters ad - dressed to San - ta Claus, and
Em7 Em11 A7(♭5) Dm9 Dm7/G
love is ev - 'ry - where you look. I guess it's just be - cause: It's
rit.
Rubato
Cmaj7 B7(♯5) Gm/B♭ A7(♭5)
Christ - mas, yes Christ - mas. The mag - ic casts its spell, when

Dm9
B♭9(♯11)
Em7
Fmaj9
F♯m7(♭5)
E/G♯
e - ven to - tal strang - ers stop to wish each oth - er well. So
Am9
Am(maj7) Am7
D/E
E7
Am
C/G
D(2)/F♯
F13
San - ta, if you're list - 'ning, please make this wish come true: Let the
C
B7(♯5)
B♭13(♯11)
A7(♭9)
Dm7
Em7
Fmaj7
G7(♭9)
C(2)
love the world is feel - ing now, last the whole year through. It's
B♭13(♯11)
A♭13(♯11)
C(2)
Christ - mas, yes Christ - mas, it's Christ - mas.
8va

IT'S THE MOST WONDERFUL TIME OF THE YEAR

By
EDDIE POLA and GEORGE WYLE

1.
170
Fm7 B♭7 G♭ Fm7 B♭7
time of the year. It's
sea - son of
E♭7 B♭m7 E♭7 A♭ A♮dim E♭/B♭ Cm7
There'll be par-ties for host-ing, marsh-mal-lows for toast-ing and
Fm7 B♭7 E♭ E♭7 A♭m7 D♭7
car - ol - ing out in the snow. There'll be scar - y ghost sto - ries and
G♭maj7 E♭m Fm7(♭5) C♭7 Fm7/B♭ B♭7 Fm7
tales of the glo - ries of Christ-mas-es long long a - go.

B♭9 E♭ Cm Fm7 B♭7 E♭ Cm
It's the most won-der-ful time of the year.
Fm7 B♭7 Fm7 B♭7 E♭ E♭7
There'll be much mis-tle-toe-ing and hearts will be glow-ing, when
A♭ A♮dim E♭
loved ones are near. It's the most
Cm7 Fm7 B♭7 E♭ C♭ A♭m E♭
won-der-ful time of the year.

JINGLE BELL ROCK

Words and Music by
JOE BEAL and JIM BOOTHE

Moderately (with a rock beat)

Chorus

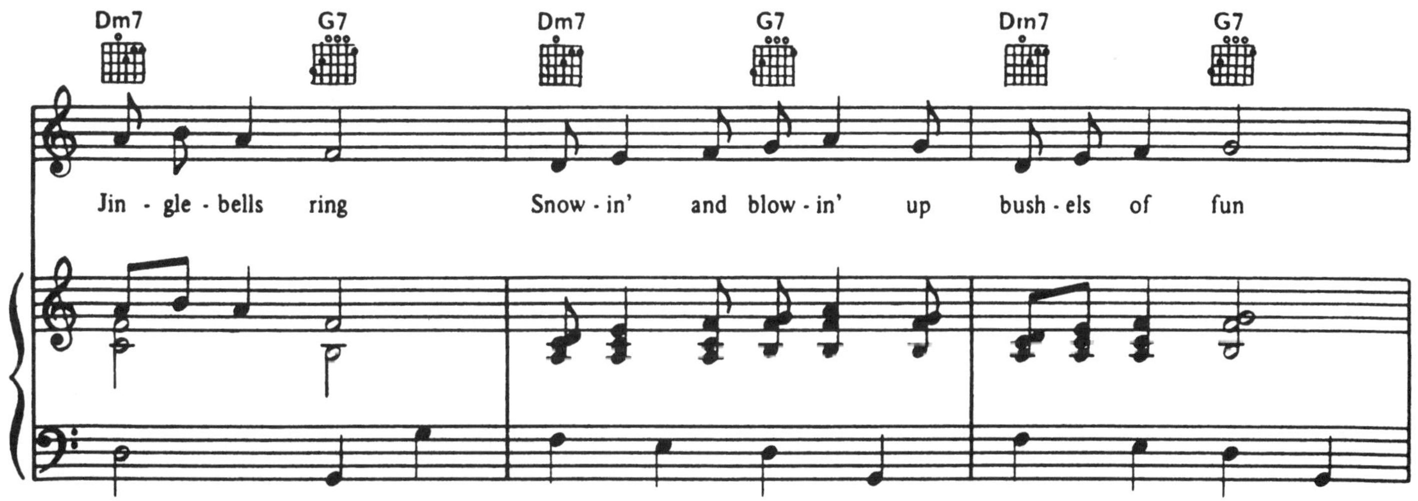

Dm7
G7
G7+5
C
Now the jin - gle - hop has be - gun
Jin - gle - bell, Jin - gle - bell,
C♯dim
Dm7
G7
JIN-GLE-BELL ROCK
Jin - gle - bells chime in Jin - gle - bell time
Dm7
G7
Dm7
G7
D7
G7
Dan - cin' and pran - cin' in Jin - gle - bell Square
In the fros - ty air
C
Dm7
C7
F
F♯dim
C
What a bright time, it's the right time
To rock the night a -

Am7 D7 Am7 D7 G7 Dm7
way___ Jin-gle - bell___ time___ is a swell time___ To go gli-din' in a
G7 C Em7-5 A7+5 A7
one-horse sleigh___ Gid-dy-ap, jin-gle horse pick up your feet___ Jin-gle a-round the clock
F Fm6 D7 G7 1 C C♯dim Dm7 G7
Mix and min-gle in a jin-gl-in' beat___ That's the JIN-GLE-BELL ROCK.___
2 D7 G D7 G7 F C Dm7 B C
That's the Jin-gle-bell, That's the JIN-GLE-BELL ROCK.___

JINGLE BELLS

Words and Music by
JAMES PIERPONT

Chorus:
D7
G
D7
G
sleigh - ing song to - night! Jin - gle bells, jin - gle bells, jin - gle all the
D7
G
A7
way, Oh, what fun it is to ride in a one - horse o - pen
D7
G
sleigh! Jin - gle bells, jin - gle bells, jin - gle all the way,
D7
G
D7
G
Oh, what fun it is to ride in a one - horse o - pen sleigh!

JOY TO THE WORLD

Words by
ISAAC WATTS

Music by
GEORGE F. HANDEL

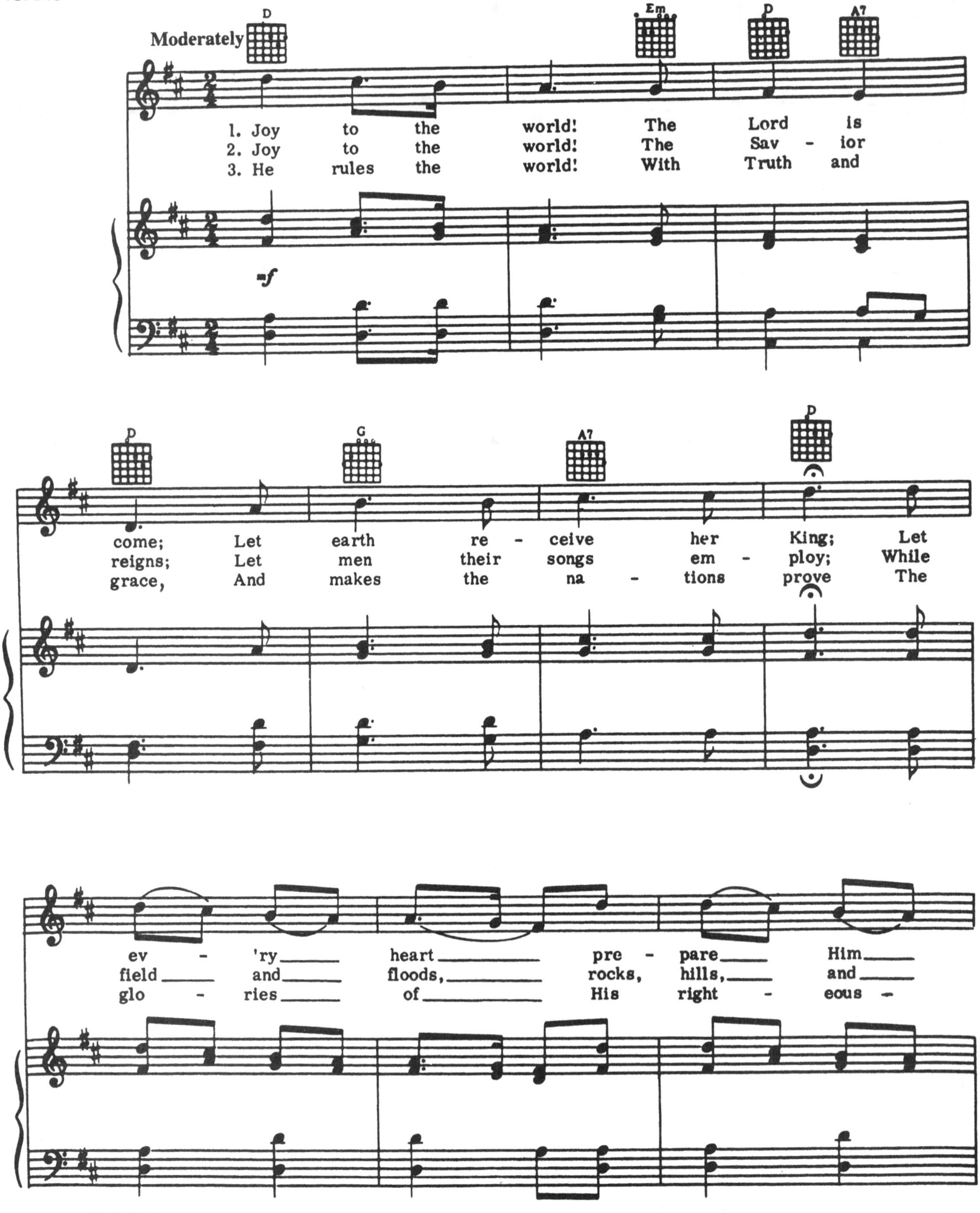

Moderately

D Em D A7

1. Joy to the world! The Lord is
2. Joy to the world! The Sav - ior
3. He rules the world! With Truth and

mf

D G A7 D

come; Let earth re - ceive her King; Let
reigns; Let men their songs em - ploy; While
grace, And makes the na - tions prove The

room, And heav'n and na - ture sing, And
plains Re - peat the sound - ing joy, Re -
ness, And won - ders of His love, And
A
A7
D
G
heav'n and na - ture sing, And heav'n, And
peat the sound - ing joy, Re - peat, re -
won - ders of His love, And won - ders,
D
Em
D
A7
D
heav'n and na - ture sing.
peat the sound - ing joy.
won - ders of His love.

JOYFUL CHRISTMAS

Words and Music by
JAKOB OLOFSSON and
ANNA OLOFSSON

*Harmony is sung 2nd time.

G/D
Am
G/D
B/D♯
1.
Em
D/F♯
G
D7/A
G/B
for un - to us a King is born this day, this Christ - mas Day.
C
Cm
C2
C
He is born this day.
rit.
2.
Em
D/F♯
G
F/A
Bridge:
G
F
G/B
F/A
day, this Christ - mas.
Joy bells are ring - ing.
G
F
Dm
C/E
Dm
Chorus:
F♯/C♯
F♯sus/C♯
C♯/B
All heav - en's an - gels sing - ing...
Joy - ful Christ - mas,

F♯/A♯
Bmaj7
B/D♯
C♯
B
F♯/A♯
D♯m
C♯/E♯
C♯
all hearts re - joice with won - der. Joy - ful Christ - mas,
F♯/C♯
B/D♯
C♯/E♯
F♯
G♯/F♯
for un - to us a King is born this day.
A/F♯
B/F♯
G♯/F♯
F♯
G♯/F♯
F♯
G♯/F♯
D♯m7
King is born this day!
G♯/D♯
B2
F♯
rit.
mp

JOLLY OLD SAINT NICHOLAS

TRADITIONAL

2. When the clock is striking twelve,
When I'm fast asleep,
Down the chimney broad and black,
With your pack you'll creep;
All the stockings you will find
Hanging in a row;
Mine will be the shortest one,
You'll be sure to know.

LET'S MAKE IT CHRISTMAS ALL YEAR 'ROUND

Lyrics by
DOROTHY FIELDS

Music by
BURTON LANE

Fm7
B♭7
E♭maj7
E♭6
Edim7
Fm7
B♭7
dance and sing of peace on earth at last. A
E♭maj7
E♭6
Gm7
C7
F7
mil - lion sil - ver bells will ring that the fear and the sor - row have
Fm7/B♭
B♭7
E♭
A♭
B♭7
E♭
passed. Oh, why is it on - ly on this day that the
A♭/C
E♭/B♭
F7sus
F7
B♭9
B♭7
A♭
E♭/G
love that is lost can be found? Some - how I know there

Fm7
Bb7
Ebmaj7
Fm/Ab
Eb/Bb
Am7b5
D7
is a way for the hearts of the world to be bound. We'll
Gm7b5
C7
Fm7b5
Bb7
Eb
Fm/Eb
just make it Christ - mas all year 'round. Let's make it
Ebmaj7
1
Fm7/Bb
Bb7
Eb
Fm6
Eb6
Bb7sus
Bb7
Christ - mas all year 'round.
2
Fm7/Bb
Eb
all year 'round.

LET IT SNOW! LET IT SNOW! LET IT SNOW!

Words by
SAMMY CAHN

Music by
JULE STYNE

Gm D+ D7 Gm Abdim C7 F
lights are turned 'way down low. LET IT SNOW! LET IT SNOW! LET IT SNOW! When we
f mf
C C#dim Dm7 G7 C
fin - al - ly kiss good - night, How I'll hate go - ing out in the storm! But if
C B+ Gm A7 D7 G7 C F C7
you'll real - ly hold me tight All the way home I'll be warm. The
mf
F C7 F Abdim C7 D7
fi - re is slow - ly dy - ing And, my dear, we're still good - bye - ing, But as
G D+ D7 Gm Abdim C7 1. F 2. F
long as you love me so LET IT SNOW! LET IT SNOW! LET IT SNOW! Oh the SNOW!
f mf sfz

LET'S HAVE AN OLD-FASHIONED CHRISTMAS

Words by
HAROLD ADAMSON

Music by
JIMMY McHUGH

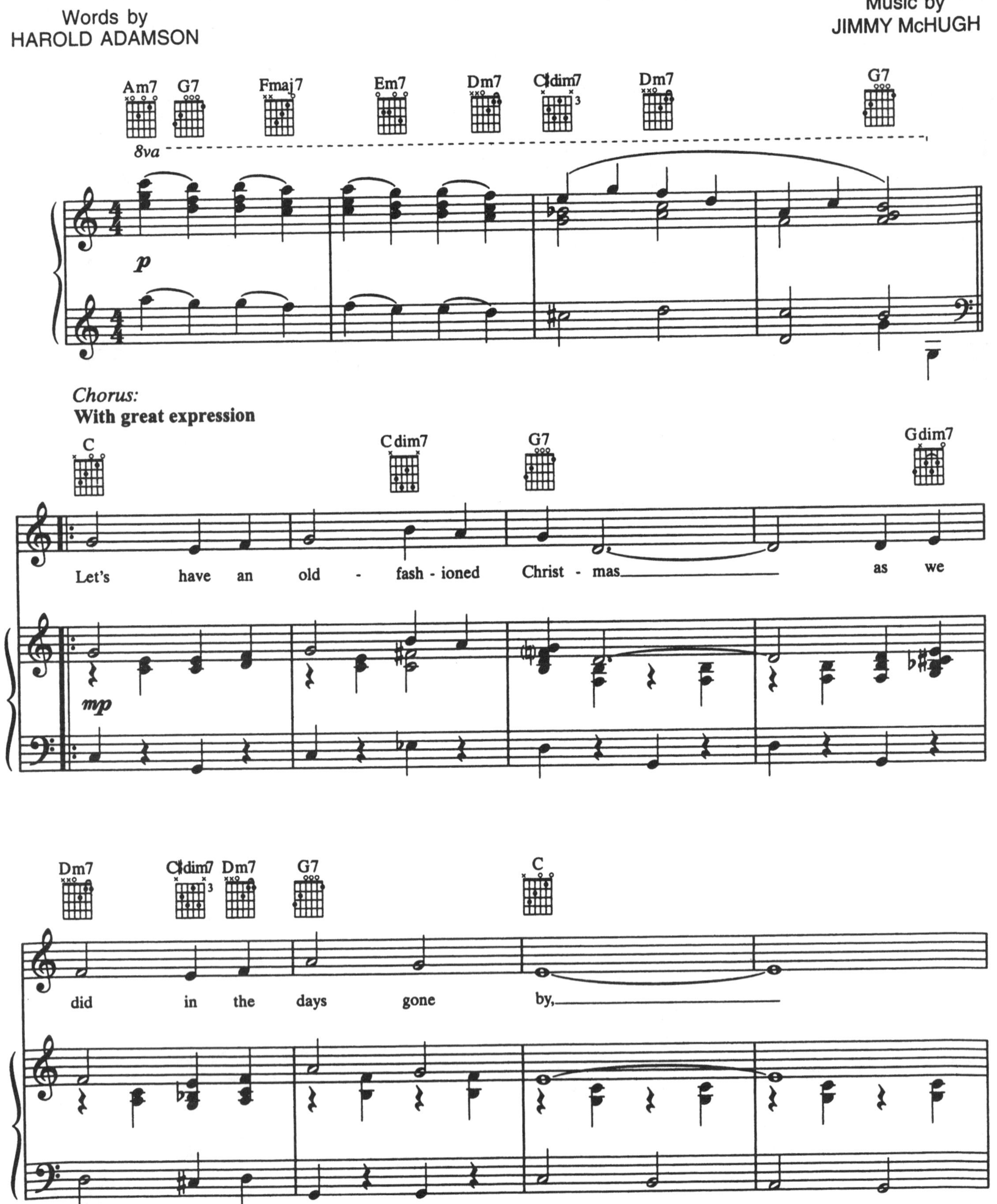

C dim7
G7
snow - flakes and San - ta, and sleigh - bells
Gdim7
Dm7
C♯dim7
Dm7
G7
C
F
and a star in a peace - ful sky.
C
C dim7
Dm7
G7
G+
Let's have mis - tle - toe, hap - py
C
C♯dim7
G7
Dm7
G7
hearts a - glow, all the things we know and

C
Cdim7
Dm7
G7
love
while each car - ol rings
G+
C
Am7(♭5)
and the king of kings
sends his
G/D
D7
G7
bless - ing from a - bove.
(chimes)
C
Cdim7
Let's stay at home by the

G7
Gdim7
Dm7
C♯dim7
Dm7
G7
fi - re with the ones that we hold so
C
Cdim7
dear. Let's have an old - fash - ioned
G7
Gdim7
Dm7
G7
Christ - mas and let's pray for a hap - py new
1.
C
2.
C
year.
year.
molto rit.
pp

THE LITTLE DRUMMER BOY

Words and Music by
KATHERINE DAVIS, HENRY ONORATI
and HARRY SIMEONE

F
B♭
rum pum pum pum, To lay be - fore the King, pa -
rum pum pum pum, That's fit to give our King, pa -
F7
B♭
F
C
rum pum pum pum, rum pum pum pum, rum pum pum pum,
rum pum pum pum, rum pum pum pum, rum pum pum pum,
F
So to hon - or Him, pa - rum pum pum pum,
Shall I play for you, pa - rum pum pum pum,
1. C7
F
when we come.

2.
C7
F
on my drum?
l.h.
f
F
Mar - y nod - ded, pa - rum pum pum pum,
The Ox and Lamb kept time, pa - rum pum pum pum.
C
I played my drum for Him, pa - rum pum pum pum,

F Bb F7 B♭ F
I played my best for Him, pa - rum pum pum pum, rum pum pum pum,
C
rum pum pum pum.
r.h.
l.h.
F
Then He smiled at me pa - rum pum pum pum,
C7 F
me and my drum.
f

A MARSHMALLOW WORLD

Words by
CARL SIGMAN

Music by
PETER DE ROSE

C Cmaj7 C6 Cmaj7 C Cmaj7 C6
marsh - mal- low clouds be- ing friend - ly In the arms of the ev- er-green
G Dm7 G G7 C Am Am7 D7 Dm7 G7
trees And the sun is red Like a pump- kin head It's shin- ing so your nose won't
Dm7 Cdim C Gm7 C7 Fmaj7 Dm Dm7
freeze. The world is your snow - ball. See how it grows.
Gm7 C9 C7 F Am7 D7
That's how it goes When - ev - er it snows. The world is your snow - ball

Gmaj7
Em
Em7
Am7
D7
G6
G7
Just for a song. Get out and roll it a - long. It's a
C
Cmaj7
C6
Cmaj7
C
Cmaj7
C6
yum - yum - my world made for sweet - hearts. Take a walk with your fa-vor- ite
G7
Dm7
G
G7
C
A7
girl. It's a su - gar date. What if spring is late? In
D7
Dm7
G7
1
C
Cdim
Dm7
G7
2
C
Db9
C6
win - ter it's A MARSH- MAL- LOW WORLD. It's A WORLD.
rit.

A VERY MERRY CHRISTMAS

Words and Music by
ALAN and MARILYN BERGMAN
and PAUL WESTON

A Very Merry Christmas - 3 - 1

C C6/9 C2 Cmaj13 C6/9 C2 C6/9 Cmaj13 C6/9
where! Mer - ry Christ - mas. Mer - ry
(Mer - ry Christ - mas.)
C2 Csus C6/9 Dm/C Am Am/G Dm7/F G/F
Christ - mas. Have you ev - er seen the chil - dren's eyes so bright? They
(Mer - ry Christ - mas.)
Em7 Dm7 G7 C Fmaj7 G/F Em7 Am/E
warm the chill in the air! Look, there's a glow in ev - 'ry win - dow and on
Dm7 G7 Cmaj9 C6 Fmaj7 G/F
ev - 'ry face you see. Seems you can feel the love that's

Em7
Am/E
C/D
D9
Dm7/G
G7
gath - ered all a - round each Christ - mas tree! Mer - ry
C2
C6/9
Cmaj13
C6/9
C2
Csus
C6/9
Dm/C
Christ - mas. Mer - ry Christ - mas. Ev - 'ry
(Mer - ry Christ-mas.)
(Mer - ry Christ-mas.)
Fmaj7
Em
Am
Am/D
Em7
F
G6
bell you hear sings a song of cheer for a ver - y Mer - ry Christ-mas and a
F
Dm7/G
G7
C
C2
C6/9
Cmaj13
C6/9
Cmaj9
Hap - py New Year.

A MEMORY OF CHRISTMAS

Words and Music by
STEVE CELI, JOHN RUSNAK
and JOSEPH BILLÉ

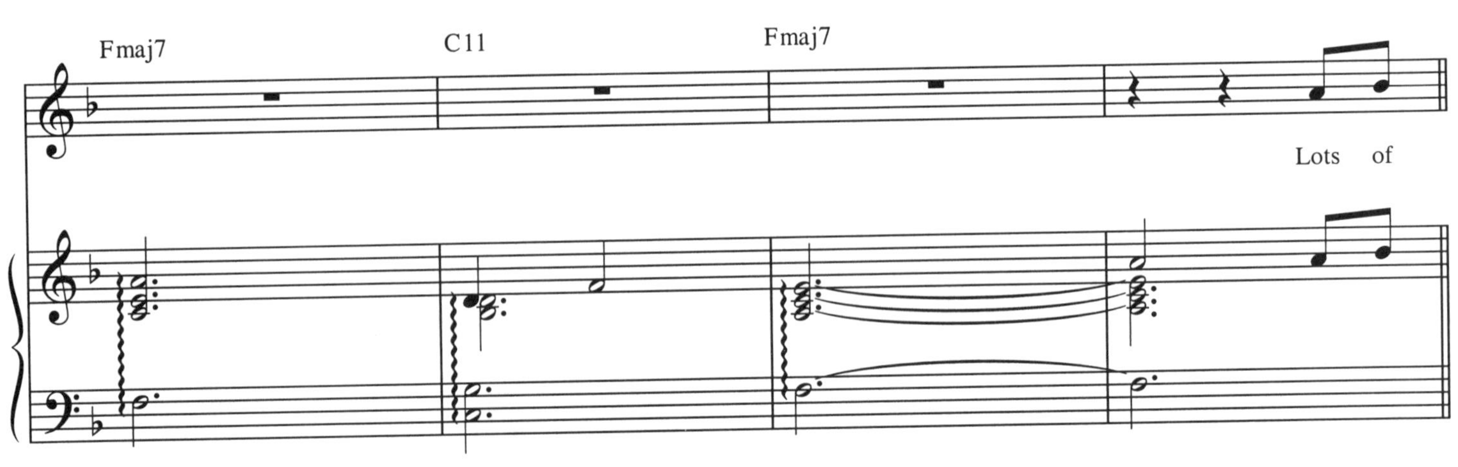

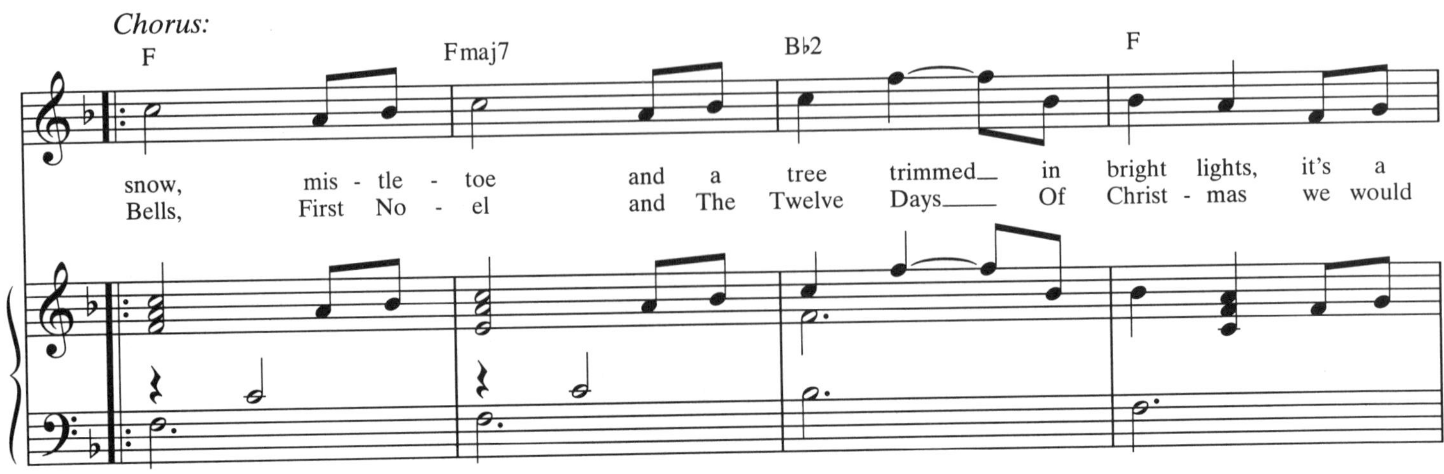

1.
2.
Dm
Dm/G
C7sus
C7
C7
mem - 'ry of Christ - mas from not long a - go. Jin - gle low. And the
sing wrapped in muf - flers in fif - teen be -
Verse:
Dm
Dm(maj7)
Dm7
Dm6
gray win - ter sky of this ice cold De - cem - ber makes me
C
Cmaj7
A7sus
A7
wish I was home safe and warm. Far a -
Dm
Dm(maj7)/C♯
Dm7/C
Dm6/B
way, far from you, I can on - ly re - mem - ber how it

B♭2 F/A E♭9(♯11) C7sus

used to be gath - ered 'round the tree. Can - dy

a tempo *mf*

Chorus:

F Fmaj7 B♭2 F

canes, frost - ed panes and the rich smell of nut - meg, just a

scenes, ev - er - greens, fro - zen lakes filled with skat - ers, it's a

Dm G9 C7sus 1. C7 2. C7

dash on the egg nog to give it some cheer. Win - ter year. In your

mem - 'ry of Christ - mas I cher - ish each

Verse:

Dm Dm(maj7) Dm7 Dm6

arms by a fire with the last em - ber glow - ing and a

C Cmaj7 A7sus A7
sweet scent of pine in the air, we en -
Dm Dm(maj7) Dm7 Dm6
joyed all the songs sung by Cros - by and Co - mo with the
B♭2 F/A E♭9(♯11) F(9)
bass down low on the ster - e - o. Christ - mas
dim.
mf
Bridge:
B♭m7 B♭m7/E♭ A♭ Fm7
Eve when the world is calm and still, when the

Bbm7
Bbm7/Eb
Ab(9)
Ab
night spar - kles right on cue, I will
Abm7
Abm7/Db
Gb
Ebm7
wish on the bright - est star and send all the
Freely
Abm7
Abm7/Db
C7sus
C13(b9)
C7sus
love that I'm feel - ing for you. Lots of
a tempo
mp
Chorus:
G
Gmaj7
C2
G
snow, mis - tle - toe and a tree trimmed in bright lights, it's a

Em A13 G/D D7
mem - 'ry of Christ - mas, a mem - 'ry this year Si - lent
cresc.
G Gmaj7 G7 Cm N.C.
Night, lone - ly night, it's a long dis - tance Christ - mas. Ev - 'ry
mf
molto rit.
a tempo
mp
Slower, freely
G/D C/E G/B Cm G/D
day, ev - 'ry sea - son I know love is the rea - son I en - joy mak - ing
Faster
D7sus G/F C/E Cm/E♭ G(9)
mem - 'ries with you.
rit.
a tempo
rit.
Ped.

MERRY CHRISTMAS BABY

Words and Music by
LOU BAXTER and JOHNNY MOORE

Bb7 Bb7 F

feel-in' might-y fine, Got good mu-sic on my ra - di - o, Well, I

C7 C7 F

want to kiss you ba-by While you're stand-in' 'neath the mis-tle-toe. Saint

Bb F Bb7 F Bb7 F

Nick came down the chim-ney 'bout half - past three, Left all these pret-ty pres-ents that you see be-fore me, Mer-ry

Bb7 F

Christ-mas Lit-tle Ba - by, you sure been good to me, I have-n't

C7 F7 Bb Bbm F

had a drink this morn-in' But I'm all lit up like a Christ- mas tree.

MY CHILDHOOD CHRISTMAS EVES

E♭
Edim7
B♭/F
F/G
Gm7
I know it's im - pos - si - ble, my wish is to
dream-ing of a mid - night ride with San - ta, and
Watch the snow that fell out - side our win - dow add
B♭/F
F7sus
1.
B♭(9)
go back to my child - hood Christ-mas Eves.
fly - ing through my child - hood Christ-mas
mag - ic to my child - hood Christ-mas
E♭(9)
2. 3.
B♭
Cm7
B♭/D
2. I'd
Eves.
Eves.
I'd
I
cresc.

Chorus:
E♭maj7
F7sus
B♭
Cm7
B♭/D
wrap my arms a-round my Mom and Dad-dy,
think I'll put a-way the old home mov-ies,
mf
hold them close and whis-per, "I love you," re-
close my eyes and drift a-way to sleep. Then for-
E♭/F
To Coda
Dm7
Gm7
mem-ber-ing the wide-eyed sense of won-der of
get-ting how im-pos-si-ble my
E♭/B♭
A♭maj9
D.S. al Coda
liv-ing in a make-be-lieve come true.
3. Then

Coda
Dm7
Gm7
E♭m/G♭
wish is,
I'll
dim.
B♭/F
F7sus
Gm7
C/E
go back to my child-hood Christ-mas Eves.
I
mp
poco rit.
Freely
B♭/E♭
F7sus
B♭(9)
E♭(9)
sure do miss my child-hood Christ-mas Eves.
a tempo
B♭(9)
E♭(9)
B♭
molto rit.

MY CHRISTMAS PRAYER

Words and Music by
GREG BIECK, E. TYLER HAYES
and BEBE WINANS

B♭ F/C F/A E♭(9)/B♭ E♭ F7 E♭/G F7/A B♭
For those that grieve, God will bring com - fort;
F Gm7 F/A B♭ F E♭ B♭/D Cm B♭/D E♭ Fsus F
laugh - ter will rap - ture there. This is my Christ - mas prayer.
Chorus:
B♭ Gm7 E♭(9) F7sus B♭ Gm7
See, I pray that love will rule and reign. And I pray that time
mf
E♭(9) F7sus E♭maj7 F/A Dm7 Gm F E♭
will rid the pain of this world as we learn to trust and care.

F7sus
Cm Dm E♭ Fsus
F
B♭
F/A
F
E♭(9)/B♭
This is my Christ - mas prayer.
Verse 2:
F7sus
B♭
F/A
F
E♭(9)
I pray for you, (Yes, I know you do.) that you
E♭ F7 E♭/G F7/A
B♭
F Gm7 F/A B♭
F
E♭
B♭/D
tri-umph and con - quer, pos-sess the strength you need to bare.
Cm Dm E♭ Fsus
F
B♭
F/A
F
E♭2
This is my Christ - mas prayer. For those in need,

E♭ F7 E♭/G F7/A B♭ F Gm7 F/A B♭ F E♭ B♭/D
there would be plen - ty___ and each oth - er's bur - dens share.___ Oh,___
Chorus:
Cm Dm E♭ Fsus F B♭ Gm7 E♭(9) F
this is my Christ - mas prayer.__ See, I pray__ that love___ will rule__ and reign.__
B♭ Gm7 E♭(9) F E♭maj7 F/A
__ And I pray__ that time___ will rid__ the pain___ of this world__ as we learn__
Dm7 Gm F E♭ B♭/D Cm Dm E♭ Fsus F
__ to trust__ and care.___ This is my Christ - mas prayer.__

Bridge:
B♭
Cm
B♭
F/A
B♭/D
E♭
So let hope fill our hearts. Yes, let hope fill our
Cm
B♭
F/A
E♭
B♭(9)
F/A
Gm
F/A
hearts. Shine the light through the dark.
All a-round the world and
E♭
B♭/D
Cm7
B♭/D
E♭
Fsus
ev - 'ry - where,
I will pray this Christ - mas prayer (prayer.
Chorus:
F
B♭
Gm7
E♭(9)
F7sus
)
See, I pray that love will rule and reign.
mp

B♭ Gm7 E♭(9) F7sus E♭maj7 F/A
And I pray that time will rid the pain of this world as we learn
mf
Dm7 Gm F E♭ B♭/D Cm Dm E♭ Fsus F
to trust and care. This is my Christ - mas,
C♯m D♯m E B/F♯ F♯ B G♯m
this is my Christ - mas prayer. See, I pray that love
E F♯ B G♯m E F♯
will rule and reign. And I pray that time will rid the pain

Emaj7
F♯/A♯
D♯m7
G♯m
F♯
E
B/D♯
of this world as we learn to trust and care.
C♯m
D♯m
E
B/F♯
F♯
G♯m
D♯m7/F♯
Fm7(♭5)
This is my Christ - mas prayer.
C♯m
D♯m
E
F♯sus
F♯
B♭
F♯/C♯
F♯/A♯
E(9)/B
This is my Christ - mas prayer.
E
F♯/E
E
B/E
E
F♯/E
B(9)
Freely
rit.
a tempo

MY VERY FIRST CHRISTMAS WITH YOU

Words and Music by
ALAN and MARILYN BERGMAN
and MARVIN HAMLISCH

D7sus
D7
G7sus
G7
E♭
E♭+
I could nev - er wait to leave. But this year I feel like a
E♭6
E♭7
Dm7
G7
C7sus
C7
child a - gain though I've known some Christ - mas - es be - fore.
F♯m7(♭5)
Fm7
Fm6
C/E
E7
Am
A♭7
C/G
C7
Fmaj7
Fm
Now it's all com - plete - ly new, it's my ver - y first Christ - mas, my
C
C7
Fmaj7
Fm6
C
Am7
Dm7
G7sus
G7
ver - y first Christ - mas, it's my ver - y first Christ - mas with

Bridge:
C Fm6 Cmaj7 Cm7 F7 B♭maj7 Gm9
you. Light cream - y egg - nogs and bright crack - 'ling Yule logs, a
Cm7 F7 B♭maj7 B♭6 D7sus D7 Gmaj7 Em9
cheer - i - ness I used to doubt. You are the rea - son the joys of the sea - son are
Dm7 G7 C7sus C7 F♯7sus F♯7 Bmaj7 B6
fi - n'lly worth sing - ing a - bout. Sweet baked Vir - gin - ia hams, marsh - mal - low can - died yams,

F♯7sus
F♯7
Bmaj7
B
Em7
A7
they nev - er tast - ed like this!
This year at last, I know
Dmaj7
D7sus
D7
G7sus
G7
why there is mis - tle - toe as we kiss.
Refrain:
Fm7
G7(♭9)
C
Fmaj7
G7/F
Christ - mas is not just for chil - dren.
I know from the way I
C/E
Gm7
C7
Fmaj7
G/F
Em7
E7
Am
feel.
Rein - deer are fly - ing and San - ta is real,

F6
E7
Am
Gm7
C7
F6
Fm6
ring - ing his sleigh - bells, and tell - ing us he'll bless us the
C
Am7
D7
G♯7
C/G
C7
Fmaj7
Fm
whole year through! I'll re - mem - ber this Christ - mas, my
C
C7
Fmaj7
Fm
C
Am7
Dm7
mer - ry first Christ - mas, my ver - y first Christ - mas
G7sus
G7(♭9)
C
Am7
Fm6
Fmaj7/G
G7(♭9)
C6/9
with you.
rit.

NUTTIN' FOR CHRISTMAS

Words and Music by
SID TEPPER and ROY C. BENNETT

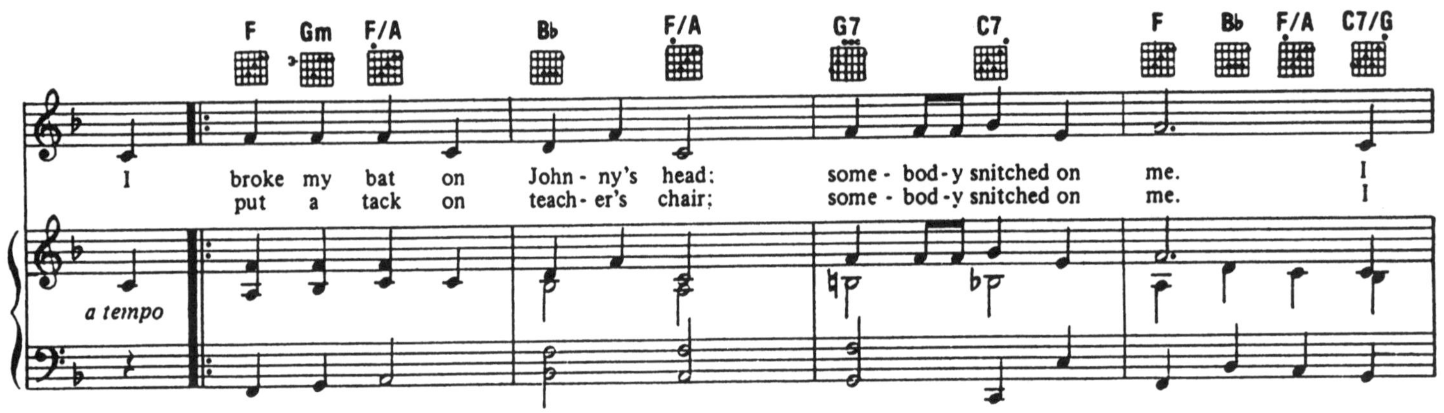

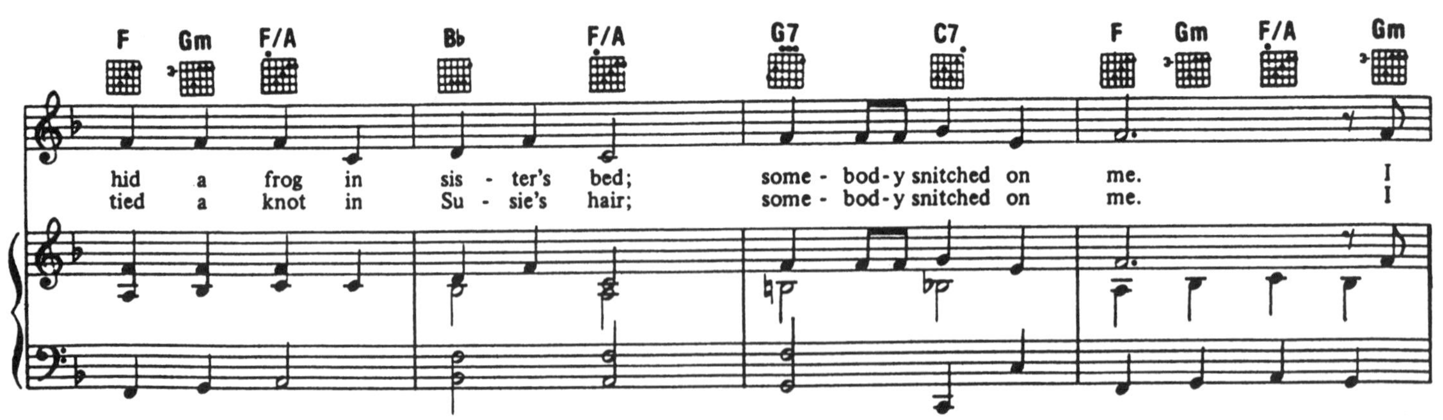

F F#dim Gm7 Gb7 Gm7 C7-9 Fmaj7 Dm7
spilled some ink on Mom - my's rug, I made Tom - my eat a bug,
did a dance on Mom - my's plants, climbed a tree and tore my pants.
Bb F/A Bb Gm7 C7/G C7 F6 C9+5
Bought some gum with a pen - ny slug; some - bod-y snitched on me. Oh,
Filled the su - gar bowl with ants; some - bod-y snitched on me. So,
F Am/E Dm7 F/C Gm
I'm Get - tin' Nut - tin' For Christ - mas. Mom - my and
Gm7/F C7/E F Am/E
Dad - dy are mad. I'm Get - tin' Nut - tin' For

3. I won't be seeing Santa Claus; somebody snitched on me.
He won't come visit me because somebody snitched on me.
Next year I'll be going straight, next year I'll be good, just wait,
I'd start now but it's too late; somebody snitched on me. Oh,

O CHRISTMAS TREE

(O Tannenbaum)

OLD GERMAN CAROL

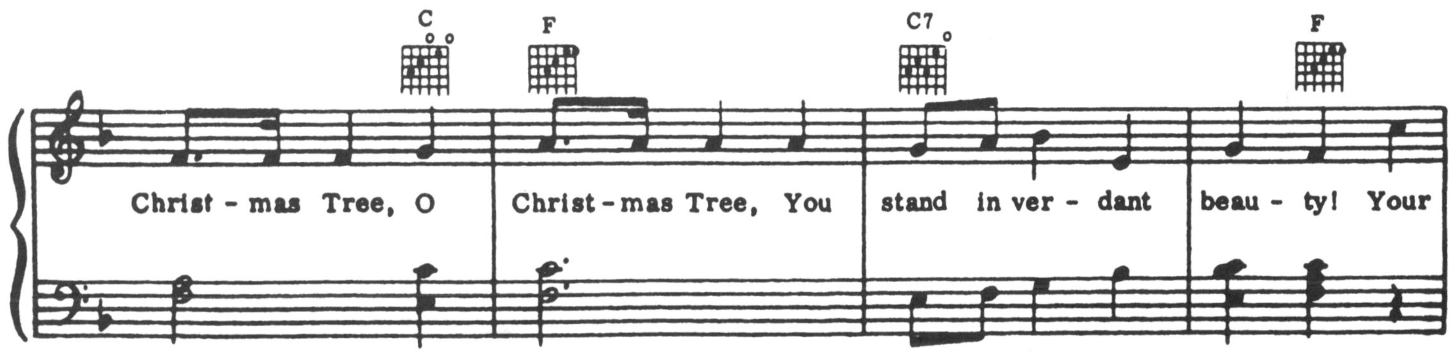

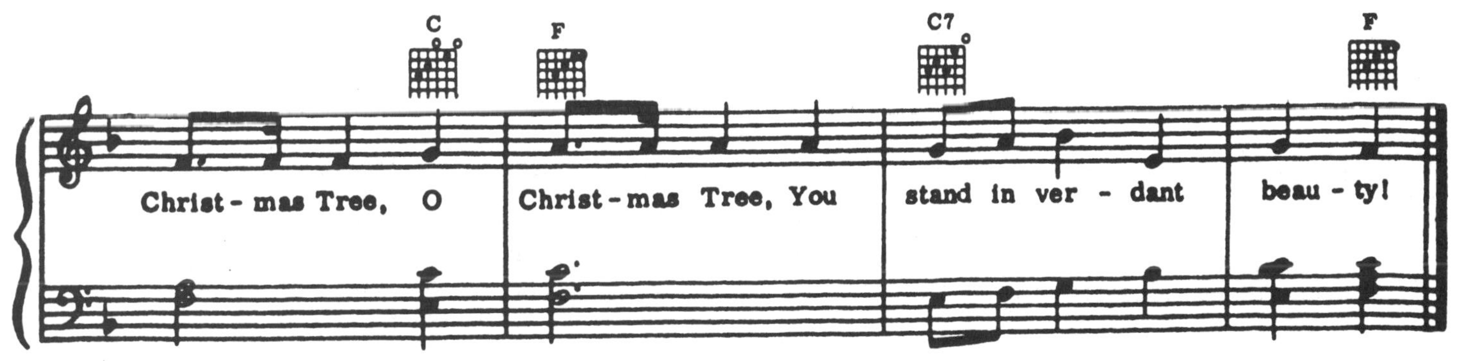

O COME, ALL YE FAITHFUL

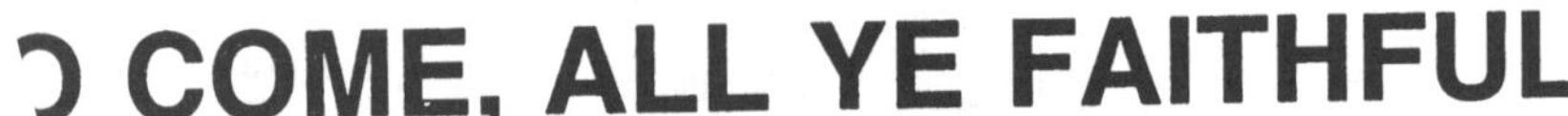

(Adeste Fideles)

EDERICK OAKELEY
JOHN FRANCIS WADE

Music by
JOHN READING

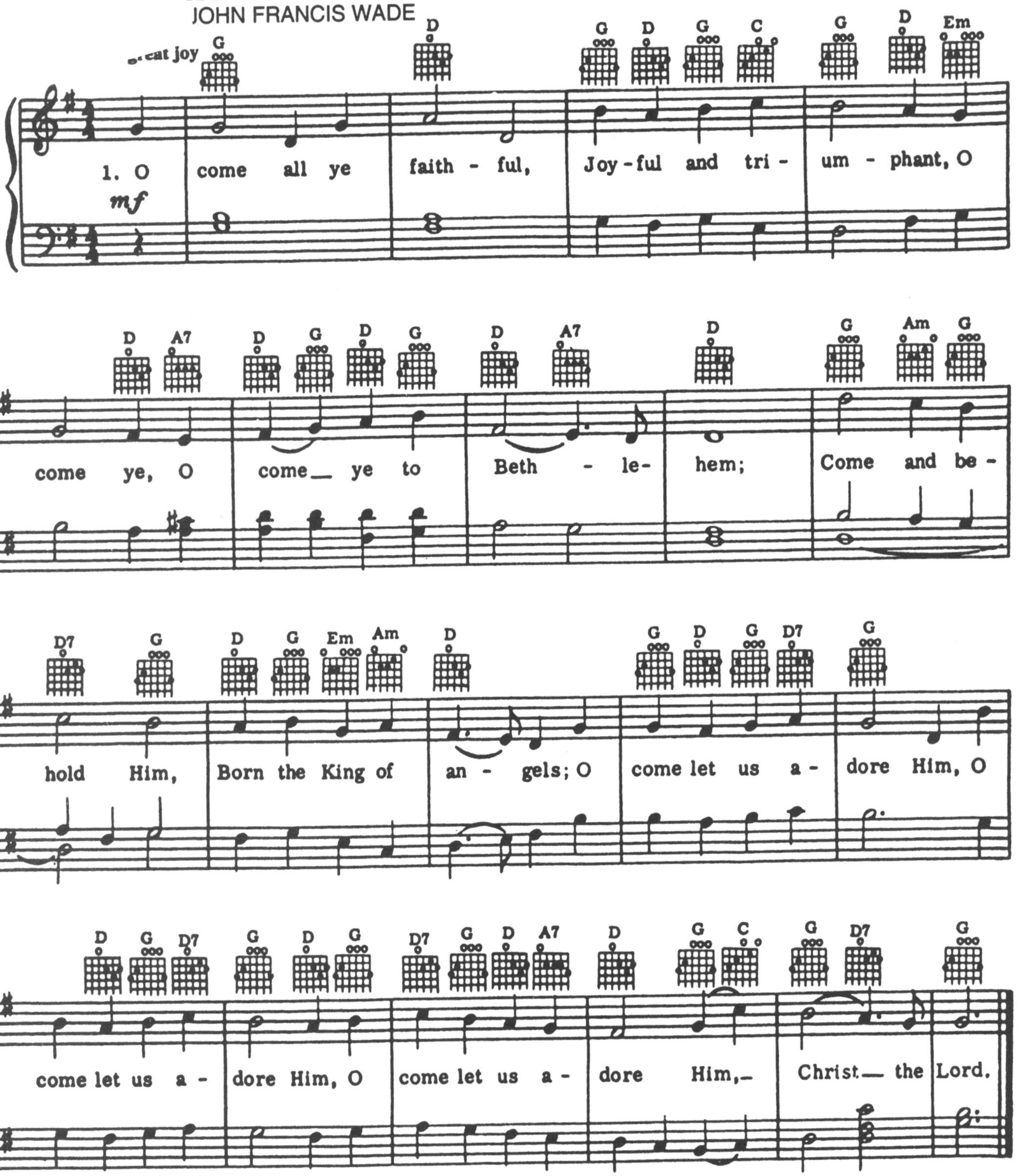
great joy
mf
1. O come all ye faithful, Joy-ful and tri - um - phant, O
come ye, O come — ye to Beth - le- hem;
Come and be - hold Him, Born the King of an - gels; O
come let us a - dore Him, O
come let us a - dore Him, O
come let us a - dore Him, — Christ — the Lord.

2. Sing, choirs of angels,
Sing in exultation,
Sing, all ye citizens of heaven above:
Glory to God
In the highest glory!
O come, let us adore Him, etc.

3. Yea, Lord, we greet Thee,
Born this happy morning,
Jesus, to Thee be glory giv'n,
Word of the Father,
Now in flesh appearing.
O come, let us adore Him, etc.

OL' KRIS KRINGLE

Words by
HAROLD ADAMSON

Music by
JIMMY McHUGH

D7
G
Em7
A7
D7
G
he can spread the Christ-mas joy to all the girls and boys. He calls on his help - ers,
Am
D7
G
Am
D7
G
Em7
A7
D7
Am7(♭5)
sing-ing mer-ri - ly, just a - bout the time that you have trimmed the Christ-mas tree. And he
D
Am7(♭5)
shouts, "Tal - ly ho! Let's go! Got a real bus - y night, you
Chorus:
D
Am7
D7
G2
know." Jin - gle, jin - gle, jin - gle, hear the sleigh bells jin - gle.
8va
molto rit.
a tempo

G
G♯dim7
Am7
D7
Ol' Kris Krin-gle's on his way.
Is-n't it ex-cit-ing?
8va
Am7
D7
Christ-mas trees are light-ing.
It will soon be Christ-mas
(8va)
G
C
G
Am7
D7
G
day.
High a-bove the chim-ney top with
rein-deers fly-ing high,
C
G
A7
D7
G2
you will hear the mu-sic of his
sleigh bells in the sky.
Jin-gle, jin-gle, jin-gle,
8va
molto rit.
a tempo

E7
A7
D7
To Coda
G
C
G
ev - 'ry - bod - y's gay. Ol' Kris Krin-gle's on his way. With a
(8va)
Bridge:
D7
D6
G/D
drum for ba - by broth - er, and a doll for sis - ter Sue, and e -
G6
F♯7
Fmaj7
E7
lec - tric trains and pep-per-mint canes and a jump - ing kan - ga - roo. With a
F♯7
Bm
F♯7
Bm
ted - dy bear for Tom - my, and a bike that's shin - y new, and I

D7
Ddim7
D.S. % al C
bet that Dad and Mom - my will get some pres - ents too.
molto rit.
Coda
G2
way, on his way, on his
(spoken) Mer - ry
way, on his way, on his
Christ - mas, ev - 'ry - bod - y!
(8va)
dim. poco a poco
G
way.
mp

O HOLY NIGHT
(Cantique de Noel)

By
ADOLPHE CHARLES ADAM

C G7 C
wear - y world re - joi - ces for yon - der breaks a new and glor - ious morn.
Am Em Dm Am
Fall on your knees! Oh, hear the an - gel voi - ces! Oh,
C G7 C F C G7 C
night di - vine! O night when Christ was born, O
G7 C Dm C G7 C
night di - vine, O night, O night di - vine.

O LITTLE TOWN OF BETHLEHEM

F
Dm
A
by; yet in thy dark streets shin - eth the
Dm
B♭
A
F
ev - er - last - ing light. The hopes and fears of
B♭
F
C7
F
all the years are met in thee to - night.

THE ONLY THING I WANT FOR CHRISTMAS

By
VICK KNIGHT, JOHNNY LANGE
and LEW PORTER

Gm
3fr.
G7
C7
F
Fmaj7
F7
garden of forget-me-not, THE ONLY THING I WANT FOR
Bb
Bbm6
F
G7
C7
CHRIST-MAS is just to keep the things that I've
F
F6
F7
Bb
Bbm6
Bbm
F
F+
Dm
Dm7
got. A friend or two, a peace-ful sky of blue, A
Gm
3fr.
C7
Gm
3fr.
Gm7
3fr.
C7
place to hang my hat, When work of day is thru, If

F
A7
Bb
D7
San - ta pass - es by my chim - ney, I'll
Gm
3fr.
G7
C7
still be hap - py like as not, THE
F
Fmaj7
F7
Bb
Bbm6
ON - LY THING I WANT FOR CHRIST - MAS is
F
G7
C7
1. F
Abo7
C7
2. F
just to keep the things that I've got. If got.

SANTA BABY

Words and Music by
JOAN JAVITS, PHILIP SPRINGER
and TONY SPRINGER

Am
D7
G
Em
Am7
D7
hur - ry down the chim - ney to - night.
hur - ry down the chim - ney to - night.
G
Em
A7
D7
G
Em
San ta Ba - by, a fif - ty four con - vert - i - ble, too, light blue.
San ta cu - tie and fill my stock - ing with a du - plex and cheques.
A7
D7
G
Em
Am7
D7
I'll wait up for you dear San - ta Ba - by, so hur - ry down the chim - ney to - night.
Sign your X on the line San - ta cu - tie and hur - ry down the chim - ney to - night.
G
Em
Am7
D7
G
B7
F♯m7
(B Bass)
B7
Think of all the fun I've missed.
Come and trim my Christ - mas tree

E7
Bm7
(open)
E7
A7
Em7
(A Bass)
Think of all the fel - las that I have - n't kissed.
with some dec - o - ra - tions bought at Tif - fa - ny.
Next year I could be
I real - ly do be -
A7
D
C#
Am7
(D Bass)
Edim
D7
just as good if you check off my Christ - mas list.
lieve in you. Let's see if you be - lieve in me.
G
Em
A7
D7
G
Em
San - ta Ba - by, I want a yacht and real - ly that's not a lot
San - ta Ba - by, for - got to men - tion one lit - tle thing a ring!
A7
D7
G
Em
Am7
D7
Been an an - gel all year San - ta Ba - by, So hur - ry down the chim - ney to - night.
I don't mean on the phone San - ta Ba - by, So hur - ry down the chim - ney to - night.
G
Em
Am7
D7
G
Em
Am7
D7-9
G

PEACE

(Where the Heart Is)

Words and Music by
JIM BRICKMAN and KEITH FOLLESE

C
G
F2
I
don't know why.
I
don't know why.
C
G
Am
F
Some-bod-y lives, some-bod-y dies. Some-bod-y wrongs and a moth-er cries. And
Best of broth-ers and best of friends. One mis-take and their sto-ry ends. And
C
G
F2
I
don't know why.
I
don't know why.
Dm
Am
G
Gsus
G
Some-things we'll nev-er un-der-stand.

Dm
Am
G
F/A
G/B
Oth - er things you change_ if you can.
Chorus:
C
Dm7
Peace, you'll find_ it where_ the heart_ is, and the heart is right_ where love_
C/E
F
F/A
G/B
_ lives, and love can al - ways find_ a way.
C
Dm7
Hope is the some-thing that_ re - minds_ us, it's not too late_ to find_

C/E
1.
F
G
F2
us. One day we may be in peace.
C
G
Am
F
C
G
F2
2.
F
G
Bridge:
F
be in peace. It's all a - bout for - give-
G
F(9)/A
G/B
A/C♯
ness. With God as my wit - ness I wan - na live to see
3

D
Em7
peace.
D/F♯
G(9)
G/B
A/C♯
Chorus:
D
Em7
Peace, you'll find it where the heart is, and the heart is right where love
lives, and love can al - ways find a way.
D/F♯
G
G/B
A/C♯

D Em7

Hope is the some-thing that__ re - minds__ us, it's not too late__ to find__

D/F♯ G A

__ us. One day we__ may__ be in

G2 D A Bm G

peace.

D A G2 D

rit.

SANTA CLAUS IS COMIN' TO TOWN

Words by
HAVEN GILLESPIE

Music by
J. FRED COOTS

Santa Claus is Comin' to Town - 5 - 1

C G7 C G7 C C/E E♭dim7
called on dear old San - ta Claus to see what I could see. He
bet - ter write your let - ter now and mail it right a - way, be -
G/D B♭dim7 Am7 D7 G G7(♯5)
took me to his work - shop and told his plans to me.
cause he's get - ting read - y his rein - deers and his sleigh.
So, you
Delicately
Chorus:
C C7 F/C Fm/C C C7 F Fm
bet - ter watch out, you bet - ter not cry. Bet - ter not pout, I'm tell - ing you why:
p
C Am F6 G7 C G7 C C7
San - ta Claus is com - in' to town. He's mak - ing a list and

F/C Fm/C C C7 F Fm C Am
check-ing it twice, gon-na find out who's naugh-ty and nice: San - ta Claus is
F6 G7 C Cdim7 C7 F
com - in' to town. He sees you when you're sleep - in'. He
mf
C7 F D7 G G♯dim7
knows when you're a - wake. He knows if you've been bad or good so be
Am7 D7 G G7(♯5) C C7 F/C Fm/C C C7
good for good-ness sake. Oh, you bet - ter watch out, you bet - ter not cry. Bet-ter not pout, I'm
p

Music box Chorus:
F Fm C Am F6 G7 C G7 C
tell-ing you why: San-ta Claus is com-in' to town. With lit-tle tin horns and
p
F C F Fm C G7
lit-tle toy drums, root-y toot-toots and rum-my tum-tums: San - ta Claus is com - in' to
8va
C G7 C F C
town. And cur-ly head dolls that tod-dle and coo, el - e-phants, boats and
(8va)
loco
p
F Fm C G7 C
kid-die cars too; San - ta Claus is com - in' to town.
8va

Cdim7 C7 F C7 F
The kids in girl and boy-land will have a jub-i-lee. They're
(8va) loco
mf
D7 G G♯dim Am7 D7 G G7(♯5)
gon-na build a toy-land town all a-round the Christ-mas tree. So, you
p
C F C F Fm
bet-ter watch out, you bet-ter not cry, bet-ter not pout, I'm tell-ing you why:
C G7 C
San-ta Claus is com-in' to town.
8va
3

SENDING YOU A LITTLE CHRISTMAS

Words and Music by
JIM BRICKMAN, VICTORIA SHAW
and BILLY MANN

Ab(9) Ab(9)/C Db(9) Bbm7/Eb
an - gel to put on a tree.
filled it with your fa - v'rite things. a
Ab(9) Ab(9)/C Db Dbm6
San - ta Claus in cray - on, to make you smile to - day,
way to say "I love you," like kiss - es through the air,
Csus C Fm Fm/Eb
while you're so far a - way.
hop - ing you feel me there.
Db Bbm7/Eb
Chorus:
Db Ab/C
So, I'm send - ing you a lit - tle Christ - mas,

B♭m7
A♭
D♭
A♭/C
wrapped up with love.
A lit - tle peace, a lit - tle light
B♭m7
Csus
C
Fm
Fm/E♭
to re - mind you of
I'm wait - ing for you, pray - ing for you. I
D♭(9)
A♭/C
B♭m7
want - ed you to see,
so I'm send - ing you a lit - tle Christ - mas
B♭m7/E♭
To Coda
1.
D♭maj7
A♭/C
till you come home to me.

2.
Bridge:
B♭m7
B♭m7/E♭
D♭(9)
2. Some till you come home to me.
A♭/C
A♭m/C♭
Home, in - to these arms of mine.
Home,
B♭sus
B♭
D.S. al Coda
Coda
where you be - long.
So, I'm
till you come
D♭maj7
A♭/C
B♭m7
E♭
A♭
home.

Dbmaj7
Ab/C
Bbm7
Bbm7/Eb
Till you come home
Dbmaj7
Ab/C
Bbm7
Ab
to me.
Dbmaj7
Ab/C
Bbm7
Bbm7/Eb
Freely (♫ = ♫)
Db
Dbm
Ab(9)
rit.

SANTA'S LITTLE HELPER

Words and Music by
PETER MATZ

Dm7
Gm7
Cm7
F7
F9(♯5)
A♭7
G7
bright shin - y rib - bon; I know it will make you so glad! I'm gon - na
Cm7
F7
B♭
Bdim7
be there when you take off the wrap - ping; I'll bet you
Cm7
F7
Fm7
B♭7
E♭maj7
E♭m6
just won't be - lieve your eyes! For what - 'll be there in that
Dm7
Gm7
Cm7
F7
Em7
A7
Christ - mas pack - age is a hol - i - day sur - prise. It

D
Bm7
Em7
A7
D/F♯
F dim7
3
comes with a life-time guar-an-tee;
you'll nev-er have to re-pair
Em9
A7
F
Dm7
Gm7
C7
it. The han-dling and the de-liv-ery are free, and I
F 7
F dim7
F 7
A♭7
G7
prom-ise you will nev-er have to share it!
1. And when you
2. And when we

Cm7
F7
B♭
Bdim7
Cm7
Am7(♭5)
D7
fi - nally__ fig - ure out___ how to use it, you'll thank the
fi - nally__ fig - ure out___ how to use it, we'll thank the
yule - tide stars a -
Gm
G♭7
Fm7
B♭7
E♭maj7
E dim7
1.
B♭/F
A♭7
G7
bove! I'm gon - na be San - ta's__ lit - tle help - er this Christ - mas:___ I'm gon - na
bring you the gift of my love.
I'm gon - na be
2.
B♭
A♭7
G7
Cm7
E♭/F
F 7(♭9)
G♭maj 9
Freely
C♭maj 9
B♭6/9
Christ - mas:___ I'm gon - na bring you the gift of my love.___
rit. e dim.
p

SILENT NIGHT

Words and Music by
JOSEPH MOHR and
FRANZ GRUBER

C
G7
C
peace, ___ sleep ___ in heav - en - ly peace! Si - lent Night,
G7
C
Ho - ly Night, Shep - herds quake at the sight;
F
C
F
Glor - ies stream ___ from heav - en a - far, Heav - en - ly hosts sing
C
G7
C
Al - le - lu - ia, Christ the sav - ior, is born! ___

G7 C
Christ,_ the sav - ior is born! Si - lent Night, Ho - ly Night,
G7 C F
Son of God, love's pure light, Ra - diant beams___ from
C F C
Thy ho - ly face, with the dawn of re - deem - ing grace,
G7 C G7 C
Je - sus Lord at Thy birth.___ Je - sus Lord at Thy birth.

SING A SONG OF CHRISTMAS

C
Am7
Dm7
G7
Cmaj7
Am7
Dm7
E7
Mu - sic of the sea - son so beau - ti - ful to hear,
Am7
F♯m7(♭5)
Am
Dm7
G7
C6
mer - ry sounds of Christ - mas, that will ec - ho loud and clear.
Fm7
B♭7
E♭maj7
Cm7
Fm7
B♭7
E♭maj7
E♭6
Sing to cel - e - brate the glo - ry of this won - drous hol - i - day.
Gm7
C7
Fmaj7
Dm7
Gm7
G♭7
F9
G13
Joy - ous cho - rus - es of hope and love will nev - er fade a - way.

C
Am7
Dm7
G7
Cmaj7
Am7
Dm7
E7
Sing a song of Christ - mas, and long be - fore you're through,
Am7
F♯m7(♭5)
D9
Dm7
church bells will be ring - ing, cho - irs will be
E7
C
Dm7
G11
sing - ing, wish - ing Mer - ry Christ - mas to
1.
C
E♭7
Dm7
G13
you.
2.
C6
C6/9
you.
rit.

SLEIGH RIDE

Words by
MITCHELL PARISH

Music by
LEROY ANDERSON

Moderately bright

f

G Am7 D7 G

mf

Just hear those sleigh bells jin - gle - ing, ring - ting - tin - gle - ing, too,

Am7 D7 G Am7 D7 G

Come on, it's love - ly weath - er for a Sleigh Ride to - geth - er with you,

B♭ D7 G Am7 D7 G

Out - side the snow is fall - ing and friends are call - ing "Yoo hoo,"

Am7
D7
G
Am7
D7
G
Come on, it's love - ly weath - er for a Sleigh Ride to - geth - er with you.
C♯m7
F♯7
B
Gid - dy - yap, gid - dy - yap, gid - dy - yap, let's go,
Let's look at the show,
C♯m7
F♯7
B
Bm
We're rid - ing in a won - der - land of snow.
Gid - dy -
Bm7
E7
A
Am7
yap, gid - dy - yap, gid - dy - yap, it's grand,
Just hold - ing your hand.
We're glid - ing a -
D7
Am7
D7
G
long with a song of a win - ter - y fair - y - land, Our cheeks are nice and ros - y, and

Am7
D7
G
com - fy co - zy are we,
We're snug - gled up to - geth - er like two
Bb
birds of a feath - er would be.
Let's take that road be - fore us and
sing a cho - rus or two.
Come on, it's love - ly weath - er for a
C
Sleigh Ride to - geth - er with you.
Just hear those
1.
2. G
you.
dim.
p
f

THROUGH THE EYES OF A CHILD

Words and Music by
ALAN and MARILYN BERGMAN
and JORGE CALANDRELLI

A7sus
A7
D
ev - er - greens watch - ing si-lent - ly. Through the eyes
Chorus:
Ddim7
Am/C
Cdim7
of a child, sweet sur - prise of a child.
G/B
C/B
There's a Christ - mas moon tin - sel bright in the night
Am7
D7sus
D7
and a sin - gle star, warm and

Bridge:
G
G7
shim-mer - y.
Love wakes the world and
Peace walks the world and
mp–mf
Cmaj7/G
B♭dim7
finds it's way Christ-mas Day, it ar - rives with the
finds it's way Christ-mas Day, brings a light to the
Gm/B♭
Cm/E♭
morn - ing sun bring - ing joy, bless - ing
dark - est place, just as love brings a
Chorus:
D7sus
G/D
ev - 'ry - one.
kind of grace.
Through the eyes of a child,
mp–f

D7sus
D7
what the world would see!
Edim7/D
G/D
Wise lit - tle child
filled with
D7sus
D7
To Coda
3
love, show - ing what the world could
Instrumental solo:
G
B7(♯5)
Em7
Em/D
A7sus
A7
A/G
be!
cresc.
mf

D2/F♯
G(9)
G/F♯
Em7
Em/D
A7sus
A7
D
D.S. 𝄋 al Coda
(end solo)
Through the eyes
Coda
G7
C/G
be!
dim.
D7/G
G
Through the eyes of a child.
rit.
p

SUZY SNOWFLAKE

Words and Music by
SID TEPPER and ROY BRODSKY

C
A7
Dm7
G7
C7
F
play with me I have-n't long to stay.
If you wan-na make a snow-man
I'll help you make one, one two, three.
If you wan - na take a sleigh - ride,
D7
C♯dim
the ride's on me.
fz
Here comes SU - ZY SNOW - FLAKE,
fp
look at her tumb-lin' down,
pp
Bring-ing joy to ev-'ry girl and boy.
1
2
Su-zy's come to town.
Su - zy's come to town.
fz

THERE IS NO CHRISTMAS LIKE A HOME CHRISTMAS

F
F+
F6
G6
G7
C
Christ-mas bells, Christ-mas bells, ring - ing loud and strong,
mf
Am
E+
Am7
D9
Dm7
C♯dim
Dm
Tacet
Fol - low them, fol - low them, you've been a - way too long. There is
mp
Gm7
C7
F-
A♭7
no Christ-mas like a home Christ-mas, for
Fmaj7
Em7
G9
Cmaj7
Fm
that's the time of year all roads lead home.
dim.
rall.
f

THIRTY-TWO FEET AND EIGHT LITTLE TAILS

(Dasher, Dancer, Prancer, Vixen, Comet, Cupid, Donner, Blitzen)

Thirty-Two Feet and Eight Little Tails - 2 - 1

C
G7
C
D7
go,
San-ta laugh-in',
Ho, ho, ho, ho,
ho, ho, ho, ho,
G7
C
G7
ho.
Dash-er, Danc-er,
Pranc-er, Vix-en,
Com-et, Cu-pid,
Don-ner, Blitz-en,
C
F
o-ver the gar-den
wall,
Thir-ty-two feet and
eight lit-tle tails an'
C
F♯dim
G7
A7
G6
all,
See 'em can-ter,
hear ol' San-ta
call,
Cm
A7
G7
C
"Mer-ry, mer-ry
cresc.
Christ-mas to you
all."
f

TOYLAND

Words by
GLEN MacDONOUGH

Music by
VICTOR HERBERT

THE TWELVE DAYS OF CHRISTMAS

TRADITIONAL ENGLISH

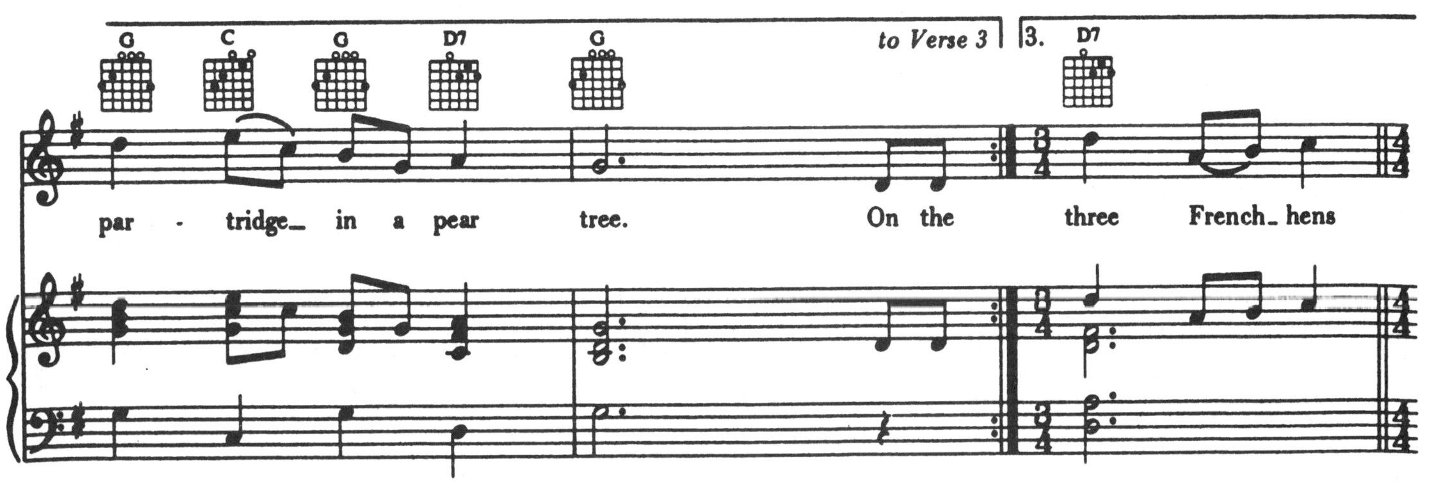

G
C
G
D7
G
to Verse 4
two tur - tle doves, and a par - tridge_ in a pear tree. On the
4.
D7
four call - ing birds, three French_ hens, two tur - tle doves, and a
G
C
G
D7
G
to Verse 5
5. G
A7
D
D7
par - tridge_ in a pear tree. On the five gold - en rings,

G
C
A7
D
four calling birds, three French hens, two turtle doves, and a
G
C
G
D7
G
End here
(after all Verses)
partridge in a pear tree.
6. On the
7. On the
8. On the
9. On the
10. On the
11. On the
12.. On the
D7
G
D7
sixth day of
seventh day of
eighth day of
ninth day of
tenth day of
eleventh day of
twelvth day of
Christ - mas my true love sent to me
6. six geese a - lay - ing. (go to ending 5)
7. seven swans a - swim - ming. (to 6)
8. eight maids a - milk - ing. (to 7)
9. nine la - dies danc - ing. (to 8)
10. ten lords a - leap - ing. (to 9)
11. eleven pi - pers pip - ing. (to 10)
12. twelve drum - mers drum-ming. (to 11)

WARMER THAN SNOW

Words and Music by
STEVE HOSTETLER

F(9)
B♭
G7sus
G7
cov - ers like a child on a win-ter hol - i - day.
sleigh ride. Glide a-long be-hind a gen-tle mare.
And to -
cresc.
Chorus:
Am
F
G7sus
C
Am
F
night the world is bright-er on the floor be-side the fi-re as we hud-dle like fro - zen Es-ki-mos.
mf
G7sus
G7
Am
F
G7sus
G7
Am
Fun-ny how the weath-er brought us to-geth-er. Does-n't
To Coda
F(9)
G7sus
G7
C/E
F
G7sus
mat-ter how the wind may blow. Is there an-y-thing warm-er than

1.
2.
C
Dm7
F(9)
snow?
2. To -
snow?
Bridge:
Gm7
B♭/C
Fmaj7
Win - ter has a way of slow - ing ev - 'ry - bod - y down;
Fm7
A♭/B♭
E♭
traf - fic on the street can bare - ly crawl.
When a snow - y cur - tain falls, there's time to look in - side

D.S. al Coda
Fm7
G7sus
where we find the warm-est place of all. To-
rit.
a tempo
Coda
Am
Am/G
F♯m7(♭5)
snow? To-
rit. e dim.
Freely
F2
G7sus
C
Dm7
night there's noth-ing warm-er than snow.
a tempo
p
mp
F2
G7sus
C
rit.
8vb

WE WISH YOU A MERRY CHRISTMAS

TRADITIONAL ENGLISH FOLK SONG

A7
D
G
B7
Em
Am7
like fig-gy fig-gy pud-ding, We like fig-gy fig-gy pud-ding and a
C6
D7
G
C
A
cup of good cheer. 4. We won't go un-til we've got some, we won't go un-til we've
D
G
B7
Em
Am7
A7
D7
got some, We won't go un-til we've got some, Kind-ly bring some out
G
B7
C
Am7
D
D7
G
here. We wish you a Mer-ry Christ-mas and a hap-py New Year.
f

From THE POLAR EXPRESS

WHEN CHRISTMAS COMES TO TOWN

Words and Music by
GLEN BALLARD and ALAN SILVESTRI

Slowly and gently ♩ = 80

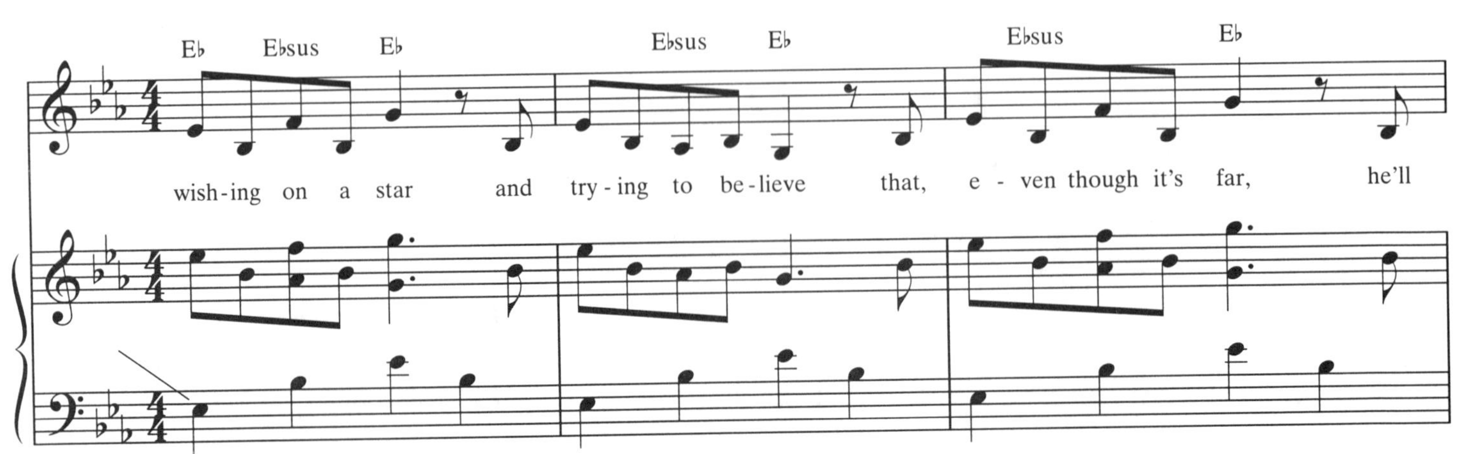

Ebsus Eb Fm7 Bb7/D Eb Eb/G Ab Eb/G
find me Christ-mas Eve. I guess that San-ta's bus-y 'cause he's nev-er come a-round. I
Fm7 Bb7sus Eb Ebsus Eb Ebsus Eb
think of him when Christ-mas comes to town. The
mp
Ebsus Eb Ebsus Eb Ebsus Eb
best time of the year, when ev-'ry-one comes home; with all this Christ-mas cheer it's
Ebsus Eb Fm7 Bb/D Eb Eb/G Ab Eb/G
hard to be a-lone. Put-ting up the Christ-mas tree with friends who come a-round, it's

Fm7
Fm7/B♭
E♭sus
E♭
so much fun when Christ - mas comes to town.
cresc.
C♭
D♭/C♭
B♭m7
E♭m
Pres - ents for the chil - dren___ wrapped in red___ and green;
mf
C♭
D♭/C♭
B♭m7
E♭m
all the things_ I've heard a - bout but nev - er real - ly seen.
Fm7(♭5)
/E♭
B♭7/D
E♭m
/D
G♭/D♭
No one will be sleep - ing on the night of Christ - mas Eve,___ hop - ing

F♯m7 B7 Fm7 B♭7sus B♭7 E♭ E♭sus E♭ E♭sus E♭
San-ta's on his way.
E♭sus E♭ E♭sus E♭ Fm7 /E♭ B♭/D E♭ E♭/G A♭ E♭/G
Fm7 Fm7/B♭ E♭sus E♭ C♭ D♭/C♭
Pres-ents for the chil - dren
B♭m7 E♭m C♭ D♭/C♭ B♭m7 E♭m
wrapped in red and green; all the things I've heard a-bout but nev-er real - ly seen.

Fm7(♭5) /E♭ B♭7/D E♭m /D G♭/D♭ F♯m7 B7
No one will be sleep-ing on the night of Christ-mas Eve, hop-ing San-ta's on his
Fm7 B♭7sus B♭7 E♭ E♭sus E♭ E♭sus E♭
way. When San-ta's sleigh bells ring, I lis-ten all a-round. The
mp
E♭sus E♭ E♭sus E♭ Fm7 B♭/D
her-ald an-gels sing; I nev-er hear a sound. And all the dreams of chil-dren, once
E♭ E♭/G A♭ E♭/G Fm7 Fm7/B♭ Bdim7 Cm F9
lost, will all be found. That's all I want when Christ-mas comes to town.

Fm7
Fm7/B♭
That's all I want when Christ - mas comes ___ comes to
E♭ E♭sus E♭
E♭sus E♭
E♭sus E♭
E♭sus E♭
town.
E♭sus E♭
E♭sus E♭
E♭sus E♭
E♭sus E♭
E♭sus E♭
E♭sus E♭
E♭sus E♭
E♭sus E♭
p

WINTER WONDERLAND

Words by
DICK SMITH

Music by
FELIX BERNARD

Winter Wonderland - 2 - 1

G
D7
G
snow - man,
snow - man,
Then pre-tend that he is Par - son Brown; ___
And pre-tend that he's a cir - cus clown; ___
Bb
F7
Bb
C7
F7
He'll say, "Are you mar-ried?" We'll say, "No, man! But you can do the job when you're in
We'll have lots of fun with Mis - ter Snow-man, Un - til the oth - er kid-dies knock 'im
Fm7
Bb7
Eb
Bb7
town!" Lat - er on we'll con - spire ___ as we dream by the
down! When it snows, ain't it thrill-in', tho' your nose gets a
fire, ___ To face un - a - fraid ___ the plans that we made, ___
chill - in'? We'll frol - ic and play ___ the Es - ki - mo way, ___
1.
2.
F7
Bb7
Eb
Eb
Walk - in' in a win - ter won - der - land! Sleigh - bells land!
Walk - in' in a win - ter won - der - land! Sleigh - bells land!

UP ON THE HOUSETOP

TRADITIONAL